"This is an innovative, interesting and creati
psychoanalytic concepts. This most signific
ber of short presentations from prestigious a
illustrate fundamental psychoanalytic conc
rary perspective. Clinical examples illustra
cal approaches that the authors follow, how they think and practise. Rooted on Freudian thinking, the reader will encounter different perspectives on concepts such as the presence of the analyst, transference, listening and interpretation, figures and forms, the frame and setting, the role of the drives, of trauma, sexualities and otherness among many other fundamental concepts. This book will be of great value to both psychoanalysts and to a wider interested readership alike."

Catalina Bronstein, Training and Supervising Analyst of the British Psychoanalytical Society and Visiting Professor in the Psychoanalysis Unit at University College London

"This is a great profoundly psychoanalytic contribution. Parsimonious, deep, insightful and introducing me to lots of things I half-knew or hadn't thought about. Good to keep by and browse at random. Will repay hours of attention."

David Tuckett, formerly president of the European Psychoanalytic Federation, Editor-in-Chief of the *International Psychoanalytic Journal* and a Professor at UCL and Training and Supervising Analyst in London

Psychoanalysts in Session

Psychoanalysis is an intimate clinical experience and the concepts that it explores aim to grapple with the specific phenomena that unfold when a patient speaks and an analyst listens. This book aims to give concrete examples of how these concepts take shape when analysts work.

The structure of the contributions presented in this book matches this concern; drawing on a fragment of an analysis, each contribution illustrates how a notion reveals unforeseen perspectives. The list of entries selected is diverse, with notions encountered in international studies since the Second World War prioritised. Certain classical concepts are nonetheless included when their significance has been shaped by the innovative rereading that contemporary authors have made of them. However, not all the entries in this glossary constitute concepts: some correspond to notions, others to intuitions, and even to recurrent situations with which the analyst is confronted. By grounding, in each entry, the theoretical reflection on a clinical case, the reader is led towards the incessant to-and-fro process that governs the analyst's reflections from clinical experience to theory.

This book therefore constitutes an essential tool for psychologists, psychoanalysts and all professionals in the field of mental care.

Laurent Danon-Boileau is a training analyst at the Paris Psychoanalytical Society (SPP); he is also Professor Emeritus in Linguistics at the University Paris-Descartes and the author of several fiction and nonfiction books.

Jean-Yves Tamet is a psychoanalyst in Lyon and a full member of the French Psychoanalytic Association (APF); he is also a member of the editorial board of the *Libres cahiers pour la psychanalyse* (1999–2014) and an honorary hospital psychiatrist.

THE NEW LIBRARY OF PSYCHOANALYSIS

General Editor: Alessandra Lemma

The New Library of Psychoanalysis was launched in 1987 in association with the Institute of Psychoanalysis, London. It took over from the International Psychoanalytical Library that published many of the early translations of the works of Freud and the writings of most of the leading British and Continental psychoanalysts.

The purpose of the New Library of Psychoanalysis is to facilitate a greater and more widespread appreciation of psychoanalysis and to provide a forum for increasing mutual understanding between psychoanalysts and those working in other disciplines such as the social sciences, medicine, philosophy, history, linguistics, literature and the arts. It aims to represent different trends both in British psychoanalysis and in psychoanalysis generally. The New Library of Psychoanalysis is well placed to make available to the English-speaking world psychoanalytic writings from other European countries and to increase the interchange of ideas between British and American psychoanalysts. Through the *Teaching Series*, the New Library of Psychoanalysis now also publishes books that provide comprehensive, yet accessible, overviews of selected subject areas aimed at those studying psychoanalysis and related fields such as the social sciences, philosophy, literature and the arts.

The Institute, together with the British Psychoanalytical Society, runs a low-fee psychoanalytic clinic, organizes lectures and scientific events concerned with psychoanalysis and publishes the *International Journal of Psychoanalysis*. It runs a training course in psychoanalysis that leads to membership of the International Psychoanalytical Association – the body that preserves internationally agreed standards of training, of professional entry, and of professional ethics and practice for psychoanalysis as initiated and developed by Sigmund Freud. Distinguished members of the Institute have included Michael Balint, Wilfred Bion, Ronald Fairbairn, Anna Freud, Ernest Jones, Melanie Klein, John Rickman and Donald Winnicott.

Previous general editors have included David Tuckett, who played a very active role in the establishment of the New Library. He was followed as general editor by Elizabeth Bott Spillius, who was in turn followed by Susan Budd and then by Dana Birksted-Breen. Current members of the Advisory Board include Giovanna Di Ceglie, Liz Allison, Anne Patterson, Josh Cohen and Daniel Pick.

Previous members of the Advisory Board include Christopher Bollas, Ronald Britton, Catalina Bronstein, Donald Campbell, Rosemary Davies, Sara Flanders, Stephen Grosz, John Keene, Eglé Laufer, Alessandra Lemma, Juliet Mitchell, Michael Parsons, Rosine Jozef Perelberg, Richard Rusbridger, Mary Target and David Taylor.

For a full list of all the titles in the New Library of Psychoanalysis main series as well as both the New Library of Psychoanalysis "Teaching" and "Beyond the Couch" subseries, please visit the Routledge website.

Psychoanalysts in Session

Clinical Glossary of Contemporary Psychoanalysis

Edited by Laurent Danon-Boileau and Jean-Yves Tamet

Translated by Andrew Weller

LONDON AND NEW YORK

First published in English 2021 by Routledge
2 Park Square, Milton Park, Abingdon, Oxon OX14 4RN

and by Routledge
52 Vanderbilt Avenue, New York, NY 10017

Routledge is an imprint of the Taylor & Francis Group, an informa business

British Library Cataloguing-in-Publication Data
A catalogue record for this book is available from the British Library

Library of Congress Cataloging-in-Publication Data
Names: Danon-Boileau, Laurent, 1946- editor. | Tamet, Jean-Yves, editor.
Title: Psychoanalysts in session: clinical glossary of contemporary psychoanalysis/edited by Laurent Danon-Boileau and Jean-Yves Tamet; translated by Andrew Weller.
Description: Abingdon, Oxon; New York, NY: Routledge, 2021. | Series: The new library of psychoanalysis | "Published in French, 2016"–Title page verso. | Includes bibliographical references and index. | Identifiers: LCCN 2020024481 (print) | LCCN 2020024482 (ebook) | ISBN 9780367185398 (hbk) | ISBN 9780367185435 (pbk) | ISBN 9780429196751
(ebk)
Subjects: LCSH: Psychoanalysis. | Psychoanalytic interpretation.
Classification: LCC BF173 .P77628 2021 (print) | LCC BF173 (ebook) | DDC
616.89/17–dc23
LC record available at https://lccn.loc.gov/2020024481
LC ebook record available at https://lccn.loc.gov/2020024482

ISBN: 978-0-367-18539-8 (hbk)
ISBN: 978-0-367-18543-5 (pbk)
ISBN: 978-0-429-19675-1 (ebk)

Typeset in Bembo
by KnowledgeWorks Global Ltd.

Contents

Editorial Committee

"An analytic concept…is…a mental tool that makes it possible
to grasp that which is not visible, to designate what
otherwise would have been ignored or unrecognised."
J.-B. Pontalis, *Perdre de vue*, 1983, p. 102.

Preface

From theory to clinical practice, and back

A large number of dictionaries or vocabularies of psychoanalysis already exist. Their usefulness and reliability are valuable for the knowledge of theory: they make it possible to locate classical notions within the architecture of the Freudian apparatus as well as to follow the trajectory of the different currents of thought belonging to the history of the discipline. However, psychoanalysis is first and foremost an intimate clinical experience and the concepts that it elaborates have a particular object: they aim to grapple with the specific phenomena that unfold in the singular space of an analysis, when a patient speaks and an analyst listens.

In this book, we consider the analytic exchange from a contemporary perspective. Our aim is to give concrete examples that go beyond fashion and polemics of how clinical phenomena take shape and are theorised by the contemporary psychoanalyst. We would like to show how analysts think, and the concepts that they employ when working with those who confide their inner life to them.

The structure of the contributions presented matches this concern; drawing on a fragment of an analysis, each contribution illustrates *how this or that notion reveals unforeseen perspectives.* It thus constitutes a testimony to the work of thinking that has its source in the concepts elaborated since Freud to organise day-to-day clinical reflections. By grounding, in each instance, the theoretical reflection on a clinical case, this glossary hopes to lead the reader towards the incessant to-and-fro process which, from clinical experience to theory, governs the analyst's reflections. Psychoanalysis, considered as a hybrid body of knowledge, half-theory, half-clinical practice, is neither a simple practice nor a philosophy that disavows its name: it may be likened to what the Greeks called *métis,* a sort of sixth sense that enabled Odysseus to appreciate the colours of time and to return to the shores of his native country after a long and costly odyssey.

Which entries?

The list of entries selected is diverse. This was bound to be the case because psychoanalysis is permeated by diverse currents and traditions that needed to be represented. However, this diversity does not amount to dispersion: as we received contributions over the course of time, it appeared that entries signed by authors of radically different horizons brought to light remarkable convergences. These obviously reside in shared convictions concerning fundamentals, and they are rooted in the Freudian heritage. This is particularly the case for certain ideas related to the transference or to psychic conflict. Others arise from the feeling that the work of elaboration that takes shape in the space of analysis, that is to say the poetics that are deployed there, depends on the particular effects of this exchange. It is embodied therefore in, and through, the discourse addressed to a transference-object. This is what constitutes the specificity of the language used in psychoanalysis. Certain literary texts or other cultural creations provide dazzling metaphors of this. Several entries have as their starting-point an artistic creation, as if it were analytic material, thus linking up with a fruitful tradition initiated by Freud.

The priority of choice was given to notions encountered in international studies since the Second World War. Certain classical concepts are nonetheless included when their significance has been shaped by the innovative rereading that contemporary authors have made of them. Furthermore, in the strict sense of the term, not all the entries in this glossary constitute concepts: some correspond to notions, others to ways of saying things or to intuitions, and even to recurrent situations with which the analyst is confronted. What seemed to justify their inclusion was the way in which each expression selected supports, but also crystallises, the inner work developed by the analyst when he or she tries to grapple with the process of a session and the movements that have unfolded in it.

The clinical fragment

Each author has organised the clinical fragment that he[1] presents according to the perspective he wanted to give to it. And yet, curiously enough, certain convergences may be observed in the presentations: after a phase of painful repetition for analyst and patient alike, an event suddenly emerges (often a form of behaviour or "acting" (*agir*) on the part of the patient, and sometimes on the part of the analyst): this irruption first produces an effect of putting the analytic frame in a state of tension, provoking an acute moment of "crisis". The analyst then shares something without knowing what is brewing. This event often conjures up the memory of a traumatic moment that had marked the history of the patient's childhood. What is remarkable is that the first phase of this process is established, for patient and analyst alike, thanks to significant manifestations that elude the register of the discourse and even seem to form an obstacle to its sequences. Finally, when the ensemble gives rise to an interpretation, the latter avoids a strict attribution of meaning. Ordinarily, it does not result, either, in a lifting of repression that allows the associative movement to get going again immediately.

The dramaturgy that we have just succinctly described is most probably linked in part to the type of patients who mobilise reflection today, but perhaps also to the language they have in common. More than the neurosis of the time of the founders of the "talking cure", the analyses that contemporary concepts account for are often those of patients affected by "*borderline disorders*". With them, the logic of trauma, the recourse to acting (*l'agir*), and the compulsion to repeat, are more prominent than in analyses in the past, which were supposedly cadenced by the adventures of speech and the pleasure principle: as a sign of the times, the interpretative field has widened.

The differences between psychoanalysts

Notwithstanding the convergences that have just been identified, differences in the way material is approached remain. It is certainly a matter of each analyst's particular sensibility, but also of different traditions depending on variations in training. Some analysts are inclined to see the effect of the unconscious in the associative networks that form the thread of the discourse; others emphasise in the speech that is addressed to the analyst the expression of a repeated situation that the patient is seeking to master; still others focus on the emergence and maturation of the affect that is felt; and others, finally, attach particular attention to the paradoxical reversals that are created by an effect of rupture. It is true that, depending on the patient and the moment in his analysis, every analyst gives priority to one of these perspectives or the other, but it is still true that the personal style that results from each analyst's training lends itself more directly to one way or the other of envisaging the work of interpretation.

From this point of view, there is a significant gap between the way that Anglo-Saxon analysts and French authors approach the session material and account for it. It lies in their training, but it is above all characterised by what one might be tempted to call a difference in styles. For British analysts, the essential material is formed in the very instant of the session; thus it can be embodied in the affects that the patient re-experiences, in his movements of love, hate, jealousy and envy. These movements of mental life are the first target of the work of interpretation. In other traditions, the focal issue may be more clearly one of the link established between what is experienced in the session and the past recomposed by the joint work. Sometimes, though, it is a matter of how, in the course of the narrative, the patient manages to put into words what is going on internally. In each tradition, the difficulties to which the symptoms observed are related can also vary. While some insist on the pains of separation and the wish to be loved, others highlight the difficulty that each one of us faces in transforming, through renunciation, wishes addressed to incestuous objects.

A history of clinical reflection

Indirectly, this book also sketches an outline of the history of clinical reflection in psychoanalysis. With the extension of psychoanalysis towards new configurations of the mind, there has been a shift in themes: hence the importance attributed to traumatic events re-experienced in analysis, the negative transference and the heterogeneity of the associative material; hence, too, the new requirements that weigh upon the analyst's listening and mode of presence. There is a shift of accent, then, towards what is happening on the analyst's side, that is to say the nature of his associations, "inner discourse", countertransference and paradoxical moments, whose incongruous and trying character he must accept. Appreciating what is happening within the analyst is necessary for re-establishing the patient's associative freedom as well as for the emergence of the very particular way of thinking that has been called "co-thinking", paradoxical transference, retrogression, formal regression or maternal reverie. It requires both protagonists to abandon the requirements of reason and to have confident recourse to "dreaming thought".

The overall presentation

A suitable way of presenting the contributions we had collected still had to be found. Rather than a simple alphabetical order, we preferred an arrangement that suggests the thematic affinities that the editorial work had enabled us to reveal. This glossary is therefore comprised of sections. Each section brings together, in alphabetical order, entries dealing with convergent preoccupations, accompanied by indications for further reading so that readers can delve more deeply into the topic if they so wish. They are organised into two main parts titled "The space of the session" and "The space of the psyche", which follow the encounter that is established during analysis and thus the meanderings of its complexity.

By passing from one entry to another through a free play of associations and networks, the reader is thus invited to form his own picture of psychoanalysis today.

LAURENT DANON-BOILEAU
AND JEAN-YVES TAMET

Translator's note

1 To avoid repetition, I have decided throughout to use "he" (rather than he/she) to refer to the analyst or patient when the gender is unknown, but of course no gender-bias is intended.

Part I

THE SPACE OF THE SESSION

1

A SPACE FOR TALKING

ACTING THROUGH SPEECH

JEAN-LUC DONNET

This notion is related to the complex issue of *Agieren* raised by Freud (1914a) in "Remembering, repeating and working-through". By indicating that transference repetition could be "enacted" in the session, Freud offered the investigation of the unconscious a new "royal path". Acted repetition manifests itself in particular at the very heart of speech, the speaker being unaware that he is repeating and also of what he is repeating. It is listening that detects this acting through speech (*agir de parole*), while the subject believes he is saying only what he wants to say.

This enunciation must be distinguished from one in which the patient speaks directly to the analyst, for example to tell the latter about his fear of being judged, criticised or rejected. In this case, speech is simply making explicit a transference displacement in which the analyst takes the place of an object of the past.

Acting though speech takes on an entirely different form. Certain enunciations that emerge unexpectedly at the beginning of analyses, and that may make one doubt the indication, make it possible to illustrate acting through speech in a way that is almost a caricature. Here are two examples:

A female patient, addressing the analyst directly, said: "I hope that you won't take this badly, but you look a bit odd."

A male patient punctuated the end of each of his sentences with, "Okay?"

In both cases, the analyst was surprised and even slightly taken aback by the incongruous nature of these formulations which openly "flout" the spirit of the fundamental rule. He felt a bit irritated and was tempted to correct what amounted to a misunderstanding, a typically countertranferential response in the form of counteracting through speech. On reflection, the analyst realised that such acting through speech corresponds to deep issues revealing archaic modes of functioning: need for control, demand for symmetry, and an ingenuous use of projection. Speech is then cut off from any metaphorical resonance and the concrete character of thought goes hand in hand with a denial of the conflictuality involved in speaking. Above all, a direct transferential register is intensified by an invalidation of the very meaning of the situation. Acting through speech appears here to be a sort of involuntary verbal sally, a blunder that the subject knows nothing about, but whose quirky, compulsive character can be perceived through listening.

By contrast, in an analysis that is evolving sufficiently, acting through speech appears in the course of the process and quite often constitutes the primary support of an irreplaceable retroactive effect of interpretation. Here is an example: the patient still had a childhood memory of a confused, almost traumatic scene in which his mother, addressing her children who were gathered together, had said to them: "If you hadn't been here, I would've written." She was expressing, in a way that was obscure for them, the regret that her maternal tasks had prevented her from fulfilling her vocation as a writer. The patient had mentioned this scene very early on in his analysis, without analysing deeply what it represented for him as a screen memory. Years later, at a time when he had to go away for a fortnight and was therefore going to miss several sessions, he asked himself out loud what his psychoanalyst was going to do with the time of his sessions during his absence. Looking around the room and noticing the desk covered with papers, he declared impulsively: "You will write." "Like your mother?" the analyst echoed. The response, totally unexpected, triggered an intense emotional upheaval that gave access to major issues of identification that were condensed in the screen memory: the patient recognised in particular the origin of a temptation in himself to make a donation of absence, a temptation whose masochistic tonality had hitherto remained enigmatic for him.

The statement, "You will write" is here unquestionably a form of acting through speech: it resembles a joke, but has a hint of injunction about it and expresses an imperative need to influence. Simultaneously, it contains, in a particularly condensed form, a considerable associative network. It is possible that its irruption was linked to withdrawal when faced with the emergence of a fantasised scene. The discreet but immediate intervention of the analyst simply made a link between the transference actualisation and the childhood memory; if it had such a decisive interpretative effect, it was because the ego's affirmation of its control was reversed, delivering up a truth of the subject of the unconscious. This reversal, through its retroactive effect, created a breach, but the cathartic discharge was prolonged in a process of intense linking. Of course, the discontinuity that was virtually equivalent to the traumatic aspects of the episode implies the continuity of an analysing situation and, in the patient, of a process of working-through, pursued in silence between the two phases of the operation of après-coup. It is significant that the *Agieren* realises its transference scenario by including it in a dramatisation that uses situation analysis (*l'analytique de situation*): the symbolic issues of the setting and the contingent characteristics of the analyst's desk contribute to a psychodramatic hystericisation of the verbal exchange.

Acting through speech often corresponds to a peak moment in the analytic action, a moment that it is important to grasp. While it may accelerate the course of the work, it can also block its advance, sometimes irremediably. The transference actualisation to which it bears witness can take on the projective consistency of a reincarnation, illustrating the statement, "It is impossible to destroy anyone in absentia or in effigy" (Freud 1912, p. 108). Ultimately, speech is addressed to the object of which it speaks, combining enunciation and representation: a conjunction that involves the risk of suspending any reference to a third party.

On the metapsychological level, acting through speech, as a form of *Agieren*, is one of the phenomena that led Freud to the notion of what lies beyond the pleasure principle, to the duality of the drives and to the second topography. It is above all directly related to the unconscious of the ego, consisting of more or less unified unconscious identifications. In experiencing this speech through which the subject is spoken, while being unaware of whom it is addressing, we can hear the voice of an unconscious identification.

Further reading

Donnet, J.-L. (1995). *Le divan bien tempéré.* Paris, Presses Universitaires de France (Series: Le Fil Rouge).
Donnet, J.-L. (2005). *La situation analysante.* Paris: Presses Universitaires de France, (Series: Le Fil Rouge).

KEY WORDS Identificatory unconscious of the ego, transference scenario.

ASSOCIATIVE SPEECH, COMPULSIVE SPEECH

LAURENT DANON-BOILEAU

When a patient's speech is sufficiently associative such that he is able to say things without logically correlating the different subjects or the transition from one subject to another, and he has recourse to the "long circuit", why interrupt and interpret? Why leave this position of witnessing a self-analysis that is happily running its course? The answer lies in the necessity of tension: an analytic process requires a degree of operant conflictuality, which cannot be the case if everything is going too well and the analyst simply keeps quiet.

A patient opened the session by speaking about stopping his analysis: "This morning, as I was coming here, I don't know why, but I felt like stopping the analysis." Then, after a period of silence and various remarks about his daily life, he mentioned a mother he saw while crossing a square. She was accompanied by a child and clearly pregnant. This evocation then led him to recall the moment when his own mother had announced to him that she was expecting a baby: "The day she told me that I was going to have a little sister, I cried." This is a classical situation. As in a dream, the consequence – the wish to stop the analysis – is stated before the cause, namely, having thought about his mother's announcement concerning the little sister while passing the child in the square. It is in this respect that speech is associative: its course follows the movement of a dream. It is also for this reason that interpretation can come in the form of an association. After a silence, the analyst said: "Stop the analysis? To avoid hearing me say that you are going to have a little sister?"

This classical interpretation was made possible by the tonality of the transference and the associativity of the discourse. It was heard and the patient responded to it by providing, by way of association, a dream.

Here, the interpretation establishes links between different tonalities of relations to the object that all infiltrate the patient's discourse, but which had hitherto been kept isolated from each other. The first part of the interpretation ("Stop the analysis?) makes it possible to place a fragment of discourse under the joint gaze of the patient and the analyst in order to constitute it as a symptom, that is to say, in a psychic creation that deserves to be examined. Here, the analyst places himself beside the analysand, side by side. The actors of the exchange become witnesses of the analytic process that is emerging from the patient's discourse.

Of course, that is not all. What is recognised by both of them is also questioned by one of them. It is this questioning that is deployed through the second part of the interpretation ("To avoid hearing me say that you are going to have a little sister?"). The content of the fantasised threat is thus brought to light. Here, contrary to the transitional side-by-side situation that preceded it, the place of the patient, who learns of the announcement, and that of the analyst, who takes over in his own name the statement about the forthcoming birth, are now established in a face-to-face situation. However, as they are united in the enunciation of the interpretation, the conflict can be formulated. At the very moment when he says "I", the analyst is referring to himself as an object present in the session (an object of the here-and-now transference), as a primary maternal object (the one who is looking with the child at what the child is producing), and as the maternal object of the infantile neurosis announcing the forthcoming birth. This announcement is the origin of the indispensable work of mourning that the patient, like every subject, will have to carry out. The deployment of the process has its source in this conflictual structure. By disturbing without creating disarray, the interpretation displaces the repetition; the discourse then rediscovers what makes it a promoter of psychic life.

Not all patients have a discourse that is constantly associative. Often, under the insistent effect of the repetition compulsion, speech is organised during the session in a more compact way. It sometimes gives rise to "acting through speech" (*agir de parole*, Jean-Luc Donnet), which is addressed directly to the object. But it can also take the form of relentless descriptions of flat, pleasureless day-to-day life where factual situations are enumerated, an indefinite repetition of a neurotic configuration with little, very little, too little, variation. This form of compulsive speech often arouses in the analyst feelings of boredom, powerlessness and inadequacy. The significance of compulsive speech is then manifested in a kind of excitation in the analyst's listening.

A 40-year-old woman of Czech origin was three months old when her parents separated. Her childhood was spent in an environment that consisted exclusively of her mother and her brother. Her father had remarried and no longer had any contact with the children of his first marriage. After 1968, when she was eight years old, she emigrated to France with her mother and brother. Her father had also settled in France and remarried, but had not re-established relations with her and her brother. It was as if they had never existed. Recently, she had made a trip to revisit the places of her past. She brought back photos of the house where she was born.

In general, she comes to her sessions extremely regularly. This somewhat excessive and ostentatious regularity is fortunately sometimes disturbed by a caustic sense of humour, tinted with a certain tenderness. And yet, when she goes into the details of daily events, an associative silence descends upon the analyst's mind, and it stands in the way of any form of representation. Her speech tends to make him just another interlocutor. The defensive quality of this discourse has been addressed in the analytic work, and today, the analyst is sometimes able to notice when it is being deployed.

In the session that I wish to speak about, the patient was talking about a family meal that had taken place on the occasion of her niece's 20th birthday party. She had given her a gift and was complaining that the young girl had never told her what she thought of it, whereas she had shared with others her reactions to their gifts. While she was speaking, the analyst gradually felt excluded. And then, suddenly, the patient returned to her niece's attitude and the atmosphere of the lunch. "It was nice and pleasant, but it's strange – my niece doesn't see me." Why, at this moment, did something induce the analyst to turn his attention away from the account of daily events towards something else? No doubt in order to thwart his sensation of feeling excluded. Could it be that she was treating him as her niece had treated her, that she was telling him things without "seeing" him?

It was thanks to an association with a reverse situation that the analyst was able to recognize his discomfort in the countertransference. Not without a sense of guilt, he recalled that he had once, in the course of this long analysis, forgotten a session after she had requested to change the time. At the time, his guilt had been reinforced by the fact that the patient had not done or said anything that would have allowed them to speak about it. He had waited, in vain. All of a sudden, the recollection of this absence came back to him. At the same time, the analyst was also recollecting something that was both cultural and personal: a passage from Virgil that describes the descent of Aeneas into the Underworld. During his sojourn amongst the dead, Aeneas meets the ghost of his father. And when he tries to embrace him, his arms pass right through the shadow of Anchises so that they cross each other on his own chest. The analyst then recalled that he had once translated this fragment of text with his son who was preparing for his Baccalaureate exam. Neither of them had said anything, but they both knew that something was going on between them. Then, returning to the session, he thought that this literary recollection probably had something to do with the sense of guilt linked to his error – he was absent; like his father, he was a ghostly father. He also recalled that the patient's mother had lost a daughter before her birth. All this happened quite quickly.

The account of the lunch continued, in the same somewhat flat mode. And the analyst suddenly said: "When she doesn't see you, your niece is treating you as if you were dead, like an older sister." To which the patient replied: "That reminds me that my niece also lost a sister between her and her brother, and that I was always told that her character was not the same at all before and after this sister's death. Before, she was quite gay and easy-going; afterwards she became distant." The analyst then added that, like her niece, he had sometimes not seen her, like the time, for instance, when he had been absent for the appointment that she had asked him to change. For the first time, she was able to speak about what she had imagined about his absence on that day. She obviously was not happy about the mistreatment to which he had subjected her; but, beyond that, something unrepresentable had also come back to her: she had perceived in her mother's gaze the mourning for this older sister that the patient had not known.

What had led the analyst to associate, and then to speak? Was it his guilt at having missed a session? No doubt. But what was it, in the patient's remarks, that had revived the process of thinking? It lay in the form of the discourse, in a rupture of the compulsive discourse. She said that her niece "does not see" her. Yet, there is something singular about the use of the present here. It would be quite different if she had said, for example: "She didn't speak to me", "She didn't address me". Or even: "It seemed as if she didn't see me." The analyst was troubled by the use of the present, the absence of any recognition of metaphor, of any formula such as, "It was as if…", "It seemed that…".

The way she formulated what she had felt marked the compulsive dimension of her speech. It was like a factual statement, like a reality outside herself, erasing any subject of enunciation, any trace of sensation, of feeling, of point of view. At the same time, it was precisely this emergence marked by compulsivity that restarted the process of joint thinking.

Further reading

Danon-Boileau, L. (2006). La force du langage. *Bulletin de la Société Psychanalytique de Paris*, 82: 19–100.

Donnet, J.-L. (1995). *Le divan bien tempéré*. Paris: Presses Universitaires de France.

KEY WORDS Acting through speech, associativity, repetition compulsion.

THE ADVERB EFFECT

JEAN-LOUIS BALDACCI

After a first promising interview, a female patient tried to block the resumption of the associative process. Indeed, in the second meeting, using speech as a form of acting, she announced abruptly: "In fact, I don't really have any big problems; I don't really need analysis. I'm just stagnating, but it's not so serious!" Taking up the adverb "really", the psychoanalyst signalled that there existed "in fact", concerning the formulation that imposed itself on the patient, a real inner debate. The adverb introduced a nuance, even a contradiction, between what was said and what was trying to express itself. While this intervention denounced a resistance against the transference, it simultaneously renounced the immediate search for its meaning. Instead, it attracted the patient's attention to the psychic processes at work rather than to their contents. Faced with the abruptness of such an enunciation by a patient, any interpretative response that directly sought the meaning would amount to counteracting because its purpose would be to convince. The result would be to reinforce the resistance that we are trying to overcome. In the opposite situation, for example, of the seductive impatience of a patient to begin the treatment, the analyst should proceed in the same way, namely, he/she should go around the resistance, here via the transference, without seeking to interpret it.

In both situations, the psychoanalyst must, therefore, make a sidestep, shifting the focus of the too positive or too negative cathexis of which he/she is directly the object, thereby directing the patient's attention towards psychic processes and not to contents and meaning. To achieve this, adverbs constitute a tool of choice, a practical means. Indeed, it seems possible to extend to them what Freud (1925) said about negation: thanks to them "thinking frees itself from the restrictions of repression and enriches itself with material that is indispensable for its proper functioning" (p. 236).

There is, however, a difference between the use of these adverbs and negation: the latter concerns a judgement of condemnation concerning the emergence of the repressed, whereas adverbs, like "still, yet or again", "a little", "perhaps", "really", "on the contrary", etc., express a judgement of concerned and wary affirmation concerning this partial emergence of the repressed. In the example chosen, the intervention concerning the adverb "really" is addressed to the ego, underlining its capacity to identify and overcome a resistance; it urges it to continue its exploration. In "Formulations on the two principles of mental functioning", Freud (1911) notes that in order to explore the relations between *Ucs./Cs.*, which he was to call in 1915 the "communication between the two systems", one is bound "to employ the currency that is in use in the country one is exploring" (p. 225). Adverbs are often part of this currency. This currency can also take on different forms: reaction formation, double negation, a parapraxis identified by the patient, or figures.[1] The list of the elements making up this "currency" is not exhaustive.

The adverb effect enables the patient to find what is already there in what he is saying. It is a form of Winnicottian found/created, but a particular form based on an appropriation of speech, its cathexis, its libidinalisation as a necessary prior phase for associative displacement. The success of the operation is marked by the development in depth and not on the surface of the associative process.[2] For his part, the analyst thereby gains a position of active neutrality. For, by refusing the direct cathexis of which he is initially the object in favour of speech, he declines to occupy the imaginary place the resistance of the superego seeks to assign to him/her through projection or seduction, the place, for example, of an omnipotent mother or of a seductive father. He thus opens up the dynamic of an interpretable transference. The analyst is then in a situation where he can construct and interpret what may prevent the patient from following the fundamental rule of analysis, in particular the sadomasochistic sexualisation of the relations between the ego and the superego. The adverb effect is thus a time of opening up the interpretative process that is particularly useful not only during the session but also during the preliminary interviews. In this case, it enables the patient to encounter his/her speech right at the beginning and thereby gives him/her the aptitude for agreeing or not to the treatment proposed.

Notes

1 Figures have the advantage of being abstract and thus of keeping repressed images, contents, at a distance, while involving associative analogies. They easily bring into play the temporality of the operation of après-coup and the relations between trauma and fantasy.

2 "When the pressure of resistance is extremely high, one meets with the phenomenon of the dreamer's associations broadening instead of deepening" (Freud, 1923b [1922], p. 110).

Further reading

Baldacci, J.-L. (2012). Dès le début l'interprétation. In: *L'Interprétation*. Paris: Presses Universitaires de France, coll. Monographies et débats de psychanalyse, pp. 53–62.

Baldacci, J.-L. (2012). Processus théorisant et processus analytique. *Partir, revenir, Libres cahiers pour la psychanalyse*, 26: 15–27. Paris: In Press.

Baldacci, J.-L. (2013). Fonctions de la Consultation psychanalytique. In: *La Consultation psychanalytique*. Paris: Presses Universitaires de France (Series: Monographies et débats de psychanalyse, pp. 11–28).

Baldacci, J.-L. (2013). L'analyse des résistances, à propos du texte de Fred Busch. *Revue française de psychanalyse*, 3: 799–808.

KEY WORDS Interpretation, neutrality, process, resistance.

LANGUAGE, A SHELL?

BRIGITTE CHERVOILLOT-COURTILLON

On the couch, he was silent. A period of time passed. Then he recounted what he had just experienced in the entrance hall of the analyst's building. As he was looking in the mirror, he saw his analyst's face appearing and felt an irrepressible urge to smash it in. His associations expressed his fear that his words, which he experienced as "empty shells", would not protect the analyst from this instinctual drive upsurge.

This calls into question the nature of the barrier protecting the subject from strong quantities of excitation, which Freud calls a "stimulus barrier". In *Beyond the Pleasure Principle* (1920), he elaborates the elementary model of the psychical apparatus and describes the functioning of psychic substance in these terms: "This little fragment of living substance is suspended in the middle of an external world charged with the most powerful energies; and it would be killed by the stimulation emanating from these if it were it not provided with a protective shield against stimuli" (p. 27).

In *Avant d'être celui qui parle,* Jean-Claude Rolland (1998) renews this approach. For him, the Freudian description is a metaphor of the "obscure relations that psychic substance has with its language surface" (p. 33). The ego would be destroyed by the repeated assaults of the unconscious if it were not helped in its task by the action of language. The latter, "like a shell", ensures a protective function against stimuli. This function is twofold: it is "both one of rejection and also of integration owing to the compulsion to represent." (p. 87). Its operation of filtering takes two directions: first, by participating in the repression of psychic traumas and in their returns; some analyses bear the marks of this in the drying up of language that occurs in them, which is completely devoted to the service of counter-cathecting repressed ideas, but also in the use of ordinary language that reduces the polysemy of its discourse in order to be communicable for others; and, second, on the analytic stage in the movements of exhuming what is repressed.

Rolland proposes a new method of investigation. In the analysand's discourse, thanks to the unbinding carried out by free association, the analyst, by virtue of his regressive and "visionary" listening, discerns repetitions that constitute "analogies between themselves".

They attest to the presence of the return of the repressed. These analogies are at the origin of his forthcoming interpretation: this is how "analogical interpretation" arises.

This actualisation cannot be achieved without the hallucinatory participation of the reliving of infantile experience. This hallucinatory wish-fulfilment "is necessary for the homeostasis of the psychical apparatus just as speech is for its surface" (p. 120). In order that this fantasy scenario may become conscious, it is sustained by the indirect work of language at work notably in the dream process. The dream thoughts, like "antenna, infiltrate the *terrae incognitae* of the mental apparatus … and bring back certain information" (p.72). For example, in the dream of the Wolf Man (Freud, 1918 [1914]), the signifier "white" plays this role. Arising from the preconscious, and "put into orbit" by the unconscious, it thereby gives the memory-trace and the drive a presentation and a visual representation or figuration. In analysis, charged with their unconscious experiences, these signifiers, like "*passeurs* between soul and psyche, open up a power of infinite significance for language" (Rolland, 1998, p. 85).

Further reading

Fédida, P. (2009). *Crise et contre-transfert.* Paris: Presses Universitaires de France.

Freud, S. (1918 [1914]). *From the history of an infantile neurosis. S.E.* 17. London: Hogarth, pp. 1–122.

Freud, S. (1920). *Beyond the pleasure principle. S.E.* 18. London: Hogarth, pp. 1–64.

Gómez-Mango, E. (1999). *La place des mères.* Paris: Gallimard (Series: Connaissance de l'inconscient).

Rolland, J.-C. (1998). *Avant d'être celui qui parle.* Paris: Gallimard (Series: Connaissance de l'inconscient).

Rolland, J.-C. (1998). *Guérir du mal d'aimer.* Paris: Gallimard (Series: Connaissance de l'inconscient).

KEY WORDS *Infans*, analogical interpretation, language, stimulus barrier.

JOKES

JEAN-PHILIPPE DUBOIS

She had the knack of misusing, generally quite involuntarily, ready-made expressions or the most varied platitudes. During an interview for a job of which she no longer expected much, she heard herself describe her interlocutor as a "delegate of Father Christmas". Between a slip of the pen and a joke, she had thus always imagined that the expression "*qui ne dit mot consent*" ("silence implies consent") was written "*qui ne dit mot qu'on sent*" (lit. "he who says nothing one can feel"), inviting the subject only to speak about well-established perceptions. In this respect, the expression seemed closer to Ludwig Wittgenstein's statement "That whereof we cannot speak, thereof we must remain silent" than to the expression of a hesitation or of a general difficulty in expressing or taking a position, in making a choice. It also seemed to her to take into account the fundamentally perceptual aspect of all language, just as it was important above all to say things that one felt strongly in order to express oneself as well as possible, in whatever way (*voie*) (*voix*=voice) that might be.[1]

As its name indicates, perhaps better in the French language than in the German language (*Witz*), the joke (Fr: *mot d'esprit*) is a matter of language.[2] It is also a matter of wit. Is it a question then of bringing out the wit of the joke or of giving the joke in question more wit than it seems to have initially? In any case, it was in aristocratic France that it was considered important to possess wit, even if this could verge on absurdity ("*ridicule*")[3] during certain bouts of verbal jousting at the King's court.

The joke disarms or defuses criticism, or censorship, diverts attention or tension. It thereby liberates an aggressive, teasing or mocking form of expression, in a side-step that tempers the attack or conceals it. Although it is aimed at one person or another, it is also generally addressed to a third party or to a public, tasked, through its reaction, with confirming its intention, sometimes double, sometimes ambiguous.

In the joke, the play on words involves a polysemy of language by means of consonances or assonances provoking effects of shifts of meaning in which the "repressed" can be revealed. The complacency of language can partially thwart the effects of a personal censorship of ideas or images that had hitherto been unconscious, like in dreams, parapraxes or bungled actions, and thus result in a partial lifting of the effects of the repression. The joke thus belongs to the register of more or less symptomatic compromise formations, making it possible to navigate between wish (*désir*) and defence.

Unlike other compromise formations (dreams, reminiscences, bungled actions or neuroses of all kinds), the joke is not essentially involuntary. Quite to the contrary, it may even be knowingly calculated in order to have an effect, to hit the mark (*faire mouche*) or snub someone (*moucher*).

An inventory of jokes could no doubt constitute a dictionary in itself ("*Witzionary*"), at the risk of toning down the effects of surprise and the situational effects of their enunciation.

This would give, for example, for the word "*impuissant*" ("impotent") the definition "*homme de peu de fois*" ("man of few times) and for "*teutons*" (Teutons) [in French, one can also hear the word *têtons*/nipples] "*cousseins germains*" [a play on words on *cousins*/cousins; *coussins*/pillows and *seins*/breasts]), the sexual character of the joke merely confirming the unconscious aspects emerging on this occasion.

Enunciation, pronunciation, accent, tone... Everything that leads someone to speak, to choose this word or that form remains underpinned by unconscious aspects or constraints that soon take on the form of inhibitions or symptoms. In his preface to a revised French translation of Freud's (1992 [1905]) Le *mot d'esprit et sa relation á l'inconscient* (*Jokes and their Relation to the Unconscious*), Jean-Claude Lavie clearly shows how the domain of Freud's study of the phenomenon "goes well beyond the restricted framework" that he seems to have given himself in order to reveal, as if as a second step and "as an inevitable counterpoint, the permanent and unconscious constraint of our words" (p. 30). One always says less than one wanted to say and more than one thought one had said, even though, it could be added, it is not necessarily a matter of "being witty".

Cutting the figure of a psychoanalyst who is quick himself to make use of jokes or humour to back up his propositions and the games of hide-and-seek of the unconscious with the use of consciousness and of language,[4] the same Lavie, during a very serious lecture he was reading to an audience of psychoanalytic colleagues, evoked his position and his emotion at thus finding himself, after so many years, "*sur le divan de la scène*".[5]

The so called "talking cure" itself puts speech on the "*divan de la scène*". Some have even imagined, taking this as a starting-point, language itself as a potential form of a generalised joke, which would amount to giving the determinism of language priority over its use and the involvement that it implies in the one who is speaking. The unconscious would therefore be nothing but a product of the structure of language (according to Lacan in particular). This form of idealisation of the signifier, which refers to a "treasure of signifiers", the tendency towards interpretation originating in forms that a priori underlie those used, can become systematic and lead to an impasse. Speech thereby loses its effect of intention, of address, of impact, and the system then is akin to the mechanism of defence: manic defence or detours of thought, which, by diverting attention, end up paradoxically putting themselves in the service of repression itself rather than in that of lifting its effects.

Used advisedly, wordplay can, however, throw light on the part played by words without our realising it in our distress, in our symptoms. The joke in itself is thus a form of potential interpretation depending on the context, in particular transferential, in which it is used. In this respect, it can prove to be very valuable for analytic interpretation. It is therefore often in the context of a form of interpretation that the joke may become highly expressive for the one who is speaking.

Notes

1 Wittgenstein also said, in so many words, that language must adapt itself to facts and not facts to language. Trying to accommodate the interpretation of a phenomenon with a language already formed and filled with a priori can only lead to false conclusions concerning the nature of things.

2 *Witz* could be translated by "funny story", "touch of humour" or alternatively "wit", which always influences its interprétation.

3 See the eponymous 1966 film by Patrice Leconte.

4 See in particular *L'amour est un crime parfait* (Lavie, 2002), a book whose title itself appears to be a joke, and one of the chapters of which, devoted more particularly to jokes, is called "*Maudit mot*" (lit. "Cursed joke", but there is also a homophonic play on *Mau* and *mot*). "In truth, the language that employs possesses him", writes the author concerning the one who is speaking. (p. 99).

5 Translator's note: "*le divan de la scène*" may also be understood phonetically as "le devant de la scène" (front stage).

Further reading

Anzieu, D. (1981). Une conclusion pour rire: le mot d'esprit, circuit court du travail créateur. In: *Le Corps de l'œuvre*. Paris: Gallimard.
Freud, S. (1992 [1905]). *Le mot d'esprit et sa relation à l'inconscient*, trans. D. Messier, preface by Jean-Claude *Lavie*. Paris: Gallimard.
Lavie, J.-C. (2002). *L'amour est un crime parfait*. Paris: Gallimard.

KEY WORDS Defences, interpretation, word play, jokes.

THE CONFUSION OF TONGUES BETWEEN ADULTS AND THE CHILD

BERNADETTE FERRERO-MADIGNIER

In a climate of unrest reinforced by misunderstandings, a few months before he died in May 1933, Sándor Ferenczi presented to his colleagues of the 12th International Congress of Psychoanalysis his testamentary article, "Confusion of tongues between adults and the child. The language of tenderness and passion" (Ferenczi, 1955 [1933]). The paper caused a great scandal and wrecked his chances of becoming president of the International Psychoanalytical Association, after he had finally decided to submit his candidacy at Freud's request. Ferenczi had already questioned, in other texts, the countertransference movements related to the treatment of patients who had suffered a real trauma. However, tormented by his wish to heal and to be healed, he exposed himself here at the same time as he was presenting his hypotheses and his interpretative proposals. His thinking bears the trace of a confusion of tongues reactivated in the transference/countertransference relationship with Freud, his analyst.

Under the guise of a style of writing that is sometimes naïve and empirical, he delineates essential questions that are raised by the encounter between the adult and the child around infantile sexuality. He describes the confusion and identification that take place and how they encourage splitting in the child when he is invaded by adult passion. In the course of his reflections, the author focuses his remarks more closely on the nature and origins of trauma: is it a fantasy or a reality? He shows that, in analysis, everything depends ultimately on the analyst's own analysis and that, for the patient, there is a great risk when the analyst is unaware of his own countertransference responses: this can result in a new confusion of tongues. To avoid this situation, Ferenczi emphasises that speech and memory can only come into play at a later stage. He also acknowledges that the trust acquired in the transference, thanks to the analyst's tact, promotes a process of healing in the patient that can extinguish or attenuate the hallucinatory reproduction of the trauma. It is, therefore, up to the analyst to guard against repeating the abuse by "penetrating" the patient with his own convictions through, or as a result of, the movements of regression initiated.

An adolescent girl came for treatment thanks to the vigilance of her father who took the initiative to set it up and accompanied her regularly in spite of his very full professional life. During the first years, she above all expressed her disenchantment with herself and with the members of her family, while gradually developing towards the analyst the seductive position of a lost and suffering adolescent. This transference movement was met with the reserve that it merited. The analyst avoided using the familiar "*tu*" form or entering into excessive complicity.

When she was very young, she had felt unloved and said she felt very uneasy when looking at photos of the past. A cathartic scene emerged regularly that ended in the convulsive complaining of a little girl being beaten by her father while her melancholic mother was looking on inertly and remaining strangely silent: she had done something silly and he had responded by dragging her to the ground and kicking her repeatedly in the belly. Each time she told this story, she seemed more submerged, beset by anger and on the verge of breakdown. She detested her father. He had no idea of his strength and could have killed her! She also hated her mother for her cowardice in not protecting her. The scene and its actualisation condensed the intensity and insecurity of the confused feelings of a helpless child faced with adult passion.

What had she really suffered? Her emotions were so strong that it inevitably raised the issue of knowing to what extent they were grounded in reality. However, it was clear to the analyst that no lapse or failure on her (the analyst's) part would be tolerable. Her whole attention was focused therefore on not reproducing the indifference experienced through contact with her mother's melancholy, on being reassuring at the end of sessions, and on saying a few words of transition emphasising the fact that now her father was very concerned about her. Indeed, he would wait for her in the waiting room while working on his files.

Finally, the day arrived when she was much calmer and lifted the veil. Behind her appearances of a young Goth dressed in black and nourished with negative thoughts, the patient was able to talk about her addictions and the extent of her self-destructive behaviour. Touched by her trust and this new burst of sincerity, the analyst at first thought she could influence her to undergo a period of weaning or a specific treatment; but in vain. The recurrent situations of danger in which the patient kept putting herself prevailed over the analyst's far too "unconditional" support. The analyst thus had to inform the patient that she refused to be the "silent witness" of these attacks on herself. If recovery was to remain a hope, the intervention of a third party was necessary and it had become urgent to speak to her parents. The patient fell silent, before repeating once again that she couldn't do it, that she didn't want to. And then she murmured that her father would kill her, which was indeed what she had believed when she was a child.

Several more weeks and an overtly suicidal act were necessary before this wall of silence was lifted and a clandestine trance repeated during the sessions led her finally to speak truthfully to third parties, her parents or others. In this analysis, wishes to calm the inconsolable tears of the little girl in distress and to address the adolescent present in the session constituted a lasting stumbling block. For a long time, these twin moments of entreaty emerged in response to the analyst's position of reserve when faced with the seductive attitudes of the patient in search of identification. Her demands – for example, where could she buy a certain item of clothing that the analyst was wearing? – certainly called for moderation with regard to the content of the response, but they also required the analyst to support the movement towards femininity that was thereby outlined. Without such support, on each occasion, the swing towards a new regression was in danger of shattering the new impulsion. The analyst's task was thus to listen in such a way as to permit the little girl and the adolescent to appear on the same stage, without however seducing the little girl with words addressed to the adolescent.

Further reading

Ferenczi, S. (1955 [1933]). Confusion of tongues between adults and the child. The language of tenderness and passion. In: *Final Contributions to the Problems and Methods of Psychoanalysis*. London: Hogarth, pp. 155–167.

Ferenczi, S. (1995 [1932]). *The Clinical Diary of Sándor Ferenczi*, ed. J. Dupont (trans. M. Balint & N.Z. Jackson). Cambridge, MA: Harvard University Press.

Freud, S., and Ferenczi, S. (1996). *The Correspondence of Sigmund Freud and Sándor Ferenczi*, vol. 2, 1914–1919, ed. E. Falzeder and E. Brabant (trans. P. Hoffer). Cambridge, MA: Belknap Press.

Freud, S., and Ferenczi, S. (2000). *The Correspondence of Sigmund Freud and Sándor Ferenczi*, vol. 3, 1920–1933, ed. E. Falzeder and E. Brabant (trans. P. Hoffer). Cambridge, MA: Belknap Press.

Granoff, W. (2001). *Lacan, Ferenczi and Freud.* Paris: Gallimard (Series: Tracés).

KEY WORDS Adolescence, splitting, passion, tact, trauma.

CASE HISTORIES

NICOLAS DE COULON

While Freud often resorted to the case history to support his thinking and confirm his views, he also drew support from literary examples. He was convinced that the psychic truth of fictional characters was no less real than that observed in analysis: the profound and fruitful intuition of certain creators makes it possible to portray immediately what psychoanalysts often take longer to understand. In substance, psychic truth and novelistic fiction are necessarily entwined.

Whereas for weeks a young woman had been recounting nothing but nightmares that paralysed her and the analyst alike, on this day she recounted a dream, a real dream, which began just after her experience of anguish, as if the nightmare had taken place before. The dream began at the moment when the person who had abducted her let her go. She felt relieved, especially as he had not wanted to hurt her. He just wanted to give her a lesson! In the dream, she was nonetheless shocked and wanted to take revenge. The police confirmed that the villain was in reality the prosecutor: he led a double life, but there was insufficient proof to foil him. She decided, therefore, to take the matter in hand herself and went to provoke him, to taunt him, in a public library. The situation was once again coloured by a sense of disquiet: the villain had become invisible; she felt she was in danger and fled the library before realising that her child was still in there. This could have ended badly again, but she found her safe and sound, and then woke up, feeling relieved.

Here we have a dream that could provide the fabric for a detective story, but the most surprising thing was that the patient associated to it spontaneously. She named the protagonists: in the prosecutor she saw her father who had mistreated her in her childhood and who, above all, had abandoned her. The police made her think of her mother (the analyst had not immediately thought of this), who had not intervened sufficiently to protect her from her father. The child in danger was thus not only her son, but the little girl she once was. This scenario sums up more than a year of psychoanalysis. An interpretation followed in which, at the level of the transference, the analyst took on something of this profoundly antipathic father in whom, up till then, he had refused to recognise himself. Finally, in the dream, the signifier public library formed a link with the consulting room for, beside the couch, there is in fact a library. In this fiction, had the analysis become the site of the crime?

This session was not selected by chance; the leading thread proposed simplifies things and erases the hesitations, the intermingled tears. However, it does not conceal what is essential. What we have is an "abbreviated" case history, summed up by a single session composed of the dream and its associations. In the interests of speed, the case history has not been related; in fact, to some extent, it tells itself, with the disadvantage that the analyst's role remains in the shadows. In a more conventional narrative, one might perhaps have provided more material, for instance, the important events of the patient's life in order to link them up with the unfolding of the analysis. Perhaps it would have been useful to present several sessions, and even details of the words exchanged. To what end, though? To avoid turning it into a novel?

Speaking about a patient, writing a case history, is an attempt to share the essence of the analytic encounter, which is clearly impossible. To put it briefly, outside the session, it's no longer the session. One cannot give an exhaustive account of the words exchanged, of the intonation, of the process, of the patient's history that is in question. However detailed it may be, the case history remains partial, selective, reconstructed, in a word: fictional.

Nonetheless, resorting to this artifice sometimes helps to throw light on the elements concealed in the session, precisely due to the effects of proximity and actuality. The fictional gap is fruitful when it succeeds in preserving the psychic link between the situation of the session and that of the narrative. Writing therefore helps the analyst to evaluate what has eluded him in the session. For it is the unknown aspects of the countertransference that organise the scenography of the writing, but it is in the narrative that they have the possibility of being named. Thus, for the patient, it was the whole question of the detective story that suddenly appeared when she wrote the narrative of her dream.

Further reading

Freud, S. (1905 [1901]). *Fragment of ang analysis of a case of hysteria. S.E.* 7. London: Hogarth, pp. 7–122.

Freud, S. (1907). *Delusions and dreams in Jensen's 'Gradiva'. S.E.* 9. London: Hogarth, pp. 1–95.

Freud, S. (1909). *Analysis of a phobia in a five-year-old boy. S.E.* 10. London: Hogarth, pp. 5–149.

Freud, S. (1909). *Notes upon a case of obsessional neurosis. S.E.* 9. London: Hogarth, pp. 151–249.

Freud, S. (1912 [1911]). *Psycho-analytic notes on an autobiographical account of a case of paranoia' (Dementia paranoides). S.E.* 12. London: Hogarth, pp. 1–82.

Freud, S. (1918 [1914]). From the history of an *infantile neurosis. S.E.* 17. London: Hogarth, pp. 1–122.

Scarfone, D. (2009). Verité d'un texte: réflexions sur ce qu'il convient d'attendre d'un compte rendu de notre pratique analytique. *Bulletin de la Société psychanalytique de Montréal*, 21(3): 40–43.

KEY WORDS Fiction, narrative, dream.

INFANS SCRIPTOR

JEAN-YVES TAMET

The man was crying, but he didn't know why. The tears were streaming down his face; he was astonished because it was something new. A few instants before, he had spoken about the death of his sick mother: he was 10 years old at the time; now he was 60. No sooner had she died than he was sent away to boarding school at the start of the following school year; he hardly cried at all and never spoke about her again. Now, a long time later, he was looking back over things, at a time when marital conflicts were making him consider a separation that he did not want. It was only now that he saw himself as having been abandoned by his mother and surprised himself as he came to an understanding of his choice of a love partner. His wife was older than him: might she be the "substitute" for his absent mother? It is possible that, in the end, this was the basis of their relationship? Now, he was finally speaking about it, daring to speak about it, daring to speak about it to the analyst. What followed was a freeing up of his speech. He could now express those very memories in which affects were buried. One was almost tempted to silence him.

We are indebted to Freud for having drawn our attention to the infantile scenarios that persist in adulthood and structure certain actions. But it was J.-B. Pontalis who portrayed this process in images by giving it forms that evoke figures of childhood, in particular that which he called *infans scriptor.* After having written many analytic texts and edited numerous French or foreign works, he published a volume (*L'amour des commencements,* 1986) that was written as a story in which his intellectual development was evoked in the light of certain aspects of his life: the book concluded with this Latin expression emphasising the emergence of words that originated from the silence of the *infans.*

Back to the analysis: Transferences act with insistence. They place the analyst in the position of a recipient of words and of a forwarding agent when the words cannot be formulated. The man who was recounting this distant memory was sincere. How are we to understand that he was able to share so quickly with someone he did not know, at the beginning of his sessions, his secret, the source of torment inherited from childhood? At this stage of the encounter, the patient must turn to the analyst, the one who makes possible a powerful lifting of repression. This is about speaking to an unknown person who listens and does not comment immediately, who does not offer an explanation right away. In the trains of yesteryear, there were corridors where, leaning onto the wooden rail and peering out into the distance, men and women talked together. Ephemeral encounters took place and secrets were exchanged. Once at their destination, these strangers, who, for a time, had been so familiar, donned once again the clothes of their daily lives and disappeared. Each session of analysis is like this, unique but repeated.

The possibility of change stems from the capacity of words to migrate, and to carry along with them the affects that they contain. The evocative power of language allows for plunges and resurrections. In this way, what has been silenced finds life. This serves as an illustration of the difficulty of breaking free from fixed aspects of oneself, something that the singular process of analysis makes possible. This opening occurs with the liberation of buried speech. Fixed forms are put back into movement and new spaces open up: what is new is hidden within what is most familiar.

Pontalis, both as a writer and as a clinician, accorded great attention to experiences of psychic walling-up, during which, in childhood, speech gets blocked or immobilised. It is not a matter of boredom or lost time; no, it is a matter of unlived, immobile time, the very time that analysis puts back into action. It consists of stupor and blank terror, which are inscribed in the psyche like foreign bodies: words are imprinted but do not migrate, and, in this sense, they are lost, at least temporarily. They can, however, rediscover their mobility and, although they seemed to be lost, begin to live again and to speak of old psychic times.

The analyst opens up a path: when he was a child, the patient had seen his father's state of total distress when faced with the ordeal of bereavement. This man had become frozen. It was no doubt in order to protect his father that the little boy, identifying with his disarray, had adopted the posture of silence. Now, factual elements of his life are allowing him to call into question this statue of the commander.

Free association has fine days ahead of it because, by favouring remembering, it develops listening to language: it wends its way by reference, from one analogy to another, and so the "muteness of language" (Gomèz Mango, 2009) constructs its "discourse" which the analyst honours with his listening. Concerning this question with respect to the *infans*, it is interesting to note the proximity between Edmundo Gómez Mango's and Jean-Claude Rolland's way of thinking to that of Pontalis.

Infans scriptor closes the last page of *L'amour des commencements* (Pontalis, 1986) but it is also present in *La force d'attraction* (Pontalis, 1990) and in *Ce temps qui ne passe pas* (Pontalis, 1997). This expression is a shibboleth of the author that one finds from one line to another. It is the precious trace of the childhood that underpins and animates the life of the adult.

Further reading

Gómez Mango, E. (2009). *Un muet dans la langue*. Paris: Gallimard (Series: Connaissance de l'inconscient).

Pontalis, J.-B. (1986). *L'amour des commencements*. Paris: Gallimard (Series: Folio).

Pontalis, J.-B. (1990). *La force d'attraction*. Paris: Hachette (Series: La Librairie du XXe siècle).

Pontalis, J.-B. (1997). *Ce temps qui ne passe pas*. Paris: Gallimard (Series: Connaissance de l'inconscient).

Tamet, J.-Y. (2014). Persistance de la photographie. *Approches. Le silence des commencements*, 160: 77–84, December 2014.

KEY WORDS Construction, repetition, time.

2

FIGURES AND FORMS

THE ACTION OF FORM

LAURENCE KAHN

The free-floating attention required of the analyst is simply the counterpart of the rule of free association prescribed for the patient on the condition that we consider that transmission always takes place indirectly, thanks to the capture and conversion of an ensemble of perceptions. Even if depth is an indispensable auxiliary representation for thinking about the architecture of the psychical apparatus, we have no other way, in practising analysis, but the psychic surface for entering into contact with unconscious structures. A surface made up of visually and auditorily perceivable formations (dreams, symptoms, parapraxes, etc.), but also constituted by the effects of acts impelled by the transference.

Now, whether it is a matter of forms that offer themselves as such or of effects of the acting of the transference, the activity of distortion imposed by the censorship scrambles the systems of semantisation directly. This is true of the disguise of the latent contents (dreams, parapraxes, symptoms) that make themselves known without the conscious mind being able to *represent* to itself what is *presented* to it in this disguised form, but the same is true of the "distortion through transference" – the transference neurosis being a "recreated" neurosis thanks to the reactivation of the repressed impulses by means of fragments of reality available in the analytic environment. Thus, the form that presents itself to consciousness is always the fruit of psychic work in which antagonistic forces, namely, the realisation of unconscious impulses and the power of resistance are entangled. Within this horizon, the performative influence of speech in the session, that is to say not only what is said, but how it is said – the rhythm, the prosody, the inflections – participates in the action of the form.

A man whose analysis was marked by intense excitation maintained by relations with multiple partners had sought for a long time to keep me on tenterhooks by telling me all about his adventures. Then it was through telling me about the violent conflict between him and his maternal uncle – a man who had in part brought him up after the premature death of his father – that he sought to create a situation of complicity with the woman or the man that I was in the transference. One thing in any case was noticeable, albeit in no way accessible: apart from a few anecdotes repeated identically, the maternal figure, always described as tender and calm, remained in the shadows, which contrasted with the effervescence lived in the sessions – sessions that he rarely missed.

The situation occurred in which he was due to be away for a long enough period of time for the problem of the payment of those sessions that were going to be missed to arise. A very hostile movement emerged when he made it clear to me that, under no circumstances, given that this absence was necessary for professional reasons, would he pay this sum. I did not give way, pointing out to him that he was free to use his session times as he wished, whether he was present or absent, which brought his anger to boiling point. In his absence? What on earth did that mean since, precisely, he would not be with me? He left after threatening to break off his treatment… and returned a few weeks later at the time of one of his sessions. The confrontation resumed once again while, at the same time, it seemed evident to him that the analyst would have waited for him and that his session times would still be available. And then, one day, he arrived very late. In spite of a meeting, he insisted, he had made every effort to come. After a while, I said to him: "So that it wouldn't be once again a session in your absence?" – "That's got nothing to do with it," he replied furiously. "I hate you having 'holes'! I feel I'm betraying you." – "So you feel you don't have to pay me for the sessions during your long absence in order to erase the betrayal." – "Whose betrayal? Yours or mine?" – I was surprised: initially because the betrayal had changed sides; subsequently, I noticed that I was disconcerted by the amenable tone in which he had spoken to me. And then there was silence; a silence whose colouring was impossible to determine, but which continued unusually for two sessions. Until the day I asked, "My betrayal?" – "Yes," he said to me, "I don't know why I said that to you, you were there when I came back; you are always there; I have checked that!" – I was once again astonished by the sweetness of the tone that contrasted with the acrimony of verification. "Checked that, precisely because I am always there, we can see the hole?" – "It's not a problem of a hole in my finances." – "It could be another?" he replied, but in such a soft voice that he suddenly became inaudible. Verification of the hole, control of violence, countercathexis of emotion? Or alternatively, a declaration of love under the cover of conflict? Or the opposite, a declaration of war under cover of affection? At the following session, he paid me. His use of speech ceased to be evanescent, but I was still impregnated by this strange presence of disappearance, which was like the inverted replica of the threat of breaking off the treatment.

About a year later – and how can I speak about the intermediate processes of weaving – for a brief period, he asked me repeatedly if he could use my toilet at the beginning of the session. He felt confused, like a child, very shameful for feeling the need like that… and suddenly, he became inaudible. I asked: "Who is speaking in such a low voice?" Tit for tat, he replied: "Like low mass… without the priest. – Alright, the priest doesn't go into the W.C., but what can he verify?" A long silence followed. I saw myself in a sort of black cassock, as a priest who was conducting the mass but who didn't understand anything. All this was mixed up with my own particular impressions in which I was preoccupied by the death of his father, his burial, and was reproaching myself in addition for insisting on the matter of verification. What came was something quite different: as a child, he checked that it didn't disappear. And what he had to make sure did not disappear was his penis at the moment when his turd detached itself. His mother was concerned behind the locked door and would try to persuade him nicely to come out of the toilet. "One piece detaches itself, but not the other", he finally said, when he got back in contact with the ambivalence bound up with the mixture of maternal softness and authority. This was the first emergence of an intense oedipal relationship, strongly sanctioned by castration anxiety that made him chase one woman after another.

The action of form does not correspond, therefore, in any way, to a reverberation from subjectivity to subjectivity: in this case, if I was the priest kept at a distance, he was the one who verified and, furthermore, who spoke in a low voice. It opens up, as it were, an indentation in the perception of the action of the transference. Something, in this case, like, "It is important not to lose that in the hole!", which had no doubt helped me to stand firm in connection with the payment of the sessions. In this indentation there appeared in a veiled form the condensation of the father and mother around the disappearance of a penis, which would have had no impact if it had not resonated with the request to go and see the hole in my toilet, mixed with the paradoxical entanglement of violence and softness. Such a paradox, the first sign of a knot, could not be elucidated in the form of a "language-sensation".

Further reading

Donnet, J.-L. (2005). *La situation analysante.* Paris: Presses Universitaires de France.

Heimann, P., Little, M. I., Reich, A., and Tower, L. (1987). *Le Contre-transfert.* Paris: Navarin.

Kahn, L. (2012). *L'ecoute de l'analyste. De l'acte à la forme.* Paris: Presses Universitaires de France (Series: Le fil rouge).

Widlöcher, D. (1991). Affect et empathie. *Revue française de psychanalyse,* 63(1): 173–186.

KEY WORDS Transference action, perception, presentation/representation, psychic surface.

THE FIGURATION OF THE TRANSFERENCE

NICOLE OURY

The erratic behaviour, to say the least, of Norbert Hanold (Freud, 1907) an unwitting lover, served Freud as a clinical example for enlarging on delusion. The deeds and acts of the hero of *Gradiva* initially seem strange to the reader: Hanold takes refuge in his work to escape his perception of his childhood love incarnated by Zoe. Now she lives just around the corner from him, but if he passes her during the day in the street, he does not see her. Fortunately, his unconscious decides otherwise and she appears to him in a dream: the figuration of Zoe is transposed to Pompeii; she is walking in the streets and is buried under the ashes of the eruption of Vesuvius. The next morning, he has forgotten the dream. Inwardly agitated, Hanold feels compelled to leave the town where he is living. He leaves "precisely" for Pompeii where, as soon as he arrives, he contemplates the relief named Gradiva. He does not recall that he has already seen at his friend Zoe's house a similar posture of the foot "lifted from the ground… [touching] it only with the tip of the toes", but it suffices to awaken the childhood impression of the beautiful girl, even if it does not reach his conscious mind. He is then able to recall his initial dream, the traces of the lost object returning to him through the visual images and the enactment of the dream, which reveal to the reader and to Hanold a former link between two childhood friends, but transposed to Pompeii and to another epoch.

It is remarkable, Freud notes, that the recollected content of this dream initiates the delusion, here a transference love that sweeps along everything in its path. Thus, when, as a result of a fortunate fictional coincidence, Hanold catches sight of the real Zoe in Pompeii, the one his unconscious tells him not to notice, he is unable to realise that it is his childhood friend, alive and real, that he has seen. He makes her incarnate the figure of Gradiva, the name of the young girl in the relief, a fine example of a negative hallucination. Zoe plays her part in the incarnation by letting Hanold believe that she is Gradiva. Like the analyst, she assumes the role of Gradiva *rediviva* so that Hanold may finally recognise his love for her and his sensory confusion. Thanks to this transition via representation, the transference love has a fictional outcome here.

The meshing of the associative chains favours the representation of the transference. Certain details belonging to childhood love-objects are transposed onto the analyst and she becomes the father or the mother. Hanold swoons in front of a stele representing a Pompeian girl. Owing to the details of the position of her foot, this attractive figure serves as a substitute and reveals to him his former love for a childhood friend. The real Zoe tries to get herself noticed (she wants to be married) and readily agrees to represent Gradiva for Hanold. The two figures are superimposed and are indistinguishable.

J.-B. Pontalis thinks that Freud derived joy from reading this text, which portrays the fact that "our most unreasonable acts are dictated by persistent and forgotten impressions from our childhood, and that tiny details – here a peculiar gait, the position of a foot – determine the choice of the love-object" (Gómez Mango & Pontalis, 2012, p. 204). In analysis, the transference neurosis favours such a process: a tiny detail suffices, a silent link is formed between the patient's past and the present of the analysis and the depiction of the transference occurs.

An excess of figuration thus sometimes leads to a dramatic turn of events in the treatment: feelings of love of which the patient is unaware are powerfully projected onto the analyst, and there is then fire in the transference. "There is a complete change of scene; it is as though some piece of make-believe had been stopped by the sudden irruption of reality as when, for instance, a cry of fire is raised during a theatrical performance" (Freud, 1915, p. 162).

Further reading

Libres cahiers pour la psychanalyse. Transferts d'amours, 23, Spring, 2011. Paris: 2013. Issue 2, volume 77, pp 585-597.

KEY WORDS Transference-love, figuration, incarnation.

THE SIGNIFIER OF DEMARCATION

PATRICK MEROT

The signifier of demarcation is encountered constantly in Proust's *In Search of Lost Time.* Traces referring to sensoriality are one of the essential motive forces that animate the narrative. Rather than the example of the madeleine, let us take Swann's evocation of the women that he has loved. Far from being unique, they are eminently contingent and have only exerted their charm through the associations that they have aroused, associations consisting of sensations and memories in which sensoriality and pleasure or sadness are mixed: "When I succumbed to the attraction of a new face," Proust writes, "… I said to myself sadly that this love of ours, insofar as it is love for one particular creature, is not perhaps a very real thing, since, though associations of pleasant or painful musings can attach it for a time to a woman to the extent of making us believe that it has been inspired by her in a logically necessary way, if we detach ourselves deliberately or unconsciously from those associations, this love, as though it were in fact spontaneous and sprang from ourselves alone, will revive in order to bestow itself on another woman" (2015, p. 239).

In Freud, we find a remarkable example of this in the text on Jensen's *Gradiva.* Norbert is under the sway of a signifier of demarcation: "The sculpture represented a fully-grown girl stepping along, with her flowing dress a little pulled up so as to reveal her sandalled feet. One foot rested squarely on the ground; the other, lifted from the ground in the act of following after, touched it only with the tips of the toes, while the sole and heel rose almost perpendicularly" (1907, p. 10). Norbert found the almost perpendicular position of the right foot exaggerated; while he found it beautiful, he regretted that, because it was created only by the fantasy or whim of the sculptor, it had not been reproduced in a life-like manner. It took all the guile of Zoe Bergang, who in their relationship has the role of the analyst, for Norbert to be able to tear himself away from the power of this signifier of demarcation and gain access, in what may be called a talking cure, to another register and really see Zoe.

The screen-memory makes it possible to discern in an almost pure form the signifier of demarcation, marked by the intensity of the images, their very clear delimitation, but also their isolation with regard to associations and other unrelated memories. Guy Rosolato (1985) gives an example of this: Why had this 70-year-old man been thinking intensely for some time now about the "crunching sound of the sand under his footsteps when he was three years old?" (p. 78).

The signifier of demarcation is constituted from the traits that make up every representation that is distinct from verbal language: visual, auditory, olfactory, contact-based (gustatory or cutaneous), intero- and proprioceptive, motor-based (Rosolato, 1992). It helps to identify and fix bodily expressions, affects and drives, as well as the perceptions and sensations that comprise the particular quality of lived experience. It also constitutes what accompanies the nuances of the information that accompanies verbal communication, gestures, facial expressions and prosody that complete the functions of speech. Objective representations, whether spatial or temporal, are completed by a unique and individual context, that is specific to each one of us. Music is a domain in which the signifier of demarcation appears in the pure state.

The concept of the signifier of demarcation is part of the extension of Lacanian theory concerning the signifier. For Rosolato, it constitutes both recognition of a fundamental concept of Lacanian theory, the signifier, and the end of a tendency to take only the linguistic signifier into consideration, which does not suffice to account for the totality of the experience of the internal world. Digital signifiers (or linguistic signifiers) only concern a very fragmentary part of psychic functioning. With the signifier of demarcation, it is a matter (or analogical signifier) of proposing a concept for what has remained unformulated and no doubt unthought in the Lacanian formula.

A first demarcation of signifiers is only possible through the initial signifying action of the mother. Very often, when they appear, the evocations of these traces remain enigmatic for the subject who experiences them. Indeed, they refer back to archaic experiences, to the first sensations with the mother, since there is a prevalence of the signifier of demarcation in the child. They are similar to Piera Aulagnier's pictograms and Didier Anzieu's formal signifiers.

The operations of metaphor and metonymy identifiable in linguistic signifiers are also identifiable in the signifiers of demarcation. This point is essential. The signifier of demarcation and the correspondences that are established between its domain and that of digital signifiers elucidate a point that is often left implicit by analytic theories, namely, the relationship between the erogenous, oral, anal and genital zones – that is to say, all the fields of the part-object – the representations that are associated with them and the series of verbal representations associated with these representations.

One of the major functions of analysis is to allow for the translation of the signifiers of demarcation into linguistic signifiers (Rosolato, 1985, p. 91).

Further reading

Lacan, J. (1966). The instance of the letter in the unconscious, or reason since Freud. In: *Écrits*, trans. B. Fink, pp. 412–441. New York, NY: Norton, 2006.

Lacan, J. (1993 [1981]). On the signifier in the real and the bellowing miracle. In: *The psychoses (1955–1956), the seminar of Jacques Lacan book III*, ed. J.A. Miller, trans. R. Grigg. New York, NY: Norton.

Lacan, J. (2006 [1966]). Seminar on "The Purloined Letter". In: *Écrits*, trans. B. Fink, pp. 6–48. New York, NY: Norton.

Rosolato, G. (1985). *Élements de l'interprétation*. Paris: Gallimard.

Rosolato, G. (1992). Comment s'isolent les signifiants de démarcation. *Topique*, 49: 65–79.

KEY WORDS Part-object, pictogram, signifier of demarcation, erogenous zones.

THE PICTOGRAM OF THE PRIMAL

MIREILLE FOGNINI

It is rare, even exceptional, that "engrams", which Piera Aulagnier referred to as "pictograms of the primal" and Freud called "memory traces", can reach a state of representable and thinkable consciousness. This is because the psychic imprints of the metabolising relationship of the primal process are deployed on the basis of perceptual and sensory emotions received by the *infans* through the impacts of the maternal and environmental relationship, at a time when the other heterogeneous metabolisations, primary and secondary, have not yet come into being. Piera Aulagnier regards them as the representation of the "image of the bodily zone", the first relational schema inscribing the "image of the complementary-object-zone".

Literature sometimes offers us fine examples of the enigmatic experience of these strange and residual sensations; psychoanalytic work also sometimes gives access to them, albeit in a way that is more or less partially identifiable and expressible.

This original concept is developed in the *Violence of Interpretation* (Aulagnier, 2001 [1975]), which offers a theory of representation illuminating the fate of the psychotic's being and discourse. The work of Piera Aulagnier (1923–1990), an eminent psychoanalyst and co-founder in 1969 of the "Quatrième Groupe (OPLF: *Organisation psychanalytique de langue française*) and of the journal *Topique*, is centred around psychosis and narcissistic pathologies in her articles and other books: *Les Destins du plaisir* (1979), *L'Apprenti-historien et le maître sorcier: du discourse identifiant au discourse délirant* (1984), and *Un interprète en quete de sens* (1986).

The first session of a patient's analysis was taken up with the account of a dream that had left her feeling overwhelmed by the "nightmarish" final element, not dissimilar to the fantasy themes dear to Edgar Allan Poe. She was lost, wandering amidst ruins when, from a vestige, a woman of fascinating and magnetic beauty appeared. Paralysed with emotion, she could neither speak nor breathe yet felt attracted to her because she was both unknown and familiar. The unknown woman joined her mouth to hers and they mingled their tongues and saliva in an infinite kiss that made her swoon with pleasure, pleasure that turned into the sudden horror of sensing that the union of their tongues had become a fusion of flesh that was disintegrating and melting in their saliva, and then that the mouths of the unknown woman and of the dreamer had vanished: they had been liquefied. The dreamer said that she no longer felt she existed; just one thing remained: a "taste of death" in her mouth, which, after she had woken up, persisted for a long time in her saliva and turned her whole body upside down.

"This taste of death in my mouth", present from the first session was to return many times during the analysis of this "borderline" patient. We thus had to discover how she had fallen blindly in love with her partner as soon as this sensation began to invade her in an imminent fainting fit during the first kiss.

In the course of time, she discovered gradually that her oral means of auto-erotic self-consolation had been the permanent sucking of her tongue aimed at compensating for her difficulties of breast feeding triggered at birth in her primal experience as an *infans.* What had happened? She had been born amid the surrounding terror of very intense bombardments of her town during which her mother had narrowly escaped death, giving birth to her amid the explosions of bombs; this extreme state of weakness, causing her to lose consciousness repeatedly, had not allowed her to hold her baby when feeding her. But some nuns had managed to save the mother and the child by keeping the baby systematically at the breast, whom they massaged diligently, so that this mother who was convinced she was dying, or already dead, could give the baby some of her milk. According to the recollections gathered in the course of the analysis by the patient from her mother, she had been a baby who did not suckle at the breast, or only with great difficulty, and who would fall asleep with the nipple in her mouth while the mother also slipped into unconsciousness, in spite of the attentive massage of her breasts by the nuns. The entire evolution of the patient had subsequently been punctuated by difficulties in eating and in relationships.

Thus, the "primal" experience of this patient had formed an engram of a deeply buried "breast-mouth" pictogram of tactile, gustatory and relational sensory perception with the body of her dying mother with her baby in a fusional "feeling-felt state of non-dissociation": a taste of death in her mouth".

Further reading

Mijolla, A. de (Ed.) (2005 [2002]). *International dictionary of psychoanalysis*. London: McMillan. (See articles: autohistorisation, infans, I, pictogram, psychotic potentiality, identificatory project and violence of interpretation).

Valabrega, J-P. (2001). Les notions de pictogramme et de potentialité psychotique dans l'œuvre de Piera Aulagnier. *Topique*, 74: 119–122.

KEY WORDS Image of the complementary object-zone, feeling-felt state of non-dissociation, pictogram of the primal, breast-mouth pictogram, theory of representation, memory trace.

THE OSCILLATION BETWEEN METAPHOR AND METONYMY

PATRICK MEROT

A man described himself as a moral masochist and said he was satisfied with his autoerotic daydreams in which he was a woman's willing slave in kissing her feet. Feeling quite satisfied with the results of his analysis and having decided to go on with it, he said: "Nothing has changed, but while before I saw myself as benefiting from my fantasies, now I see myself as their victim." Thus, the day came when, having met a woman in reality, he was able to have access to real sexual relations. This meeting had an impact on his fantasy, but admittedly without really modifying it. What he liked about this idealised woman was her body: her feet, "of course", her thighs and her breasts; but her sexual organs remained a part that he left between parentheses, that he still found unsightly, even repugnant, and that he strived not to see. In short, they were unbearably ugly and the object of absolute horror. This obliged him, in the act of "coitus" (his language was always extremely precise), to engage in rather complex mental gymnastics, which he described with humour. This involved an oscillation between real sexual organs that were terribly metonymic, with which he was obliged to be in the greatest contiguity, something he could not accept, and a woman whose foot – and by default a part of the body – embodied ideally, and metaphorically, the object of his desire.

With the fetish, we are dealing both with an ordinary, and even trivial, object that permits disavowal (*Verleugnung*) and, at the same time, with the object that represents the maternal penis and which, in its uniqueness, and in an exclusive way, is the condition of jouissance. It is between these two senses that the oscillation between metaphor and metonymy is played out for the subject with very great precision and fragility.

In its simple metonymic sense (an immediate sense: the boot, in Luis Buñuel's 1964 film *Diary of a Chambermaid*), the fetish brushes aside the sexual and, in its metaphoric sense, it is what realises the presence of the maternal penis (the phantasmatic sense, as access to jouissance). As Guy Rosolato (1978b [1968]) writes, "the known (the penis) crushes the unknown (the mother's sexual organs) and what is recognised (these same sexual organs without a penis) is rendered unknown by the sight of the fetish that cancels it out" (p. 263). The metamorphosis appears to be a fullness of meaning, an idealisation, like a marvellous revelation. Therein lies the metaphor.

In Alfred Hitchcock's 1954 film, *Rear Window,* we can see how this concept of oscillation between metaphor and metonymy, which is based on a broad conception of both, can throw a great deal of light on the singular position of the subject. The state of immobility to which the character played by James Stewart, with a leg in plaster, is condemned, is translated by a psychic excitation that transforms him into a fanatical investigator. The multiple windows that he notices from his place of retreat function like little theatrical scenes in which many private stories are played out – stories without words – whose meaning he tries to reconstruct. He identifies without difficulty a succession of narratives that may be called metonymic for, in the series of scenes that he observes, the gestures of the various protagonists impose a translation, an immediate sense: a musician organising parties, amorous encounters at a dancer's home, etc.

In one of these windows, the dealings of a couple having a dispute provide a mass of observations that remain enigmatic: a disappearance, suspect suitcases, multiple telephone calls, nocturnal movements that give rise to an intense metaphorical-metonymic interplay until a meaning takes shape thanks to an imaginative leap, representing a creative metaphor.

This mechanism can be found at the heart of the approach to works of art and aesthetic jouissance, whether it is a case of interpreting a painting, listening to music, or of literature. In a text devoted to John Cowper Powys, Rosolato (1993 [1985]) highlights an interplay between the metonymy of raw perception and the metaphor of an experience of plenitude that can be evoked by the contemplation of nature: devoting oneself to the contemplation of nature and of the inanimate (a section of wall, an opening where there is a play of light), as well as to moments of ecstasy in which contraries meet, gives a sense of deliverance and reorganisation of the forces of being, serenity and happiness in a moment of delight in harmony with earthly powers. In this movement evoked by the writer, between raw perceptions of the inanimate and the aura of both intimate and limitless evocations, between united contraries, we can detect a metaphorical-metonymic oscillation that provokes a sense of joy comparable to that which comes from contemplating a work of art.

The concept of metaphorical-metonymic oscillation is part of a bipolar approach to associative functioning that employs the two modes of metaphor and metonymy, an explicit reference to Roman Jakobson and Jacques Lacan.

Metaphorical-metonymic oscillation occurs when an undecidable situation arises in the search for meaning. Consequently, in the attempt to bring out meaning, which is impossible to reach by means of the successful employment of the habitual combination of metaphor and metonymy, a sort of panic occurs, an oscillation between the two poles. Thus, it is when the interplay between the two associative modes is constantly renewed and finds no outcome that we can speak of oscillation.

Metaphorical-metonymic oscillation was first described by Rosolato in two specific contexts, in the clinical study of perversion (Rosolato, 1967) and in the origins of aesthetic joy (see Rosolato, 1969a [1965], 1969c [1963], 1969d [1960]), but it is encountered in many other situations. In this oscillation, it is a matter both of abolishing and maintaining the significations that emerge.

Further reading

Lacan, J. (1966). The instance of the letter in the unconscious, or reason since Freud. In: *Écrits*, trans. B. Fink, New York, NY: Norton, 2006, pp. 412–441.

Lacan, J. (1966). Metaphor of the subject. In: *Écrits*, trans. B. Fink, New York, NY: Norton, 2006, pp. 755–758.

Lacan, J. (1993 [1981]). Metaphor and metonymy I and II (Chs. XVII and XVIII). In: *The psychoses (1955–1956), the seminar of Jacques Lacan book III*, ed. J.A. Miller, trans. R. Grigg. New York, NY: Norton.

Rosolato, G. (1967). Étude des perversions sexuelles à partir du fétishisme. In: *Le Desir et la Perversion*. Paris: Seuil, pp. 7–52.

Rosolato, G. (1969 [1960]). Technique d'analyse picturale. In: *Essais sur le symbolique*. Paris: Gallimard (Series: Connaissance de l'inconscient, 1969 (reprinted Series: Tel, 1979), pp. 139–157.

Rosolato, G. (1969 [1963]). Les arts plastiques dans un système des beaux-arts. In: *Essais sur le symbolique*. Paris: Gallimard (Series: Connaissance de l'inconscient, 1969 (reprinted Series: Tel, 1979), pp. 129–138.

Rosolato, G. (1969 [1965]). Difficultés à surmonter pour une esthétique psychanalytique. In: *Essais sur le symbolique*. Paris: Gallimard (Series: Connaissance de l'inconscient, 1969 (reprinted Series: Tel, 1979), pp. 121–128.

Rosolato, G. (1993 [1985]). John Cowper Powys: l'extase préméditée. In: *Pour une psychanalyse exploratrice dans la culture*. Paris: Presses Universitaires de France, pp. 113–122.

KEY WORDS Aesthetics, metaphor, metonymy, perversion.

THE ANALOGY

CLAIRE TREMOULET

A young woman had difficulties in separating. It was the last session before the summer holidays. She began: "When you opened the door to come and get me from the waiting room, you were wearing a blue T-shirt, which made me think about the one that I put on my son this morning... my son, my baby... the thought came to me again that he could disappear, die, like the dog that I adored when I was small." The analyst said to her: "I have the same blue T-shirt as your son and I am going to disappear for a while during the holidays, but I will come back and I will be here after the holidays, on the date agreed. I will be waiting for you." She sighed. A moment of silence followed. And then she said, "I just fell asleep momentarily... I could see the face of my much loved mother."

The analogy, a word of Greek origin, appeared in French around the 13th century. According to Alain Rey (2005), "[i]n its first sense it is the identity of relationship between four or more elements, taken two by two. This notion of mathematical origin, employed in arithmetic as in geometry, seeks to designate any resemblance established between two pairs of terms, then between two terms. It refers, finally, and particularly, to the reasoning with which the human mind deduces from a similarity observed between several objects an unobserved and unverifiable similarity. In this sense, the analogy is one of our most essential and most uncertain modes of reasoning" (p. 300).

This common word is taken up by Jean-Claude Rolland to clarify his conception of psychoanalytic interpretation. He develops his ideas on this subject and offers a meticulous analysis of it in several of his books and articles. Initially, his remarks are based on the Freudian conception of language, bringing the various aspects of it into play and enriching it gradually. "Language," he writes," opens itself to the memory of the infantile because it has an aptitude for regression analogous to that which authorises the dream-work" (Rolland, 1998, p. 98). He then goes on to establish the link between interpretation and analogy: "Every time the analyst has the joy of hearing this creation of analogy and every time, through his interpretation, he simply brings its terms into a closer relationship, there appears, as its third unconscious term, a psychic formation to which access to speech had hitherto seemed absolutely closed: a dream, memory or thought. It is this form of interpretation that I propose to call analogical interpretation; it is notable for the efficacy and economy of means that it achieves" (p. 169).

Having posited in this way the "analogical interpretation", he provides the reader with elements that make it possible to liken the analogical interpretation to the joke, the *Witz*: "Analogical interpretation is an operation that has a certain similarity with that of the *Witz*." He adds: "The enemy of psychoanalytic thinking is common sense, which is unwilling to attribute wit, that is *Witz*, to words... Wit is the capacity of speech to take up the correspondences that flow secretly within language and to reveal, in a flash, a new meaning which immediately finds its clothing of words" (p. 174).

Further on, the sense of the initial conception of his finding is broadened by linking it up with transference regression and the compulsion to repeat before proposing another term that is personal to him, namely, that of the compulsion to represent, which he sees as a solution to the repetition compulsion. He writes: "The new power struggle introduced by the transference regression in the psychic conflict, the instinctual drive renunciation necessarily involved in undertaking an analysis, call forth the hypothesis that the compulsion to repeat, to which unconscious desire or drive demands are regularly subject, is substituted in analysis by a compulsion to represent, in which the first, as it were, develops itself, elaborates itself, satisfies itself *in effigie*, sublimates itself" (p. 235).

For Jean-Claude Rolland, analogical interpretation becomes one of the axes of change and evolution in analysis that permits an unconscious content to become conscious; this was the effect of the analogical interpretation that was given to the patient mentioned above.

Analogy is thus directly linked to the transference relationship. It is accompanied by a relative and temporary destructuring of the discourse, when the manifest content of the discourse, linked to an unconscious impulse and charged with visual images, satisfaction or fulfilment, albeit without any capacity for representation or enunciation, finds itself charged with a capacity for expressing infantile experience. At this precise moment, "the production of analogies [by the psychoanalyst] tends to compensate for this lack" (p. 235). Beyond repetition, the capacity for representation through the putting into words, into speech, of analogical interpretation, opens up.

Starting from the various links proposed by the author, analogical interpretation is based on a hidden community of meaning between two signifiers, on a mere homophony, on the contrary expression of opposite meanings, or alternatively on the rudimentary mechanism of contiguity.

Should this conception encourage us to consider analogical interpretation as a concept? It is not certain that this is a concern of the author, for he is more interested in sharing with us what, based on clinical experience, is useful to him, and perhaps to other analysts. Furthermore, is it not the case that we regularly use analogical interpretation in analysis, as Mr Jourdain[1] did with prose, while knowing nothing of it? Like prose, the practice of psychoanalysis gains from being deployed in all its complexity. This is precisely where the interest of Jean-Claude Rolland's work lies, that is, when he transforms a word of everyday language into a word that enriches the experience of analysis, as well as our own, through this original contribution. Is this not how theory progresses?

Note

1 Reference to Molière's (1660) *Le Bourgeois gentilhomme.*

Further reading

Hoffstadter, D., and Sander, E. (2013). *L'analogie, cœur de la pensée.* Paris: Odile Jacob.

Rolland, J.-C. (1998). *Guérir du mal d'aimer.* Paris: Gallimard.

Rolland, J.-C. (2003). L'analogie dans la situation analytique: un processus. *Libres cahiers pour la psychanalyse*, 7(1): 99–124.

KEY WORDS Compulsion to represent, analogical interpretation, transference.

THE IMAGE

OLIVIA TODISCO

Pierre Fédida's thinking on the image is dominated by melancholia and the dread of dying. The dream, as a model and experience, is fundamentally a work of mourning, mourning the unforgettable. Events but also, and above all, the face of the forgotten-unforgettable dead have a central place in what is unforgettable. That is why the image, in its essence, "touches the dead person", "for the dead person as a face … – forgotten by the living as a name – is the face that the dying man seeks to meet up with so as to appropriate his own death, while he still hopes that the living will grant him the grace to let himself form an image of his face in them, that which will write itself and inscribe itself for the time of the memory of the mourning" (Fédida, 2009a, p. 216).

Extending Freud's thought in *The Interpretation of Dreams* (1900), he emphasises that, if the dream image is presence, it consists, including plastically, in its visuality, of forgetting, that is, forgetting that once upon a time it was clairvoyant and that it saw. Fédida takes up the term "*voyance*" from Arthur Rimbaud (Correspondances [Letter to Paul Demeny dated 15 May 1875] in Rimbaud, 2009 [1972], p. 249), a term that would be developed by Jean-Claude Rolland to designate the "visionary" state of the *infans,* before being one who speaks.

Citing Walter Benjamin in his article "La régression", Fédida (2009c) expresses perhaps more clearly than in his philosophical and analytic article titled "Le souffle indistinct de l'image" (2009b) his thinking on the image, whether it be a memory image or a dream image; he develops the importance he accords to the places of infantile memory more than to its objects, which he calls the "genealogy of oneself". This is what Benjamin (1934) wrote: "Memory… is the medium of past experience, just as the earth is the medium in which dead cities lie buried. He who seeks to approach his own buried past must conduct himself like a man digging. He must not be afraid to return again and again to the same matter; to scatter it as one scatters earth, to turn it over as one turns over soil. For the matter itself is only a deposit, a stratum, which yields only to the most meticulous examination what constitutes the real treasure hidden within the earth: the images, severed from all earlier associations, that stand – like precious fragments or torsos in a collector's gallery... And the man who merely makes an inventory of his findings, while failing to establish the exact location of where in today's ground the ancient treasures have been stored up, cheats himself of his richest prize" (pp. 400–401).

The difficulty of the text titled "Le souffle indistinct de l'image" lies in part in the fact that in it, Fédida conducts a long philosophical reflection mixing image, dream image and painting, and evokes a variety of authors from Paul Klee to Pierre Boulez, including Freud. Generally speaking, the image is presented as a chiaroscuro, as a "hermetism" of which the dream image is the apogee, because it allies extreme sensory clarity with the deep obscurity born of the processes of condensation that it comprises. Thus, the dream becomes for him a theory of the image correlative to a theory of memory and language, its solipsism highlighting the sensitive quality of the image. For its part, the latter becomes a sort of presence, that is, the temporal form of the wish which is fulfilled in it, but also a kind deprivation of an interlocutor. For Fédida, "deprived of words", it is "bereft of a gaze". A connection can be made here with his theory of the images that are at work in the transference, considered as a series of copies, imitations, masks.

François Mauriac (1968 [1964]), continuing his autobiographical project in the *Inner Presence. Recollection of My Spiritual Life,* speaks of his relations to the dead in terms of certain aspects that complete the thinking of Fédida: "My mind could never encompass death. Yet the dead I call mine have never left me. At every moment of my life I seem to have been hemmed in by their constantly increasingly throng. But those from whom I was separated in my youth remain the closest, despite this uninterrupted increase. If my memory should fail, if one day I should lose control and succumb to forgetfulness, the dead who left me first would also be the last to be erased from my memory. Not a day or night passes, I believe, without their faces looming up, if only for the space of a sigh. Sometimes it is one, sometimes another, some of them at long intervals. And it is not always the faces of those we most loved that are called to mind; it is as though the fact of having been a part of the life of a child or youth was enough to give them the right of priority. Some of them whom I regarded with indifference at the time have become dear to me, upon reflection, if I may put it that way. I offer them now what they expected of me when they were still on earth – an affection I did not dream of giving" (pp. 54–55).

Further reading

Didi-Hubermann, G. (1992). *Ce que nous croyons. Ce qui nous regarde*. Paris: Minuit.

Fédida, P. (2009). La régression. In: *Le site de l'étranger*. Paris: Presses Universitaires de France, pp. 221–244.

Fédida, P. (2009). Le soufflé indistinct de l'image. In: *Le site de l'étranger*. Paris: Presses Universitaires de France, pp. 187–220.

Fédida, P. (2009). Rêve, visage et parole. In: *Crise et contretransfert*. Paris: Presses Universitaires de France.

Perret, C. (1992). *Walter Benjamin sans destin*. Paris: la Différence.

KEY WORDS Mourning, death, dream.

THE POLYPHONY OF DREAMS

MIREILLE FOGNINI

During a "fourth analysis",[1] an analyst spoke about the strangeness of her experience when a patient recounted a nightmare to her. The night before, this analyst had had a dream that had a direct bearing on her personal history and it had made her think immediately about this patient towards whom she felt a great sense of empathy. This patient had, in fact, just suffered a sudden trauma: the loss of an adolescent child. The analyst found her patient's dream as poignant as her own. The patient described how she was on her knees, with her head on the analyst's knees, in front of the door of her office. She was like a little girl sobbing without being able to stop. A continuous whimpering sound came from her throat. In the dream, the analyst was much older than she was in reality; she did not speak, but she had placed her hand on her hair. People were coming and going all around without paying attention to what was happening. Suddenly the patient cried out: "But why? Why? Why?" As a result of her cry, she woke up in tears. The aged analyst reminded her of her grandmother who had partly brought her up but had never been capable of making any gesture of affection. Moreover, the patient herself would never have dared to make such a gesture of abandonment with her.

The analyst was troubled by the proximity of this dream with the one she had had the same night. A long time ago, she herself had lost a young child and had then felt very alone. Her patient's trauma had reopened a wound in her. In her own dream, a very old woman was rocking her gently like an infant. She was indeed feeling sad and lost. Around her people from her family and colleagues were passing by; they were indifferent and seemed not to notice anything; her husband was also there, wearing a haughty and cold expression that she had never seen before. Bursting into irrepressible tears onto the old woman's shoulder, she repeated the words: "Why? Why?" After hearing the old lady explain to her kindly and firmly: "No, it is not: 'Why?' Now, it is, 'How?', she woke up with her eyelids stuck together by the dry salt of her tears.

Impressed by the enunciation of the words "It is: 'How?'" and by her patient's dream, the psychoanalyst, after working on the scenario of her own dream, concluded that both for herself and for her patient it was a matter of finding the means to metabolise the nameless sorrow that the death of one's own child causes a mother.

This clinical situation is comparable to that evoked by René Kaës (2002) in *La Polyphonie du rêve*. He shows that, in such situations, the psychoanalyst can work on "cross dreams in analysis" in what he calls the "common and shared oneiric space of the dream", since, for him, the privileged relationship of analysis makes it possible to develop a "common psyche between the analyst and the analysand". To the dream navel, "the tangled network of the world of our thoughts" whose total intrapsychic investigation Freud had already suggested was impossible, Kaës adds the existence of an "interpsychic fabric", where the dream, "resting on the unknown aspects of linking" succeeds in establishing a second navel, in the hollow of this common and shared space (pp. 64–78).

The first accounts of dreams, those of the Epic of Gilgamesh (see Fognini, 2008), like those of other mythical or religious narratives of certain civilisations, were, as Kaës points out, narratives intended to be shared with close relations or other people important to the dreamer who recounted them, within his own culture. The dreamer is considered here in his relationship to his or her community and to the organising principles of the world. (Charlotte Beradt [2002] considers from this perspective the influence of a genocidal dictatorship on individual dreams.)

Western culture has gradually recentred the dream around an intimate subjective process and Freud treated it in particular as an "egotistical" formation of the unconscious. However, psychoanalytical clinical work with groups has led Kaës (2001) to observe that the dream is not only this intrasubjective formation. The expression and function of the dream in the transference/countertransference space and time of analysis, its manifest interactivity within family or therapeutic groups and the reparative and transforming creativity of its internal theatres on the psychic stage, lend greater complexity to the approach to its motive forces, sources and relations, since, from birth onwards, the emotions, thoughts and identity of the subject interact with his environment.

The dream, then, is not, merely an "egotistical" creation: it turns out to be "deeply woven into intersubjectivity". At the heart of its inter- and intrapsychic interactions, the dream organises itself in the dreamer as a combination of several voices in which waking residues, nocturnal paths and traces of sleep interpolate each other, at the confluence of the internal and external worlds. And like a palimpsest in all its polyphony, this raw matter becomes transformed with the dreamer's nocturnal work as well as with his conscious waking account of it.

These hypotheses that emphasise the place of intersubjectivity in the deployment of the dream and its associations open up new meta-psychological perspectives for its understanding, its investigation and its interpretation.

COMMENTARY

RENÉ KAËS

The clinical evocation offered by Mireille Fognini introduces us pertinently to the issue and concept of the polyphony of dreams. What is reported here corresponds to the configuration of cross-dreams, which are highlighted in a remarkable way in the dream narrative by the signifier that I understand as the conjunction or articulation of I-We – the patient reports that she found herself on her knees, with her head on her analyst's knees, in front of the door of her office – but which may also suggest a scene/painting of Pietà or alternatively maternal support in front of the door of another scene. Of course, we do not have at our disposal here the analysand's associations or those of the analyst in a "fourth analysis" who shares this account with us. It is nevertheless true that the transference and countertransference elements mentioned delineate a common and shared oneiric space organised by this double dream navel that I have tried to distinguish: that which, according to Freud "reaches down into the unknown" and has its roots in the mycelium of the unconscious of each patient; and that which nourishes itself on our unconscious intersubjective relations.

As is often the case, the active traces of a traumatic experience that has affected both of them in their relationship to the dead child, and to what is associated with this in their own childhood, find in these cross-dreams a container and significant predispositions that the third function of the fourth analyst who listens to the account of the session is able to receive and transform into meaning, for each of them and for their common transference space.

The analyst noticed the sense of disarray and abandonment of her analysand and her call for help, an appeal to another when faced with a vital threat and the distress linked to it. The dream portrays this recourse against feelings of helplessness, no doubt through the figure of a tutelary grandmother who, in silence, "places her hand on her hair". It is the function of formal signifiers, described by Didier Anzieu (1987), to constitute psychic representatives of the qualities of psychic containers.

That the analyst is troubled by the proximity of this dream with her own dream, the same night, is a constant in such experiences: what seems to me to be involved is the blurring of the limits of the oneiric envelopes. Each of the two women knows – no doubt knowledge of which they are unaware, as Freud would say – what is implied by the loss of a child and the search for consolation.

Note

1 The "fourth analysis" (*analyse quatrième*) is the "theory of the '*contrôle*', that is, of the situation of supervision... which takes into account all the scenarios and persons who intervene in it, as well as their visible or hidden interactions". Taken from the site of the "Fourth Group" (*Quatrième Groupe*): http://www.quatrième-groupe.org

Further reading

Fognini, M. (2007) (Ed.). *Frondaisons et arborescences des rêves: nouvelles perspectives. Le Coq-Héron*, 191. Paris: Érès.

Fognini, M. (2007). Un troisième ombilic du rêve gestateur de l'émergence de myths? *Les hauts-lieux et non-lieux du rêve, Filigrane*, 16(2): 62–75.

Kaës, R. (2002). *La Polyphonie du rêve. L'expérience onirique commune et partagée.* Paris: Dunod.

Kaës, R. (2007). Les rêves en heritage. La possibilité et l'impossibilité de rêver. *Les hauts-lieux et non-lieux du rêve, Filigrane*, 16(2): 5–14.

Kaës, R. (2012). Polyphonie et polytopie du rêve. *Rêves, cauchemars et mythes en famille, Le divan familial*, 19(2): 137–157. Paris: In Press.

KEY WORDS Common and shared oneiric space, interpsychic fabric, unconscious intersubjective links, mycelium of the subject's unconscious, cross-dreams, second dream navel.

THE DETAIL

CLAUDE ARLÈS

As soon as this patient had made an appointment, the analyst was struck by his belief that he was being judged, justifying his willingness to fight. From the outset, the patient drew attention feverishly to the weight of his name and the negligence of his interlocutors with regard to spelling it properly. In his first session, a detail moved the analyst deeply, without his being able, at this stage, to grasp its full import. Noticing a sardonic smile on his analyst's face, the patient suddenly got carried away and evoked the irreducible state of conflict uniting him and his father, whom he presented as an intransigent man who was often belittling and invariably disappointed by his children and their perception of their father's prerogatives. This outline of an inaugural construction blurred a more furtive, and swiftly repressed, variation of this same detail.

During the session, an untoward thought came to the analyst's mind. With such a surname, how could one escape the inevitable evocation of the worst atrocities of war and of a heritage – his name – that was inescapable? This detail then assumed various forms and the analytic work slowly outlined the motif of his crusade. It organised for a long time the patient's relationship with the analyst and the content of his grievances: his opinions about globalisation, about the sharks that financial analysts are, about the future of the planet, about his phobia of school, where he always felt he was constantly being judged, or about a more current variation of this phobia, which, for the same reasons, concerned women and fed his sadness about not really being able to commit himself. He also expressed his hatred of the governing classes and of dissymmetry, or his refusal to have children so as to spare them an inevitably sordid fate and the presence of a father who would bring them nothing good.

For a long time, this form of fighting governed the sessions. The patient was testing the analyst. He had assigned him the role of a judge who was attentive to his requisitions while hoping not to be judged, condemned or worse, dismissed. During the analysis, however, his anger abated and he discovered the intense erotic attachment that he felt towards his father whom we had already glimpsed in the first session through this detail. Up until then, he had only been able to approach him through the idea of being judged, and above all beaten, and he displaced this conflict on to political, historical or family representations.

Albeit a word in ordinary language, the detail is not an analytic concept as such, and we are indebted to Daniel Arasse for its usage in the pictorial domain. This specific attention nonetheless has an important place in the analyst's listening, and then in his interpretations. Whether it concerns a word, an attitude, a voice inflection, a minimal or secondary element of the discourse, or what may be left aside and buried by the painstaking description of an event or memory that holds the analysand's attention, the analyst accords details special attention, especially if he perceives a movement, in himself or in the analysand, that seeks to brush them aside or tone them down. Good examples of this are slips of the tongue or incidental ideas. The repressed is condensed and, thanks to its emergence into consciousness, the incidental idea becomes rather like a symptom that the analyst waits for and scrutinises in his listening. Thus, psychic events that are as incongruous as they are cumbersome, and fleeting fantasies, are woven with unconscious representations and traces that repression pushes into the background so that they remain invisible.

In his study called "Heurs et malheurs de l'anachronism", Arasse (2006a) defines the anachronism in painting by the fact that the conditions of visibility transform what the spectator can see. A Renaissance painting is not seen in the same way in an art gallery as when it was hanging high in the dim light of a church or a castle (pp. 219–231). This modification of the conditions of visibility due to a real change of context is quite similar to what the analytic situation seeks to promote. The discovery by Daniel Arasse of a detail of an Annunciation painted by Fra Filippo Lippi may be compared with the emergence of an (un)expected ([*in*]*attendu*) psychic event in analysis. Sitting in the calm of a courtyard, with her face tilted forward, Mary is looking at a dove, a common visual representation of the Holy Ghost, which is observing her and seems to be suspended in its flight a few inches above her knees. When observing the painting more closely, we realise that this dove is flitting around, and that golden rays fan out from the bird and disappear into in the folds of her dress at the level of her belly. At this spot there is a hole in her garment, a barely visible buttonhole.

With acuity and erudition, Arasse interprets this detail of the painting as a fantasy concerning the nun who served the artist as a model. Through this detail, painted so as not to be seen, the artist lets us get a glimpse of his relationship to painting and to the enigma of the female body (see Arasse, 1992, pp. 326–327, and 2006b, pp. 111–124). For the psychoanalyst and reader of Arasse, Filippo Lippi painted an Annunciation whose technique is rather classical but, concerning this detail and the venial impulse that took hold of him, which he only allowed himself to express because he thought that this detail would not be seen, he was not aware of what he was painting when he painted this detail. Present in the very centre of the painting, the detail appears to be a truly enigmatic message that many art critics and historians did not notice for many years until one day, when the painting was being taken down or rehung, it was noticed.

Further reading

Arasse, D. (1992). *Le Détail. Pour une histoire rapprochée de la peinture.* Paris: Flammarion.

Arasse, D. (2006). *Histoires de peintures.* Paris: Gallimard.

Arlès, C. (2014). Un amour lointain. *Libres cahiers pour la psychanalyse, Le moi et l'objet*, 29, pp. 113–125. Paris: In Press.

Gómez Mango, E. (2009). L'émotion poétique. In: *Un muet dans la langue.* Paris: Gallimard, pp. 35–36.

KEY WORDS Detail, incidental idea, interpretation, enigmatic message, representation-transference.

PROJECTIVE IDENTIFICATION

NICOLE OURY

An adolescent girl, aged 13, was in individual analytic psychodrama. The first months were marked by the enactment of one of her symptoms: a female voice would speak to her, making death threats and scornful insults. In the scenarios that she played out, she was in a state of confusion between two representations: that of her accusing mother and that of the attacking daughter. She sometimes seemed relieved and calm when this voice was embodied in a scene between a mother and a daughter played by two therapists or she was in collusion with one or both of them, in echolalia. Her sense of identity was far from being assured: a part of her psyche was entangled in fantasy with the representation of a bad mother. We may assume that this internal confusion stigmatised by this delusional voice was the result of projective identifications arising from links with a maternal imago that was itself struggling with a confusion of identity. The young girl in the psychodrama made desperate efforts to control this voice whose manifest expression emerged in the form of insults and scorn.

After a few months, she was able to internalise this voice and, caught off guard by her confusion, she talked for the first time about the role of a grandmother and her granddaughter to one and the same therapist. The "inheritance" of this voice then clearly appeared to contain the unconscious identifications of the bad mother with the unconscious offshoots of the grandmother's psyche, projected into the adolescent or reappropriated by her. Her maternal grandmother had been hospitalised on several occasions for delusional episodes, events that had stigmatised the maternal line of descent. This inherited voice of the offshoots of unconscious impulses persecuted the young girl from the inside, possessed her, but did not belong to her completely. It represented progress for this adolescent girl to be able to incarnate, that is to put outside herself, to project onto one and the same person, the confusion that reigned in her between two internal agencies: a persecuting omnipotent superego and a masochistic ego, entangled and assimilated with confused internal mother/daughter representations (Freud, 1922, pp. 226–227).

The unexpected departure of one of the therapists made it possible, outside the sessions with the patient, to elaborate intertransferences coloured by persecution, and was associated with the death, which had never been explained, of one of her mother's sisters. The projective identifications directed at the therapists thus made it possible to elucidate the identifications they were carrying and, at the same time, the persecuting voice evolved towards a civilising superego (see Bion, 1970, pp. 125–129; Oury, 2013).

Projective identification, a Kleinian concept *par excellence,* can assume several meanings, depending on the authors, and is linked to three fields: the psychic development of the child, the understanding of psychotic and delusional processes, and finally child psychoanalysis. Briefly stated, the subject lends to others elements of his own ego with which he cannot coexist.

Melanie Klein (1932, 1946) analysed the psychic development of the child from the standpoint of his structuring relations with his mother: identification occurs insofar as the self is projected into the other as if into a mirror. The mechanism of projection involves projecting outside what the subject refuses in himself, namely, the aggressive and negative aspects. Initially, the child keeps in his own psyche what is good and projects into the maternal imago what is bad. Subsequently, he identifies with this projection. Thus, the aim of the process of projective identification in normal development is to reappropriate what initially was most reviled.

In 1946, Klein described the pathological projective identification at work in psychotic processes. She showed how the "prototype of the aggressive object-relationship" has as its aim the denial of reality with, as its corollary, an impoverishment of the ego through discharge into the other: the subject tries desperately to take control of the thoughts of others by offloading into the other what he cannot accept in himself, to the point of thinking that he is hurting the other in this way. The other thus becomes dangerous because he is the depositary of what belonged to the subject, while denial prevents the latter from recognising this.

This domination by the mind of the other is natural and spontaneous in the mother/child relationship. Theorisations in psychoanalysis of the child look at the vicissitudes of the child's psychic development in the light of the processes of projective identification (see Tamet, Oury & Villand, 2012). Jean Laplanche (2013) explored the unconscious identifications between parents and children as well as their evolution: in the first years of its life, the child "is in the presence of the adult and receiving messages from him or her that are not raw facts but must be translated" (p. 80). Laplanche argues "that finally the adults in the child's presence will above all reactivate their infantile sexuality" (p. 83). What counts is the way that the child interprets, translates and appropriates the message originating in the parental unconscious, which can range from projective identification to a simple enigmatic message. The child is the natural locus of projection for the parental ideal ego and, owing to its affective dependence, it conforms to what is unconsciously expected from it. "Early in my career," D.W. Winnicott (1958 [1948]) related, "a little boy came to hospital by himself and said to me, 'Please, Doctor, mother complains of a pain in my stomach', and this drew my attention usefully to the part mother can play" (p. 92), indicating thereby the colouring of family relations by mutual projective identification between mother/child psyches.

Further reading

Bion, W. (1970). *Attention and interpretation.* London: Tavistock.

Freud, S. (1922). *Some neurotic mechanisms in jealousy, paranoia and homosexuality. S.E.* 18. London: Hogarth, pp. 223–232.

Klein, M. (1932). *The psychoanalysis of children.* London: Hogarth.

Klein, M. (1946). Notes on some schizoid mechanisms. In: *Envy and gratitude and other papers, 1921–45. The writings of Melanie Klein*, Vol. III. London: Hogarth Press, pp. 1–24.

Laplanche, J. (2013). Le genre, le sexe et le sexual. In: *Sur la théorie de la séduction, Libres cahiers pour la psychanalyse, Etudes.* Paris: In Press, pp. 69–103.

Oury, N. (2013). Sonner à plain souffle du cor! Paper read at a meeting of analysts of the l'Association Psychanalytique de France (APF) in Lyon, 16 March 2013 on the theme "L'appel du vivant".

Tamet, J.-Y., Oury, N., and Villand, M. (2012). *Inquiétudes des amours enfantines.* Paris: Presses Universitaires de France.

Winnicott, D.W. (1958 [1948]). Reparation in respect of mother's organized defence against depression. In: *Through paediatrics to psychoanalysis: Collected Papers.* London: Tavistock, pp. 91–96.

KEY WORDS Identification, projective identification, intertransferences, projection, civilising superego, transmission.

THE CENTRAL PHANTASY OF ACTED VIOLENCE

ROSINE JOZEF PERELBERG

Sometimes, we can have access to the central phantasy of patients who resort to violence that is acted out. This phantasy is often an account of the primal scene in which their pre-oedipal and oedipal theories appear. In Freud's work, moreover, it is almost exclusively within the context of the primitive scene and Oedipus complex that the term "violence" (*Heftigkeit*) appears.

In the very first meeting, the patient communicated a question that, for him, amounted to an obsession. He was wondering about his parents' sexuality. He was convinced that they indulged in sadomasochistic games. He had always "known" this. When he was a young child, he and one of his sisters would hide behind the bedroom door to listen to them. They had caught them reading out loud passages from a book that described games of this kind. Later, they had heard them putting them into practice.

During this first consultation, the patient's account was extremely confusing. When he talked in confidence about the scene in which he was spying on his parents with his sister, it was as if he was speaking of a screen memory that allowed him to project an initial depiction of the primal scene. Then he talked about his own violent behaviour. At university, he took part with other young people in various disturbing practices and, with a girlfriend, he had organised games based on a constant escalation in sexual violence. In the course of the analysis, what was quickly striking was the fact that each time an interpretation helped the patient to understand what was happening in him, he had the feeling he was going mad and immediately had to retreat. If not, he ran the risk of ceasing to exist. As soon as he had the impression that the analyst understood him, he felt he had to take leave of his sessions for a while. He was capable of missing a whole week of sessions without being aware of the time that had gone by. Often, he would fall into a deep sleep from which nothing could awaken him, neither the alarm clocks placed around his bed nor his mother's yelling. Alternatively, he would play compulsively with video games in which robotic violence was exerted against enemies deprived of all humanity.

To begin with the interpretations pertained to his complete avoidance of the experience of analysis as well as of the obstacles that he met with in his relationship with the analyst. The patient's sleep, devoid of any dreams, was also a way of retreating from experiencing his capacity to think. He regularly talked about his wish to meet women as well as of his need to flee from them. To protect himself from the terror that they inspired in him, he resorted to behaving violently towards men. It was partly fantasy-based and partly acted out. This was no comfortable form of refuge because he found himself immediately faced with his drive impulses.

The analyst's careful interpretations helped him to get a sense of the correlation between his violence towards men and his terror of women. However, in the transference, the slightest interpretation reinforced his fear of intrusion and led to a flare up of his violence. Incidentally, he told the analyst one day that he had bought a pistol and some bullets that he kept at home. It was clearly a way of keeping her hostage with a part of himself and, at the same time, of remaining at a distance from the terror that his own destructiveness inspired in him.

Drawing on the anxiety that she felt in the countertransference, the analyst was able to show him that he wanted to see if he could terrify her in order to protect himself against the fear that she inspired in him. He got rid of the pistol but deprived himself in so doing of the capacity to terrorise her. So now he was lost, abandoned and deeply depressed.

To counter his depression, he then got involved in delinquent activities. Without really realising what he was saying, he said that he felt more comfortable coming to his session after having indulged in some dangerous activities such as reselling stolen diamonds. It made him feel omnipotent. The analyst pointed out to him that that this was probably a means of reducing his fear of the power that she could have over him. Among other transference meanings, these offences were aimed at putting distance between them, and especially of avoiding having a meaningful emotional experience with her.

From a technical point of view, the situation was delicate, as is always the case when patients resort to this kind of primitive narcissistic destructiveness to protect themselves. For the patient, the emotional experience of shared understanding in the transference was unbearable. Opening himself to genuine exchange involved the risk at any moment of being submerged, and the risk of his fragile sense of identity being destroyed. Each time the analyst tried to understand him, he experienced it as a manoeuvre of seduction and felt involved in a relationship that risked costing him his life, drowning his contours, and making him disappear. Faced with this danger, he swiftly took refuge in what he believed was the robust and virile world of delinquency. Paradoxically, this world of delinquency had his mother's backing (she agreed, for example, to cover the patient when he had resold stolen jewels). And, of course, this backing meant that he found himself confined in a perverse situation with her.

The patient was constantly confused. If the analyst pointed out contradictions between his different projects, and contrasted the analysis and his university studies with his delinquent activities, he did not understand. For him, everything had the same value, without differentiation or separation, in the image of his inner chaos. This plunged him into constant reversals. Whenever he tried to establish a relationship with a woman, the patient would succumb to the terror of his poisons, artifices, and perversion. He would then immediately try to flee from any female creature (woman, analyst, girl), which plunged him into shame, humiliation and confusion. When, on the contrary, he threw himself into his delinquent activities with his male friends, he was then caught up in anxieties related to his homosexual desires. He disentangled himself from this through aggressive and violent acting out, which once again terrorised and persecuted him. The same seesaw movement was present in the sessions: he was constantly buffeted by anxieties connected with an archaic oedipal configuration from which he could not free himself.

In the transference, the situation was equally delicate. If he had the impression that the analyst was getting close to him, he experienced it as an attempt by a phallic mother to control him. This led him to take refuge in a world of men, but there the relationships were also caught up in fantasies of violence and murder. Conversely, if he felt that the analyst was leaving space between them, he experienced it as abandonment in the face of the terror that his fantasies of sadomasochistic relations aroused in him. In order to defend himself against closeness, he was potentially capable of responding by committing murder, but equally too much distance could lead him to suicide.

Consequently, in the course of the work, recourse to a certain degree of acting out was difficult to avoid. It was the only way of keeping at bay the danger of an explosion of violence during the session. For the patient, the danger resided as much in the analyst as in himself.

However, as the treatment went on, increased understanding emerged. It often manifested itself before the process of elaboration itself and provided him with salutary support. In this way, the acting out – his absences, for example – could be brought back within the space of the session and worked on. Gradually, the analyst realised that the patient was using them to preserve the process. And, when he returned, it became possible to speak about it.

Then, one day, he finally managed to speak more extensively about his childhood. He even made a slip of the tongue: "The problem with my stepfather," he said, "is that he can't get used to the idea that he wasn't there when I was conceived. There was just me and my mother, he wasn't there." Suddenly realising what he had just said to me, the patient found himself for the first time in contact with his central fantasy, namely of witnessing his own conception and of excluding his stepfather. Furthermore, he immediately felt imprisoned in a world where there was just him and his mother, and saw himself reduced finally to being nothing more than the plaything of her desires. "That's why she would've liked me to be a girl or a homo," he said. "For her, homos never leave their mother."

That day, the patient noted his slip of the tongue immediately. More time was needed, though, before he was able to fully appreciate the significance of what he had said. A few months later, a dream made it possible to take up these fantasised convictions in the transference. He was then able to appreciate their implications. In this dream, he was looking for his father, but only he and his mother were represented. He felt confined in a world controlled by his mother or by the analyst. And in this world, any form of questioning concerning his father was impossible for him. Everything was blocked. When the analyst pointed out that for him it was as if he had not had a father, he replied: "It seems astonishing, but up until now I have never thought of myself as someone who had a biological father. I realise that that is what is changing today, and that it will change my life." It was true. It was a turning-point in the analysis. The patient was subsequently able to come more regularly to his sessions.

At the root of all violent behaviour, it is as if there is an intrigue or narrative that is seeking to express itself. This unconscious narrative is sometimes expressed in a screen memory that takes up an "event" from childhood (real or fantasised). It provides an explanation that the subject gives to himself or his existence. Sometimes, this recourse to enacted violence is the only means that the subject has to communicate how he sees his existence, his relationships with others, and the mythical narrative that he can establish of his origins. The analytic process must then follow the associative chains that manifest themselves through violent acting out, as well as transference acting, in order to gradually allow this narrative of the subject's origins to express itself.

Further reading

Perelberg, R. J. (Ed.). (2004). *Violence et suicide.* Paris: Presses Universitaires de France.

Perelberg, R. J. (2009). Murdered father; dead father: Revisiting the Oedipus complex. *The International Journal of Psychoanalysis*, 90: 713–732.

Perelberg, R. J. (2013). A father is being beaten: Constructions in the analysis of some male patients. *The International Journal of Psychoanalysis*, 92(1): 97–116.

KEY WORDS Depression, destructiveness, murder of the father, archaic Oedipus, acted violence.

THE BEATEN FATHER

ROSINE JOZEF PERELBERG

With certain patients, analytic work brings out, in different forms, the fantasy of "a father is being beaten". What I am referring to does not necessarily mean that it is the father who is being beaten. It is more a matter of a construction derived from free associations and dreams, the fruit of the analytic encounter, that is obtained thanks to the work of interpretation. This configuration corresponds, if you like, to a moment in the analysis that makes it possible to organise a broader role for the symbolic father in the subject's psyche.

This man had been the victim of an accident the week before. His car was written off, but he was not hurt. Shortly before the accident, the analyst had felt that he was overcome by a certain degree of apathy, as if he had ceased to take interest in things. She linked this partly to a forthcoming change in his work as a teacher. In her countertransference, she also felt a loss of interest and had linked this to the approaching summer holidays and the feelings of insecurity that can be attached to it. After the accident, the day before the session that I am going to report, the analyst had pointed out that this accident might be related to his wish to have an analyst providing the role of a protective father. The next day, the patient came in and lay down on the couch. He said he had found a car on the internet. It was in good condition. It belonged to a policeman, which made him feel confident. He then added, with excitement, that he had had a dream, after several weeks during which he had not had any.

> "We were in a car. I was one of the passengers and I was with my family, my mother and my brother. We were adolescents. We arrived at an open market. There were costumes from George Lucas' *Star Wars* (2008–2014) guards' uniforms, with their empty masks. They were more or less lined up beside each other, but all of them were missing something. One of them had no boots. We stopped to get out. I then realised that we were wearing long trench coats. When I was a child, we often went to the market in a neighbouring village, and I would buy clothes. I loved rummaging through piles of things; it was incredible what one could find in the way of junk and even good things. I used to buy long coats; they were very practical and warm for wintertime. I liked

> them very much. In the dream, we were wearing them. Then, in the third part of the dream (the first part unfolded in the car, the second at the market), the crowd of people was dispersing. I needed the toilets. Finally, I found them. I opened the door. There was an old man and his penis was hanging out. I passed in front of him. He seemed to get animated, but then he left. In all that, there was no excitation; rather, a sense of disgust."

There was a moment of silence. Then the patient thought about a female teacher who had just arrived at the *lycée*. She had recently bought a Darth Vader toy for her son. He associated to her arrival at the *lycée* that morning: he had seen a young workman who was really handsome. Then he explained: "Darth Vader is in fact the father of one of the characters in the film. He represents both authority and evil. The guards are clones of this character. They are all dressed like him. All these masked characters, these empty uniforms, seem rather inhuman to me. In the dream, they look like shells.

The analyst interpreted: "You are all dressed in these long coats, like when you were children… like Darth Vader, and there are all these bits that are missing… the uniforms are empty on the inside."

Later during the session, the patient added: "This reminds me of my own father, who did not see his children again. For her part, the analyst heard: "who does not see his children" and thought about Darth Vader's mask, about this face with pierced absent eyes concerning which it is not possible to know if they can see you.

> This dream seems to depict the quest for the father, for a protective father, a quest that is constantly disappointed because the dreamer finds himself constantly faced with a castrating, castrated, empty father. Associating, he said that when he was a child, he dreamed that later he would be an adult wearing a uniform. But in the dream, all the uniforms had something that was missing. It was clear to the analyst that these feelings of emptiness and loss were linked to the real absence of his father in his history and no doubt, to the fact that for him, his accident was linked to a lack of paternal vigilance on the analyst's part. All that created the image of a father who was not there to see his children, who was not a witness of their relationship with their mother. All these empty uniforms point towards a hollow or negative father, a non-father; that is to say, a father that is still not in the position of a third party

> in the subject's psyche and who does not ensure the dual function of an erotic father and a prohibiting father.

The patient associated to his childhood as well as to the beginnings of our transference relationship, but everything took on substance in the actuality of the session, as he was telling the dream, in the evocation of this paternal image that appeared through Darth Vader and the universe of *Star Wars*. It is a universe of war, of trenches, echoed by the adjective "trench" in "trench coat". And the man who exhibits his penis in the dream is also a father figure, but an evil and perverse father figure who exhibits his power while being, in spite of that, a desired/expected father. The sense of disgust felt by the patient in the dream seems also to be a reaction against the desire he nourished towards his father.

> In the following session, he continued with a new dream: "There was a group of men. One of them had been accused of something. He had broken a law or something like that. Another got hold of him, and hit him and kicked him so much that he was left lying unconscious on the ground. Then a woman appeared; she was with the man who had been beaten up. And yet she did not come to his help immediately. She was trying to discuss with the leader of the group. She was trying to get on with him and to promise him something. Her companion was still lying on the ground. I don't know if she abandoned him or if she was doing that to help him. The leader went away and she went with him. I left. On the road there was a Turkish bakery. I saw a spinach and feta fritter. There were lots of good things. I passed in front of it and told myself I had gone out for the evening and that now I knew where I could find something to eat. I thought about this group of men. Usually, one does not get beaten up for breaking the law. They belonged to a sort of primitive society, a gang of outlaws, dominated by the survival of the fittest. When this woman tried to win favour with the leaders, there was something sexual involved. That disturbs me a lot."

Apparently, if the dream depicted the situation that the patient was experiencing in the transference, the analyst's interpretations were for him like an avalanche of sadistic blows that were designed to leave him "unconscious" on the couch. They were also like the bewitching woman who was trying to seduce the leader of the gang to divert his anger. At the same time, the patient identified himself with the different positions: he was both the violent man who was doing the beating and the one who was masochistically being beaten. The polysemy of the image is emphasised by the fact that it was a group of men who were beating up the main character. Echoes of the brothers of the primal horde are not far away. The dreamer is also the witness of the whole of this scene which, in short, illustrates the fantasy "a man is being beaten". The associations show that there is a link between the man who is beating or who is being beaten and the father, Darth Vader. Seen from a passive position, the scene is homosexual, with the mother looking on. This scene seems to be like a transformed version of that of the accident.

The father was absent in this man's life and was only present as a facet of his mother's desire. This absence was also linked to the violence exerted towards his mother. Consequently, it is difficult for him to mobilise both his aggressiveness and his desire. His experience of the mother/son, analyst/patient relationship is one of a bond between two persons that leaves no way out. There is a relationship between last night's dream, the accident of the week before, the transference and the experience of a perverse and seductive, as well as containing, mother. Infantile experiences that were previously unrepresentable thus acquire representations retroactively in the analytic process.

My clinical experience leads me to think, for my part, that the fantasy "a father is being beaten" constitutes a crucial elaboration in the analysis of many male patients, the expression of awareness of ambivalent feelings towards the father.

The fantasy of the "beaten" father can open the way towards the reinforcement of a male identification, the mobilisation of feelings of rage and violence, and the possibility of using aggressiveness in a more creative way.

Further reading

Bion, W.R. (1963). *Elements of psycho-analysis*. London: Heinemann.

Bollas, C. (1992). *Being a character*. New York: Harper Collins.

Bollas, C. (2008). *The evocative object world*. London: Routledge.

Chabert, C. (2005). Clinical and metapsychological reflections on "A child is being beaten". In: *Freud: A modern reader*, ed. Perelberg, R.J. London: Routledge.

Freud, S. (1920). *Beyond the pleasure principle. S.E.* 18. London: Hogarth, pp. 1–64.

Kristeva, J. (2008). A father is beaten to death. In: *The dead father: A psychoanalytic enquiry*, ed. Kalinich, L., Taylor. S. London: Routledge.

Perelberg, R.J. (Ed.) (2004). *Violence et suicide.* Paris: Presses Universitaires de France.

Perelberg, R.J. (2009). Murdered father; dead father: Revisiting the Oedipus complex. *The International Journal of Psychoanalysis*, 90: 713–732.

Perelberg, R.J. (2013). A father is being beaten: Constructions in the analysis of some male patients. *The International Journal of Psychoanalysis*, 92(1): 97–116.

KEY WORDS Construction, paternal function, foreclosure, dead father, narcissistic father.

3

LISTENING

REVERIE AND ALPHA FUNCTION

MICHAEL PARSONS

Towards the end of Chapter Twelve of *Learning from Experience*, Wilfred R. Bion (1962) asks the following question: "When a mother loves the infant, what does she do it with?" And he replies: "Leaving aside the physical channels of communication my impression is that her love is expressed by reverie" (pp. 35–36). Then he emphasises the link between this reverie and what he calls "alpha function". According to him, our psychical apparatus cannot directly process the experience of raw reality. The elementary fragments of this experience cannot, for instance, be the object of a thought, give birth to a dream or find a place in memory. As such, these fragments that he calls "beta elements" cannot produce anything. If the psyche is to be able to take possession of them actively and do something with them, they must first be converted into alpha elements. These, on the contrary, can be subject to psychic transformations.

Bion proposes the term "alpha function" to designate the process that makes it possible to transform beta elements that cannot be assimilated by the psyche into alpha elements that can be thought or used in the imaginative world or in dreams. The development of the infant's alpha capacity depends on its mother's capacity for reverie. This capacity enables the mother to receive any psychic object from the infant and to submit it to the process of transformation of her own alpha function. The result is something that the infant will then be able to make use of in his inner life.

Bion did not go further in elaborating the concept of maternal reverie, but this description and the links that can be established with the analytic situation make it a concept that is rich with echoes. We are quite close here to what D.W. Winnicott called "primary maternal preoccupation". For him, the expression refers to a particular state of receptiveness, a specific sensibility of the mother to the demands of the infant's inner state. And what he calls the "elaboration in fantasy of concrete experience" is also comparable with the work of alpha function and the transformation of beta elements that it makes possible.

In many respects, the analyst's psychic state in the session belongs to the register of maternal reverie. In its psychoanalytic sense, this word does not refer to a vague withdrawal or a state of daydreaming. It is a way for the analyst to bring into resonance all the levels of awareness of his being (mental, affective and physical) in order to be available for any experience he may encounter coming from the patient or from what he feels inwardly. This requires a sort of inner clarity, not in the sense in which we speak of that concept, but rather in the sense that the term has when it refers to an opening of space, a transparency, just as when we speak of water or sky being clear. Reverie is at once a state and a process. It is a specific state of alert receptiveness combined with the activity that needs to be deployed to maintain oneself in this state.

Analytic sessions are often permeated by powerful emotions. And yet even when storm clouds accumulate and the wind is whipping the surface of the lake, underneath, the original clarity of the water remains. It is there, within reach. When an analyst is caught up in his efforts to interpret a patient's attacks, whether he is trying to contain the patient's provocations or to elucidate the complex feelings that the patient is making him experience, his reverie remains active, both as an internal state and as an effort to maintain this state. In music, the equivalent of reverie would be basso continuo. It supports the melody of the highest pitched voices, whether peaceful or troubled. It deploys them. The analyst's reverie is thus not a defence; nor is it a way of resisting troubling or painful transference experiences or a means of avoiding an overly direct identification with the violent impulses enacted by the patient. Rather, it is a process that leads the analyst to understand the experience with which the patient is confronting him. Above all, it is what guides the analyst in his search for an adequate way to communicate with the patient concerning this experience.

In the analyst's psyche, the departure point for any interpretation is an experience originating in the patient, but as such it is a beta element. The analyst thus finds himself faced with an aspect of the patient's functioning, but if he tries to present it to the patient directly, he finds himself in the position of the removal man who picks up a piece of furniture to move it from one place to another. Bion drew attention to how psychotic patients strive to evacuate the beta elements that encumber them by projecting them into the analyst. Analysts constantly run the risk of doing as much with their interpretations by evacuating them into their patients. This danger exists above all if they do not bring their alpha function to bear sufficiently on the experience that they want to give back to the patient before communicating it to him. The experience that the analyst has of what comes from the patient cannot have any effect on the patient if it remains purely and simply what the analyst has experienced. To interpret what he has experienced, the analyst must make use of his alpha function. It is this that gives his experience the transformational and evolving potential of interpretation.

A patient, who is a teacher, said that, one day, during his class, he suddenly "let go". Ideas came to him that were original and stimulating both for him and his students. He knew that he was going to take part in a conference one week later. Could the magic of words reproduce itself? At this conference, a colleague that he knew would be present and he feared that this would break the spell. "I can only let go when I am alone," he said. "If there is a colleague in the room, everything collapses and rivalry prevails". The transference allusion is clear.

Imagine that the analyst wants to reflect something of this back to the patient. He could say to him for example; "You probably see me as a rival and you are afraid that I will spoil your creativity or deprive you of it." Even without complementary material, it is a possible interpretation. Let's call it A. At first sight, it seems more pertinent than something like: "There are two of us in this room." This second way of formulating things (let's say, formulation B) is not very explicit. If one just expresses it because one vaguely has the feeling that there is some rivalry in the air and that it is necessary to say something, it is likely to come to nothing. The patient may even experience these words as aggressive. Let's call this interpretation (and the way it is received by the patient) interpretation B1.

Now, let's look at the situation a little differently. Suppose that the analyst thinks that the content of A is pertinent, but that he is unwilling to use it as such because he feels that the formulation is too explicit, too clear, that it restricts things too much, that it closes the range of internal movements that the patient can offer in response. He may then have recourse to his alpha function and try to conserve the essence of what he wanted to say, leaving aside everything which, in the formulation A, restricts the openness of the patient's psychic responses. This can lead to an interpretation that might then be: "There are two of us in this room." Let's call that interpretation B2. The words of B2 are strictly identical to those of B1. And yet the interpretation is completely different, both from the analyst's and the patient's point of view. If the patient responds, for example, by saying that he has suddenly realised that he sees the analyst as a rival, the idea that was contained in A may have been for him the object of a discovery. If the patient says nothing of the kind, but the analyst considers nevertheless that rivalry is the essential point, he may interpret the way in which the patient gets around it and say: "You seem not to want to consider that you might see me as a rival." The possibility of revealing the idea at the centre of the formulation A is thus not lost. Other paths also remain open and the patient can make something of my interpretation that the analyst had not expected. The closed horizon organised by the formulation A leaves little chance for the shared discovery of something initially unknown to the patient and analyst alike.

The analyst's employment of his capacity for reverie requires real confidence in the analytic process as well as in his way of going about it. One must trust oneself. This might seem to refer to a passive quality, while failing to recognise the real work of the analyst. And yet the psychic work that leads to the formulation B2 is infinitely more demanding than that which leads to A. The analyst is not passive, but the nature of his work remains strangely invisible. The affective experience that the patient has of B2 is different from that which he/she can have of B1, even if the words corresponding to B1 and B2 are the same. The same is true for the experience that the baby has of food: this experience depends on the internal state of its mother, and not simply on what she gives it to eat. A and B2 are not simply different interpretations because their contents are different. They are different because their origins in the psyche of the analyst are different. B1 and B2 are identical from the point of view of their contents, but they are different interpretations because their points of departure in the psyche of the analyst are different. This way of seeing things coincides with what Sacha Nacht said when he insisted on the "deep state of the analyst" at the moment of making the interpretation. Reverie is what brings the analyst's alpha function into play. It is the process that makes it possible for the beta elements that the analyst receives from the patient to become alpha elements, which can then give birth to a productive interpretation. In the example with which we began, the interpretation must evolve in the analyst's mind and pass from A to B2. This is not, however, a matter of conscious work on the formulation: it can only occur by bringing into play a larger and deeper capacity, namely, the capacity for reverie.

Further reading

Bion, W.R. (1962). *Learning from experience.* London: Heinemann.

Nacht, S. (1962). The curative *factors* in psychoanalysis. *The International Journal of Psychoanalysis,* 43: 206–211.

Ogden, T. (1997). *Reverie and Interpretation. Sensing something human.* Northvale: Aronson.

Parsons, M. (2014). What does interpretation put into words? In: *Living psychoanalysis, from theory to experience* (Chapter 10). London: Routledge.

Winnicott, D.W. (1958 [1954]). Primary maternal preoccupation. In: *Through paediatrics to psychoanalysis: Collected papers.* London: Tavistock, pp. 300–305.

KEY WORDS Internal setting, analytic listening, alpha and beta elements, interpretation, primary maternal preoccupation.

NEGATIVE CAPABILITY AND CAPACITY FOR REVERIE

RÉAL LAPERRIÈRE

A patient presented herself at her morning session in a completely distraught state. She had been crying, as often happened to her, during much of the night, in a state of despair devoid of any thought. It was "extreme suffering" about which she could not say anything. Gradually, she was able to put together a few words and organise a few ideas in an attempt to understand this state. It was to do with the uncertainty of the current situation in her life: the sale of her house, a professional move, a trip with a girlfriend... No assurance anywhere... "It's too much!" she said. "So you should wait," the analyst replied. She then burst into tears: "Waiting... Waiting... It's unbearable! It's helplessness!"

What prevented her from accepting feeling helpless for a while? For her, this question was inadmissible, unthinkable; for helplessness, even transitory, brought about a catastrophic experience. The uncertainty plunged her into the void. Waiting was synonymous with total disarray. Without the capacity to dream of a happy outcome, the suspense became in the strict sense unliveable: it reminded her of radical disarray and emptiness of thought. She therefore had to avoid any situation of uncertainty, mystery and doubt. The discovery of her psychic reality was therefore equally compromised.

Another patient had dreamed the night before that her boyfriend was cheating on her with another girl. When she woke up, she telephoned him, saying: "I know you've been cheating on me!" Her boyfriend's reaction of surprise, his questions as to the reasons for such an accusation, and then the soothing tone in which he told her that she was mistaken did nothing to change her conviction: "Well, then, you're intending to do it!" The analyst tried to get her to think about her dream and to see how it might portray what was happening in her, but in vain; instead, she took these suggestions as an attack on her narcissism. According to her, the analyst was calling into question faculties of "intuition" that had never let her down. He was not acknowledging this exceptional gift that she had always made use of to take decisions in love, friendship and in her professional life. There would be no use in pointing out that it was precisely what had often led to failure. She remained convinced, unshakeable. Her intuition was an objective fact. It could not be the sign of a psychic reality to be discovered: it was like that, just as uninterpretable as the external world.

What both these patients were lacking was what Wilfred R. Bion called "negative capability". The capacity for reverie that he associates with it is (in a circular fashion) both its foundation and consequence.

It was from John Keats that Bion borrowed the term "negative capability". For the poet, the term refers to the state in which "a man is capable of being in uncertainties, mysteries, doubts, without any irritable reaching after fact and reason" (Letter to George and Thomas Keats, 21 Dec 1817, [Wu, 2005, p. 1351]). Keats sees it as the "mark of the man of accomplishment". For Bion, it is also an essential condition of the analyst's work in the session. It enables him to tolerate, with patience, security and confidence (but not without anxiety), the frustration of not being able to understand as well as the need to remain in a state of uncertainty and waiting. It is necessary for the later emergence of the "selected fact" that will serve as a basis for interpretation. Admittedly, this negative capability is based on the analyst's confidence in the analytic method, but it also depends on the analyst's aptitude for investing in his capacity for "reverie" in the session – just as much, moreover, as it is a condition for it.

This pair – negative capability/capacity for reverie – proves to be decisive with certain patients in whom the emergence of meaning and the illusion anticipating satisfaction are constantly impeded by the unconscious belief that there can be no happy outcome for their wishes. A radical pessimism bars the way to any possibility of anticipatory illusion coming into play. This was the case with the first patient. She cannot face uncertainty because the unconscious thought of the worst impedes her from dreaming about a happy outcome that would help her to wait. The lack of anticipatory illusion and of negative capability is no less important when, for the patient, the most important thing is to be right, as this is what "guarantees her narcissistic integrity", as Wilfrid Reid (2008, p. 71) writes. Inner reality then acquires an intangible de facto status, and the resistance to doubt, to waiting, to uncertainty in the appreciation of this inner reality bars access to any discovery of her psychic life.

Further reading

Phillips, A. (2003). *Trois capacities negatives*. Paris: L'Olivier.

Reid, W. (2008). Un nouveau regard sur la pulsion, le trauma et la méthode analytique. Première partie: une théorie de la psyche. *Filigrane*, 17, 2008/1, *Une théorie de la psyché*, pp. 68–94.

Reid, W. (2008). Un nouveau regard sur la pulsion, le trauma et la méthode analytique. Deuxième partie: une théorie de la méthode. *Filigrane*, 17, 2008/2, *Une théorie de la psyché*, pp. 70–98.

KEY WORDS Disarray, anticipatory illusion, helplessness, psychic reality.

THE INNER DISCOURSE

JEAN-YVES TAMET

The notion of inner discourse proposed by Jean-Claude Rolland (2002) extends the notion of countertransference. It is based on his listening in analysis to movements experienced by the analyst and secondarily relayed to the patient. A short clinical sequence will help to situate the establishment of this singular listening and its development during the analysis.

A modest man, who had a good understanding of himself, had been coming to analysis for a long time. On the basis of what he had said about his current difficulties and his internal experience of traumatic events linked to his early childhood, the analyst had formed a version of this patient's history in his mind. This was the history that the patient himself was unable to talk about freely in the sessions. This narrative – for its form had become the equivalent of a text – featured a silent pain that had overwhelmed both the child that he was and his parents. It was linked to health and had evolved against a background of stoicism consisting of abnegation, courage, and also discreet seduction. In short, *never explain, never complain* could have been the motto of these childhood and parental universes. However, for a long period, this representation remained inaccessible during the sessions. A state of shock repeating the initial wound put the same silence at the heart of the transference.

The analysis nonetheless unfolded at its own rhythm and, gradually, by paying attention to associative openings, elements forged at the heart of the analyst's listening could be introduced. The patient was then able to appropriate these elements and link them up with his conception of his own past. One day, the analyst's silent narrative was used and embraced within that of the patient: evoking a silent mother figure going away sadly, the analyst made a connection with the patient's mother going away in the evenings from the place where he had been hospitalised as a child, leaving her child there alone. This connection facilitated the recognition and then the appropriation of shared pain. As if liberated, the patient recollected his mother's sadness and the conflict of being both the seductive child and, because of his bodily affliction, the disappointing child.

The evolution in the analyst's constructions has its counterpart in the patient. This was a symmetrical work of elaboration, with the sole reservation that the analyst attributes a different value and significance to this emergence in himself. "At a given moment the discourse supplants psychic experience and becomes its representative and, furthermore, its substitute," Rolland (2002, p. 95) noted. He thus attributes considerable value to those thoughts, ideas and impressions that colonise the psychic functioning of the analyst during the session. They are the manifestations of underground work, violent, even insurrectional, effected by language that operates by mingling unforeseen visual or linguistic percepts or fragments. Sometimes, and this is what we call interpretation, words are articulated out loud, as if driven by an exigency, and directed towards the patient, bringing the fragments of signifiers into closer relationship along the analogical path.

We hypothesize that these constructions have a structural connection with the fantasy life of the patient during the session, and call into question the presence and representation of the object with regard to both its historical determinism and its economic cathexis.

In this analysis, the childhood scenario, and its trail of disappointment from which seduction was not excluded, was there, silently, and this silence was strongly based on an oedipal pleasure that continued to have for him an exquisite and transgressive dimension. To approach it, the regressive path of analysis had to go back through long periods of concealment. It was these periods that, in silence, engulfed the inner discourse, a space of figuration or of breakdown, but also of unknown subversion.

In another elaboration of the countertransference, Michel de M'Uzan (2013 [1976]) has described a similar state, that of the paradoxical transference, a sporadic and violent emergence that is more akin to a hallucinatory moment. On the contrary, the inner discourse, though marked by moments of searing intensity, is more of a slowly forged construction.

Do all analyses evoke an inner discourse? Sometimes, time is needed before this narrative is established, as if there is a strong and muffled opposition to the transition of images into words: the recognition of the presence in oneself of this discourse is the sign that the transference has taken hold and that the sexual has attained a status that permits its construction and elaboration.

Further reading

Jablonka, I. (2013). *L'histoire est une littérature contemporaine*. Paris: Seuil.
Quignard, P. (2014). *Mourir de penser*. Paris: Grasset.
Rolland, J.-C. (2015). *Quatre essais sur la vie de l'âme*. Paris: Gallimard.

KEY WORDS Construction, countertransference, inner discourse, interpretation, object relation, silence.

CO-THINKING

FELIPE VOTADORO

Daniel Widlöcher has suggested the term "co-thinking" to describe a reciprocal process of the development of associative activity that is made possible by the double fundamental rule in the analytic situation. The involvement of the thinking person of the analyst, through the induction effect that makes him the receiver of what is thought by the analysand, invalidates the idea of "pure" listening: the roles of "interpreter" and "interpreted" are thus made more complex, for the analysand also "listens" to the analyst. The task carried out by the psychoanalyst/observer thus consists in perceiving an effect of transmission induced by the analysand. It is situated beyond words, for although they are conscious, words acquire their meaning within the associative contextual network, which implies the employment of preconscious and unconscious elements. Thus, co-thinking may be considered as the vehicle of unconscious to conscious communication, the illocutionary framework of which the interplay of the transference and countertransference is a part. The author contends that the term "co-thinking" should provide a response to the questions raised by the "vague" and scarcely Freudian character of terms such as "intersubjectivity" or "empathy", and also stands in contrast to a model of attentive listening to the "plays of the signifier" alone.

For him, the session should be considered as the locus of a succession of mental acts that are associated with each other. "What in a given event and context gives birth to the following event is the force of meaning [the associative force] that evokes this new act; it is not a matter of temporal causality, but rather of a mutual attraction" (Widlöcher, 2003, p. 61). The association between two thoughts may thus be explained by their latent connection, their structure and by the cathexis of this link, the actualisation: a double mechanism is thus involved. The associative dispositions depend on formal analogies, past habits or purposive identities, but these do little more than outline the current flowing through the cathexis. However, associativity does not involve the space of just one psychic apparatus, and it is in this respect that there is "co-thinking".

However, co-thinking is not empathy. Thus, there are "moments when co-thinking diverges and when the representations that are forged in the analyst's mind recede or separate radically from the analysand's associative network" (p. 61). Empathy, then, reveals its non-analytic character: understanding the feelings of others or sharing the same emotions, as in sympathy, "is not a problem in itself, but the discovery of derivatives of the formations of the unconscious alone is a psychoanalytic question" (Widlöcher, 1998, p. 10). In short, "for the psychoanalyst, the experience is more one of the opaqueness of someone else's mind, and certainly not of its transparency that can be read like an open book" (Widlöcher & Delattre, 2003, p. 72), and it is this opaqueness that initiates analytic work that is accomplished by two people.

Here is a clinical illustration offered by Widlöcher himself.

> The patient, a teacher in her fifties, reported a dream at the beginning of a session: she had the task of giving lessons to the granddaughter of her former teacher. But the latter had died a long time ago and had never had a child. The patient still had a sense of boundless gratitude and admiration for her. She owed her everything, her professional success, but above all an intellectual filiation that had never faltered. The fact of having, in turn, to give lessons to her granddaughter was a situation that was both touching and comical. Indeed, it was as if she had become her own teacher's teacher, the analyst said to her. The patient was startled: "What you are saying is astonishing." She seemed troubled, but then suddenly she said: "What a coincidence! In my bag I've got a reprint of an original edition of Freud that I wanted to offer you. I didn't know if I would have the courage to give it to you or even speak to you about it!"

This might be regarded as a small example of telepathy. Of course, it is easy to identify the associative paths in it. One might suppose that this patient was presenting herself extremely submissively, while at the same time feigning to know nothing about psychoanalysis. Recently, she had dreamed that another teacher of hers, a man this time, was welcoming her warmly. She had made this link with the analyst, while emphasising that she in no way feared a closer relationship with him.

In terms of transference and countertransference, and what may be called drive transference, there is much that could be said: to what extent is the analyst addressed as a maternal imago? Is this a matter of phallic rivalry or does it fall within a more clearly oedipal perspective? In both cases, what she has in her bag is unquestionably the phallus that she possesses and that she lets him desire.

What is worth noting here is another form of involvement of the psychoanalyst's thinking, another form of involvement of his person, through which he is led to think out an interpretation that immediately gives meaning to the fact that the patient possesses in her bag precisely what she has power over, while allowing herself to offer it to the analyst.

The mind of the patient could not, throughout the session, or in the hours (or sessions) that preceded it, have failed to be preoccupied by what she had in her bag and by the fantasy that expressed this. The dream could only be the expression of this fantasy. In formulating the interpretation "being the analyst of her own analyst", the latter was simply expressing the induction effect of what was on the patient's mind. It is not surprising, then, that the actual fact, the book in her bag, "the phallus in her pocket", directly echoed what underpinned the associative course of her thoughts (Widlöcher, 2003, p. 90).

Further reading

Widlöcher, D. (1986). *Metapsychologie du sens.* Paris: Presses Universitaires de France.

Widlöcher, D. (1996). *Les nouvelles cartes de la psychanalyse.* Paris: Odile Jacob.

Widlöcher, D. (2003). *La psychanalyse en dialogue.* Paris: Odile Jacob.

Widlöcher, D. (2010). *Comment on devient psychanalyste… et comment on le reste.* Paris: Odile Jacob.

KEY WORDS Association of ideas, analytic communication, countertransference, empathy, negative empathy, transmission.

THE CHIMERA

DOMINIQUE TABONE-WEIL

This patient needed several years to settle into a stable setting; at the beginning, it had been intolerable for her and she had attacked it constantly. Today, she freely invests interest in her sessions and engages in them, whereas the dominating theme of her entire life up until now has been one of non-engagement. But nothing is acquired once and for all and this analysis is still in "danger" of being broken off. This session was the last before the analyst was due to be absent for a week, an absence that had been announced a month before, during which the patient had planned to make a trip with a girlfriend.

She arrived feeling "encumbered": she had not felt like coming and did not feel like going away with her friend either. She came with a heavy heart, just like when she had to go to school as a little girl. Her associations revolved around the fear of being disappointed by her loved ones, in her relationships, in her undertakings, and of "making a bad choice". A girlfriend of hers, who was pregnant, had returned to live with her with only a few euros per month to live on (the price of the patient's analysis); she thought this was a very bad choice. The session was rather laborious; she did not talk much and stopped in the middle of sentences. The analyst had the feeling that the patient was censoring herself constantly, and began to feel a bit discouraged. At the same time, she told herself that the patient was once again on the point of losing interest in the analysis and of stopping. During a silence, the analyst was wondering about the pertinence of the analysis for her, and about its pertinence in general. She had the depressing thought it was perhaps all a vast sham, and the distressing feeling of not having access to what would give or restore meaning.

Suddenly, an image of flying heads crossed her mind, like in a ball game. The analyst recognised a dream she had recounted to her own analyst more than 10 years before, which he had commented on by saying: "I'm making fun of you" ("*Je me paie votre tête*"). She then had a sudden doubt. Had he not in fact said, "You are making fun of me?" ("*Vous payez ma tête?*") This would be more logical because, when one does an analysis, one does in fact pay for someone's "head" (*on se paie la tête de quelqu'un*) (his/her thought, listening, knowledge). The analyst then wondered if her patient was not making fun of her, among other things with these long silences during which she actively resisted the fundamental rule, beginning each sentence in response to the analyst's "Yes?", inviting her to say more, by saying: "*No,* I was just thinking about...". Unless, in fact, it was the analyst who was making fun of her by agreeing to let her use the couch as she had requested, when it was not a "good" indication. The analyst was led to think about the way she paid for her sessions, at the beginning of the month, which had the hallmarks of a magical act. Elements from previous sessions also came back to the analyst's mind: the patient had said that she could only accept an invitation to travel from her stepmother if she paid her own ticket herself, so as not to owe her anything.

At this point, the analyst invited her to continue with her usual, "Yes?" to which the patient replied to her great surprise: "I've just had a flash, I saw my stepmother's head and I said to myself: At least, that's done." In fact, she said, she was wondering if she still needed to come to her sessions. She wasn't sure. She had succeeded, for example, in resolving the problems with her stepmother.

"You have got rid of the stepmother and you are wondering if you might not get rid of me as well, which would avoid the risk of depending too much on me or of being disappointed with the trip, even if you pay for your ticket yourself," the analyst said.

This image, apparently unrelated to what was being said, arose as a condensation of what was going on between the patient and the analyst. The feeling of discouraged helplessness that she made the analyst feel, echoing her own doubts, caused this forgotten and violent image of flying heads to emerge and recalled the exchange in which the analyst was making fun of her own analyst, in which he was making fun of her, in which all that was pointless. In the present session, the analyst had a moment of decathexis, echoing that of her patient, a moment that confronted both of them with the risk of abandonment, fusion or disappointment.

It was Michel de M'Uzan who invented the concept of the chimera, which he defined as a monstrous entity born of the relationship between the unconscious minds of the two protagonists. Here, it was a matter of the friend's baby who, stuck to her mother, was perhaps a representation among others of the monstrous child that the analyst and patient were in the process of creating together. The chimera is related to issues of identity. In the session, it activates in the analyst regressive modes of functioning in which there is a volatile state of the distinction of identity for the purpose of understanding the other and of getting to know him thanks to the collaboration of the respective unconscious minds that give birth to an entity that begins functioning for itself. This process is thus clearly different from that of projective identification. In the latter, the subject seeks to project and control in the other, whom he keeps clearly distinct from him, something that he refuses to recognise in him.

De M'Uzan also insists on the appearance of pictorial representations that help to understand what is going on in the patient and that are liable to lead to precise interventions. The occurrence of an image without any apparent relationship to what is being said is a surprising emergence of primary functioning, which often makes it possible, subsequently, to return to it in a form more redolent of secondary level functioning.

In the example proposed, the patient often complained about a certain blurring of identity. The session was thus centred on the problem of blurring and fusion with the analyst in the maternal transference and the anxiety that she engendered. We can see the expression of the patient's unconscious desire for there no longer to be any boundaries with the other, as well as the fear of non-differentiation, of solitude or abandonment.

Using the expression "*se payer ma tête*" is a way of establishing distance, a boundary – here the obstacle of anality via the question of payment ("*paying for* my head"/*se payer* ma tête), an obstacle that halted a regression that would otherwise have been too dangerous.

In this instance, it was at the end of this session, as the patient was paying for the month to come, that the analyst noticed once again the intensity that she put into this act, and how important it was for her.

Paradoxical thoughts and the paradoxical system belong to the same register of identity as the chimera.

Further reading

M'Uzan, M. de. (1994). *La Bouche de l'inconscient.* Paris: Gallimard.

M'Uzan, M. de. (1999). L'interprétation? Question de formulation. In: *Interprétation I. Un processus mutatif.* Paris: Presses Universitaires Française.

M'Uzan, M. de. (2004). Pour une cohérence théorique et doctrinale de l'interprétation. Interview with Marie-Françoise *Laval*-Hygonenq, May 2004. In: *Débats de Psychanalyse.* Paris: Presses Universitaires Française.

KEY WORDS Collaboration of unconscious minds, blurring of identity, regressive functioning of the analyst, paradoxical.

PARADOXICAL THOUGHT

ALICE BAUER AND JOSEPH TORRENTE

Before the patient could get down to writing his graduation thesis, he had to trace out his future and choose between the legal profession and his passion for fencing: it had always been like that, for as long as he could remember. He then described the obsessional world in which he was trapped: his constant ruminating, the hesitations that made him weigh up the pros and cons of any situation indefinitely. Likewise, how could he find a way to combine his activity as a high-level fencer with his legal career? The conflict that had been partially avoided up until then seemed insoluble this time. Rumination became a feature of the sessions. The analyst was gradually feeling caught in the trap of this binary and deadly world. As for the patient, his associations and dreams became increasingly rare, while his defences became more rigid; to the point even that the analyst sometimes spent whole sessions wondering inwardly what choice her patient should make, letting herself get caught up in a game that immobilised her own associative capacities and keeping her stuck to the literal nature of the discourse. There was then an alternation between moments of "collage" and moments when, in order to escape this situation, the analyst began thinking about something else, but always very concrete things. The field of the session dried up, turned into a desert.

It was in this context that the appearance of a paradoxical thought in the analyst would permit the resumption of a work of working through. As, once again, the patient talked about his thesis that wasn't advancing, and her doubts, the analyst suddenly stopped listening to him and let herself enter into a curious, and even frightening feeling, namely, the almost physical sensation of another presence in the room. The word that came to her mind to describe what she had perceived was "ectoplasm". This paradoxical thought occurred to her without being induced by any conscious association; it seemed foreign to the analyst who did not know where it had come from and who was surprised by what was going on. It was previous experience of moments of this kind, with all the depersonalising aspects that they can involve, that led her to think that what had happened was connected with her patient and to tolerate the strangeness of it. She then heard herself say: "One can't make an omelette without breaking eggs." A sentence that was just as strange as the feeling that had preceded it. After a very peaceful silence, the patient replied: "It's me who broke the egg." He fell silent again and it was the end of the session. At the next session, he took up again where he had left off: "There's one thing I haven't told you about." I never speak about it, and would like to forget about it, but I think about it constantly; it haunts me. In fact, I should've had a twin sister; there were two eggs. It was my mother who told me about it. When I was little, she talked about it all the time. But the egg did not develop, and the doctors said I had eaten it… they even spoke of cannibalism. My mother was constantly reproaching me for having deprived her of her daughter. I have felt monstrous ever since. Sometimes, I tell myself that perhaps I've got a little bit of my sister somewhere in me. I have the feeling I know her; she keeps me company. It's curious; I don't know what to think about it: I like to feel her close to me, but at the same time she prevents me from living. It's a ghost that I cannot get rid of. Perhaps I don't really want to."

From this point on, he began to evoke behaviour of a perverse kind: regularly and in a compulsive way, he would dress up as a woman and observe his reflection in the mirror. This behaviour was so split that it took the analyst some time to be able to picture him, dressed as a woman, in search of his twin, encysted in him. He spoke of these moments that were very painful for him as well as of his connection with his dead twin, who was both him and not him incorporated in the primary sense of the term, something he had never done up until then. This behaviour disappeared quite quickly. The patient was finally able to express a certain amount of aggressiveness towards the external world, without being obliged to restrict himself to its very controlled expression in the form of fencing. He completed his studies successfully and finished his thesis in the university year. He could attack and appreciate the analysis, without fear of destroying it. He had an experience of the third party and of rivalry.

Returning to the concept of paradoxical thought that he introduced in 1976 (see de M'Uzan, 2003 and 2013 [1976]), Michel de M'Uzan explains that at certain moments, during certain sessions, strange images emerge unexpectedly in the analyst's mind. Fleeting, polymorphous, generally speaking expressed in images and endowed with a strong hallucinatory character, but sometimes expressed in language, these representations develop against the background of a slight depersonalisation and in parallel with a regressive movement. Responding to psychic processes that belong to the analysand, they unfold in the analyst, anticipating the possible intellectual understanding of the clinical material presented. These images are characterised by the variety of their form and especially by their dynamism. They announce an inaccessible phantasmatic potentiality whose unconscious dynamic can be restored by interpretation.

Paradoxical thought may be considered, in short, as the extreme form taken by the countertransference when the analyst's psychic apparatus puts itself entirely in the service of the patient's psychic functioning. The mechanism underlying it remains mysterious. De M'Uzan sees it as part of a paradoxical system which he situates between the unconscious and the preconscious. De M'Uzan also suggests that what is involved is a particular movement of the narcissistic libido; this is paradoxical because its expression is at its acme here, permitting the analyst to function entirely in the service of his analysand, while in doing so he dispossesses himself of his status as a libidinal object.

Further reading

M'Uzan, M de. (1977). *De l'art à la mort*. Paris: Gallimard.

M'Uzan, M de. (1994). *La Bouche de l'inconscient. Essais sur l'interprétation*. Paris: Gallimard.

M'Uzan, M de. (2003). La séance analytique, une zone érogène. *Revue française de psychanalyse*, 67(2): 431–439.

M'Uzan, M de. (2005). *Aux confins de l'identité*. Paris: Gallimard.

M'Uzan, M de. (2013 [1976]). *Countertransference* and the paradoxical system. In: *Death and identity: Being and the psycho-sexual drama*. London: Karnac, pp. 17–32.

KEY WORDS Countertransference, psychic functioning of the analyst, interpretation, paradoxical system.

RETROGRESSION

ALICE BAUER AND JOSEPH TORRENTE

The notion of retrogression (*régrédience*) refers to a particular psychic movement and quality. It is clinically inseparable from its result, the work of figurability, whose major manifestation is the dream: these two notions have their place within a theoretical ensemble that aims to account for the coherence of endo-hallucinatory phenomena.

Proposed by César and Sára Botella, this notion is to be clearly distinguished from that of regression, both that of the libido as defined by Freud with the oral, anal and genital stages and that of D.W. Winnicott called "regression to dependence". Here, it is a matter of regular modes of psychic functioning in its potentiality of expression, and more particularly those that concern thought. Retrogression is thus akin to topographical and formal regression (Freud, 1914a) as well as to that which he calls "material regression" (1917). It proves fundamental for the study of psychic creativity.

Retrogressive psychic functioning is complementary to progressive ("*progrédient*") functioning, which extends from the wish to its enactment or representation, while the retrogressive movement extends from the wish to its endo-hallucinatory realisation, figurability.

As a movement and dynamic, retrogression provides a canvas allowing for the formation of *figurations* and establishes the loom on which ideational contents are deployed. It allows for the linking up of heterogeneous psychic elements, "all the elements present at a given moment, regardless of their origin: representational, perceptual or motor; regardless of their quality: conscious or unconscious; and of their sometimes radical heterogeneity: perception of the sense organs, intrapsychic perception; as well as of their heterochrony: a current thought, a recollection, a repressed childhood wish, a future project. Defined by the simultaneous coexistence of all the components of equal value, of all the psychic elements present at a given moment, retrogression can, in one and the same movement, give rise to numerous new links, even where there were none, thereby creating new causalities" (Botella, 2001, p. 1179).

Its clinical interest also lies in the fact that it emphasises the psychoanalyst's capacity during the session to let himself enter a state that may give him access to a work of figurability based on the material brought by the analysand, when he is unable to communicate his ideas or images and so is not in a position to elaborate by means of language. In the face-to-face situation of treatments with so-called borderline patients, it sometimes occurs in a stranger way: an idea or image emerges, which gathers up and gives shape to all the issues of the session, throwing new and unexpected light on it. The retrogressive process tends to create intelligibility where suffering, associated with a barely organised state, had reigned. It thus makes it possible to gain access to infantile traumas experienced before the advent of speech, but cannot be reduced to that. An atmosphere of unease, anxiety and even depersonalisation often characterises these states.

A patient, an elegant and apparently well-adapted woman, albeit with a false-self presentation, had been in analysis for two years. She complained that she suffered from chronic depression that made her life, she said, "flat, like a landscape with no relief, no great joys, no great misfortunes either. I no longer know what powerful emotions are." She did not know "why or how" this had begun. She associated it perhaps, without much conviction, with the beginnings of her shared life with her partner, even though this was going well.

There was little relief in her "flat" manner of presenting her biography: her parents both worked and there was a good understanding between them. Her elder sister suffered from cerebral-motor disability and had been placed in an institution quite early on when the patient was in preschool. She nonetheless returned home regularly and the whole family also often went to visit her.

The patient, who was about thirty years of age now, had been living for a while with a man whom she met during her studies: their relationship seemed stable and they were planning to have a child.

The analyst was also finding things a bit "flat". This had been going on for two years and nothing was happening: she complained constantly about a sort of rampant depression that did not shift and the analyst had the intuition that something of her "demand" had not yet been elaborated, as if it were suspended.

During a session, the patient talked about her plan to have a child and, for the first time, explained her hesitations. She associated them with her sister's pathology: she was wondering about the possible genetic character of the disability and asking herself how and through whom it might have been handed down, whether through her mother's or father's respective families. How could she know what the risks were if she herself had a child?

As the analyst was listening to her, she noticed that a familiar tune was running through her head, a tune that took her back to her own past: the song of the *Wizard of Oz*. She did not push away this apparently incongruous element, but accepted this retrogressive moment and also let the images of the film run through her mind. She then recalled that what had deeply moved her at the time was the scene in which the wicked neighbour, who was to become the "Wicked Witch of the West", had just "arrested" the heroine's dog with a mandate from the sheriff: the dog was judged and condemned because it would slip under the fence to enter her house. Nobody was able to save the dog from the judgement. So, he was taken away from Dorothy and placed in a home. The adults were powerless to do anything about this decision.

The analyst then asked her patient: "What happened when your sister was put in an institution?" The patient broke down, sobbed with tears, at length and without restraint. Then, in a broken voice, she spoke about her feelings of incomprehension, anger and terror when her parents went to place her sister in an institution. For her, this was a real betrayal, an abandonment. She had never been able to say anything about it but she began to live in terror of being "placed" herself as well if she disappointed her parents. Shortly after, she started resorting to conjuratory rituals and also recalls having had nightmares in which her sister was calling to her for help.

The analyst's moment of retrogression and the figurability that resulted from it allowed the early infantile trauma to emerge: it permitted a resumption of the weaving of links with the present state. Shortly after, the patient evoked her wish to have a child which, previously, had no doubt silently played a part in reawakening her trauma. In the analysis, this particular analytic moment led to a resumption of the whole process during which it became possible to work on themes ranging from oedipal guilt to the idea of becoming a mother. Gradually, this young woman gained access to her desire and emerged from her state of depression.

Further reading

Botella, C. (2001). Figurabilité et *regrédience. Revue française de psychanalyse*, 65(4): 1149–1239.

Botella, C. and Botella, S. (2007). La figurabilité *psychique*. In: *Explorations psychanalytiques*. Paris: In Press.

KEY WORDS Psychic figurability, retrogressive functioning, hallucinatory perception-representation.

4

INTERPRETATIONS

THE DECISION

NICOLE OURY

A patient, who usually was sparing with words, arrived at her session in a very animated state. She expressed herself strongly: she had decided to dispense with her current prescribing psychiatrist because, like the ones before, he had made a diagnosis evoking delusion and schizophrenia. She, however, did not recognise herself in these symptoms, though she readily admitted that all areas of her life were pervaded by a longstanding lack of pragmatism. She had even been thinking, she said, of stopping her sessions. The analyst told her how lively she was when she was angry. She replied that each time she spoke it cost her a lot because she lacked vocabulary and that making herself understood, establishing links between words, was too much effort for her. She would prefer, she added, not to recount dreams in which she killed her father and mother, or to have to express her terrifying fear of being suffocated by her mother. The crude and greedy anger present on the analytic stage through the narration of her anxieties actualised itself in the transference onto the person the analyst embodied, namely, a parent who was repeatedly clumsy in the way she listened to her psychic reality.

At the next session, she reported a scene in which, for the first time in her life, she had been able to express in words her anger, which she admitted was exaggerated, towards her father, in a dream in which she portrayed the risk that he might kill his wife. The work of elaboration enabled her to say that she had made the decision to go and see the prescribing psychiatrist again, and also to affirm her wish to continue to see her analyst. This initial step towards culture and civilisation stood in contrast with massive phobic tendencies that swept every act of thinking along with them. The transference towards the analyst, marked by repeated destructive attacks, created the space in which a decision could be taken, namely, confronting her murderous anger towards her father and recognising oedipal wishes.

Psychoanalysis is indebted to Wladimir Granoff (1975) for having stressed the importance of "decision", to which the author devotes a long chapter at the end of his book *Filiations* (see, pp. 518–549). The texts in this book bring together, in chronological order, the faithful accounts of 23 seminars on the theme of the Oedipus complex. The last chapter, "La decision" presaged a pursuit of these reflections centred on thinking and the feminine (Granoff, 1978). Decision – a term taken from Freud's *Moses and Monotheism* – delimits the moment when, one day, it is necessary for man to progress in the life of the mind. It involves leaving the sensory world of mothers and the evidence of the senses and turning towards higher intellectual processes: "It consists for instance in deciding that paternity is more important than maternity, although it cannot, like the latter, be established by the evidence of the senses, and that that is reason is why the child should bear his father's name and be his heir" (Freud, 1939, p. 118). This decision results from a cutting off, an active setting aside of (*Beseitigung*), the mother, and creates a link of spirituality in the relationship with the father. It is remarkable to note that, in the dynamic of the development of Granoff's theses, he closes a stage in his reflections on the Oedipus complex with this high point of the importance of decision (leaving the sensory world of the mothers and turning towards higher intellectual process) in order to open his research towards the feminine and thinking, and to direct himself towards other obscure strata of the mind from which, precisely, it is necessary to cut oneself off.

The French word "*decision*" is a noun. However, Freud in his text, employs a verb to name this act. What interests Granoff is what this decision tends towards, its outcome: it favours intellectual processes at the expense of the evidence of the senses which affirm with complete certainty who is the child's mother. The term encompasses the act of choosing a path and its outcome. In this sense, the attribution of the article "*la*" to the word "*décision*" brings together this unique moment in which man extracts himself from the individual Oedipus complex and takes his place within the patrilineal descent.

Granoff looks at the issues relating to the image of the father, thus his visual representation, and the question of the father, and the lines of exploration that arise from it. The subject comes into being as such, if he is located within a double lineage resulting from the intersection of the Oedipus complex and its decline and the question of inheritance in a line of descent where history and death exist side by side. Thus, taking the decision of naming a child leaves a trace: the name is trace and decision. The destiny of the child is also weighed down by the unrepresentable place of his origins: the desire between a father and a mother. To get free of these tutelary influences, there is only one way: the intellectual work arising from the psychic space where the decision is made and sometimes extracted.

In the clinical sequence, the first decision to leave the prescribing psychiatrist, and then the analyst, may be understood as acting out in reaction to the transference, a reaction towards which the patient had felt pushed. Then, the second decision – not to break off the analysis – was made in quite another context, that of the outcome of a transformation, of a small gain in psychic autonomy. The ambivalence with regard to the paternal complex of the patient shows the necessity of a decision whose purpose is to restore the father after having excluded him. This was the path travelled from *Totem and Taboo* (Freud, 1913) to *Moses and Monotheism* (Freud, 1939).

Further reading

Freud, S. (1939). *Moses and monotheism. SE.* 23. London: Hogarth, pp. 1–137.
Granoff, W. (1975). *Filiations: L'avenir du complexe d'Œdipe. S.E.* 7. Paris: Minuit, pp. 518–549.
Granoff, W. (1978). *La pensée et la féminin*. Paris: Minuit.

KEY WORDS Ambivalence, parental complex, decision, Oedipus.

LISTENING TO LISTENING

HAYDÉE FAIMBERG AND LAURENT DANON-BOILEAU

The analyst's work is based on listening and interpretation. But each interpretation risks promoting in the patient the illusion of an omniscient analyst who can determine the truth of the unconscious of the other, without even having recourse to the patient's associations or psychic work. This narcissistic fascination must be renounced in order for the patient to recognise that interpretation actually arises from the union of his words with the analyst's listening. The transition to the oedipal register can only occur if the patient is aware of the fundamental incompleteness of each of the parties taking part in the analytic encounter. For this dimension of disillusionment to lead to a fruitful experience of mourning, Haydée Faimberg has suggested that it is necessary for analyst and patient to have recourse to "listening to listening". For the analyst, this consists of being sensitive to the way in which the patient reinterprets what he hears (sometimes even the analyst's silence "speaks") so that he can appreciate the nature and scale of the psychic work involved in the process. Sometimes, listening to listening can be the object of sharing.

Here is a session. As we shall see, it contains a first interpretation that was rather badly formulated. The patient was speaking about the different relations that she was having with the sole aim of getting pregnant, as if she attributed no importance whatsoever to the father of the baby. Her tone was provocative, apparently devoid of affect. She told her analyst that she expected her to take the high moral ground by drawing on a theory that emphasised the importance of the father. Then she talked about bad-smelling situations while associating to the bad smell of her last partner. She would no doubt have had a child from him if there hadn't been this smell! Perhaps she just needed to find him a good deodorant, she added, sarcastically. A silence followed. As it continued, the analyst felt herself becoming indifferent to the suffering that she was displaying. But an interpretation did not come to her mind. With hindsight, it was no doubt the patient's manner of making the analyst into an indifferent witness that should have been the object of an interpretation. Finally, the analyst ventured to make an interpretation that was in fact poorly formulated: "You were speaking about bad smells and of your wish to be pregnant, as if you felt that there was a link between the two, as if you thought that something about this smelt bad." She replied: "You have no right to say that, and I feel like insulting you." A question then came to the analyst's mind that she communicated to her: "You said with anger: 'And I feel like insulting you.' This 'and' suggests to me that you heard my interpretation as an insult." The patient was thus asked to listen, retrospectively, to the way that she had heard the interpretation.

The words of the interpretation, which, up until then, had been equivalent for her to acts (in this case insults), initiated a transformation: they gradually became words that said something. This led the analyst to continue: "It may be that through my interpretation we (you and me) were hearing someone who treats you as if you had no value. If that was the case, I wonder who that could be." This last question did not call for a response, but it created an opening, an unconscious association. And the patient continued: "When I was an adolescent, one day, my mother told me that I should take care of my teeth, because girls always inherit their father's teeth. I protested saying that we both had good teeth. Thereupon, she left the room after telling me carelessly that the person I called my father was not in fact my biological father. And when I asked her later for explanations, she avoided the issue. She told me that I was making a fuss about nothing, adding that my Dad had promised to recognise his paternity of me so that she didn't have to have an abortion." The account of this memory was the unconscious response to the conflict that had arisen in the transference. It was the sharing of listening to listening that made it possible after the event to reveal this new meaning.

Initially developed as a clinical concept in analysis, the concept "listening to listening" was extended by Haydée Faimberg to the work of clinical reflection between analysts. In interanalytic workgroups, listening to listening makes it possible to focus on the recognition of the misunderstandings that arise between participants; this in turn makes it possible to elucidate their implicit theoretical presuppositions and to recognise the specificity of the point of view of the analyst who is presenting the material.

Further reading

Faimberg, H. (1994). L'enigme que pose le transfert. In: *Colloque sur "Nouveaux Fondements pour la psychanalyse*, eds. Laplanche, J. et al. Paris: Presses Universitaires de France, pp. 211–221.

Faimberg, H. (2005). *The telescoping of generations. Listening to the narcissistic links between generations.* London: Routledge.
Faimberg, H. (2009). Après-coup et construction. *Revue française de psychanalyse*, 2: 473–486.
Faimberg, H. (2010 [1993]). Malentendu et vérités psychiques. In: *Avancées freudiennes. Revue française de psychanalyse.* Paris: Presses Universitaires de France, pp. 237–244.
Freud, S. (1937). *Constructions in analysis. S.E.* 23. London: Hogarth, pp. 255–269.

KEY WORDS Listening, listening to listening, interpretation, misunderstanding, transference.

SATURATED AND UNSATURATED INTERPRETATIONS

MICHAEL PARSONS

A patient dreamed that he saw himself as a filmmaker filming a marching army. He framed his shots adventurously, taking risks. This began with a close-up shot of a soldier's hand. Then he raised the lens, taking a wider shot of other soldiers and finally the heads of all the men. At this point, he picked up the camera and climbed onto a crane to get an overview of the whole army and take a long panoramic shot. All this was in just one sequence. He associated to the image of another dream: some birds on the ground were taking flight; pale yellow and particularly beautiful birds. Their heads were completely featherless. For him this was somehow connected with the soldiers' helmets. All this probably had something to do with images of circumcised and uncircumcised penises, he added. The remark was no doubt pertinent. Moreover, it echoed other elements of the material. Everything was there, ready for interpretation: his way of filming, which was equivalent to an erection; we can even go further and see the filmmaking as an act of sexual intercourse.

And yet the patient's initial comments, however exact they may have been, felt conventional and lifeless. The analyst did not take them up. So the patient went on. The day before, he had played squash; to begin with, he had played classically, which resulted in him losing. Then he stopped playing correctly and hit a series of original and rather unorthodox shots. To his great satisfaction, they worked. He noted that in his dream, when he was filming, he had had the same feeling of pleasure, namely of doing things in a slightly unpredictable and risky way. I then intervened to take up the connection he had made between the heads of the birds and the soldiers' helmets. This was not in order to attribute some sort of meaning to it, but just to highlight the freedom the patient had shown in passing from one dream to the other. He then associated to the impact that the images of certain films had had on him, adding that there was something marvellous about the link between the pale-yellow birds and the marching army. And suddenly, he realised that this creativity that he wanted so much to be able to employ in his artistic work was in fact something that he possessed already and that was expressed in the first dream as well as in the link that he established with the birds taking flight. This clinical sequence may seem very simple, but it had a considerable effect in mobilising the affects of the patient.

Here is an example that stands in contrast with the one before. It concerns a woman who has sexual problems and little capacity for association. She reported a dream. She had to take the train to Glasgow, but her luggage was stolen by supporters of the Liverpool Basin football club. She was going to lodge a complaint with the police inspector. She was desperate because she had packed her cases carefully and everything in them was absolutely indispensable for her. But it was only clothes, after all. Moreover, even if all of them were essential for her, she could manage to get by without certain garments. She had taken a pair of trousers that made her look larger than she was and a sweater that was too small. While she was telling her story to the police inspector, she broke down into tears. The analyst then pointed out to her that she did not seem to know whether these clothes were indispensable or superfluous. She replied by saying that the sweater gave her big breasts and she wondered what had made her take it. It was at this point that a scene from the evening before came back to her, when she and her husband had got undressed in the sauna. This had excited him. Then she had dived naked into the big pool (*grand bassin*) and had a lot of pleasure in doing so. She further recalled that when she was small, her father would often go to Glasgow on business. The analyst then pointed out that he was like an inspector whom she spoke to about what bothered her. He could have stopped there without telling her what had come to his mind concerning the implication of her remarks, but given the type of patient she was, he had the feeling that he needed to be more explicit. He drew her attention to the word play around "*bassin*" (pool or pelvis) and showed her that apart from her fear of sexuality, the dream showed her desire to be excited and to show her breasts. He added that her conflictual feelings to do with her body seemed to be related to her desire to be close to her father.

These two examples show the extent to which an analyst can be led to change his vantage point. With the first patient, the concern was to avoid saying anything that might hinder the unfolding of the psychoanalytic process and impede it from finding its own direction. The analyst did not want to exploit the movement in order to obtain from it some gain of knowledge or of insight. By keeping in the background without interpreting, the analyst let the link with the scene of squash and the unusual shots that the patient had made emerge. This is what helped the patient come into contact with his creativity. With the woman patient, it seemed on the contrary that at the point she was at in her analysis she needed me to suggest a meaning that she was not able to identify herself. It was also necessary to make her realise that there were more things going on in her head than she imagined.

Depending on the vantage point one has, the interpretations that one is led to formulate present different degrees of saturation and explicitness. However, one point of view, one type of formulation, does not exclude another. The analytic work plays on both and all the harmonics between them. The position of the analyst must constantly fluctuate between the extremes evoked here in the examples. Of course, patients differ. And, above all, one and the same patient may change register at any moment, scarcely without noticing it. The analyst, on the other hand, must be aware of this and be able to modify his interpretative point of view, shifting along the whole range that goes from the more or less explicit depending on the position of the patient in the present moment, but also taking into account the requirements of the analysis in the long term.

Further reading

Ferro, A. (2009). *Mind works. Technique and creativity in psychoanalysis.* London: Routledge.

Parsons, M. (2000). *The dove that returns, the dove that vanishes. Paradox and creativity in psychoanalysis.* London: Routledge. See in particular, Chapter 11: "The Dove that Returns, The Dove that Vanishes".

Parsons, M. (2014). *Living psychoanalysis. From theory to experience.* London: Routledge. See in particular Chapter 10: "Raiding the Inarticulate: Internal Analytic Setting, Beyond Countertransference".

KEY WORDS Interpretation, point of observation, analytic process, dream.

INTERPRETATION AND TRANSFERENCE

DOMINIQUE TABONE-WEIL

An interpretation is characterised by both its target and the place assigned to the analyst by the patient at the moment when he speaks. It is in these different respects that Jean-Luc Donnet differentiates between interpretation *in* the transference (*interprétation dans le transfert*), *of* the transference (*interprétation du transfert*) and transference interpretation (*interprétation de transfert*). As we shall see, each of them gives a different weighting to the three essential motive forces of every interpretation.

Interpretation *in* the transference

"You must think that I am really hopeless (*indécrottable*),[1] she said repeatedly. You must find me useless; you must find me boring.

"I must?" the analyst asked, leaving the patient nonplussed for a moment.

"You must…? she responded, suddenly meditative. The analyst had simply taken up the patient's words and extracted them from the opaque wrapping of their apparent banality in order to let them deploy new meanings.

The patient did not say: "Perhaps you find me boring?" She did not formulate a hypothesis, but an order. The analyst "must". Here the interpretation led her to realise that she was trying to induce something in her analyst, and then to ask herself what she had against the analyst or what she wanted from her. The dimension of control masked by her grievance and masochistic position were also revealed, but without violence because the patient may not have heard the brief repetition of her words. This was an interpretation *in* the transference. Its primary aim is a quality of the relationship to the analyst established on the stage of interlocution: "Interpretation *in* the transference is an interpretation in the *here and now* of the session, where the intervention concerns at the manifest level the transference relationship" (Donnet, 1995, p. 184). It does not evacuate the latent content, everything that stems from the subject's infantile history and manifests itself at this moment in the analysis in the words "you must". This simply remains in the background.

Two other examples with the same patient will illustrate the two other perspectives of transferential interpretation.

Interpretation *of* the transference

The same patient, at the beginning of the analysis this time, had just expressed the ideal expectations that she fostered in relation to her analyst, who intervened by asking: "As if I was going to be the ideal parent that you would've liked to have?"

Apparently trivial, the question possessed a considerable effect of interpretative destabilisation. Its aim was to foster awareness of the transference and of the particular quality that it had at that moment – in this instance, the massive idealising projections that accompanied it.

"Because that's not the case?" the analysand might have replied, somewhat disconcerted. In fact, just when she was celebrating her analyst as a perfect object, capable of repairing her experiences of all those, present or past, who had disappointed or betrayed her, she heard the analyst retorting in substance by saying: "I am not who you think I am." The interpretation *of* the transference destabilised her.

Perhaps the patient would be able, at a later stage, to express the hostile feelings she was experiencing in relation to the oedipal frustration with which she was thus confronted. Perhaps she would be able to see in it the echo of the infantile disappointments that she once experienced when faced with the impasses of her oedipal wishes. It is for the analyst to identify their manifestations and to know how to interpret them.

According to Jean-Luc Donnet, interpretation *of* the transference, of which I have just given an example, proves useful at the beginning of an analysis in order to make the patient aware of his resistance *to* the transference or, conversely, at the end of the treatment in order to deal with resistances *through* the transference. It makes the analysand aware of the nature of what he is experiencing and re-establishes the dimension of "as if". Here, the patient believed she had found the object capable of satisfying her infantile impulses, but the interpretation *of* the transference challenged this illusion.

The transference interpretation

This is the fundamental transference interpretation. It presupposes that the analyst is speaking *from* the place of transference object assigned to him by the patient, as well as *from* his place as an analyst. It is this particular situation that enables him to link the *here-and-now* of the session, the actuality of the transference relationship, with the other space and other time of the infantile history that the patients' words have just reactualised.

The patient was complaining about insomnia, bouts of suffocation, and coughing spells, accompanied by extreme anxiety. "The other night," she said, I was almost suffocating, I thought I was going to die and I thought about you with a lot of anger. I said to myself that it wasn't possible, that you couldn't leave me like that!" In this instance, behind the night anxiety, the words "like that" referred to many other things: the pain of an unhappy love relationship (she experiences her partner as a frustrating narcissistic mother) and beyond that a helpless state of despair, verging on helplessness.

> "I am a very bad mother!" the analyst replied. "And a very poor father too, who doesn't protect you from that mother or give you any consolation."

Through this transference interpretation, several registers are associated: the archaic and oedipal dimensions, the sexual demand, and the vital urgency of the plea addressed to the analyst. What the analyst is drawing attention to in the background is the representation of a primal scene in which the parents, occupied with their lovemaking, let the distressed infant suffocate without coming to her aid. In what the patient says, there is a mixture of a demand for bodily relief, presence and concern, but also a demand for sexual relief – irritation of the bronchial tubes, of the throat, symbolising through displacement the overwhelming and unsatisfied drive excitation, whether from the mother, the father, the analyst or the husband. The analyst responds from the place of object that this plea assigns to him. And it is in this respect that what he says has the effect of a transference interpretation.

However, whatever the perspective is, all forms of interpretation are established in the transference. And all comprise the three dimensions that I have tried to distinguish here. Thus, even interpretations that are aimed at the surface of the transference relationship (interpretations *in* the transference) pertain in different degrees to interpretation *of* the transference or transference interpretations (*interprétations de transfert*). In the first clinical fragment above, the interpretation *in* the transference also takes on retrospectively a colouring of transference interpretation (*interprétation de transfert*) or interpretation *of* the transference. Who, in fact, is the character who "must" find the patient boring? In which infantile scenario is he participating? And what does the word "*décrotter*" (to remove the dirt from something), to which the word "*indécrottable*" is related, open out onto?

Note

1 Translator's note: in the word *indécrottable*, one can hear the word *crotte* = dung, dropping, dirt, as well as *décrotter* = to remove the dirt from something.

Further reading

Urtubey, L. de. (1999). *Interprétation I. Aux sources de l'interprétation: le contre-transfert*. Paris: Presses Universitaires de France.

Donnet, J.L. (1995). *Le divan bien tempéré*. Paris: Presses Universitaires de France.

Sechaud, É. (2009). Le maniement du transfert dans la psychanalyse française. *L'Année psychanalytique internationale*, 2009(7): 161–181.

Strachey, J. (1934). The *nature* of the therapeutic action of psychoanalysis. *International Journal of Psychoanalysis*, 15: 127–159.

KEY WORDS Here-and-now: analytic interpretation par excellence.

THE INDEXATION OF INTERPRETATION

MICHEL ODY

The patient had been in analysis for a few months. On that day, he was speaking about his sense of liberation in the relationship that had recently been established with his line manager. But at the beginning of the session, he had referred to an event that had occurred before he arrived for his session: a dead mouse he had noticed in the corridor of the metro. He was afraid he might leave traces of it on my couch with his shoes. The associative sequence led him to a sense of guilt concerning a part manufactured in the company where he was working. He had learnt that it could be the source of an accident. He went on to imagine that this would amount to a murder. The analyst asked him: "With traces left by shoes?" First indexation: he laughed. Then he added: "If you say so!" Assisted by the transference connotation, he returned to his boss, to the conflict that had been overcome and to its liberating effect. Noticing a painting on the wall, he then remarked: "It's a bit old-fashioned." The analyst asked: "Close to death?" A new indexation: he laughed again. Then, after a moment of silence, he added: "You are right." This was not his customary way of expressing himself.

A few years later, he was clearly confronted with the "demonic" aspect of the drive. Up to then, he had never been able to form a couple that lasted, but now he had found a woman with whom he had established a satisfying relationship on most levels, until the day when he was invaded by an impulse that was driving him to destroy this relationship. "Why do I feel like breaking up this magnificent relationship?" he asked. And he continued: I don't know what it's all about... Perhaps happiness is unbearable for me." One thing leading to another, he talked about his disappointment, the day before, about not having pursued a reflection on the comparison between two civilisations of Antiquity. The analyst said: "The reflection was not magnificent..." A further indexation: he linked up this movement through the signifier "magnificent" with a "destructive impulse" (these were his words) and added: "Yes, I was disappointed by my girlfriend, just as I was by my mother."

The term "indexation" refers here to what follows an analyst's intervention or interpretation, irrespective of the analytic setting, whether it is with a child or an adult and irrespective of the content of what follows, whether it be silence (whose quality, moreover can be varied), or any positive or negative element. André Green used it in a paper he read in a work group on the absence of the transference neurosis and the absence of infantile neurosis at the 39th Congress of French-Speaking Psychoanalysts in 1979. He had been led to do so in order to clarify the psychic movements at work during the session in borderline cases in comparison with cases characterised by neurotic states. His reflections began with the central question of the relationship between the subject and his discourse. He asked himself what the subject's coefficient of indexation to his own discourse was. Did he really adhere to what he was saying? Was he saying yes and/or no? And Green added that it could be that and/or the contrary. "At that moment," he wrote, "intelligibility continues to pertain to the contents but not to the elements that govern the associativity of the contents" (Green, 1980, pp. 1092–1093). This is a crucial point, because in a certain way it announces the question of the relationship between process and content. In the rest of this article, he posited the existence of tertiary processes regulating the relation between primary processes and secondary processes.

It was my practice with children that led me to employ the term indexation to refer to the observable effects of the analyst's interventions. What is particular to the child is the variety of his expressive registers: he can pass from verbal expression to acting out, to drawing, writing, and to the play that is characteristic of a child. This variety and rapidity of the changes that take place often lead the analyst to dwell less on the contents than to follow the process and even the microprocesses that are unfolding, while taking into account the possible manifestations that occur. Noting or pointing up one of these manifestations as the trace of something, as the visible emergence of an earlier movement that is in fact infiltrated libidinally and/or destructively, makes it possible to draw the patient's attention to an unconscious logic. This can give rise to an associative sequence ranging from the most positive to the most negative. What has been referred to since Freud as "free association" constitutes the most mentalised manifestation of the general process of associativity that can be designated by the term indexation.

Further reading

Green, A. (1980). Intervention. *Revue française de psychanalyse*, 5–6: 1092–1093.

Ody, M. (2019 [2013]). *The psychoanalyst and the child*, trans. A. Weller. London: Routledge.

KEY WORDS Indexation, interpretation, content/process relationship.

ENACTION

MARIE-LAURE LÉANDRI

A mother requested a consultation for her son, aged 11. She came without her husband, the child's father. She had been worried for several months about his moodiness and his withdrawnness, which stood in contrast with their former mutual trust. He was also manifesting quite acute anxieties at bedtime and experiencing moments of searing anger that were having a negative impact on his parents, as well as his brothers and sisters, and himself. He was no longer the gay and adorable little boy that he had been. While his mother was speaking, the child was getting impatient and expressing this by being agitated. He repeated some of the things his mother had said and offered a commentary in a clearly provocative tone. His mother spoke intelligently and tenderly about her son, their relationship, as well as his relationship with his father. She then went on to say that they were extremely "different". At this moment, she accompanied her statement with a peculiar gesture: she put her hands together, the right hand in precise contact with the left. There was no difference; they matched perfectly. This gesture and the liveliness of the problem of separation that it expressed were striking. At this precise moment, the analyst felt in her body an emotion that accelerated her heart beat for a moment and experienced inwardly a sense of sad anger.

Deciding that she would intervene, she said to the mother and child that, although they were different, they seemed to have difficulty accepting it. She pointed out that it would not have been possible to slip a piece of cigarette paper between these two joined hands. Separating them would have been almost impossible. She added that in any case they seemed to be going through a painful period. It is true that the child was growing up and would soon be entering 6th grade in France (6th grade Junior High School in the USA and Year 7 High School in the UK); Growing up, yes, it means separating from one's mother; and separating, was perhaps frightening for both of them. They might never find each other again, they might lose each other. So they had to think of themselves as twins who would always like to be united. At this point, the mother looked at the analyst intensely, interrupted her, and, sobbing painfully, said: "I lost my twin brother when I was very young." The bodily experience of sad anger thus had an object.

Enaction is a concept introduced by Serge Lebovici (1994) that was the fruit of his therapeutic consultations with babies and their families. It arises from the strong emotion felt by the analyst in his body at a certain moment in the consultation. Emotion and bodily sensations thus become a source of new representations. What is involved, Lebovici suggests, is a controlled action of the analyst's body, where the idea, thus thinking, is a-corporated. A passage from the body towards the psyche thus occurs in the analyst, which differentiates *enaction* – even though it involves a physical movement – from the *passage à l'acte* and from acting out. Indeed, there is no short-circuit of the capacities for representation here. *Enaction* is an action of language with bodily roots. To deploy this perspective, Lebovici draws on the notion of "enactment" first introduced by Theodore Jacobs. In English, the verb "to enact" belongs to legal vocabulary, where it means to promulgate a law. However, it also used in the theatrical register, where it means to "represent", to "play a role".

It was in the course of his practice of parent/baby consultations that Lebovici was led to develop this concept. Starting from the observation that the psychoanalyst's access to the baby does not only depend on the parents with whom he is speaking, thereby making the baby an "interlocutor" in its own right, he sees *enaction* as a crucial process that permits the analyst to link up parental fantasies and the protorepresentations of the baby. The resultant metaphorisation concerns the father/mother/baby triad. *Enaction* is not unrelated to D.W. Winnicott's notion of the sacred moment and brings into play the question of the countertransference and of empathy. It is nonetheless true that in this interpretative moment, the analyst is directly in connection with the immediateness of the interaction in the session and consequently further removed from considerations of the work of the operation of après-coup.

Further reading

Angelergues, J. (2005). Peut-on parler de processus psychanalytique dans les traitements parents/bébé? *Perspectives Psychiatriques*, 44(5): 400–405.

Jacobs, Th. (1986). On countertransference enactments. *Journal of the American Psychoanalytic Association*, 34: 289–307.

Lebovici, S. (1994). Empathie et 'enactment' dans le travail de contre-transfert. *Revue française de psychanalyse*, 58(5): 1551–1561.

Lebovici, S. (1998). *L'Arbre de vie. Paris*: Érès.

Missoninier, S. (2004). L'empathie dans les consultations thérapeutiques parents/bébé: l'héritage de Serge Lebovici. *Revue française de psychanalyse*, 68(3): 929–946.

Rabain, J.-F. (2001). Psychodrame psychanalytique et 'empathie métaphorisante. *Champ psychosomatique*, 23(3): 69–84.

KEY WORDS A-corporation, parent/baby therapeutic consultations, metaphorising empathy.

THE VIOLENCE OF INTERPRETATION

MIREILLE FOGNINI

The violence of interpretation described in the eponymous work by Piera Aulagnier (2001 [1975]) concerns neither the "wild" interpretation nor the "violent" interpretation that might be proffered by a psychoanalyst to his analysand. It is a matter of understanding in the emerging psyche the complex and sometimes seriously impeded path "from pictogram to statement", as the subtitle makes clear; in other words, of following the vagaries of the psychic birth of a subject "I" to his own speech, the emergence from the primal "pictogram", the inexpressible imprint of the perceptual and sensory experience of the *infans*, towards a form of autonomous thought that can be enunciated as such. This gradual negotiation of the metabolising processes, primal, primary, and then secondary, is exposed to many factors of disturbance of a relational and environmental nature that are more or less combined or dominant. If, after birth, the maturing *infans* remains subject to the univocal power of the "thought of the other", that is, of a mother who continues to exert this sort of "primary violence" beyond her necessary and primordial prior concern for the baby's survival – if, therefore, the infant remains under the weight of the maternal interpretative injunction of the external and relational world, this excess imposes real violence on the developing psyche. Under such circumstances, the "psychotic potential" that is latent in each one of us may turn into manifest psychosis in its various forms, hallucinatory, delusional or compulsive.

Different stages open up the paths of metabolisation of the function of psychic representation until it gradually becomes expressible for a subject who is supposed, in the best of cases, to gain access to an existence that has already been thought about and that becomes thinkable for the subject in the external world as well as in his internal world. It is with the primal process that is active at birth, determined by the state of "helplessness" of the *infans*, that the pictogram is engrammed, and that a pictographic representation, generally speaking inexpressible and unthinkable, remains enclosed within experiences of fusion, where the mother exerts an inevitable primary violence through her interpretation of the world. Then the primary process develops through which the fantasmatic representation is formed, namely the fantasy that "rejects the reality principle" imposed on the psyche by what is "outside oneself". With the establishment of the secondary process a task of "giving meaning" to the ideational representation and to the expressible statement of an "I" takes place. Contrary to the primal stage, the primary and secondary stages produce accessible data that can be visually represented and thought about.

Imprisoned in an infantile psychosis that entailed multiple early measures of re-education, a young androgynous-looking woman spoke, in the course of her intensive psychotherapy, of a life trajectory punctuated by her repeated attempts to become an autonomous and thinking subject. In spite of significant advances in this respect, which helped to extricate her temporarily from her psychotic invasions, she would regularly fall under the sway again of the interpretative injunctions of different encounters, which took her back to the violence of maternal interpretation that she continually complained about, while provoking it at the same time.

While going through a new delusional interpretative episode that had led to the loss of her precarious employment, she experienced a tricky period clinically in which the fragile reconstruction of her reference points with regard to external reality had been shattered, even though the framework of her psychic treatment – without hospitalisation – had not thus far been affected. But then she suddenly decided to reduce, and then to break off, her psychotherapeutic sessions as well as the drug treatment prescribed by the psychiatrist. She feels that she has been doing very well since then, and especially since she has been seeing on a daily basis "an old alchemist guru" who administers her with herbal teas and aromatic plant baths, teaching her to relax and sleep better. He is a marabout whose language she does not understand, and of the same oriental origin as her ex-husband from whom she is divorced.

How could she be persuaded to postpone this total suspension of treatment in order to better contain her delusions? Much less talkative than usual, and certain that she was being listened to by her guru through the walls of my office – "because he is an alchemist" – she assured me that she would get in contact again if necessary. "You will know, of course, without my needing to tell you…" she added. There were reasons to be concerned here, and I suggested another appointment in about a fortnight's time, which she firmly declined.

In the previous meetings, I had noticed the persistence of a particular perfume she was wearing, and that day this fragrance similar to that of aromatic plants was intense. It was still lingering in the air after the session; it reminded me of a detail in her childhood during which she had suffered from the litigious divorce of her parents who used her as their object at stake in a battle of appropriation full of hatred. When she stayed with her father, he imposed on her the ritual of only wearing clothes chosen by her paternal grandmother; but she had always managed to secretly keep in her clenched fist a tissue impregnated with her own mother's perfume, which the latter sprayed abundantly on all her body linen to *assure her of her constant presence.*

I wondered if during her meetings with this "alchemist guru" providing her with infusions of herbal teas and strongly perfumed baths, she rediscovered the perfumed trace of the fragrant oriental flower that had governed her mother's choice of her first name from *One Thousand and One Nights,* a rhinencephalon injunction already revealing the mother's relational interpretative mode to the *infans*, fixed to ineffable feelings that were part of her own history. This mother – who had been married via a classified ad for barely 18 months – had requested that the infant be registered under this name only, denying the father and the paternal family any right to register the baby under the name predetermined by their ancestral tradition. In spite of this single first name registered on the birth certificate, this family and its father never ceased calling the child by "their" other first name. Thus, in addition to the obligatory ritual of changing her skin of maternal clothing into the other paternalised skin for her monthly visits to her father, she had to hear herself called by a different name.

Was there a link between her unilateral breaking off of her treatment, which was a new event and had never occurred before during her long therapy, and her sudden ruptures and successive separations, even if they did not last very long, with each of her parents? Did the analyst, with the regular rhythm of the sessions (perhaps reminiscent of the obligatory visits to her father), represent for the patient feared contacts with external reality and with her psychic reality that was marked both by splitting and fusion? Did she experience her treatment as being under the sway of an intolerable sphere "outside herself", breaking with the primal perfumed idyll, whose new hold on her, supporting her delusion, really worried me?

How could one fail to think that her decision to totally suspend her psychic treatment was part of the repetitive processes of unbinding and her inability to give meaning to her reality as a subject in relation to external reality?

Was her new guru, the "alchemist" who spoke a foreign language and perfumed her, not the new "spokesman", an implicit duplicate of the "primary violence of maternal interpretation" that was kept alive in her, barring her access to the non-excluded third element, to reality, to the other, of which the analyst (with the psychiatrist), was the current representative, and in whose office she secreted the essence of her perfumed tissue?

Was not the analyst for her both the other of external reality, a combined father and grandfather figure, who, in her delusion, could be controlled through the walls by the guru/mother, but also the omnipotent figure of a mother of a newborn baby who was able to discern the need for help and recourse against psychic death or confinement within shared madness? In any case, this is an example of the complexity of the mobile and paradoxical cathexes of psychotic personalities.

Further reading

Aulgnier, P. (2001 [1975]). *The violence of interpretation: From pictogram to statement*. London: Routledge.

Aulagnier, P. (2001). *Topique*, vol. 74. Paris: L'esprit du temps.

Mijolla, A. de. (Ed.). (2005). *International dictionary of psychoanalysis*. New York: Thomson Gale. See the following entries: "Self-historicisation", "Infans" "Je", "Pictogram", Psychotic potentiality, "*Identificatory* project" and "Violence of interpretation".

Mijolla-Mellor, S. (1998). *Penser la psychose. Une lecture de l'œuvre de Piera Aulagnier.* Paris: Dunod.

KEY WORDS From pictogram to statement, state of "helplessness", shared madness, spokesman, psychotic potentiality, pictographic representation, secondary process work of sense-making, perceptual-sensory experience, primary violence.

5

THE PRESENCE OF THE ANALYST

THE BASIC TRANSFERENCE

LAURE BONNEFON-TORT AND VINCENT PÉLISSIER

This term, suggested by Catherine Parat (1976), concerns that part of the relationship with the analyst that is not reducible to the transference movements classically developed in a transference neurosis. She describes it as cathexis by the patient of the person of the analyst. This cathexis is tinged with trust, and is the basic background against which projections and positive and negative transference movements develop. Basic transference has often been likened to the notion of therapeutic alliance with a "healthy" or "rational" ego. However, the term "transference" makes a difference here, as it places the emphasises on a cathexis involving the transference/countertransference economy. From the point of view of the countertransference, the basic transference nourishes the feeling in the analyst that it is possible to work with this or that patient. It supports the benevolence that colours neutrality. From the patient's point of view, it is fuelled by narcissistic resources and a tender, non-eroticised instinctual drive current, but also by the introjection of qualities that belong to the analyst and his function. Even when the patient seems to accept the setting, the trust necessary for the development of speech in analysis is not necessarily assured. And while the setting establishes the formal conditions of possibility of the analytic process, the basic transference permits the establishment of the psychic conditions that are necessary for it to unfold.

It is not easy to grasp this basic aspect of analytic work because it is often silent or virtual. While it is more clearly required in face-to face work, it is in the margins or manifests only at certain critical moments of classical analysis. It is entangled with projective and narcissistic residues and so can be difficult to discern. For Parat, the basic transference can also persist after the end of an analysis and must then be relinquished by the analysand. Certain renewed contacts in a face-to-face setting after a classical analysis reveal the intensity of a basic transference and make it possible to distinguish it from the projective residues that it once contained.

Another question remains, moreover, concerning this intermediary concept: should we see it as an inherent factor in the initial encounter or, on the contrary, as an effect of the process of analysis? As we shall see in the clinical fragments that follow, it is often difficult to tell.

On leaving a session during which the analyst had remained silent, a patient, whose language was usually polished and whose fantasies of anal intrusion were patiently and painstakingly elaborated, said to himself, "What an asshole!" It was wintertime. A few days later, having reported this thought, not without an element of shame, and associated to it – speaking of his fears of being ripped off, of not receiving as much as he gives – he suddenly remarked: "You know, it's warmer in here than outside..." As he was complaining again about how difficult it is for him to talk, the analyst suggested that what one keeps inside is nice and warm. The patient then associated to his pleasure in choosing words and also to what he "made the analyst pay" by sometimes making him wait for him to speak. In the following session, he noted again the warmth. He said he was happy to have been able to formulate "dirty words" and that the analyst had accepted them. He spoke about some school memories. He remembered a teacher who read stories when it was too cold to go out into the playground. He felt sheltered in the analyst's office, in his den (*antre*), in his belly (*ventre*)... A certain euphoria thus countercathected the hostility and the fantasy of penetration. He was nonetheless able to recall his ambivalent feelings towards his schoolmaster – his authoritarianism, his injustices. A bit later in the session, he recalled his first appointment with the analyst, the impulse that had stirred him to undertake this analysis, and he added with a note of derision: "I think that I also want to say that, even though you were silent, I did find you warm."

After several years of psychotherapy, a young woman wanted to begin an analysis. She suffered from very crippling anxiety attacks when she was unable to remain alone and needed physical containment from her companion. The situation improved and she wanted to stop her psychotherapy. She was very surprised by the ease with which her therapist had let her leave, practically from one day to the next. Her attacks resumed with more intensity.

The analysis began without discussion once the proposed setting had been accepted. She was fully involved in her sessions and associated with great ease. However, a phenomenon soon manifested itself. All of a sudden, without warning, she started to miss sessions – sometimes one, sometimes more. When she returned, she apologised, paid for the missed sessions, and resumed as if nothing had happened. Various hypotheses were explored: gradually, she understood that, in spite of the reasons she gave for her absences (work, looking after the children), something much deeper was going on. The analyst had noticed that these absences often occurred after a particularly rich sequence in the analysis. So he said to her: "It is as if you feared that things might go too well between us, that we might get too close, just as you felt when you were living alone with your mother." This interpretation led her to make very enlightening associations concerning her anxiety attacks, but changed nothing in terms of her absences. The analyst went through a variety of states: He was at first concerned, then guilty, then incredulous and, finally, disinterested. This last state alerted him: he experienced her absences as disappearances and, no doubt in order to protect himself against them, realised that sometimes he was no longer in the psychic state of waiting for her at the time of her sessions. He then made a connection between this and what she had experienced as a child: regularly, her father would cancel his scheduled visits to her at the last minute. She was now making the analyst experience this situation and he suggested this connection to her. This time, the intervention was effective; she was thereafter able to come to all her sessions. Trust had been established.

This young woman constantly oscillated between the fear of being too close to her mother and the fear of not existing for her father. Establishing the basic transference based on the interpretation of a projective identification consisted here in weaving this in-between state of the right distance in the face of the terror of incest and the unthinkable of the void.

Whether it is present from the outset or constructed, the basic transference can prove to be fundamental in clinical situations that seem antithetical.

A passionate transference in a face-to-face analysis can sometimes be talked about serenely, many years afterwards, in a new tone: "I told myself a lot of stories about us. For a long time, I came mostly to see you and hear the sound of your voice. I provoked you, but I knew that you would hold out and I always felt that there was a zone of safety in your office. For you, that probably wasn't easy."

Is it not this dimension of basic transference that serves as a basis for the help that is felt, often quite rightly, to be received by patients who come very regularly to their sessions without saying more than a few words in them, or who only sporadically bring meagre accounts leaving no room for any possible interpretation?

Further reading

Godfrind, J. (1993). *Les deux courants du transfert*. Paris: Presses Universitaires de France.

Parat, C. (1995). *L'affect partagé*. Paris: Presses Universitaires de France.

KEY WORDS Therapeutic alliance, process, relation, basic transference.

THE ANALYST'S SENSITIVE PRESENCE

JACQUES PRESS

This term refers to an often-neglected component of the transference/countertransference interplay that concerns the analyst's élan towards his patient, the quality of his investment. This aspect plays a particularly important role in narcissistic and identity-related issues, but it is active in every analysis.

Here is an example. It concerned a young woman with a painful history combining early narcissistic and sexual traumas. As is classically the case, she tended to repeat both of them beyond the pleasure principle in her affective life, which stood in striking contrast with her brilliant professional career. She felt a constant need to test not only the constancy of the analyst's investment during his absences, but also the nature and quality of his presence during the sessions. From thereon, they moved on a ridge line between two major dangers: disinvestment on one side, and instinctual drive violence on the other.

During this difficult process for both partners, the analyst felt on a day-to-day basis that presence and absence, passivity and activity, should not be opposed term for term, but on the contrary that they formed a complementary pair underpinning his functioning during the session. As much as it was important for the analyst to let himself follow his inner movements associated sometimes with bodily sensations or with quasi-hallucinatory experiences, equally he soon realised that the quality of his presence, including physical, of his way of speaking, of choosing his words, of expressing them neither too strongly nor too neutrally, played a central role. At certain moments, he was almost painfully sensitive to his own bodily presence, and this feeling formed the basis of the constructions communicated to the patient as well as his way of putting them.

In a session that took place during a particularly critical period of her analysis, the patient declared that "it had gone on long enough" and that she preferred to return to her solitude rather than run the risk of being "mortally disappointed". The analyst then felt in an acute way a sort of hollow in his stomach when thinking again about the multiple experiences of abandonment that had marked her history. Shortly after, as if in passing, she made an allusion to her solitude as a child – a recurrent theme between them. An image then welled up in the analyst's mind of photographic precision concerning the patient, as a child, in a state of absolute solitude, staring into the distance with an empty gaze. It was at this point that he intervened: "You have just talked to me about your solitude as a little girl and today you are asking me to let this child go. I cannot prevent you from leaving, but do not ask me to be an accomplice in this abandonment." She was taken aback. Moreover, this moment was to remain an anchor point for the rest of the analysis.

The relative poverty of the literature bearing on issues related to the analyst's presence seems to be linked to the very conditions that governed the discovery of psychoanalysis. By inventing the couch/armchair setting, Freud carried out, in effect, a foundational operation with far-reaching consequences. The fact that the analyst remains hidden from the analysand's view pushed the founder of our discipline as well as his successors to develop a conception of psychic activity based on the efficacy of a certain negativity. This line of thinking gave rise to fundamental developments, particularly in French psychoanalysis, whether those of André Green on the work of the negative or those of Michel Fain suggesting that the "prelude" to fantasy life is based on the discontinuity of the maternal presence and the active conflictuality in every woman between the mother and the lover.

This way of thinking about the birth of the psyche has nonetheless led analysts to neglect a central fact: before a healthy negativity can be established, opening the way to the unfolding of fantasy life, the quality of the maternal presence must first be sufficiently assured. Or more exactly, presence and absence can only be thought about in a dynamic dialectic.

Two notions are useful for following this path. The first is that of Ferenczian introjection. Contrary to Freud, Sándor Ferenczi considers introjection as an expansion of the potentialities of the ego in contact with the object and in its presence. As for the second notion, that of holding described by D.W. Winnicott throughout his work, it involves a complexity that is too often underestimated. On the one hand, holding only has value inasmuch as it is animated by maternal love, including the conflictuality between mother and lover mentioned earlier. On the other, it engages all the sensory-motricity and corporeity of the two partners in a genuine choreography (Roussillon, 1999).

And because the analyst does not physically touch his patients, it is through other channels that this aspect of the relationship must be expressed. In the couch/armchair setting, it is the analyst's way of expressing himself, the tonality of words, the effort to find the right word and, more profoundly, the analyst's élan towards his patient that make his presence "sensitive". In the face-to-face situation, his facial expressions, way of moving and of being actively present, his expressivity, are in the foreground.

Further reading

Braunschweig, D., and Fain, M. (1975). *La Nuit, le Jour.* Paris: Presses Universitaires de France.

Fain, M. (1971). Prélude à la vie fantasmatique. *Revue française de psychanalyse*, 36: 291–364.

Green, A. (1999 [1993]). *The work of the negative,* trans. A. Weller. London: Free Association Books.

Press, J. (2010). *La construction du sens.* Paris: Presses Universitaires de France.

Roussillon, R. (1999). *Agonie, clivage, symbolisation.* Paris: Presses Universitaires de France.

Winnicott, D.W. (1958). *Collected papers: through paediatrics to psycho-analysis.* London: Tavistock.

KEY WORDS Countertransference, holding, Ferenczian introjection, presence.

PRIMARY SEDUCTION

NICOLE MINAZIO

"[T]he child's mother...not only nourishes but looks after it and thus arouses in it a number of other physical sensations pleasurable and unpleasurable. By her care of the child's body, she becomes its first seducer. In these two relations lies the root of a mother's importance, unique, without parallel, established unalterably for a whole lifetime as the first and strongest love-object and as the prototype of all later love-relations – for both sexes... And for however long it is fed at its mother's breast, it will always be left with a conviction after it has been weaned that its feeding was too short and too little" (Freud, 1940b [1938]), pp.188–189). Such is the overview that Freud gives of what is commonly called primary seduction.

Today, clinical psychoanalysis is particularly sensitive to the effects of external realities on the internal realities of the subject. And the concept of primary seduction is particularly pertinent when thinking about the entanglement of these two registers. Primary seduction gives us an idea of the complexities of the primary relationship in the *infans* with its object, while according full importance to the place of the repressed traces of infantile sexuality.

In the initial stages of life, an essentially dissymmetrical relationship is established between the infant and its mother. By loving her infant, the mother unwittingly seduces it and leaves it with the stamp of the marks of her own repressed infantile sexuality reactivated during her close physical relationship with the baby. In its passivity, the baby cannot evade a potentially traumatic seduction by the mother. Through her caresses, her facial expression, the nipple that she puts in its mouth, the mother inaugurates an emotional bond of shared pleasure from which the constitution of an erotogenic body will emerge for the infant.

Primary seduction is thus established in an atmosphere of excitation, of instinctual drive force, of fantasies in a dissymmetrical intersubjective relationship, woven in a network of intra- and interpsychic complexities: the infant's desires are matched by the mother's desire. The mother constantly seeks to decipher the infant's instinctual drive impulses and then to transform them. However, the effects of this primary seduction clearly depend on the quality of the mother's response. D.W. Winnicott is attentive to the following fact: for seduction to be operative, the mother must be able both to survive the violent instinctual drive impulses that the infant expresses towards her and to enable it to find an object that is sufficiently close to the one that its fantasies have led it to create in its mind. When this conjunction between the created and the found occurs, the infant can then gain access to an area of illusion that is indispensable for its psychic birth as well as to the sense of continuity of being. Nonetheless, at the dawn of life, the infant is constantly threatened with disorganisation and the adult psyche is constantly animated by the repressed traces of its own infantile sexuality. Thus the relationship of primal seduction is often the locus of painful experiences, of lack or excess. This can result in deficiencies in the subject's capacities for representation and thinking.

During the session, this is often expressed by a dominance of the perceptual/motor and hallucinatory register. The analyst's listening and psychic functioning are then put under considerable strain. The incomprehensible aspects and strangeness of the psyche of the other feature at the heart of the transference/countertransference interactions. Something comes from beyond words and the search for meaning. It becomes impossible to avoid the dominance of the sensory and perceptual dimensions and of the act. Prosody then loses its conventional function and becomes music. Words once again become sensation, thing, and act. The analyst's response consists in providing an affective and emotional quality for what cannot be said or represented. What we are dealing with here is the first psychic lineaments, the first traces of instinctual drive movements in search of the object. In this type of situation, the risk is one of yielding to a form of seduction in which the infantile produces its effects without either of the protagonists realising it. It is a question, then, of permitting a gradual liberation from this shared sensory dimension through the gradual construction of a tolerable gap between perception and thought. What is involved is a process of experimenting together, understanding, seeing and understanding how the psyche manages to free itself from the body in order to metaphorise it and open itself to representation. Far from being a regular method, the process often emerges from the hiatus between what was expected and what is perceived, between what is and what was or was not, between what is known and what is unknown both with regard to oneself and the other.

A little less than a year ago; A young girl had been seriously traumatised and deprived of the presence of her mother who had died in extremely violent circumstances. The father had disappeared and, after spending some time in institutions, she was adopted. She was nine years old when she saw the analyst for the first time.

The analyst had to invent a way of approaching her in order to tame her. They were able to make contact with each other through the medium of soft and pliable modelling clay. She did not really speak, but murmured little inaudible words. She seemed animated merely by a faint breath. To avoid increasing the gap between the registers of touch and sound, the analyst also had to be careful to use a soft voice and to listen flexibly. By respecting her silences and her murmurs, and also by speaking to her softly and slowly, it became possible to introduce the first words of a therapeutic voyage which was to last almost 10 years. Initially, the sessions consisted essentially of games of collage and envelopment. She would sniff the modelling paste or 'play dough ' before handling it. She was also sensitive to the modulations of the analyst's voice, and then later on to the nursery rhymes that the analyst asked her to sing; she enveloped herself with this music to calm herself and make links. Gradually, the sounds, rhythms and silences became differentiated, acquiring an affective and relational value.

The first games were sensorial. They were set up as a mirror of their shared impressions by producing echoing gestures and sounds. Then, words provided a new extension to this first mode of exchange. For a long time, bodily expression remained the essential support. The girl sometimes wanted the analyst to be mobile, sometimes immobile, controlling her varying degrees of closeness or distance, as well as her speech and silences. She let her make comments within the context of play, but rarely outside it. When the analyst offered her an interpretation, she would often stop her ears even if, a moment later, her play seemed to provide an illustration of it. Even though she modulated her interventions, the analyst was inwardly assailed by violently intrusive images.

In the course of the work, the girl also practised opening and closing her orifices. She visibly took pleasure in doing so, venturing to make sounds with her mouth, to emit various sounds or, on the contrary, a single, continuous and monotone vibration, which saturated the space. The analyst first interpreted these noises as if they allowed the girl to keep her words at a distance. Later, it seemed that there was also an experience of sensory pleasure involved, that she needed to feel her flesh and her tongue vibrating, to make her mouth resound, as a first outline of autoerotic pleasure.

Gradually, within the framework of the session, a scenario of her games emerged; then, the beginnings of a relationship with the analyst took shape. Her instinctual impulses, which she had previously felt to be dangerous, began at certain moments to deploy themselves. However, it did not take much for the analyst to feel once again that she was being breached or intruded upon by a monstrously seductive and intrusive mother/analyst. In these moments of crisis, she had the image in her mind of an envelope for their two merged bodies. The girl would then throw herself on the analyst, crying out and groaning, as if what she had projected outside her ego had returned and obliged her to identify herself with an aggressor to whom she could only attribute cries and groans owing to her absence of language. It was as if she was trying to enact a situation suffered in the helplessness and distress of early childhood, at a time when she was incapable of describing anything, of differentiating anything.

These resurgences occurred violently, like muddled catastrophes, involving confused feelings about what came from her and from the other. To give them meaning, she certainly needed a reliable external object. However, it was above all necessary to create a space first that could modulate the violence of these clashes. Gradually, the experience and testing of the bodily limits of each protagonist could occur. What initially was simply a repeated multiple crash, became a rhythmic and sung dance attesting to the emergence of pleasure in the relationship. She invited the analyst to dance opposite her, to sing and to give rhythm to their sentences while observing her own tempo. Even though she demanded perfect synchrony, she slowly accepted that the melodic contents were not identical.

A joint rhythm thus emerged from the individual rhythms, uniting and separating at the same time. It provided the transference/countertransference relationship with the support of gestural, musical and visual communication created by both protagonists, but whose pauses, high points and sighs the analyst had to respect. When the trace ceased to imply for her the murder of the thing, she began to draw. The verbal exchanges became more consistent. She was then able to use words to communicate. Language then gained momentum.

Further reading

Freud, S. (1905). *Three essays on the theory of sexuality. S.E.* 7. London: Hogarth, pp. 123–243.

Freud, S. (1939). *Moses and Monotheism. S.E.* 23. London: Hogarth, pp. 1–138.

Freud, S. (1940 [1938]). *An outline of psychoanalysis. S.E.* 23. London: Hogarth, pp. 139–208.

Laplanche, J. (2007). *Freud and the sexual: Essays: 2000–2006*, trans. J. Fletcher, J. House, N. Ray. New York, NY: International Psychoanalytic Books.

KEY WORDS Instinctual drive force, illusion, primary object, primary seduction, infantile sexuality.

THE THERAPIST'S MATERNAL FUNCTION

DIANA TABACOF

In the 1980s, Pierre Marty formulated the idea that in psychosomatic clinical practice, the work with the patient ranged "from the maternal function to psychoanalysis" (Marty, 1990, p. 95). The therapist's maternal function, from Marty's economic perspective, is required with patients whose psychic apparatus has been overwhelmed by traumas (recent or distant), thus making the full use of their mental functioning unavailable (either temporarily or regularly). The analyst then finds himself faced with an "operational" (*opératoire*) type of functioning, for defensive purposes, characterised by a very factual discourse centred on current events, while associative work remains quite limited and affects are massively suppressed.

A man came for a consultation with a medical prescription, not for his psychic suffering but due to the serious consequences of a somatic illness. After one year of psychotherapy, this is how one of his sessions unfolded.

The patient said: "I finally went to see J. We signed the papers and I left immediately. I was calm. I took the papers directly to the lawyer. There we are, it's done." "You were afraid you wouldn't be able to remain calm?" the analyst asked. "Well, yes," the patient replied, "I was afraid I would not be able to control myself, as we said here, but now it's done, one file less on the pile. It was quite a headache, but the following day I didn't think about it anymore". He continued by recounting the events of the week, but he couldn't find a comfortable position in his chair, and kept moving and frowning. The analyst intervened as soon as he made a pause: "It looks as if are feeling a lot of pain today." "Yes," the patient said, "this weekend I tried to saw off the branches of a tree; it wasn't easy." The analyst replied: "Perhaps try leaning back in your chair a bit more. (The analyst leaned back in her chair at the same time.) What could you do to make things better?" "I would need to go back and see my dear osteopath," the patient said. "To tell you the truth, I'm afraid: I have the feeling that I've got a very thin thread in the spine. And yet, I know she is very careful, that she goes about things very gently." "Well!" the analyst said. "A little bit of gentleness in this world of brutes!" "Yeah, because I no longer have my mummy," the patient replied, feigning a childish voice, which evoked the picture he had of himself as the only son of a depressive mother and an alcoholic father.

The analyst's cathexis of the patient's body and pains served to make a psychic object of them attracting associations. Her suggestion about seeking treatment for them evoked anxieties in the patient linked to the passivity and reliability of the object, because the lateral transference onto the osteopath might lead to autoerotic behaviours and fantasy scenarios. The aim of this work, which was to reinforce the patient's narcissistic foundations, impacted on the patient's capacities for mentally elaborating his erotic and aggressive instinctual impulses.

The session continued. The analyst asked her patient about his sleep and nightmares. "Still the same horrors," the patient said, "but now I think of you and I tell myself that it's OK, that I'm not going mad. There was J., obviously! I saw myself knocking him to the ground and…". (He mimed a punch accompanied by a facial expression that revealed the instinctual violence with which he had fought.)

Marty defines the therapist's maternal function in terms of the maternal function at the beginning of life, which is based on the maternal instinct for preserving the species, but is also dependent on the mother's instinctual drive development and capacities for identification. A major constituent of the maternal function is the "affective appreciation of the needs and desires of the infant in the light of the signals perceived thanks to deep identification with the mother, and the regulation of the times and modes of intervention or non-intervention at the levels of the multiple communications with the infant" (Marty, 1985, p. 125). Faced with patients like this one, in whom narcissistic fragility and anti-traumatic defences are in the foreground, Marty recommended employing the "caution of a mine-clearing expert", surveying the variations in the sources of excitation, and good management of silence and frustration. The therapist's role as a stimulus barrier and his attuned accompaniment of the patient, within a relationship involving both verbal and sensory-motor exchanges, makes it possible to bind stimuli into affects and representations; the economic excesses can thus be gradually broken down into smaller elements and treated psychodynamically. Giving the instinctual drive force and its links with an object's psychic status, at the heart of the maternal function, will provide the basis for increasingly thorough psychoanalytic work.

In their developments on the subject of this notion of Marty, Michel Fain and Denis Braunschweig point out that there is no maternal function without a third element. In this sense, the therapist's concern for the patient's body may be seen as equivalent to the threat of castration by the father, for whom the mother is a messenger. Between seduction and the threat of castration, for these authors, the superego becomes a component of the maternal function.

Further reading

Braunschweig, D. (1993). Implications techniques de la théorie en psychosomatique. *Revue française de psychosomatique*, 3: 21–31.

Fain, M. (2001). La fonction maternelle selon Pierre Marty. *Revue française de psychosomatique*, 20: 47–52.

Marty, P., de M'Uzan, M., and David, C. (1962). *Sept observations cliniques. L'investigation psychosomatique*. Paris: Presses Universitaires de France.

KEY WORDS Shared affect, censorship, traumatic state, stimulus barrier.

THE PLIABLE MEDIUM

DOMINIQUE TABONE-WEIL

Introduced by Marion Milner (1955) in her article "The role of illusion in symbol formation", translated into French for the *Revue française de psychanalyse* in 1979 (Milner, 1979), this concept was taken up and developed by René Roussillon in his book *Paradoxes et situations limites en psychanalyse* (1991). According to Roussillon, it is a "transitional object of the process of representation", a bridge between internal reality and external reality, like the medium used by artists to give shape to objects in their internal world. It is particularly useful when the analyst finds himself at grips with the difficulties of a countertransference endangered by negativity.

For Roussillon, it presents five characteristics: it is indestructible, very sensitive, unconditionally available, indefinitely transformable and endowed with its own life (while being transformable, it remains itself). These characteristics are interdependent and they result in the capacity to transform quantitative variations into qualitative change, just as the material earth, if it is given a violent blow (quantitative), is transformed by being flattened out (qualitative).

It is the "good enough mother" at the beginning of life who is the pliable medium par excellence for her baby. When this quality has been absent, it is for the object-analyst to provide it, thereby permitting the subject to experience, alternating between fusion and defusion, the process of separation and differentiation that did not take place at the time. It is a foundational experience of illusion (total control over the object which is both outside and a part of the subject) followed by progressive disillusionment, which does not require the subject to adapt to the object and external reality in a forced and immature way in order to survive.

A young woman has been in analysis for several years. She is very involved in her sessions, but we are always on the verge of a negative therapeutic reaction, and, more generally, under the threat of worrying negativity and destructiveness (self-sabotage, suicidal plans, risky behaviour, ruptures, withdrawal).

She idealises the analysis as being too good for her, as well as the analyst, while at the same time, she sees herself as being persecuted by malevolent figures, "real" or imaginary, which often appear in the accounts she gives of readings, films or dreams. These figures correspond to a very negative maternal imago formed on the basis of a defective primary object experienced as entirely bad, insensitive, and impossible to change. Underlying destructive rage is noticeable, directed at this object to whom she feels obliged to adapt absolutely and at her own expense. This prevents her from making use of her sessions, in the sense that D.W. Winnicott gives to the term "use", that is, by expressing what she feels without seeking to adapt herself to the object (out of fear of reprisals: judgement, abandonment, or even destruction of the subject). Splitting protects the analyst precariously, who is prey to growing feelings of helplessness and disquiet; she feels she is the victim of a sort of latent blackmail, for the patient is very susceptible and the slightest false step involves a risk of transference rupture, or worse. At the same time, the analyst notices that she sometimes hopes this rupture will occur, saying to herself: "After all, she can go to the devil! If she doesn't want my help, too bad."

Analysis of this countertransference reaction of revolt gradually revealed to the analyst her own need to be the good object for this patient, the saving and redemptive object (a manifestation of the "perfect" narcissistic mother), which ran counter to the patient's (denied) need to see the analyst as the bad and hateful persecuting object and to experience her capacity to accommodate and survive the patient's instinctual violence, the only possible way to construct a good enough and really reliable object.

The analyst understood that by showing her silently that nothing she offered her was usable, and that she was "incurable", the patient was making her experience the maternal rejection that she had always felt she had suffered and was putting up defensive opposition to any change, for change was felt to be equivalent to submission to the maternal desiderata. (To be accepted by the object, she would have to be different.)

From thereon, the analyst interpreted in small doses the negative transference that was both patent and denied wholesale, while taking care to point out the defensive use that she was trying to make of these interpretations that she "transformed" into reproaches.

The concept of pliable medium helped the analyst here to free herself from unconscious demands that led her to want to be a perfect analyst, that is, quite the contrary of a good enough object, and to disarm the patient's anti-processual negativity. For her part, the patient was gradually able to withdraw her projections and reduce her splitting, which allowed for an internal reconciliation that was expressed by an apparently "magical" reduction of tensions in her hitherto very painful relations with those around her, and also a liberation of her sublimatory capacities.

Further reading

Milner, M. (1955). The role of illusion in symbol formation. In: *Psychoanalysis and art. Kleinian perspectives*, ed. Gosso, S. London: Karnac, pp. 85–109.

Milner, M. (1979). Le rôle de l'illusion dans la formation du symbole. *Revue française de psychanalyse*, 43(5–6).

Roussillon, R. (1991). *Paradoxes et situations limites de la psychanalyse.* Paris: Presses Universitaires de France.

KEY WORDS Good enough mother, characteristics of the medium, use of the object.

6

THE ORDEAL OF TRANSFERENCES

THE PRECESSION OF THE COUNTERTRANSFERENCE IN RELATION TO THE TRANSFERENCE

LAURE BONNEFON-TORT

It was Michel Neyraut (2004 [1974]) who introduced, running contrary to commonly held ideas, the notion of the precession of the countertransference in relation to the transference. As he points out, the etymology of the term "countertransference, transposed from the German *Gegen übertragung,* suggests that "the countertransference is opposed to the transference, occurs after the transference, is determined by it [and] is essentially second and reactive" (p. 14). Now, even in its extended sense, which includes in the countertransference everything that occurs in the analyst, this does not account for the "conflictual and dynamic relationship that is formed in the analytic situation" (p. 16).

In his approach to the transference, it is essentially this dialectical character of the analytical encounter that Neyraut highlights. He shows that it is the transference that comes second in two respects: as a concept, it appeared retrospectively; in analysis it cannot be first because it occurs during the analytic process. "If psychoanalytic thinking," he writes, "is constituted essentially by a response, we are obliged to note that sometimes the response precedes the question and that this is a first form of countertransference" (p. 18). This conception reveals the fundamental ambiguity of the countertransference and makes our approach to it considerably more complex because it also locates the demand on the analyst's side. This can be illustrated by a clinical sequence that seemed particularly enigmatic at the time.

The analyst had just opened the door to receive a patient for a first interview. A man entered. Their eyes met and at that very moment, a thought crossed the analyst's mind: "Yet another drug addict (*Encore un toxico*)!" The interview then unfolded perfectly normally. After the event, however, she still felt affected by this incomprehensible "psychic incident" that had occurred before the man had even said anything.

Why "yet another"? It did not correspond to anything: the analyst was not seeing any patient at that time who could have been described as an addict (*toxicomane*). The term "*toxico*" seemed to have emerged from nowhere and, in its abridged for, it seemed strangely aggressive. The analyst had no reason, it seemed to her, to feel as overwhelmed as a consultant in a specialised service for addicts at the end of the day. It was all the more troubling in that this inopportune thought was totally contrary to the ideal of benevolence with which she had wanted to welcome a new demand.

This man had nothing about him of a marginal. On the contrary, he was brilliantly successful professionally. That was not the problem. He had spoken about his solitude that went back as long as he could remember, how he had collapsed when his last love affair broke up, and his impression that he would never manage to establish a stable relationship. The first interviews opened out onto an enriching analysis during which all the threads gradually led back to the major event that had marked his history: the early death of his mother.

What had happened, then, at the moment of meeting, in that fraction of a second during which something had silently occurred? What had the analyst perceived in the patient's eyes? Certainly disarray, the intense nature of his lack, and the expression of the feeling of being lost. To which she had responded inwardly: "Yet another drug addict!" As Neyraut writes, the response here preceded the demand.

After reading the text on the precession of the countertransference, the analyst remembered, in echo with this first session, a formula that had come to her several years earlier during the last sessions of her own analysis, in which the transference was associated with a hard drug. She had responded to her patient with her prior subjective knowledge of the process of the transference, of the state of dependence that it induces. The weakness that she had no doubt perceived in his eyes had made her understand that she was going to be put under severe pressure in the transference. And she had probably experienced a movement of retreat, of withdrawal, faced with this process whose outcome she anticipated: yet another future addict of the transference, yet another! (*encore un future drogué du transfert, encore un!*) The ambiguity lay in the fact that this "yet another" (*encore*) included the analyst without her realising it and that it had reminded her of her own journey as a patient, of the affects that she had experienced in her analysis, and of those that she was feeling now in the transference of her patients and of her wish that it should continue, *again and again*.

Further reading

Bouvet, M. (1959). *Œuvres psychanalytiques*, vol. 2. Paris: Payot.

Freud, S. (1915). *Observations on transference-love. S.E.* 12. London Hogarth, pp. 159–171.

Neyraut, M. (2004 [1974]). *Le Transfert*. Paris: Presses Universitaires de France.

KEY WORDS Countertransference, dependence, process, transference.

DEFERRAL AND THE QUIPROQUO

ANNE MAUPAS

In his book *Le Transfert*, Michel Neyraut (2004 [1974]) states: "Transference is the *quiproquo* (*displacement*) of the unconscious" (p. 7). It is a deferred displacement whose resolution consists in returning it to whomever it concerns and to wherever it comes from. He goes on to ask himself: "Why is there this quiproquo in man and why does man, who loves discriminating between things, have this capacity within himself to confuse them, to the point that, without this capacity he would perhaps be mad? It is a strange contradiction" (p. 7). He compares transference to animistic thinking, according to which spiritual beings animate human beings in such a way that souls can migrate from one body to the other. Animistic thinking is governed by the omnipotence of ideas and present in all the neuroses. It leads the patient to mistake someone who is there now for someone else (quiproquo) who was there then (deferral: at a different moment).

The patient sat on the couch, then suddenly got up again and hurried towards the door: "I have to go to the toilet!" she said. The analyst was taken aback. She felt ill-at-ease, invaded by the disagreeable impression that she was witnessing a totally quirky scene that had emerged from elsewhere, from another time and from another place, with other protagonists. Trying to regain her composure, she told herself that this patient was clearly inhabited by parental imagos that had been intruding upon her analysis since the beginning: the inadequate mother who was unable to contain her and the seductive and exciting father who had precipitated her flight towards the toilet. Knowing that the transference reactualises an infantile relationship in the context of a contemporary conflict, the analyst wondered how to interpret her act in the transference by "returning it to whomever it concerns and to wherever it comes from".

The patient returned to the couch, taking up the associative thread of the last session. She said: "I am gender-neutral... Born with something more and something less. Something less: I am the failed boy of my mother.[1] Something more: I am my father's boy."

At this moment in the session, the analyst pictured the little girl with an irrepressible need to urinate, running to the toilet to discharge the excitement and, in the same moment, being confronted with her anatomy, and, by extension, by the difference between the sexes. This countertransference experience had the advantage of lowering the erotic charge that was directed to the analyst and placing the patient's act back within the associative chain.

After a silence, the patient said that she loved to be naked in her bath and to imagine being noticed by her neighbours. She added: "I was looked at before looking. Someone looked at me in an unhealthy way… a mixture of desire and disgust." The analyst intervened: "When you went to the toilet just now, you put me in the position of the one who may have looked at you in an unhealthy way. Were you trying to make me, like your mother or your father, put you in the position of having something more or something less on you?" The patient continued: "What is a woman's body without a man's sexual member? I prefer to invest the *nothing* rather than this ridiculous little thing that is the clitoris. This part of my body disgusts me; it's so *useless* that it doesn't interest me." The analyst replied: "You'd rather be gender-neutral than have a 'little thing'!"

The interpretation of the transference thus made it possible, at least temporarily, to put the lost representation back into context. My witnessing of her race to the toilet was her way of acting out the fact of being looked at. This was a representation voided of affect. The circumstances that would have allowed her to address this affect with the real person in the real time were repressed because they were too close to the central conflict. By helping the patient become aware of this deferred quiproquo, the analyst helped her to associate around her incestuous desires and to restore the containing function of the maternal imago.

For Neyraut, the countertransference precedes the transference: the transference is addressed to the psychoanalyst and only exists because there is the context given by the psychoanalyst. The context is comprised of the involvement of the analyst as a person and his understanding of psychoanalytic theory. The countertransference is both a response and an expectation. The analyst waits for the appearance of the transference manifestation and addresses it. It is this which, in meeting that of the patient, is the basis of the therapeutic alliance. We can see how the countertransference can give rise to the transference or, conversely, present an obstacle to the deployment of some of its modalities. Transference and countertransference both carry strong resistances. The reactualisation of infantile sexuality and primal phantasies can awaken affects that are so painful that they risk impeding the process of the analysis by establishing a negative transference. That is why the transference, whatever its nature, is only of value if it is interpreted and if it maintains the possibility of a new response. "The organisation of the transference neurosis," Neyraut writes, "implies that there are at least two people involved" (2004 [1974] p. 241). But it also implies that the displacement onto the person of the therapist is conceived as symbolic and leaves the therapist the possibility of remaining himself, which gives this deferred quiproquo its full dialectical and spatiotemporal dimension.

Note

1 "*Je suis un garçon manqué par ma mère*" There is also a word play here because *un garçon manqué* means a tomboy.

Further reading

Neyraut, M. (2004 [1974]). *Le Transfert*. Paris: Presses Universitaires de France.

KEY WORDS Transference neurosis, countertransference, transference.

THE CRISIS

OLIVIA TODISCO

This concept embraces different senses in Pierre Fédida's work, from the most ordinary – crises in the inner history of a life or moments of rupture in analysis – to the most complex, if we limit ourselves exclusively to the level of psychoanalytic theory. Here it is the transference that is a crisis, and the events that intersperse the sessions – slips of the tongue, bungled actions, forgetting, dreams, sudden idea – are to be thought of as a critical process, that is, as likely to induce a crisis in the ego or alternatively, as Fédida formulates it, in the occult theory that the subject has of himself.

In what respects is the transference a crisis? First and foremost because it evokes remembering and therefore dreams that constitute our true memory. For Fédida, it is the compulsion to remember induced by the transference that proves to be traumatic, much more than what is discovered. He breaks, therefore, following Freud, with the model of hypnotic remembering concerning the hysteric, and extends the considerations of "Remembering, repeating and working-through" (Freud, 1914a) in his article titled "Restes diurnes. Restes de vie" (Fédida, 2009d). There, he develops the idea that the psychoanalytic situation establishes a temporal crisis, and that a given event is always to be thought of historically in analysis as "to come", even if it presents itself in the form of the concealing temporality of the present of the transference as causality of the past. A corollary of this is the fact that the analyst, by his presence, is in fact the author of it instead of being the recipient.

A man came for analysis because, ever since the death of his little sister when he was about three years old, he felt he had never emerged from a long sleep. He worked but did not really live or wash himself as he still felt so shocked that his death wishes, quite ordinary when all is said and done, may have caused a catastrophe. Only his animated language, almost animistic inasmuch as it *showed* the thing that he was talking about more than it helped him to think about it, had "saved" him.

After a few years, he began to suffer from feelings of helplessness, without however managing to feel them fully. And as the figure of a powerful and cruel father was becoming more prominent at the same time, the analyst made a connection between the two motifs by uttering the word "amputation".

The patient arrived at the following session with a crutch and his ankle in plaster. He then reported the following sequence which he had experienced, in his own words, "as if it had taken place in a dream": the evening before, in a café, he had got into conversation with one of the "drifters" at the bar; then he left, the man had followed him and the patient, feeling his anxiety rising, had tried to lose him. The other man started running after him in the night calling him by his first name; overtaken by feelings of panic that he did not understand, he had jumped over the park railings and then slept under a bush. At dawn, he had once again climbed over the railings and, in jumping, had broken his ankle. He added that he was happy to be here and to report his "heroic" deed.

Without having decided to do so, the analyst treated the sequence as a day residue, examining the different elements, which gave rise in the patient to the elaboration of the equivalent of a dream during the session, whose text included the session of the day before in which a great leader had uttered a "diabolical" word, the word "amputation". The current session ended on his feelings of disappointment because he thought he could perceive perplexity in the analyst's silence, even though this "life event" had concerned him.

This dream during a session had permitted, for the first time, the keen recollection of the immortal child that he had been obliged to be after the death of his sister. Now he had never been aware of having been this child, in spite of his certainty concerning the force and the magic of his death wishes. This "life event" had caused a crisis at the foundations of his being, making him enter the human order.

Further reading

Fédida, P. (2009). "Crises et metaphores" et "Restes diurnes. Restes de vie". In: *Crise et contre-transfert.* Paris: Presses Universitaires de France.

Rolland, J.-C. (2006). *Avant d'être celui qui parle.* Paris: Presses Universitaires de France.

KEY WORDS Event, remembering, transference.

THE NARCISSISTIC TRANSFERENCE

ALICE BAUER AND JOSEPH TORRENTE

A man sought analysis because he felt ill-at-ease and had the impression that his relational and affective life was unsatisfying. Above all, it seemed to him to be very out of step with his success in the professional domain. From the outset, the account that he gave of his difficulties introduced a sort of boredom into the listening. His fragility was, however, evident. The edifice of his psychic organisation was precarious; he constantly doubted his capacities, called into question what he was doing, his choices, and so on, and when he had success it was, he said, "a coincidence". In spite of everything, in appearance at least, the analysis began and the patient started associating, dreaming and remembering.

And yet a sense of malaise was still present. After reflecting on the fact that he did not feel very touched or moved by his patient, the analyst felt trapped. He was unable to identify which object his analysand was addressing. He did not feel free to say anything. Every interpretation, moreover, was rejected. The patient could not tolerate him introducing any new element into what he said. Conversely, he reacted sharply if the silence lasted. He got angry. Clearly, the analyst did not understand him: "If it's to have the impression of speaking in a void," the patient said, "there's no point in continuing." The analyst sometimes felt that he would have to achieve perfection to meet the needs that were thus manifested. For how could he find a way of making a presence felt that was not hurtful owing to its very otherness? His interventions remained brief. They were limited in most cases to taking up certain words, to discreet support.

For quite a long time, it was important to play this role of narcissistic double that this patient, who was so wounded, required. This stage in the process was necessary in order to respect the narcissistic equilibrium of this man, until he was able to invest in others ways of living, As a result, the recognition that he received slowly helped to free him from the false relationship to life that he had developed – a life that he sometimes described as a fragile edifice in which he was not certain that he had a place. Subsequently, the analytic work unfolded in a more confident manner, focusing on intrapsychic conflicts that were less inaccessible and less threatening.

The first obstacle that arose in the initial stages of this analysis was undoubtedly linked to the intensity of the narcissistic transference. Even if the employment of narcissism is part and parcel of the analytic process, its topographical definition does not seem to enjoy a consensus. For some, it constitutes an independent organisation of the three classical agencies of the second topography (id, ego, superego) and is organised along a specific developmental line culminating in the constitution of the self. From this perspective, developed in particular by Heinz Kohut, the notion of self, as Paul Denis (2012) writes, refers to the whole personality, to psychic functioning as a whole, to the bodily self as well as to better defined elements, such as the representation of oneself. It can also be associated with the love of the ego, with all the semantic ambiguity that the term "ego" takes on here, designating as much the psychical agency as the whole person.

The expression "narcissistic transference" thus refers to a certain type of transference in which the ego's needs are reactualised and repeated, because hitherto they have remained suspended during the course of psychic development. More than a reproduction of object relations transferred onto the person of the analyst, the transference relationship takes on a particularly striking narcissistic colouring. At the heart of the narcissistic transference, Heinz Kohut (1971) distinguishes between the idealising transference and the mirror transference. In the idealising transference, the ego idealises a narcissistic object in order to appropriate it ("you are perfect and I am part of you"). In the mirror transference, the ego develops its own sense of value under the gaze of the narcissistic object while awaiting its confirmation ("I am perfect and I need you to confirm it"). The links between object transference and narcissistic transference are complex. During the analysis, they are so entangled that it is sometimes difficult to differentiate them. The feelings in the countertransference may provide a clue: tension, impatience and boredom are often marks of the narcissistic transference. It is true that such feelings are also attached to moments of conflict, which constitute the very essence of the dynamics of analysis.

Further reading

Denis, P. (2012). *Le Narcissisme*. Paris: Presses Universitaires de France.
Grunberger, B. (2003). *Le Narcissisme*. Paris: Payot.

Kohut, H. (1971). *The analysis of the self.* New York, NY: International Universities Press.
Oppenheimer, A. (1996). *Kohut et la psychologie du self.* Paris: Paris: Presses Universitaires de France.

KEY WORDS Narcissism, self, transference.

THE NEGATIVITY OF THE TRANSFERENCE

NICOLAS DE COULON

In *Moderato Cantabile* by Marguerite Duras (1980 [1958]), Anne Desbaresdes takes her much loved little boy to have a piano lesson. She hears a scream and rushes into the bar below. A crime has been committed: a man has killed his wife. The following day, she returns and meets another man. She is troubled and drinks wine. He listens to her, and a dialogue ensues, slowly and interrupted by silences. It is repeated on the following days, oscillating between two themes: on the one hand the crime of passion and, on the other, the life of this unhappy woman. About the man we learn nothing or almost nothing, he remains in the shadows. This may be seen as a metaphor for the analytic session. Soon, what makes Anne continue to come is no longer the child's piano session, but rather the moment in the bar when she speaks to this unknown man. The traumatic dimension emerges in the dialogue. It has all the strangeness of consultations. And like analysis, it is repeated day after day.

The nature of the relationship between Anne and the man who listens to her is not clear. We can feel that there is a sensual attraction and the first image that comes to mind is, of course, one of an emerging love affair, a romantic encounter. Is it a real encounter? Uncertainty reigns: we never know how this couple, who have difficulty forming a relationship and who meet at fixed times and for a determined period, will evolve. There is one feeling that remains throughout our reading: the expectation that something will happen. What is going to happen? This expectation is trying, unpleasant, irritating; the relationship needs too much alcohol to function.

What's more, negative images are permanently cropping up due to the very skilful overlapping of two sequences. For there exists a double of the couple formed by the protagonists, that of the man who killed his wife in the very place where they are meeting. This dramatic past infiltrates the present of the narrative. The reader cannot help asking himself whether the outcome will be a sexual relationship or a murder; love is united with death.

What the writer shows us in halftones are aggressive erotic affects, of which jealousy and hate are examples. What we have is a sort of enactment or depiction of a negativised transference whose repressed instinctual side is illustrated by the "old" murder, the traumatic background that returns in the present relationship between Ann and the unknown man and that contributes to making it profoundly unsatisfying. We also learn, indirectly, and in small steps – this is the author's art – that Anne is discontent with her life, that she does not love her husband, that she tries to protect herself through the fusional relationship with her child who was supposed to play a Sonatina *moderato cantabile* to make life less boring or less tragic. Indeed, some of our sessions seem to unfold in a *moderato cantabile* atmosphere, while in the background a story as tragic as a crime of passion is unfolding, and perhaps being repeated *sotto voce* in the transference.

The image of a marvellous transference sustained by feelings of love is an idealised and simplified vision of what happens during the session. During an analysis, the transference does not always manifest itself with the positivity that we would like: a well-tempered transference love that allows for regular processual progress and its interpretation. We can therefore speak of "negativity of the transference". What is displaced onto the person of the psychoanalyst is subjected to the uncertainties of the hollow, the blank, the contrary, and destruction. All the forms of negativity can be found in it. As André Green has pointed out, reflections on the transference must take this work of the negative into account. Its clearest form is certainly that of the negative transference. It would nevertheless be a bit hasty to conclude that it is the only expression of negativity in the field of the transference. That would be to forget that the negative can feature even in "simple" clinical situations, for example in the various forms taken by resistance or in the non-encounter that is observed when the transference-object becomes totally inaccessible for the patient.

In certain pathologies, such as borderline states, the entire range of the transference pertains to the negative. Splitting, the deployment of hostile forces, the constant tendency towards breaking off relations, shows this quite clearly. In this register, some have spoken of the replacement of the model of the dream by that of the act, given that the patient resorts so much to evacuating drive impulses through action or through the body. The negative therapeutic reaction may then result in the analysis being broken off. It would nonetheless be a shame if this manifestation of the negative turned out to be the tree hiding the forest of the infinitely complex forms that negativity can assume in the psychoanalyst's clinical experience.

In *Beyond the Pleasure Principle*, Freud (1920) considers binding and unbinding as the characteristics of Eros and the death drive. What we know is that unbinding also belongs to the paradoxical expressions of the attachment to the psychoanalyst. The patient should count on the clinician, trust him and even, typically, fall in love with him or her. Yet what we often observe is attacks, domination, hostility and destructiveness or, which is more difficult to evaluate, a withdrawal, a void, an absence. All the forms of opposition and lack can be found in the transference. It is nevertheless the major tool of the psychoanalyst, whatever forms and colourings it takes.

Further reading

Duras, M. (1980 [1958]). *Moderato cantabile.* Paris: Minuit.

Freud, S. (1915). *Observations on transference-love. S.E.* 12. London: Hogarth, pp. 159–171.

Freud, S. (1920). *Beyond the pleasure principle. S.E.* 20. London: Hogarth, pp. 1–66.

Green, A. (1999 [1993]). *The work of the negative*, trans. A. Weller, London: Free Association Books.

Pontalis, J. B. (1981). Non, deux fois non. *Nouvelle Revue de Psychanalyse*, 24: 53–73. Also In: *Perdre de vue.* Paris: Gallimard, pp. 73–100.

Pontalis, J. B. (1988). Ce transfert qu'on appelle négatif. In: *Perdre de vue.* Paris: Gallimard, pp. 101–105.

KEY WORDS Splitting, negativity, novel, transference.

NEGATIVE TRANSFERENCES

THIERRY BOKANOWSKI

Classically, negative transferences develop as a counterpoint to positive aspects of the transference: as the negative pole of the positive transference, they are inherent to the unfolding of the process. They arise from the inevitable repetition in analysis of experiences of frustration and lack linked to the feeling that the object is neither satisfying nor able to live up to infantile expectations. They translate movements of opposition in connection with the instinctual drive ambivalence that infiltrates the unconscious/preconscious relationship between the subject and his past objects and thus, in the context of the analysis, between the subject and the analyst today.

In *The Dynamics of the Transference*, Freud (1912), describes the effects of the function of the transference in the analytic process as being both the major obstacle to, as well as the essential instrument (a real tool) of, progress in analysis, and distinguishes between two types of transference, two "currents" of transference: one, consisting of friendly or affectionate *positive* feelings; the other of hostile, *negative* feelings, sometimes with an erotic colouring. They may manifest themselves openly or remain concealed, cloaked in other garments such as a transference love in its eroticised form.

However, negative transferences are not only defined by the negative or violent quality of the feelings they express, but also by the force of their movements which impede the unfolding of the process (Bouvet, 1959). Thus, it is important to distinguish between the quality of affects that are negative from the negative effects of the transference that slow down, impede or sometimes immobilise psychoanalytic work: in other words, the negativity of the transference depends less on the sign attributed to its content than on the negative quality of its effects.

This was the case for a patient whose analysis was not making progress, even though things had seemed promising at the beginning. While a basic positive transference seemed to have been established, the analyst nonetheless had the feeling that the analysis was not reaching the patient in spite of his apparent willingness to conform to the conditions of the frame and to report, in keeping with events, material that concerned many aspects of his life. After a certain time, his defences of a narcissistic character suggested that he was coming to his sessions to be listened to more than being really "heard". This was linked to his fear of "being understood", that is, of "being caught" in the negative complexities implied by the idea of finding himself, as in the past, in a passive and submissive position in front of his father who, each time he asked him questions about himself or about life, always seemed to reply in a way that still seemed to him today to be very enigmatic.

The analysis thus seemed to be getting bogged down, and this was especially true in that the analyst was having less and less pleasure in listening to him. Sometimes a deep sense of boredom (negative countertransference) invaded him as he was listening to the patient's repeated complaints that as a child he was "not understood" by his father. And furthermore, it was out of the question that any aspect of his person reflected his father. This boredom was also linked to the fact that, when some affective or emotional expression appeared in him – either positive or (and especially) negative – it was immediately suppressed, when it was not disavowed.

It was when he recounted a dream – there had been very few of them since the beginning of the analysis – that certain threads of the negative transference, silently hostile and immobilising, began to be disentangled, permitting the beginnings of a change in his mode of functioning and economic organisation. In the course of the week before, the analyst had asked him, exceptionally, if they could change the time of a session, usually in the evening, to lunch time; moreover, in the session the day before, the analyst had interpreted the patient's difficulties in getting in touch with his affects. He was particularly afraid of them in that they seemed to him just as enigmatic as the answers his father used to give to the questions of a curious child, replying systematically, "Well, read *La rivière aux castors*!" a book by Alain Surget (2001) that he had never, either then or since, tried to read on account of this response.

By pointing out this connection, the analyst was showing the patient how he identified with the aggressor. To this transference analysis through an operation of reversal, he responded the following day by bringing the following dream, which had astonished him greatly: *"He had killed someone and had to eat this person's body as quickly as possible because he knew that if he did not get rid of the evidence of his crime in this way, he would be discovered and put in prison. He forced himself to eat the remains of the corpse, but he told himself that if he didn't manage to swallow them all he would have to accept that he would be discovered and imprisoned for life…"*

His associations led him to evoke his recent reading of *Pourquoi j'ai mange mon père?…* by Roy Lewis.[1] Was it the combined effect of different complex feelings that the analyst experienced when faced with the cannibalistic, necrophiliac, coprophiliac and melancholic fantasies that this dream had aroused in him? Or was it the need to overcome a state of immobility that was felt to be close to that of a corpse? In any case, it was at this moment that the analyst moved in his armchair. And the patient reacted painfully, reproaching him for "not listening to him" and of "turning away from him".

> "Just at the moment when you are nourishing me with a dream in which you are feeding yourself on me?" the analyst asked, before adding: *Pourquoi j'ai mange mon père?…* It's true that I offered you a session at meal time!"

At that moment, something entirely new happened in the atmosphere of the analytic relationship hitherto established: for the first time since the beginning, the patient began to cry silently; and a long silence followed. Before the session ended, he said: 'I can see that I don't really let myself speak about my feelings. I'm afraid that things will become profoundly chaotic."

The rest of the analysis – which was long – revealed that what he wanted to avoid, for he would then have felt he was in the chaotic situation of having been both "discovered" and "uncovered" – was the seemingly "devouring" love that he felt for his father and the fear that he had of feeling enchained forever by the very object of this love. Behind this father, there was the figure of a seductive and attractive, yet depressed mother, for however many obvious signs of love she received, she was never satisfied; in other words, a sentimental mother hungry for affection.

So it can be argued that the analysis of negative transferences is the *spearhead* of analysis, just as it is one of the central aspects of analytic work. Inscribed at the level of Eros and anchored in instinctual drive binding, they maintain transferability. As movements *counter* to the process (*resistances*), their psychic expressions – fuelled by manifest or latent reproaches (preconscious or unconscious) – are addressed to the transference object and the object of the transference (*l'objet de, et du, transfert*). They pertain to psychic suffering, in contrast with psychic pain, suffering that is linked to castration and penetration anxiety as well as to separation anxiety, which is related to mourning.

Just as dream interpretation, as Freud says, is the "royal road" to the unconscious, it may be argued that the interpretation of negative transferences is the royal road of the analytic process.

Note

1 Original English title: Lewis, R. (1993). *Evolution Man: Or: How I Ate My Father.* London: Pantheon Books,

Further reading

Bokanowski, T. (2017 [2015]). *The analytic process: Journeys and pathways.* London: Karnac.

Bouvet, M. (1959). *Le Transfert. Œuvres psychanalytiques*, vol. 2. Paris: Payot.

Couvreur, C. (2000). *La Polarité de l'amour et de la mort.* Paris: Presses Universitaires de France.

Freud, S. (1912). *The dynamics of the transference. S.E.* 12. London: Hogarth, pp. 99–108.

KEY WORDS Affects, cannibalistic fantasies, analytic process, psychic suffering.

NEGATIVISING TRANSFERENCES

THIERRY BOKANOWSKI

Negativising transferences – or transferences of the negative – must be distinguished from negative transferences proper. Linked to a negativity in the transference that is often difficult to reverse – or to a negativisation of the transference – they neutralise the process by annihilating its transformative capacities, by devitilising it and emptying it of its richness – a sterile approach that culminates in anti-processuality. They are at the basis of the questions and theoretical/clinical advances concerning certain aspects of psychic functioning which may appear, in the course of the analytic process, to be borderline or non-neurotic.

They are a defensive manoeuvre in the subject who seeks to preserve – when faced with the dependence implied by the transference-object and the object of the transference – his narcissistic integrity by deploying a destructive narcissism (Green, 2001 [1983]; Rosenfeld, 1987) which may only become apparent during the analysis because the drive mobilisation induced by the encounter with the other becomes threatening. Hence the destructive opposition to any form of "introjective" availability in the transference (resistance to change due to painful separation and/or intrusion anxieties. The destructive attack (full of hatred) is directed against the link uniting the patient and the analyst. This makes interpretability all the more uncertain in that the subject no longer seems capable of displacing cathexes that would mobilise the expression of affects in other ways than against a background of pain. This pain is sometimes so intense that it can lead to the subject's incapacity to utilise transferability.

While they are noisy in cases of transferences of an erotic or passionate type, they can also be silent and thus give the analyst the feeling that the analysis is repudiated, and the analyst, neutralised in his otherness, may then feel powerless and "dissociated from his function" (Neyraut, 2004 [1974]).

This is what seemed to be happening with a female patient who, at certain moments, gave the impression that she experienced the analytic approach itself – its structure, its method, its limits – as a threat, in spite of having found some relief from it. Notwithstanding her conscious desire to do her analysis, and a few changes that had occurred in her life since starting it, which she saw as positive, she seemed to react to it quite negatively. In particular, she seemed, overall, not to be very interested or intrigued or challenged by her psychic productions. A background noise, which was not immediately identifiable, nonetheless emerged: it seemed linked to points of narcissistic and identity-related tension that had appeared quietly, creating notes of discordance in a process which, initially, seemed to manifest the vicissitudes of a transference neurosis.

Furthermore, she sometimes gave the impression of trying to thwart attempts to make sense of the material she reported. She seemed to misunderstand interpretations; she "misinterpreted" them, or worse treated them in a subtly scornful and murderous way with remarks such as: "I don't remember...", "I don't know...", "I don't see..." or "I don't understand...". In other words, she was constantly saying, in effect: "I hear what you are saying; you may be right, but that has no meaning for me."

Somewhat disoriented, the analyst began to have serious doubts about the relevance of the indication of analysis, and even about that of the indication of the analyst. "Who is speaking about what to whom? Who is hearing what? What is being heard by whom? What's it all about, in fact? Who is it really all about?" he asked himself. These questions reflected the fact that this patient never gave the impression of being able to give the analyst access to the destiny of her cathexes concerning her internal objects. She only introduced them into the session in order to bring them to life again within the conflictuality of a relationship that had to be solely confined to the here-and-now of the session, while asking implicitly that their enigmatic status be respected.

Among other things, she had entered analysis in order to gain understanding of searing suicidal anxieties that had appeared in adolescence. Initially, they could be understood as a retroactive effect of the trauma linked to the suicide, in dramatic circumstances, of one of her very close relatives during her childhood but, when faced with any attempt to make connections, she seemed to try to systematically "suicide" ("*suicider*") such attempts.

Not long after complaining at length about not feeling understood and that nobody, the analyst no more than anyone else, could understand the torments of her pain, she concluded that there was no point in continuing her analysis, which had proved futile, and then reported the following dream: *"I had the task of watching over a vicious little girl who was determined to kill someone. I tried to extract a confession from her for her own good, but without success. In the dream I saw a man observing me while I was trying to strangle this little girl so that she wouldn't carry out her plan. Just when the little girl was on the verge of dying, I woke up."*

As a result of this dream and in the sessions that followed it, it became possible, with the help of her associations, to get some idea of the split image that she had of herself: she saw herself as being both protective and, at the same time, a vicious little girl driven by murderous wishes (reversal of suicidal anxieties) towards certain people around her who had been unable in the past to protect her from the traumatic effects engendered by the suicide of a very close relative. Moreover, as a backcloth to murderous wishes to attack the analysis and the analyst, this dream contained a scenario of seduction highlighting elements of a primal scene involving the analyst, a scene in which he was the subject and the object. This was what he subsequently tried to explore with her.

Was he wrong to do so? For, in so doing, he activated drive impulses which undermined her frantic neutralisation of the transference relationship, which, at the same time, created a breach in what seemed to be a defensive system driven by narcissistic omnipotence. In any case, in the weeks that followed, she decided to "execute" (*sic*) the plan that had appeared before the dream not to continue her analysis and she fixed the date of her last session.

On that day, she came with a new dream: *It was very cold. She passed a blind man in the street who asked her for directions and she found it very difficult to give them to him. At the same time, she checked that the coat she was wearing was well buttoned up.*

It was not possible to determine during this last session who (she or the analyst) was the blind man asking for his way, nor which of them who had difficulty in giving directions to him. Placing emphasis on his words, the analyst asked her: "Very cold?" She replied with what might be seen as a witticism: "Don't worry, my coat is well buttoned up."

During processes that involve negativising transferences, the analyst is very likely to find himself confronted by the patient with the pain of solitude or of psychic exclusion, because his attempts to achieve emotional contact and sharing are rejected, abolished and evacuated. But the paradox is that it is also hate that maintains the relationship to the object. In this sense, here it is stronger and more vital than love. Resistance to the transference, which, in itself, is a form of transference, reveals a split (notably a narcissistic split, according to Sándor Ferenczi) that serves to conceal an intolerable narcissistic wound associated with a feeling of dependence that in the past led to unconscious hatred of the other, as well as self-hatred.

Further reading

Bokanowski, T. (2017 [2015]). *The analytic process: Journeys and pathways.* London: Karnac.

Ferenczi, S. (1988 [1932]). *The clinical diary of Sándor Ferenczi*, ed. J. Dupont, trans. M. Balint and N.Z. Jackson. Cambridge, MA: Harvard University Press.

Green, A. (1999 [1993]). *The work of the negative*, trans. A. Weller. London: Free Association Books.

Neyraut, M. (2004 [1974]). *Le Transfert.* Paris: Presses Universitaires de France.

Rosenfeld, H. (1987). *Impasse and interpretation: therapeutic and anti-therapeutic factors in the psychoanalytic treatment of psychotic, Borderline, and neurotic patients.* New York, NY: Tavistock/Routledge.

KEY WORDS Narcissistic splitting, psychic pain, self-hatred, narcissistic omnipotence.

7

FRAME AND SETTING

SITUATION ANALYSIS

JEAN-LUC DONNET

This notion (*l'analytique de situation*) is intended to highlight what the dynamics of analysis owes globally to the structured situation in which it unfolds. It stands in a dialectical relationship with the interpretative function, which it supports and completes. Situation analysis refers implicitly to the intrinsic value of the lived experience of the session. It underpins the transference dynamic inherent to the encounter between the patient and the overall means offered by the analytic method. In a more objective manner, in this or that privileged moment, situation analysis refers to the identifiable role played by the ensemble of the analytic site in the enactment of the transference intrigue.

Here is an example of a moment when the suspension of the interpretative register makes these issues immediately comprehensible. The patient had been in analysis for several months. He respected the analytic frame scrupulously and seemed to have invested intensely in his sessions; essentially, he was taken up with an activity of remembering, evoking the characters of his history, and sketching out constructions related to his past. He gradually let himself think more associatively but, in spite of the spontaneity of his speech, his discourse was marked by a certain vigilance.

One evening, when his session finished at 8 p.m., he fell silent just before the end. And in the silence that followed, the church clock nearby chimed eight times; a few seconds passed, the patient seemed tense and, impulsively, exclaimed, addressing the analyst directly: "But… I don't want you to give me more than my time!" He fell silent, feeling a bit embarrassed, but apparently relieved. The analyst ended the session as usual.

For the analyst who was attentive to the transference neurosis that was developing, it was clear that the circumstances had evoked in his patient feelings of anxiety linked to the fantasy of seduction by the adult – anxiety that there was no question of interpreting at this stage of the analysis. It was only much later on, retrospectively, that the meaning of his acting through speech (*agir de parole*) became accessible to the patient thanks to the analysis of the transference. It turned out that the negation involved in the words "I don't want" expressed, in a manner that was projected onto the analyst, the wish and fear that the session might continue, the effect of a demand for love from the distant past. The eight chimes of the clock, evoking the inexorability of time, separation and death, had had a subtraumatic resonance.

The meaning of the episode had remained in latency, as the analysing situation requires and permits, but the fact that it was deferred did not prevent this brief episode from constituting for the patient a particularly significant moment. It even took on the significance of a crucial point of reference in, and for, the appropriation of the intrinsic functionality of the situation, that is to say, the introjection of a "situation analysis". The compulsive formulation, addressed directly to the analyst, stood in contrast with the patient's usual discursive mode, as is often the case with acting through speech. It had even surprised the patient himself, who had experienced it as transgressive. On leaving the session, he had the conviction that something unknown and slightly strange had happened in him, but also between the analyst and him. His verbal gesture had taken on the significance for him of a symptom that would one day acquire meaning. On returning in the next session to what had happened, the patient recalled having felt that the total sense of conviction that he had had in the moment his words surged forth had dissipated during the brief course of their enunciation, which had then become enigmatic for him. The trace of this inner experience was inseparable from the perceptual aspects of the scene: the shared hearing of the eight chimes of the church clock, with their affect of nostalgia, the anxious tension of the brief period of waiting, the relaxation after acting through speech. The impression of having crossed a boundary was based, in the heat of the moment, on the sudden, albeit duly functional, actualisation of all the elements of the analytic site: the frame (the programmed end of the session), the setting (the scene is unthinkable without the couch and the imminence of the transition to the upright position), the silent analyst (projective object of the transference, then rediscovered guardian of the frame), and the fundamental rule (which, paradoxically, legitimised the transgressive statement). The patient had the confused feeling of having made use of the situation in a way that was both improvised, creative, and yet perfectly in keeping with its vocation. The word "use" could take on here its Winnicottian meaning, insofar as the patient had the impression of being the author of the situation, of having created it, even though he had found the elements already there. This conviction coexisted with the subjectively enigmatic dimension of the scene.

Such a contrast shows how the sense of transgressing a boundary, of appropriating what makes one an analysand, is not necessarily linked to a meaning attributed by interpretation, even if it foreshadows and prepares it. In these cases, there exists a correlation between the desubjectivising moment of acting through speech and the subjectivising value of the situation analysis.

Let's imagine that the same patient, further on in his process, had been in the position to say: "I am feeling anxious about the idea that you could prolong the session." Or even: "I have the fantasy that you could prolong the session." Both these formulations, which imply a reflexive position, could have led rapidly to an interpretation of the unconscious issue at stake. However, the opaqueness of the patient's acting through speech presented the inestimable interest of finding expression in a temporary projective confusion between the analyst and the object of the transference. Compared with a simple moment of coming to awareness, the brief regressive subversion of the ego made it undergo an irreplaceable experience, that which Freud (1912) referred to, in connection with transference actualisation, by stating that: "It is impossible to destroy anyone *in absentia* or *in effigie*" (p. 108). In the crucial moments of the analytic process, in particular each time that an incident of the frame occurs, we can appreciate the intrinsic functionality characteristic of situation analysis, whether interpretation is brought into play or remains latent. Outside such moments, situation analysis corresponds to the transferential cathexis of the analytic frame or, more broadly of the analytic site; it contributes to silent working-through and constitutes an essential support for the interpretability of the transference onto the analyst. In a sense, situation analysis is the precipitate of a subjectivised utilisation of the site that permitted the structuring of an analysing situation: it is on the introjection of its own temporality and of its diachronic reference points that the analysand's confidence in the expectation of the retroactive effects of interpretation.

Further reading

Donnet, J.-L. (1995). *Le divan bien tempéré.* Paris: Presses Universitaires de France (Series: Le Fil rouge).

Donnet, J.-L. (2005). *La situation analysante.* Paris: Presses Universitaires de France (Series: Le Fil rouge).

KEY WORDS Processual dynamics, working-through, analytic site, analysing situation.

THE TUB

JEAN H. GUÉGAN

The moment when an analytic treatment begins is rarely contemporaneous with the decision to have regular sessions. A busy "business man", with an overloaded schedule, who seemed to have little interest in the existence of other human beings, entered analysis. There was only one "obstacle" for him, his migraine pains, which were the alleged reason for his seeking treatment. The sessions continued, totally taken up with his "professional concerns", as if he was trying to pour into the analyst's mind what was at the origin of his blockages. There seemed little hope of making use of any of these elements in his external daily reality and the rare allusions to other scenes closer to his inner life were also treated as his own "business". For a long time, this factuality dominated the sessions and confined him within the distressing impression of not really being able to gain access to his psychic life. The initial statement of the fundamental rule as well as further reminders of it seemed to have no effect. Thus, a sort of strangeness was established which, at the beginning of each session, created in the analyst a certain anxiety that gradually appeared to be the sign of an incomprehensible transference action.

One day, as he was giving an account of a family meal, he named (in Italian) a traditional dessert on his mother's side of the family that he appreciated particularly. To his great surprise, the analyst repeated part of this name, pronouncing it in the French way, *"castagne"*. The polysemy underlined by this reprise thus engendered a surprising mutation: it was as if an entire network of associativity had suddenly been mobilised. There then appeared, in a complex enactment, strongly contrasting parental imagos, between an extremely cold mother and the exciting figure of a father "of the horde", then diverse associations related to long concealed infantile bodily anxieties, which no doubt lay behind the headaches. Starting from this inflection point crystallised by the pronunciation of this word, the analytic situation was transformed, opening the way for the working-through of drive and libidinal impulses during what was eventually a long analytic journey. By turning the perceptions of the outside towards the inside, the word "*castagne*", helped to localise the tub ("*baquet*"), in the sense that Jean Laplanche gave to this term.

For him, the "tub" circumscribes the asymmetrical space of encounter that is established between patient and analyst when the access to internal processes, their temporality and their transference deployments succeeds in ensuring a transition towards internal representation.

By using this word which, in the French language, designates a recipient in common use, even if it also means "belly" in slang, Laplanche sought to modelise the analytic situation by following the movement that Freud initiated by means of different schemas aimed at giving his theoretical thoughts a spatial form. If an analyst's empty consulting room can be photographed, the analytic frame and the analytic situation cannot be reduced to a visible materiality on a photo or in a cinematographic work as has sometimes been attempted. On another level, metapsychological this time, this virtual tub schematises the arena of the infantile drive forces that meet when their traces are actualised in the transference action.

The term also alludes to the interest shown historically by Freud in the mysterious machine that Franz-Anton Mesmer (1734–1815) had built at the beginning of the 19th century, a sort of tub conducive to exciting the minds of the participants during sessions of "hypnotic magnetism", but above all designed to concentrate the practitioner's or wizard's power of suggestion. Of course, the sense of the concept of tub proposed by Laplanche to characterise the analytic site is poles apart from such an apparatus and, while it seems more inspired by the meaning of the English expression "to kick the bucket" – the equivalent of the French expression "*casser sa pipe*", which suggests the fragility of the inner vital equilibrium – his intention is quite different. In the theoretical developments he offers on the tub, the concept appears as a modelisation of the boundaries between inside and outside that determine the tangential position of the self-preservative position with the internal drive ensemble arising from infantile sexuality. It accounts both for a process, a psychogenesis and a clinical situation – the setting – which is repeated in analytic treatment. The proposition thus makes it possible to associate method, clinical experience and theory, while maintaining a tension of incompletion that is contrary to everything that makes us resort to a catalogue of technical procedures.

Further reading

Freud, S. (1900). *The interpretation of dreams. S.E.* 4 & 5. London: Hogarth.

Hennebelle, G. (1989). *CinémAction, 50, Cinéma et psychanalyse.* Paris: Corlet.

Laplanche, J. (1987). *Problématiques V. Le baquet-transcendance du transfert.* Paris: Presses Universitaires de France.

Laplanche, J., and Macey, D. (1989). *New foundations for psychoanalysis.* London: Blackwell Publishers.

Laplanche, J. (2011 [2007]). Dream and communication. In: *Freud and the sexual*, trans. J. House & N. Ray. New York: International Psychoanalytic Books.

KEY WORDS Language, psychoanalytic method, symptoms, transference.

THE CENTRAL LABORATORY[1]

LUCETTE NOBS

A young girl came across as a gloomy, observant and tense "kid", on the margins of family life, with an unpredictable, capricious and disturbing mother, a tender but rather unavailable father, and siblings for whom she was an enigma. Her melancholic withdrawal, the manifest symptom of her phobia, was inhibited speech. Silence was the mark of her presence which was sometimes ridiculed and sometimes neglected by others. She seemed neither to want nor expect anything from the world. Nevertheless, she accepted an invitation by her brothers and sisters to attend a theatrical production. Fascinated, she came into contact with the theatrical way of life in which words and roles are given. She projected herself into it, saw herself in it and saw in the manner of a revelation the place that she could have in it. The appeal was irresistible: she would go into theatre! How does one inhabit the stage? How does one exist in this space where only the specific magic of the place and of the theatrical phenomenon seemed to her to be able to offer the wished-for yet inconceivable metamorphosis of her nagging disquiet?

When she joined the theatre troupe, it was her name that turned out to be unpronounceable! She could not say who she was. She stumbled over each letter. The ordeal was infinitely painful, but not prohibitive: she was accepted. Initially, she was able to give herself with passion to her lifelong activity/passivity, that of a spectator, of a bulimic voyeur disengaged from the life of others. Then she had the opportunity to go on stage and to face the challenge of having to speak and render the text of the character that she was playing; which she did, but mechanically.

This was how Esther Kahn, a troubling character in the 2000 film of the same name by Arnaud Desplechin, makes her entrance upon the stage as in real life. Theatre is her "central laboratory", which she invests in as a space and time that are conducive to learning and to experiences favoured by the existence of a frame and rules that she can gradually understand and appropriate.

In the film, whatever happens, the acting does not go beyond the scope of the scene and its reality. There is no off-camera. The screening seems to contain the totality of tangible experience for the one for whom there is no distance between her own identity and the role. Esther is reassured. And yet she seems very far removed from what is being asked of her.

It was the theatre scene from which Freud drew inspiration for the metaphor of the transference as a sudden cry of fire during the production. The words and the way they are addressed, the bodies and their presence, the fire and its danger, are inherent and common elements of the analytical and theatrical settings.

The reference to the fiction portrayed by Arnaud Desplechin pursues the analogy of the theatrical form with the analytic situation as evoked by J.-B. Pontalis in "Le laboratoire central" (2001) in response to André Green who was concerned about the future of psychoanalysis. The term expressed both the ambition and the modesty of the analytic experience, but above all it indicated the place given to creativity in the analytic method when its dominant codes and knowledge are undermined. By creativity, I mean the aspect of discovery in the absence of any purposive idea, the bringing into play of what the subject believes in, that is, his illusions or hopes, and the anxieties that nourish the uncertain text of his own life. This issue will be common to the patient and the analyst during the treatment. Like a laboratory experiment, far from the noise of the world, speech, during the session, summons the essence of the world itself, taking the risk of being listened to in a completely new way. Like Esther Khan, between risk and necessity, the patient will invest in multiple points of view of the landscape that constitutes him and that emerges through and in the text he addresses to the analyst. The path he pursues is determined even if it often proves to be painful, straining towards a laborious field of creation of a space "for oneself" in the presence of the other.

Pontalis told the editors of the review *Penser/Rêver* in 2012 that the idea of a laboratory, which he had had for a long time, was particularly suited to restituting the implementation and study of unconscious phenomena in the analytic situation.[2] It was also a reference to Max Jacob, whom he had known, and in particular to his collection of poems bearing the title *Le Laboratoire central* (Jacob, 1921). "A sort of friendship was formed between this old man and the very young man that I was," he added.

In the fictional story, neither the development nor the transformation of the young girl would be possible without the presence near her of a *passeur*, of an experienced, attentive, demanding and sensitive actor – a salutary figure of the *Nebenmensch* – who has decided to transmit to her the meaning of acting, that is, the playing of a role and the possibility of speech: understanding the rules of the movement of bodies on a stage, initiating one's own movements, letting oneself be permeated, surprised by words before being able to say them in an intelligible way. Henceforth, the elements of the transference interplay, between desire and resistance, regression and sublimation, are brought into play.

The story of Esther Khan is thus one of the involvement of another person in the relationship of the subject tormented by desire and its misrecognition. It is also what occurs in the space/time of the session condensed in this idea of the "central laboratory" that welcomes human passions in order to construct and transform their expressions, images and words, to make them liveable with. Pontalis (2012) defines it as follows: It is a laboratory in the sense that it is there that appear, in the most tangible, demonstrative and intense form, a certain number of processes, phenomena and psychic formations, just as a well-conducted experiment is purer than the natural phenomenon (pp. 36–37).

Notes

1 Title of the article by J.-B. Pontalis that was published in 2001 in the *Revue française de psychanalyse* (special edition, pp. 311–317); it also features in *Le Laboratoire central,* Paris: L'Olivier (Series Penser/Rever, 2012).

2 See "Nous, lecteurs de vous", *Le Laboratoire central,* pp. 185ff.

Further reading

Delacomptéé, M., and Gantheret, F. (Eds.) (2007). *Le Royaume intermédiare. Psychanalyse, literature, autour de J.-B. Pontalis.* Paris: Gallimard (Series: Folio essais).

Pontalis, J.-B. (2000). L'affirmation negative. *Libres cahiers pour la psychanlyse,* 2: 11–18.

Pontalis, J.-B. (2012). *Le Laboratoire central.* Paris: L'Olivier (Series: Penser/Rêver).

KEY WORDS Laboratory, session, theatre, transference.

CHANGING LOCATION

BRIGITTE DOLLÉ-MONGLOND

When the analyst changes his office, the very function of the frame as a container of the psychic processes at work in analysis is brought into play. In its first sense, the frame is an ensemble of technical modalities that organise the meetings between the analysand and the analyst, a formal and contractual arrangement designed to promote the establishment of the process. Its essential dimension belongs therefore to the register of temporality, as is emphasised by the fixed number of sessions per week and the regular duration of each of them.

However, the frame also implies a *place in external reality.* As such, it is a space that is cathected, into which a set of representations, often unconscious, are projected, which pertain to the very history of the subject. In this respect, the place where the session takes place embodies psychic space for both protagonists of the situation. It also constitutes the *in-between space (l'entre-deux)***,** which can return both in memory and in dreams, an *immemorial place* or, finally, the theatre set that organises the stage on which the two psyches enter into dialogue.

The place of the session also raises the question of intimacy. For the analysand, the material frame is an anonymous place where he is carried away. He adorns it with imaginary elements deposited unwittingly in his internal universe. For the analyst, it is the place where he spends most of his time in his daily practice and where he reveals something of himself, even when he strives to observe the appropriate neutrality which his profession legitimately requires of him. On the analysand's side, two transference poles are constantly involved: onto the real person of the analyst, that of daily life, and onto the object that is the depositary of multiple transference movements. The equilibrium between the two dimensions varies according to the power of the ritual punctuating the session. With regard to the frame, they feature as time and space. Here, the two categories echo each other. The frame is both the before and the after of the session in which, like a sign of temporal fracture implied in the daily and inner life of the analysand, a sense of before/after marks the symbolic mourning of certain representations. However, it is also the path taken to get to the fixed appointment, all the gestures that precede and accompany the analysand's arrival in the analyst's office. Often, this arrival is punctuated by small rituals: the coffee one drinks, the moment that one preserves for oneself, sometimes diverted by the telephone call in the car that is parked not far away so as to respect the time of the session, and so on.

So, when the analyst says he is changing address, it results in a sudden modification of the ritual and a loss of familiar bearings. Often, this irruption of external reality comes as a surprise for the analysand and initiates a whole set of projective movements, as well as stimulating transference/countertransference processes. What is involved in the force of the transference takes on a tangible form here: we get a measure of its incarnation.

An analysand had been asking himself for several weeks where he was at in his work with the analyst and the latter heard his hesitation about the frame as a deeper question concerning the end of his analysis, involving a mixture of desire and fear. The analyst wondered, then, how the analysand would react when she announced the change of address of her office, and anticipated the return of movements in which what is commonly called a "negative transference" would manifest itself. In fact, if the notion of end surfaced at this point in the analysis, it was also because of certain indications: the flow of words was dwindling, associativity was becoming more tenuous, and the irruption of a thought into consciousness, the *Einfall,* dear to Freud, increasingly rare. In the session that followed the change of location, this is what the patient said: "You surprised me when you said that you were moving… That means new constraints. And then, it's further away for me in relation to my work, more complicated… I will no longer be able to come on foot. I said to myself: It's better to stop at Christmas. And then, I thought again."

Feeling uneasy, another patient questioned this announcement of change through a dream that he reported in the following session: "It didn't look like here. Without thinking too much, I entered the office; you were telling me that we could discuss Spinoza [there was a journal on Spinoza in the waiting-room]. As I did not understand your allusion, you suggested that I could continue the work with your replacement, Marie. There was the fear of stopping, the fear that you would put an end to your activity, and the first name Marie brought to mind the word "*mari*" (husband). The change of location could also mean going to your home", he said. The analyst drew attention to the strangeness of his association in which several paths were condensed, including a recurrent questioning about his life trajectory (whether to marry or not?).

Finally, another patient also responded to the announcement of change through a dream which she communicated in these terms: "I arrived in this new place that was different, and you were different; you displayed form of familiarity that I didn't recognise. You spoke to me as if I was a colleague, and the exchange was more cordial. I was surprised, embarrassed, as if you were asking me to stop this work, and I did not agree with you; I didn't feel ready." She was therefore confronted with her fear of losing the potential offered by our meetings as they had been defined hitherto, and the oscillation concerning the frame and the nature of the work she had begun.

These different sequences are all organised around a metaphor or a central signifier referring to the end of one thing and the beginning of another, to a turning-point in the course of an analysis, to the loss of a known and familiar object, constantly pointing towards a melancholic dimension that is consubstantial with the course of every analysis. Beyond the significations specific to each of the three patients, we can see in these sequences a particular illustration of the activation of both transference and countertransference projections that constitutes the very heart of the analytic situation. The particular vibration of a specific décor and the effect of its change in the course of an analysis thus raises numerous questions, and particularly the following one: what is the role played by the *body*, by the *person* that the analyst also is, in the organisation of the analysis and its progress?

Further reading

Donnet, J.-L. (1995). *Le divan bien tempéré*. Paris: Presses Universitaires de France (Series: Le Fil rouge).

KEY WORDS Incarnation, technical modalities, ritual, transference.

THE END OF AN ANALYSIS

BRIGITTE DOLLÉ-MONGLOND

After several years of analysis, an analysand could clearly identify her anxiety about ending the analysis, without however stating the reasons for this possible termination. When she said, "I have built my life", one could hear, through this moment of denouement and these sessions, a barely perceptible statement: "I don't know what I can still analyse, but I cannot leave you." She did not want to break off this relationship with the analyst because it strongly reactivated a relationship to the "maternal other" and would, in addition, be taking one step further towards "being an analyst", which was what she had in mind, but could not yet authorise herself to do. Envisaging a tangible term for the analysis a few months earlier had led to a resurgence of symptoms, to an unexpected episode of depression: how could this sudden emergence of such a sensation of breakdown be explained except by throwing light on the impediment contained in the planned termination of the sessions? It was impossible to stop the analysis in such a situation, the analyst told her clearly. The patient replied: "You are not helping me much to separate from you. What do I need to work on in order to help me negotiate the separation?". The mysteries of these ambivalent tendencies need to be explored in their different possible forms.

If the notion of the end of analysis has given rise to multiple contributions in the literature, it is difficult to find an approach to it in a dictionary of psychoanalysis, since a potential definition implies, if we think about carefully, a whole set of analytic concepts that themselves need to be defined. This question amounts to a tautology: it remains a question, raising by its very essence different scenarios referring to the analyst's clinical intuition, which is itself caught up in a constellation of theoretical elements.

It is worth recalling the famous ambiguity highlighted by Freud, which served him as inspiration for the following joke: "Analysis is terminated when the analyst and the patient cease to meet each other for the analytic session" (Freud, 1937, p. 219). Put briefly, this notion refers to the moment when the analyst and analysand stop seeing each other. Either there is a natural conclusion (as Sándor Ferenczi puts it, "when the analysis dies of exhaustion, so to speak"

[Ferenczi, 1955 [1928], p. 85]) or, on the contrary, the termination is precipitated and skewed by passionate vicissitudes or setbacks. This moment, which is as necessary as it is difficult, like every ending in the course of a life, involves both generalisable laws for the human being and a fully singular tonality. The accent can be placed on what is at stake in the transference process between the two protagonists and on the question of separation, for it is a matter, first and foremost, of separation in the transference. But transference, by its very nature, does not like separations, "and it is its function to reject them", according to Michel Gribinski (2002, p. 8).

In this respect, the end of analysis is apprehended in terms of the theorisation of the transference, or transferences in the plural, on the basis of which the analyst works, depending on the point of reference – Freudian, Kleinian, Lacanian – to mention only a few major directions within the object-relations perspective or that of the supposed subject of the knowledge of the unconscious becoming the missing object. This specific moment may thus be said to designate the peak of this necessary entanglement between clinical practice and theory, reflecting the powerful strangeness of the transference love correlated with recovery.

What indicators or criteria can be used to determine the end of an analysis? As this notion eludes any codifiable nomenclature, apart from the aim of introducing normative criteria – criteria that are variable depending on the authors, related to the clinical and social improvements of the patient, as well as to the processual progress of the analytic couple – it appeals more to a *metaphor of departure* that implies a set of imaginary processes accounted for by the Freudian formulation "infinite and finite"[1] (see Pommier, 2002) containing an uncertain, unknown dimension. It requires the patient to face up to finiteness, while at the same time a certain degree of autonomisation has to occur.

At the end of an analysis, there is a condensation and playing out again of what has unfolded during it, namely, the very core of a set of conflictual issues, diverse forms of investment, and what a process of separation implies exactly for the analysand and the analyst: the end of the analytic relationship, the untangling of an intertwining of two psyches over the course of a long period of time that has created its effects of potential influence for the two protagonists of the situation, who, in the best of cases, take a decision about when to terminate. The end of the analysis may, in some cases, reveal certain vicissitudes of the negative: these clinical situations involve instances of acting (in or out) or a *passage à l'acte,* the only outcome possible in transference impasses with all that is implied in terms of violence and destructiveness. This marks the premature end of the analysis propelled by the manifestations of a negative transference that has not been elaborated by either party, or the effects of a passionate relationship with its dimension of idealisation and dependence.

In its complexity, this question is thus to be apprehended by the yardstick of relativity and of an internal movement that must be dialectalised: end and beginning, notably, the beginning of the analytic process that may refer to the preliminary interviews or to a turning-point in the work situated beyond them; an end subsequent to a multiplicity of endings (beginning and end of the session). It highlights a confrontation with the following contrasting pairs, which are organisers of psychic life: known/unknown, familiar/uncertain, completion/incompletion. Just as the analysand must free himself from the ties that alienate him in his quest for psychic autonomy, he will also have to free himself from this place where he has deposited his personal world of fantasy.

If we return to Freud's contributions, from the logic of the first topography to the second with the introduction of the death drive, his positions evolved over time. Initially, two criteria were put forward: first, the reduction of the symptoms that gave rise to the treatment, a sufficient lifting of the repressed, and a sufficiently solid and stable situation of the ego faced with the demands of the id and superego; and secondly, as his work advanced, the objectives of civilisation with the aim of being able to "love and work", which confers on psychoanalysis two central directions: the circulation of the libido between narcissism and object-relations and the decisive place of the fusion and defusion of the drives.

Such an advance cannot, however, provide us, in terms of explicit statements, with criteria for satisfying results, the best termination possible being in reality the acquisition by the subject of a capacity to continue a process of self-analysis alone; this itself will be subject to permanent adjustments and constant transformations, which involves the famous "knowing how to deal with one's symptom, how to manage it, how to handle it" advanced by Jacques Lacan.[2]

It is this confident self-evaluation that is sometimes missing in certain clinical situations: the sequences that come to the analyst's memory tend to involve those difficult endings that provide material for successive decodings and indicate by their very nature a stumbling block in the analytic work. Like a frozen image, a period of time is still necessary for forming the outline of a nucleus that may seem impossible to elaborate, echoing situations that feature specific difficulties: in particular, the effects of a passionate transference in Piera Aulagnier's sense, the residues of a negative transference that had unfolded and been worked on during the analysis, the productions of separation anxiety and object loss.

For the analysand, approaching the term already decided upon reactivates all sorts of anxieties, but anxieties that have mourning as a common point, symbolic mourning that marks the beginning of the analysis and reawakens the other experiences of mourning in life. The fear of the unknown prevails: not knowing whether one can continue alone, facing up to the negative in oneself and around oneself. By introducing into the course of a life an effect of before/after, it implies a confrontation with the unrepresentable dimension of the last time, which refers implicitly to finiteness and death, and may resound as a "loss object".

For the analyst, the task is reactivated: how does a process begin that inevitably contains a work of mourning, pertaining both to the transference-object embodied by the analyst and to the setting of the analysis as a container of psychic processes? How does this effect of swinging back and forth between a before and an after occur, which bears witness to this potential transformation of a subject, along with the idea of incompletion that stems from it. This crucial moment, fully constitutive of analysis, leads the subject to reconsider the manifestations and residues of this psychic issue, the contours of his own theoretical hypotheses concerning the handling of the transference, the obscurities of his own decoding in this encounter that has created in him multiple points of resonance, and finally the activity of the work of interpretation.

Later on, a dream foreshadowed a certain maturation that was unfolding: "I was planning to stop during the course of the year and you had to consider giving my place to someone else. When I woke up, I was feeling a sense of loss, and so sad. I was going to leave you."

Notes

1 "Infiniteness of its very finiteness" according to Gérard Pommier's (2002) line of thought.
2 Lacan made this proposition concerning the relation of identification with the symptom on November 16, 1976. See also "The moment of concluding" (Session of January, 10, 1978) in "Logical time and the assertion of anticipated certainty", (Lacan, *Écrits,* pp. 161–175).

Further reading

Angelergues, J., Papageorigiou, M. eds t. RFP 72 n°1 (2008). *La fin de la cure. Revue française de psychanalyse*, 72 (1).
Aulagnier, P. (1979). *Les Destins du plaisir.* Paris: Presses Universitaires de France (Series: Le Fil rouge).
Freud, S. (1933 [1932]). The dissection of the psychical personality. In: *New introductory lectures on psychoanalysis. S.E.* 22. London Hogarth, pp. 57–80.
Freud, S. (1937). Analysis terminable and interminable. *S.E 23*. London: Hogarth, pp. 216–231.
Ferenczi, S. (1955 [1928]). The problem of the termination of the analysis. In: *Final contributions to the problems and methods of psychoanlysis*. London: Hogarth, pp. 77–86.
Gribinski, M. (2002). *Les séparations imparfaite.* Paris: Gallimard (Series: Connaissance de l'inconscient).
Pommier, G. (2002). La fin relative de l'analyse. *Figures de la psychanalyse*, 6(1): 123–143.
Quinodoz, M. (1991). *La Solitude apprivoisée.* Paris: Presses Universitaires de France (Series: Quadrige).

KEY WORDS Separation anxiety, psychic autonomy, mourning, transference.

Part II

THE SPACE OF THE PSYCHE

8

TRAUMATIC EXPERIENCES

PRIMITIVE AGONY

DOMINIQUE TABONE-WEIL

This concept, Winnicottian originally, may be likened with what Freud calls primary anxiety. The prototype of this traumatic anxiety is birth and refers to the state of *Hilflosigkeit,* of the primary helplessness of the infant overwhelmed by a wave of instinctual drive activity that it cannot deal with by itself over and above a certain intensity and a certain lapse of time if the environment does not come to its help.

It is in "The fear of breakdown" that D.W. Winnicott (1974) speaks of these primitive agonies. We may ask ourselves in passing if the French translation of the English term agony by "*agonie*" is really pertinent, as the French word indicates "atrocious anxiety, suffering" (Larousse). In its usual French sense *agonie* means death agony. The term "*angoisses disséquantes primitives*" (lit. "primitive dissecting anxieties") is also used in French.

The fear that certain patients experience of having a mental breakdown exists in each one of us, but in very variable ways quantitatively speaking. According to Winnicott, this fear projected into the future concerns in reality something that has already happened, but which the subject was not in a position to experience and think about when it occurred. He links it to a failure of the primary environment and to a traumatic swamping by the instinctual drives that could not be contained. What we are faced with here is the compulsion to repeat, traumatic experience, and the register of psychotic anxieties. "There are moments," Winnicott writes, "when a patient needs to be told that the breakdown, a fear of which destroys his or her life, *has already occurred*" (p. 104, Winnicott's emphasis) and that it is a fact he carries in his unconscious, fearing to see it well up *from the inside.*

It is this "practical" side of things that came to the analyst's mind concerning a young patient, an anaesthetic nurse by profession, whose sessions are always crammed full with factual (but rich) material. Essentially it concerns emotionally very intense professional situations in which there are constantly issues of life and death (he works in intensive care). The material is not very associative, he talks continuously, in a dense and closely controlled fashion, leaving little room for the analyst to intervene. Nevertheless, he is very clear that "something is happening", that the transference has taken hold and that, in spite of the predominance of factual and perceptual material, a process has begun. And yet he misses many sessions, frequently arrives late, and makes regular "threats" to break off the analysis. These covert threats are expressed in an indirect and recurrent way, and everything is regularly linked to external conditions (the "environment", as it were), which creates impediments.

All this seems to correspond to a tight defensive organisation linked first and foremost to a deep fear of dependence, but which is related more deeply to the fear of breakdown, of intolerable, disintegrating anxiety threatening the ego's unity and belonging to the category of "agonies" of which Winnicott speaks.

He also says that, if the therapist has understood what is involved and if the patient is "ready for some kind of acceptance of this bizarre truth" (p. 105), then the way is open for the agony to be experienced in the transference in reaction to the analyst's failures and mistakes.

The patient can cope with these mistakes when they occur in reasonable doses; that is to say, when, each time a technical error occurs, he can attribute it to the countertransference. In other words, he gradually brings the original failure of the facilitating environment into the area of his omnipotence and into the experience of omnipotence that is characteristic of the state of dependence (a mark of the transference).

The first epiphany of primitive agony occurred one day when the analyst was obliged to cancel a session by telephone two hours before and when, in so doing, she repeated her "first technical error" (being absent) by a second "error", which was no doubt a result of her own momentary emotional reaction. She found herself at the hospital emergency department where she was accompanying someone close to her and did not know when she would be able to get away. Instead of keeping this to herself, she told the patient something about it, but it was sufficient to worry him, which was a sign that her negative countertransference had not been elucidated sufficiently. It should be noted that it was also countertransference guilt that led her to "act badly": the "pressure" felt by this demanding patient, with the feeling that the slightest failure would be fatal, led her to want to do too much, to justify herself with a valid reason (the hospital emergency department from which one never knows when one will leave) and thus to act technically and ethically in a questionable way.

This led to a state of total panic in the patient that lasted for several sessions. The analyst thus learned that for a long time he had been coming to sessions feeling anxious, that he could not stand the slightest delay in receiving a response after ringing the bell, and that this anxiety had become unbearably intense since this "failure". Likewise, the prospect of the analyst's departure on vacation or of her absences for whatever reason had engendered, and continued to engender, anxiety and repeated absences. Was the analyst dead? Gone forever? Had she been killed by another patient or by a jealous husband? Catastrophic fantasies abounded, providing plenty of material to work on.

The idea (communicated to the patient, who accepted it) of relating these extremely violent and paranoid anxieties to an unintegrated primitive experience made it possible to organise the work accomplished in connection with them. Given the history of this patient, the original failure of the facilitating environment had, without any doubt, repeatedly played an important role; moreover, traces of it could be found in the events of early and later childhood, making it possible to reconstruct what had no doubt taken place in prehistory.

As is suggested by Winnicott's way of presenting things, this also makes it possible to form a therapeutic space of progressive "taming", a shared work in which the pleasure of understanding, integrating and appropriating what was unelaborated and unelaborable gradually becomes vital and a source in itself of progress, of insight and subjectivation. The dimension of play appears and transforms the tonality of every analysis from which the tragic dimension gradually recedes, making more and more room for a certain pleasure in living and thinking.

Further reading

Freud, S. (1926). *Inhibitions, symptoms and anxiety. S.E.* 20. London: Hogarth, pp. 75–174.

Roussillon, R. (2012). *Agonie, clivage et symbolisation.* Paris: Presses Universitaires de France (Series: Quadrige Essais Débats).

Rosenberg, B. (2014). *Le moi et son angoisse.* Paris: In Press (Series: Explorations psychanalytiques).

Winnicott, D.W. (1974). Fear of breakdown. *International Review of Psychoanalysis*, 1: 103–107.

KEY WORDS Primitive agony, fear of breakdown, failure of the primary environment, elaboration of trauma.

THE BASIC FAULT

DOMINIQUE TABONE-WEIL

The concept of the basic fault was elaborated by Michael Balint (1896–1970), a psychoanalyst of Hungarian origin who practised primarily in England, where he belonged, with D.W. Winnicott, to the Independent or Middle Group arising from the split in the British Psychoanalytic Society, following the divergences of opinion between Anna Freud and Melanie Klein. His second analyst was Sándor Ferenczi and this filiation can easily be recognised in his way of considering the analytic relationship.

This concept refers to severe narcissistic defects and to the way they manifest themselves during an analysis, a certain change of tonality indicating that the patient has regressed to what Balint called the "area of the basic fault", a fault attesting to a seriously and chronically defective tuning between the infant and the primary environment. He proposes a new topography, defining an area of the psychical apparatus where there is a "two-person" relationship and where pre-oedipal functioning predominates. It is a matter of identifying the moment when this area is "disturbed" in order to respond adequately by adjusting technique to the patient's needs for whom it is necessary to provide the equivalent of favourable primary environment that did not exist or not sufficiently. Alongside the basic fault, there is the oedipal area involving three-person relationships and the area of creation where the subject is alone. It should be noted that Balint rejects the Freudian notion of primary narcissism, recognising only primary love; for him, narcissism is always secondary, a withdrawal into the self, following a disappointment in relation to the object.

The patient in question was a woman whose narcissism was fragile. The analyst sometimes asked herself if she was going to be able to tolerate the frustrations inherent to the analytic situation. The patient's obsessive jealousy and her mistrustful, suspicious, querulous and even procedural side also led the analyst at certain moments to fear an evolution towards an invasive persecutory experience. A certain irritation on the analyst's part in the face of her repeated complaints and her demands infiltrated with denied aggressiveness and reproaches (she idealised her analyst a lot, while constantly denigrating her), combined with a sense that the process was blocked, made the analyst wonder what was going on and suggested she needed to modify her inner attitude (tendency to be tense, feelings of impotence) towards the patient.

Transference interpretations (regarding people who did things behind her back or the fact that she cried like a little girl who wanted to be held in someone's arms) did not suffice to calm her anxiety or to get the process going again. Moreover, as Balint says, they are often experienced as hurtful criticisms, reproaches, correctives regarding inadequate ways of expressing oneself. They therefore revive the feelings of inadequacy that the patient often experiences. Sometimes, on the contrary, though this was scarcely more fruitful, she went through moments of exaltation with a "manic triumphant" colouring, provoked by interventions that she experienced as gratifying and which, she said, "re-energised her completely". The need for dependence and the terror that this need aroused in her were also in the foreground.

She also expressed the feeling that she was lacking something, that she had a loose screw, so to speak, and that, in spite of all the efforts she had made to make up for this deficiency she had the impression that it was useless: it would always be like that. There was no doubt that this patient had suffered from severe deficiencies in her early childhood and that the adjustment of her primary object to her needs was no more than approximative. The rest of her history, which was more directly accessible to memory, confirmed the suspicion that she had had immature parents. Her mother was still an adolescent when she was born; she was very narcissistic, with little ability to take care of her child, for whom she largely ditched her responsibilities by entrusting her to a wet-nurse who, fortunately, was warm and loving. This represented both an abandonment and an opportunity for this little girl, who nonetheless found a way to construct her identity quite well.

In any case, the idea that the analyst had to adjust to her needs without responding directly to her manifest and rather compulsive demands (for advice, solutions, practical responses, flexible session times) became increasingly present. Balint (1968) writes that "the analyst must sincerely accept all complaints, recriminations and resentments as real and valid and allow ample time to his patient to change his violent resentment into regret" (p. 182). This way of formulating things helped the analyst a lot and reduced her irritation, making way for the feeling that this patient needed benevolence more than neutrality and that this need had to be heard.

Concerning her need for the analyst to hold her in her arms, hold her hand or caress her forehead, it was sufficient to take note of the need, that is, to formulate and interpret it. Neither a blanket nor a cup of tea, and even less mutual analysis, were necessary. On the other hand, the fact that she wanted the analyst to be really interested in her fate, to really want to understand her and help her get better was perfectly acceptable as such: the analyst's task was to assume, for as long as was necessary, the position of a good enough primary object, and to interpret this need at the appropriate moment. The analyst "contented" herself with listening to her, accompanying her psychic movements, providing her with the favourable environment that she needed in order, as Balint would say, to be in contact with herself, to find herself, to rediscover herself, which seemed to make her "content" too.

This change of attitude on the analyst's part seemed to be an adjustment to her needs without being a response to her manifest demands. This seemed to have a beneficial effect on the process, which got going again in a relatively calm atmosphere in which the elucidation of infantile conflicts could continue in a more fruitful way.

For the first time in her life, this patient discovered that she could have confidence in herself, that she was no longer the child or adolescent undermined by feelings of insecurity and inferiority that had seemed to her to be inevitable and definitive. She tried out a whole range of interactions with those around her, free of the fear and sense of helplessness that she had felt hitherto. The analyst's sense of helplessness was also attenuated and she felt less tense and anxious.

In the part of his book devoted to the basic fault, Balint writes that there are "strong indications that for the analytic therapy of regressed states, its interpersonal aspects were more important" (1968, p. 159) and that "although, as a rule, it is not stated quite so explicitly, we are compelled to recognize that the two most important factors in psychoanalytic therapy are interpretations and object-relationship" (p. 159). He speaks of a therapeutic atmosphere that is favourable to the patient's regression, offering him the good enough primary environment, to use Winnicott's term, that he did not have, which will enable him, when he is ready, to emerge from it reassured and transformed, which he calls the period of "new beginning".

Further reading

Balint, M. (1952). *Primary love and psychoanalytic technique.* London: Tavistock.
Balint, M. (1968). *The basic fault: Therapeutic aspects of regression.* London: Tavistock.

KEY WORDS Defective adjustment of the primary environment, topographical change, narcissistic flaw, regression.

ESSENTIAL DEPRESSION

MARIE SIRJACQ

Early in his work, a patient described how he organised his life in such a way as to "smooth everything out", to reduce to a minimum all perceptual, sensorial or motor excitation because it caused him chronic and uncontrollable pain (fibromyalgia). This was why he had lowered the ring tone on his phone and was using earplugs (*boules Quiès*). Rather than playing on the polysemy of the word he employed by repeating "*Qui est-ce*?", the analyst chose to make an intervention that opened out onto affect and resituated the object: "When the telephone rings," she said, "we can ask ourselves who is calling before answering. We are in a state of waiting or apprehension…". The patient replied: "Ah, yes, I hadn't thought of that… Perhaps I am afraid that it will be my business partner; I am finding it difficult to break off relations with him." "Breaking off all contact, so as not to suffer", the analyst commented.

Hanna, the heroine of *The Secret Life of Words*, a 2005 film by Isabel Coixet, has become absent from her own existence. Taciturn and withdrawn, day after day she goes from the factory to her home where she repeats the same gestures unfailingly, like an automaton, in a mechanical and disembodied way.

This is a remarkable illustration of the typical "operational" (*opératoire*) mode of functioning of a patient affected by essential depression. For Hanna, the libidinal decathexis, both object- and narcissistic-related, affects both external objects and internal objects, and even the ego itself. This is the fundamental characteristic of essential depression, associated with a lowering of vital tonus. This extinction of psychic life is underpinned by the destructive drives and constitutes a survival mode of functioning.

When her boss suggests that she should take a holiday, go and rest somewhere in the sun, his words seem to reach Hanna emptied of their meaning and their capacity to arouse ideas or images in her. The words are reduced to their perceptual, phonetic dimension, as if Hanna has become estranged from her own language, repeating without understanding the things said to her. "Is it really necessary to get exercise?" she later asks, with a blank voice, evacuating any dimension of pleasure.

In the course of the film, she arrives at the bedside of a third-degree burn victim. He has lost his sight in an accident on an oil platform, in the middle of nowhere, a fine metaphor of the absence of links with the world. Hanna proves to be a competent and efficient nurse. She administers medical care perfectly, but without showing the slightest reaction or emotion. She seems cold and remains silent, as if indifferent to the pain of her patient and to his attempts to communicate with her. Her essential depression makes her insensitive to everything that occurs. Her affects are abraded, suppressed, frozen. She feels neither sad nor depressed. She does not complain. She does what has to be done, technically. That's all. From a clinical point of view, Hanna does not present any positive symptomatology. As occurs in essential depression, she is perfectly asymptomatic.

Listening to a patient in an "operational" state (*état opératoire*), whether it is transitory or more permanent, does not entail any interpretative activity on the analyst's part. In *L'Investigation psychosomatique,* Pierre Marty (Marty, de M'Uzan & David, 2010 [1963]) prefers to speak of an "associative expression of the investigator", a mode of communicating a meaning that is accessible to the patient. The conversion into language, which the patient lacks, occurs in the analyst on the basis of everything his patient shows him and makes him feel, including at the somatic level. What he communicates to the patient will be infiltrated by his affects mobilised in the presence of that particular patient, in the face-to-face setting. The lifting of the radical suppression of emotions and sensations is a long process. For Marty, it is a matter of "reanimating" these patients by enabling them to rediscover the links which belong to different periods of their life; the links between ideas and affects, between things and words, between ideas themselves. In Isabel Coixet's film, the tenacious interest that the burn victim shows for Hanna (Who is she? Where does she come from?) remains undiminished. In spite of her unresponsiveness, he is insistent and manifests continuous interest in her. It is only when he tells her about a traumatic episode of his own life, expressing it with emotion albeit not without humour, that a breach opens up in Hanna's defensive shell. Gradually, she reveals to him the traumas that have made her cut herself off from the world.

Reanimating a patient who suffers from essential depression requires taking an interest in him, thereby providing him with an erotic source as well as the means to make use of it to bind the effects of the destructive impulses that inhabit him.

Further reading

Marty, P. (1968). La pensée opératoire. *Revue française de psychanalyse*, 32(3): 593–598.

Marty, P., and M'Uzan, M. de. (1963). La dépression essentielle. *Revue française de psychanalyse*, 28: 345–355.

Marty, P., de M'Uzan, M., and David, C. (2010 [1963]). *L'Investigation psychosomatique. S.E.*, 7. Paris: Presses Universitaires de France (Series: Quadrige).

(2009). *À propos* de *l'investigation psychosomatique. Revue française de psychosomatique*, 35 (1). Paris: Presses Universitaires de France.

KEY WORDS Lowering of vital tonus, decathexis, operational thinking, suppression of affects.

HOT TRAUMA AND COLD TRAUMA

CLAUDE JANIN

This now classic distinction was introduced in 1985.

First of all, in order to define the field of trauma, in the psychoanalytic sense of the term, it may be argued that many patients suffer from that which is unrepresentable and come to analysis in order to find a way to represent it: herein lies the traumatic aspect of psychic life.

These patients, for whom the maternal object did not constitute itself as a "framing structure" playing the role of a container of representative space (André Green, 2001 [1983], p. 77), expect analysis to offer them the possibility to put into the form of history the "blanks" created by the vagaries of their early psychic development. They hope to obtain representations of it. Among these vagaries, the inadequate, "not good enough" in D.W. Winnicott's terms, parental responses to the needs of these patients when they were children constitute the cold nucleus of the trauma.

By means of libidinal co-excitation,[1] these patients transform this *cold nucleus* into a *hot nucleus.* On the clinical level, the "hysterical solution", as a cover for depression, is a typical example of these traumas and of their transformations.

A young woman, aged 35, was apparently satisfied with her personal and professional success but there was something, nonetheless, that worried her: she could not stop herself from verifying – and for her it was "child's play" – her powers of seduction by consuming untiringly, like a drug addict, lovers whom she never kept for very long. The moment of the conquest was all exaltation and triumph; this was followed by depression, self-disgust and separation. Then there was a period of calm, an "*anaesthesia* of feelings", she said, until "*it* begins all over again".

Speaking about her parents, she mentioned a brilliant but distant father, who was completely absorbed in his own affairs and who was mainly interested in her younger brother. Her mother was overshadowed and depressed. During the first years, the analysis brought to light a typically neurotic style of mental functioning and she came across as a hysterical patient. But after a long period of analysis, there was no change, in spite of having elaborated, in all their complexity, her oedipal conflicts, sexual theories, infantile sexuality and imagoes. There were, however, she said, things about which she felt ashamed, thereby drawing attention to some important narcissistic issues that her sexual hyperactivity both emphasised and concealed. It was necessary to wait until she could speak about it.

Finally, one day, an external event helped her to do so. She arrived at her session feeling deeply moved: she had just been to see Bergman's (1978) film *Autumn Sonata*, and what she had seen of the relations between this brilliant and distant mother and this depressed daughter – the negative side, therefore, of how she presented her mother and herself – had given rise to a cascade of affects of sadness, and then of despair. Above all, something one of the two heroines had said constantly came back to her mind: "I can't recall my mother ever having touched me." She uttered these words and then cried interminably.

After a few sessions in this register, she was finally able to speak about the cause of her shame, which she had been unable to formulate hitherto. A few years earlier, in the context of her work, she had been very moved by a young person of her own age who had been left quadriplegic following a motorcycle accident, and whose "immense *distress* one could sense", she said. She had taken care of her a lot, even helping her with her daily toileting routines, something her professional status did not oblige her to do. In doing this, she had felt, she added, a certain "sexual unease", followed by an acute sense of shame.

Seeing Bergman's film, hearing the words "I can't recall my mother ever having touched me", and the hospital scene, which was obviously traumatic (the "sexual unease", the shame, the ensuing silence over this scene), made it possible to construct *another infantile scene* in which her depressed and phobic mother reduced bodily care to the minimum, and in particular the washing of genital organs: the young quadriplegic girl represented the young woman herself as a baby, in a state of complete inner distress.

We can see, then, how, through the interplay of libidinal co-excitation, the symptom had been formed: the *first stage* consisted of an early trauma linked to the lack of maternal care giving rise to both internal excitation and a narcissistic wound. This is the *cold trauma*. The *second stage* consisted of the subsequent trauma in which the first scene was played out again through a mechanism of identification with the young patient whom she was caring for, along with the co-excitation that was involved. The sense of "sexual unease" was the retroactive effect of the internal excitation caused by the lack of maternal care for, by avoiding the task of washing her daughter's sexual organs, the mother designated them *negatively*, as a locus of excitation: this is the *hot trauma*.

Note

1 According to Freud (1924), libidinal co-excitation may be described as follows: "in the case of a great number of internal processes sexual excitation arises as a concomitant effect as soon as the intensity of those processes passes beyond certain quantitative limits" (p. 163).

Further reading

Freud, S. (1924). *The economic problem of masochism. S.E.* 19. London: Hogarth, pp. 155–170.

Janin, C. (1985). Le chaud et le froid: les logiques du traumatisme et leur gestion dans la cure psychoanalytique. *Revue française de psychanalyse*, 69(2): 125–134.

Janin, C. (2015 [1996]). *Figures et destins du traumatisme.* Paris: Presses Universitaires de France.

KEY WORDS Libidinal co-excitation.

THE BAD APRÈS-COUP

RACHEL ROSENBLUM

An American living in France sought a consultation in connection with anxiety attacks and minor sexual disturbances. During the preliminary interviews, the analyst learnt that, although he had no accent, he was Czech and Jewish, and that he had survived internment in a concentration camp. He was 15 years old when the camp was liberated by American troops, for whom he became the mascot. On becoming an adult, he had acquired American nationality and joined the army. Then he got married to a German woman who was sometimes anti-Semitic and was unaware that her husband was Jewish. The couple engaged in sado-masochistic relations in which the man had the position of the victim and found it particularly exciting to be called Jewish.

The analysis took place on a three-times weekly basis and seemed to progress normally. After about five months, he started having a lot of nightmares in which he relived his experience of the camps. The patient told the analyst that he suffered from a fish allergy that resulted in a swelling of his lips. In one of his nightmares that was particularly intolerable, he was attacked by a giant fish and had woken up with swollen lips. The analyst saw the connection with the allergy and asked him what came to his mind when he thought about the signifier "fish". This suggestion triggered a series of extremely violent associations during which the memory of the following episode emerged.

The scene took place in Czechoslovakia on the eve of a Jewish festival. In the bathroom, the carp that was to be used for the festival meal was swimming in the bathwater. Then, the Nazis burst into the family apartment. The patient fled into the living room, but could hear his mother screaming. The soldiers had just killed his father with their bayonets. The room was full of blood. They beat his mother and the patient was taken away. He would never see her or his sister again.

At the end of the session, he began screaming and hitting the walls with his fists. The analyst tried to see with a colleague if he could be treated with medication, but it was too late. Plunged into a severe psychotic state, he was transferred to Sainte Anne's hospital in Paris, where he was diagnosed with persecution delusion.

This is the account given by Sidney Stewart (2009 [2002]) of this psychoanalysis in *Mémoire de l'inhumain*. This dramatic effect of analytic treatment invites us to reflect on the failure of a therapy that seemed to have begun well. The analyst noticed the inadequacy of a strategy that had led him – perhaps too quickly – to destroy the rampart that the young Czech had built in order to protect himself from this intolerable experience. A child had witnessed the bloody execution of his father and simultaneously lost his mother and his sister. By its very dimension, such a trauma seems beyond any possibility of elaboration. This kind of trauma sometimes gives rise to a change of identity. In this case, the patient changed his name and created an assumed identity, becoming an American citizen without origin and without accent. By playing with different registers of identity and with those that permit perversion, he managed to get by. He demonstrated a certain amount of resilience and invented a solution.

What happened when he was invited to associate to the theme of fish? Stewart turned to a strategy of elaboration of decondensation, of lifting repression. However, it was certainly not a case of repression here. Far from repeating the initial trauma in "more favourable" conditions – as in ordinary cases when the operation of après-coup can be put in the service of the progression of the analysis, the work did not lead here to the transposition that dreams usually make possible, but to the brutal violence of the nightmare and the threatening return of the fish. Protective anxiety – which can have a warning role – was replaced by terror. The frozen image of the fish induced a reduplication and aggravation of the repudiation of reality. The unfreezing of affects and remembering found expression not in a reduction of suffering but in a renewed experience of trauma.

Encouraging elaboration when faced with a massive trauma often amounts to pushing the survivor into the "eye of the cyclone". Faced with the dangers that such a situation presents, some analysts recommend a strategy of accompaniment that can even include a "loan of psyche" in which the analyst shares his own experiences with the patient. This is what Stewart was to do in another case, sharing his own experience as a survivor of a concentration camp in Manchuria. Others suggest that the therapist should corroborate the historical reality of the intolerable situation. It is a matter of responding to the risks posed by the entanglement of unconscious phantasies and the event relived in the transference. Thus the aggression suffered from the fish also relates to the more strongly suppressed wishes of the patient: his death wishes towards his parents who left him an orphan, desperate, alone and abandoned, or towards those whom he wanted to die and whom he had "betrayed" by disowning his identity.

In the text that served here as a basis for reflection, Stewart questions the validity of his choices. Should he have been more cautious? Would it have been wiser to see the patient in the face-to-face setting? Should he have given priority to everything that made it possible to restore narcissism?

At any rate, the analysis of this man leads us to reflect on the pertinence of the process of the operation of après-coup in the evolution of traumas whose magnitude leads the patient to mobilise processes of dissociation or splitting. Some patients can only escape the intolerable situation by refusing to believe it really happened. Others must have made themselves psychically absent at the time it took place. For such subjects, the operation of après-coup that occurs in analytical therapy no longer plays the role of the attenuated repetition of a painful event nor that of a lifting of repression. Faced with the unfreezing of affects, in a situation where defences are no longer mobilised, the traumatic event reverberates with all its force, in a sort of new first time. As Sándor Ferenczi had already pointed out, repetition may prove to be worse than the original trauma. And far from revealing itself to be salutary, the operation of après-coup that takes place in analysis can have the effect of a coup de grâce engendering disastrous consequences.

Further reading

Rosenbaum, R. (2005). Cure ou repetition du trauma. *Revue française de psychosomatique*, 28: 69–90.

Stewart, S. (2009 [2002]). *Mémoire de l'humain: du trauma à la créativité.* Paris: Campagne Première.

KEY WORDS Loan of psyche, trauma.

9

DRIVES

LIBIDINAL CO-EXCITATION

ALICE BAUER AND JOSEPH TORRENTE

The term "sexual co-excitation" (*Miterregung*) only appears rarely in Freud's work. We find it essentially in *Three Essays on the Theory of Sexuality* (Freud, 1905), and then in *The Economic Problem of Masochism* (Freud, 1924).

In *the Three Essays*, it is used descriptively. It is a matter of highlighting the sexual excitation concomitant with a certain number of activities of the child. It appears when the internal excitation is too strong. Freud notes its existence in connection with affective, intellectual and motor phenomena, and names this phenomenon "libidinal co-excitation". He thus places this phenomenon at the crossroads of the psychic and the somatic. Sexual excitation arises, in fact, "as soon as the intensity of those processes passes beyond a certain quantitative limit" (1905, pp. 204–205). Thus, any event of life whatsoever, whether it is pleasant or unpleasant, providing it is intense, can give rise to co-excitation.

In *The Economic Problem of Masochism*, he treats it as a fundamental mechanism of erotogenic masochism. He sees it as an "infantile physiological mechanism which ceases to operate later on" (1924, p. 163) but which can always enter into action again. Co-excitation is thus what makes it possible to bind the destructive impulses thanks to the establishment of erotogenic masochism and therefore of erogenisation.

A very young girl, aged 3½, came for a consultation with her parents, who said they were overwhelmed by her "huge bouts of anger" that left them feeling helpless. They were also worried about how she liked "making dark eyes" and always wanted to play the role of the villains in her games with other children. She exhibited, moreover, quite tight obsessional defences that caused her difficulties at school and in her relationships with others.

She was a very intelligent girl who established good quality contact, but experienced major difficulties in separating, particularly from her mother. The therapy could only really begin when her father agreed to accompany her to her sessions.

Although she very much liked playing with puppets, she and the analyst were unable to create a scenario. At the beginning of the sessions, she chose some for her and the analyst, and showed a certain pleasure in handling them. Generally speaking, it was two children, a boy and a girl, playing together. She did not accept any of the interventions concerning the possible relations between them. Very quickly, moreover, she introduced the crocodile that always entered the scene in a violent way, like an uncontrollable oral impulse; it recalled her "huge bouts of anger" that were as violent as they were incomprehensible in a child who was otherwise quite calm and pleasant. Of course, she did not let the analyst say anything about these eruptions of violence.

During a session in which she seemed overwhelmed by her own impulses, her sexual excitation suddenly became obvious. While she was handling the crocodile, she was twisting on her chair, with movements that clearly suggested masturbation. This time, nothing could be done to stop the crocodile: it devoured everybody and destroyed everything that was taking shape between the puppets. And when the analyst tried once again to say something about it, the patient promptly destroyed the rest of the game.

As the work continued, efforts were obviously directed at binding these bouts of violence. It took time before she was able to acquire the possibility of cathecting masochistically something in the order of waiting. Gradually, she learnt to tolerate frustration, to delay. Her "huge bouts of anger" disappeared, creating the space that was necessary for being open to activities at school as well as to the pleasure of thinking.

Further reading

Freud, S. (1905). *Three essays on the theory of sexuality. S.E.* 7. London: Hogarth, pp. 123–143.

Freud, S. (1924). *The economic problem of masochism. S.E* 19. London: Hogarth, pp. 155–170.

Ody, M. (1991). Période de latence, vie sexuelle, co-exciitation sexuelle. *Texts of the Alfred Binet Centre*, 19: 11–21.

KEY WORDS Binding, erotogenic masochism.

THE ANARCHISTIC DRIVE

MARIE-FRANÇOISE LAVAL-HYGONENQ

The anarchistic drive, a notion introduced by Nathalie Zaltzman (1979), operates within the context of the death drives. It is a drive of unbinding whose destructive exigency ruins any fixed relationship to the object when the libidinal tie is lived in the register of mastery, with the risk of self-nullification. As a current of the death drive with a liberating rather than deadly aim, this drive must be recognised for its function of individuation and self-preservation, for it seeks to open up a life solution where a critical situation is closing in on a subject and threatening him with death.

Zaltzman was interested in the analysis of the death drives in relation to the libidinal drives; she sees them as belonging to the register of self-preservation, distinguishing the register of need from that of desire. Thanks to the notion of anarchistic drive, she emphasises how important it is to recognise the patient's appeal at the level of need when a vital struggle is engaged against death, and deplores the misunderstanding regarding "libidinal taming", which risks depriving the death drives of their destiny, one that cannot be reduced to a deadly aim. She points out that it would be a misunderstanding to deprive these drives whose aim is unbinding of their particular paths of elaboration that can open up in fantasy the space of many liberating possibilities; she rejects the "libidinal taming" that seeks to confine them too quickly within new forms of binding experienced as restrictive, reductive or totalising, and even deadly. It would thus be a misinterpretation to analyse predominantly anarchistic unconscious material, that is to say, involving a vital struggle against death, in the oedipal libidinal register. Forced libidinalisation, the "quilt of Eros" according to Zaltzman's expression, could endanger the self-preservative function of this type of death drive. She describes as "irreducible" patients whose lives are subordinated to survival and whose destiny is linked to what she calls the "destiny of extreme experience" (*expérience limite*), with reference to Maurice Blanchot. Unbinding is life in all its splendour, while binding is its suffocation. Psychic functioning under the primacy of destruction evokes the problems of anorexia and alcoholism, which can go hand in hand: "I am mistaken about my need; I drink instead of eating," said an alcoholic patient.

The question of libidinal taming could be raised in relation to childhood rebellion and suffering. Sometimes, a child's distress is not recognised, or worse, those around him find it amusing. When the *Nebenmensch* does not accomplish the task of mutual understanding necessary for the establishment of primary narcissism, when the loved object disavows the traumatic experience of the child, then the child suppresses it. Forced libidinal taming thus deprives the child of the subjective elaboration of his suffering and aggressive impulses, which will continue to operate quietly and be expressed in deadly repetition-compulsion. How can the analyst accommodate these first experiences of rage, hate and distress, these experiences of profound injustice and jealousy, these excesses of all kinds which are primarily an expression of a vital quest for identity rather than a libidinal quest? "I hate everyone who wishes me well," said this same alcoholic patient who engaged in risky forms of behaviour. He had defeated all the psychiatrists he had consulted and his life was marked by ruptures. This hatred was directed at his analyst as well as his parents, with whom he found refuge in the worst moments, without obtaining any recognition because his feelings of hatred and injustice were so powerful. The lasting relationship established with the analyst was a relationship of dependence in which rupture was always a possibility. These are situations where, for Zaltzmann, the transference object imposes itself as an object of need. The analyst must then respond to the urgency in order to deal with the radical nature of the psychic dimension of survival, which may be expressed in the form of action.

The anarchist drive is one that is anchored in the self-preservative hatred that seeks to lift deadly denials. That is why, even if it is difficult to describe on a clinical level, its activity seems to me to throw light on a certain number of difficulties encountered in analyses. For example, when a lasting therapeutic relationship is experienced as a confinement, it explains the difficulty some patients have in understanding the rule of paying for missed sessions, *irrespective of the reason for their absence,* because it establishes continuity in the work. Paying the analyst when the absence is recognised by the patient as having been his own decision poses few problems in general, but paying when it is not "his fault" can create strong feelings of injustice, which hark back to the sufferings of childhood mentioned earlier, entailing a risk of the analysis being broken off prematurely. This is no doubt the reason why many analysts feel more comfortable replacing the missed session than making the patient pay for it, which is regrettable for the future of analysis.

A patient telephoned to say that she would not be able to come to her session because she was still in the provinces due to a meeting. At the following session, the analyst pointed out that she had not paid for the missed session. She replied that she did not think she had to pay for it because this absence did not depend on her, something that we often hear, accompanied by the argument of reciprocity, referring to the rare cancellations of sessions by the analyst. This patient added: "Paying, whatever the reason for the absence, is a commitment I cannot make, it's a bind, it confines me. The idea that there is no way out, that I must commit to not missing sessions will lead me to break off the analysis." The analyst noted that she understood the obligation to pay as a prohibition against missing a session rather than as giving her the freedom to miss a session. She recognised that she had taken this "liberty", but it was not a choice because she had been obliged to be present at this meeting; she added: "It's a double penalty: not being able to come and paying nonetheless." The symbolic existence of absence or presence cannot be decreed; if existence cannot be conceived of in terms of continuity, absence is a hole, a trauma that must be recognised in its reality and the payment is experienced as a negation of absence; the negation of presence then emerges. "In that case, all I need to do is to pay without coming to my sessions!" replied the patient to show how absurd the rule was for her. Thinking of this movement of rebellion as a manifestation of the anarchistic drive makes it possible to recognise it as an appeal of the patient, to locate it in the register of need and not to experience it simply in its destructive dimension. The suspension of a payment until understanding is possible can avoid a rupture and help the patient get beyond the level of a power struggle, free him from the experience of domination and dependence, and discover more psychic freedom. It is worth noting here the paradoxical use of freedom in alienation.

As Zaltzman (1979) writes, "in analytic experience, we need to understand the deadly risk that a project of commitment constitutes for certain subjects and to respect the dimension of rupture not as a resistance, an inaptitude for analysis, but as a vital measure of protection which is part of the project of survival" (p. 61). The anarchistic drive propels the urge for freedom and provides the necessary energy needed for the struggle for survival. The black flag of anarchism thus becomes a symbol of the struggle for life and death.

Let us recall with Zaltzman the history of the cry *Viva la muerte,* which metaphorises these all too possible vicissitudes of the death drive, a libertarian cry of survival and a cry of death: it was the rallying cry of the national insurrection of the Spanish against Napoleon. It was already a cry for freedom. It was taken over by the Spanish anarchists, half a century later, as a revolutionary expression against a life of injustices, and then turned round by Franco's supporters against the anarchists, as the other vicissitude of the death drive, namely, as a deadly destructive drive.

Further reading

Zaltzman, N. (1998). *De la guérison psychanalytique.* Paris: Presses Universitaires de France (Series Épîtres).

Zaltzman, N. (Ed.) (1999). *La Résistance de l'humain.* Paris: Presses Universitaires de France (Series: Petite Bibliothèque de psychanalyse).

KEY WORDS Libidinal taming, mastery, self-preservative function, survival.

MASTERY

LAURE BONNEFON-TORT

A familiar phenomenon referring to the relations of power and domination between individuals, mastery seems to be well known; and yet, albeit introduced by Freud, the notion of a drive for mastery seems subsequently to have been neglected. By placing the notion of mastery at the heart of metapsychology, Paul Denis (1997) has given this question a central place once again. In the analytic field, *emprise* is the French translation suggested by Bela Grunberger of the Freudian term *Bemächtigung*, which Lytton Strachey translated by mastery. Denis has pointed out that it is necessary to distinguish two levels: a phenomenological level, that of the relationship of mastery, which Roger Dorey describes and considers as a characteristic of perversion, and a metapsychological level, that of Freud's drive for mastery.

It is this latter notion that Denis develops by introducing the idea of a formative component of the drive for mastery ("*formant d'emprise de la pulsion*"), a component that can be found in each drive movement and, consequently, in everybody. He thus proposes a new model of the drive: the drive is formed from the combination of two currents of cathexis "in the form of mastery" and "in the form of satisfaction". From this perspective, the only thing that can stop the efforts to achieve mastery is the experience of satisfaction or the reestablishment of a function of representation. This theoretical model proves to be particularly fruitful because it makes it possible to decondense a certain number of clinical situations.

A moment in the analysis of a patient may serve to illustrate this point. The analytic process seemed subject to the ebb and flow of particularly powerful drive movements. Everything was unfolding in a tormented atmosphere from which it was difficult to escape. In reality, a sequence repeated itself: the patient would first be plunged into despair and then accompany what she said with recurrent suicidal threats, such as: "I don't do anything", "I feel useless", "Nobody is interested in me", "I want to die". A phase would then open up in which she expressed her contentment: "Fortunately, you are here", I have been waiting for my session all day", "The last session really gave me some relief". Suddenly, this moment was interrupted by a movement of rebellion. She felt infuriated by the constraints of analysis: "I can't stand this analysis any more, I feel I am a prisoner, I want to stop." After a few sessions in the same register, she acknowledged that she absolutely needed her analysis, but relapsed into her initial despair.

The sense of helplessness felt by the analyst was, of course, the direct consequence of the efforts she was making to exert her mastery. But understanding what appeared to be a relationship of mastery at the phenomenological level was not enough to overcome the impasse. It was the rereading of these movements in the light of the theoretical model of the drive for mastery that was necessary.

The movements of the analysis were interrupted because this patient experienced the analytic situation as one in which she was being dominated by the analyst without any compensation in return. By rebelling against the constraints of the frame, she was expressing the fact that she could not bear being dominated by the analyst. But, as Denis points out, while the latter certainly exercises power with regard to the frame he imposes (times and duration of the fixed sessions, payment for missed sessions), it is to preserve his patient from possible arbitrary decisions and potential attempts to exert power that would be even more alienating. The unfolding of analytic therapy thus requires that the patient, by accepting the frame, is able to tolerate a minimum of domination.

This is where the difficulty with her lay. Of course, this patient had accepted the analytic contract, but she was unable to tolerate the frame, because she had the impression that she was at the analyst's disposal, just as in the past she had felt she was at her mother's disposal. It is possible, under these conditions, to speak of a circular movement of mastery: the cycle of sessions of this patient only acquire meaning if we understand the extent to which she was trying to dominate the analyst just as she herself had once felt dominated. These crises of despair were the means that she had found to acquire power again and to place the analyst under her control. When she had the feeling, after a soothing intervention, that the analyst had been with her sufficiently, she obtained satisfaction and could momentarily calm down and express her gratitude. Nevertheless, her feelings of dependence soon caused her terrible anxiety and precipitated her into fantasies of rupture.

Thus, the progressive elaboration of her identification with her mother, an abandoned and inconsolable woman, helped to liberate her from this movement that she was repeating in the transference. At this point, the scenes that her mother used to make at times of separation came back to her: tears, emotional blackmail, suicidal threats. These were all elements that featured in her sessions. Re-establishing the function of representation loosened the grip of mastery and opened the way towards other horizons.

Further reading

Denis, P. (1997). *Emprise et satisfaction. Les deux formants de la pulsion*. Paris: Presses Universitaires de France (Series: Le Fil rouge).

Dorey, R. (1981). La relation d'emprise. *Nouvelle Revue de Psychanalyse*, 24: 117–140.

Freud, S. (1905). *Three essays on the theory of sexuality. S.E.* 7. London: Hogarth, pp. 123–143.

KEY WORDS Drive, representation, satisfaction.

10

SEXUALITIES

GENDER

JEAN-YVES TAMET

This term has gradually emerged as a counterpoint among many notions that deal with the relations between the feminine and the masculine. *Genre* (gender) comes from *"gendre",* which was in use until the 16th century and is derived from the Latin *genus,* "race", "birth". In philosophy, it is opposed to "species"; the sense of race has disappeared as well as that of sex, which is now only present in "engender" or "generation". What dominates is the idea of grouping or category: thus we say *genre humain* (the "human species"). The sense of sort or type appears in *genre de vie* ("way of life"), *bon genre* ("right kind") or *mauvais genre*), "bad kind").

This term made a comeback in the 1960s in the United States under the influence of Robert Stoller (1968) who described "gender identity", even if he acknowledged that Evelyn Hooker was the first to introduce this notion in her correspondence with John Money. It has since enjoyed great success, largely thanks to gender studies that have developed a line of reflection with multiple aspects and orientations.

It is worth noting that in the course of the debates, the term gender has many different definitions depending on the author. While psychoanalysis is concerned by this approach, it does not make a univocal usage of the term. As for the current adherents of the term gender, they do not use its Freudian sexual component in their conception of psychic life. Jean Laplanche has suggested a notion of gender that would include the field of sexology and a linguistic gender linked to language. This division clearly expresses the difficulty surrounding the issue. In another order of ideas, Juliet Mitchell has proposed a reading of D.W. Winnicott that understands gender as "social sex", even though he himself did not use this term. On the other hand, in a fragment of analysis that has since become famous (Winnicott, 1971), he plunges us into the heart of his interpretative style when he considers a male patient's identity disorder.

A brief clinical history will help to highlight how, in practice, this issue can sometimes be encountered. For many years, on the initiative of her endocrinologist, a woman who had previously been a man was seen in psychotherapy: she was isolated and felt bad; she was prey to anxieties and she wanted to talk. Establishing a regular frame is often a delicate matter with certain patients and, in this case, it was arranged for her to have regular sessions, but to space them out. But there was an immediate problem: intense effort was necessary to avoid calling her "he"! This tension undoubtedly had its origin in the singular history of this sex change and reinforced what was revealed about her childhood. The little boy, who was often mistreated, had a sad father who committed suicide in the family home. The boy could not make friends and have straightforward relations with the adults at school because his belief that he was becoming a woman had established itself imperceptibly and had become an overwhelming preoccupation.

This radical solution gave rise to the idea of taking revenge on this childhood. The sessions gradually brought back into memory this masculine childhood from which the new woman had not separated. We may wonder, moreover if it was possible for her to do so? The insistence on calling her "he" was simply aimed at lifting a repression, as the analyst told her. Imperceptibly, she assumed her new female identity with more tranquillity, leaving an unstable in-between position.

Established in an atmosphere of great perplexity, these sessions made it possible, classically speaking, to lift a repression and, in this sense, to leave aside the dimension of gender transformation in order to find the partition created by psychic bisexuality that was undermined by the anatomical transformation.

With his *Three Essays on the Theory of Sexuality* (1905), Freud wrote a revolutionary book, something James Strachey pointed out very early on. We would do well not to forget that humans always defend themselves against the extraordinary and iconoclastic dimension that it contains, namely, of thinking about the child with the polymorphous manifestations of his sexuality and also of laying down the foundations of psychic bisexuality. It seems that the notion of gender often diverts psychoanalysis from its own roots.

Further reading

André, J. (Ed.) (2007). *Les sexes indifferenciés*. Paris: Presses Universitaires de France. (Series: Petite Bibliothèque de psychanalyse).

Barbin, H. (1978). *Herculine Barbin, dite Alexina B.*, presented by Michel Foucault. Paris: Gallimard.

Butler, J. (1990). *Gender trouble: The subversion of identity*. London: Routledge.

Butler, J. (1997). *The psychic life of power: Theories in subjection*. Stanford: Stanford University Press.

Freud, S. (1905 [1901]). *Three essays on the theory of sexuality*. *S.E.* 7. London: Hogarth, pp. 123–143.

Laplanche, J. (2003). Le genre, le sexe, le sexual. In: *Libres cahiers pour la psychanalyse, Etudes dur la théorie de la séduction*. Paris: In Press, pp. 69–103.

Mitchell, J. (2006). Utiliser Winnicott pour comprendre le genre (sexe social). *Figures de la psychanalyse*, 14(2): 119–131.

Stoller, R. (1968). *Sex and gender. The development of masculinity and femininity*. London: Karnac.

Stoller, R. (1985). *Presentations of gender*. New Haven: Yale University Press.

Tamet, J.-Y. (Ed.). (2012). *Différentiation sexuelle et identités*. Paris: In Press.

Winnicott, D.W. (1971). Creativity and its origins ("The split-off male and female elements to be found in men and women"). In: *Playing and reality*. London: Tavistock, pp. 72–79.

KEY WORDS Bisexuality, sexuality, transgender.

CRUELTY

JEAN-MICHEL HIRT

There is no better testimony on cruelty in love than letter 141 in *Dangerous Liaisons* (Choderlos de Laclos, 1782), sent by the Marquise de Merteuil to the Vicomte de Valmont, with whom she was in love, urging him to break off his relationship with the Présidente de Tourvel. She dictates to him a "little epistolary model" linked to the repetition of a sentence: "It's not my fault." It begins thus: "One tires of everything, my angel; it is a law of nature. It is not my fault. So if I am tired of an affair which has preoccupied me totally for the last four boring months, it is not my fault… It follows that I have been unfaithful to you for a while now. But to some degree your relentless tenderness has forced me into it! It is not my fault. Today a woman I am madly in love with demands that I give you up for her sake. It is not my fault… Farewell, my angel. I took you with pleasure. I leave you without regrets, I shall perhaps come back to you. That is the way of the world. It is not my fault" (2007 [1782] p. 346). The cruelty of this "story" told by the Marquise serves Valmont's own cruel purposes and he "quite simply" copies this model and sends it "quite simply" to the Présidente, his lover. It is a transfer of love under the aegis of cruelty which – we may reassure ourselves – will be the undoing of the three protagonists.

Human cruelty (*Grausamkeit*) raises all the more questions in that Freud perceives in his *Three Essays on the Theory of Sexuality* (1905) the "intimate connection" that exists between "cruelty and the sexual instinct" (p. 159). In this work, he conceives the sexual act as an element of aggressiveness striving for complete union and notes that the connection established in childhood "between the cruel and the erotogenic instincts" is likely to prove "unbreakable in later life" (p. 193). He thus links the instinct for cruelty, characterised as a part-instinct, to the "need for overcoming the resistance of the sexual object" (p. 158). In Chapter Six of *Civilization and its Discontents* (1930), he adds that sadism "[is] clearly a part of sexual life, in the activities of which affection [can] be replaced by cruelty" (pp. 117–118).

It would be an error to reduce cruelty to its perverse manifestations, sadism or masochism, to confuse it with the destructiveness of the death drive or alternatively to see in it only the perpetuation of a part-drive impulse at work in infantile sexuality. Rather, cruelty appears much more to be one of the components of the sexual drive. As the latter can never completely reach its object, except by extinguishing itself in it, it constantly pursues it ever further, even at the risk of endangering the narcissistic foundations of the subject – the myth of Tristan and Iseult affords a striking illustration of this, because the cruelty inherent in their love is one of the motive forces of the passion animating these lovers.

Insofar as a cruel trend manifests itself as a necessary dimension of sexual love life, and even as the condition of its movement and its accomplishment, its contribution must be taken into account. Accepting the role and importance of cruelty, not as an aberration of love but as an aspect of its power in the mind, informs us about the excesses that can result from it. Only the link between tenderness, sensuality and cruelty, along with the resultant conflicts, confers love with its capacity to move the flesh by its power over bodies.

While cruelty remains linked to the two other trends of love life, sensuality and tenderness, it does not lead to attacking oneself or the other. On the contrary, it allows for recognition of the strangeness of the other and not its reduction to the same. Nothing is harder than maintaining the link between these three trends. As soon as love life is immobilised in one of the three only, it is threatened with death.

Reflecting in *Civilization and its Discontents* on the precept of love, which is proper to Judaism as well as Christianity – "Thou shalt love thy neighbour as thyself" – Freud considered that such an ambition regarding someone who is a stranger to us is generally beyond our strength. It is an impractical commandment, in his view, in view of the fact that the instinct for cruelty is so quick to unfurl itself against any stranger. He writes: "As a result the neighbour is not only for them [people] a potential helper or sexual object, but also someone who tempts them to satisfy their aggressiveness on him, to exploit his capacity for work without compensation, to use him sexually without his consent, to seize his possessions, to humiliate him, to cause him pain, to torture and to kill him" (p. 111). From a clinical point of view, taking cruelty into consideration as a drive helps us to better appreciate the innumerable forms of the relations of mastery as well the "psychic crimes" that escape all condemnation. It cannot be overlooked in the pathologies of narcissism, and, more generally, in the composition of the superego.

In his seminar on the ethics of psychoanalysis, Jacques Lacan (1997 [1986]) returns to the "vehement rebellion" that the love of one's neighbour evoked in Freud. Drawing on his reading of Sade, he considers that if each one of us recoils from such an injunction, it is on account of the cruelty and jouissance at the expense of the neighbour that it implies, thus of the need to retreat from it as if it were something evil. "I retreat," Lacan declares, "from loving my neighbor as myself because there is something on the horizon there that is engaged in some form of intolerable cruelty. In that sense, to love one's neighbor may be the cruelest of choices... We retreat from what? From assaulting the image of the other, because it was the image on which we were formed as an ego... We are, in effect, at one with everything that depends on the image of the other as our fellow man, on the similarity we have to our ego and to everything that situates us in the imaginary register" (pp. 194–197). In other words, he suggests here that cruelty offers a major possibility of calling into question the image of the ego, a construction realised during the mirror stage in connection with the image of the maternal other. The unbinding of cruelty favours attacks against the similar other as an image of the ego. Consequently, in order for love to come into existence, the knotting point between the ego, the similar other and the Other must first free the subject from narcissistic projection as well as from the savagery of jouissance without another.

We can see that literature and cinema are particularly suited to deploying in a fictional mode the multiple aspects of cruelty and of procuring jouissance from it in the register of the imaginary realm. Choderlos de Laclos' 18th-century novel, *Dangerous Liaisons,* provides a very eloquent testimony to this. It recounts the positions of desire and love not only in terms of the difference between the sexes, but also of the binding and unbinding of sensuality, affection and cruelty. A veritable treatise on sentimental education, it prefigures the analyses of Georges Bataille on eroticism and evil by showing how cruelty, if it is not to sink into destructiveness, must be linked to the violence of speech: the field of cruelty has little worth if it is not expressed within a discourse, if this instinctuality of the body does not become speech. It may be argued that the uncanniness that cruelty establishes in a loving relationship is the paradoxical condition for the perpetuation over time of a pair of lovers.

Further reading

Choderlos de Laclos, P. (2007 [1782]). *Dangerous Liaisons.* London: Penguin Classics.

Freud, S. (1905). *Three essays on the theory of sexuality. S.E.* 7. London: Hogarth, pp. 135–244.

Freud, S. (1930). *Civilization and its discontents. S.E.* 21. London: Hogarth, pp. 64–145.

Hirt, J.-M. (2007). *L'Insolence de l'amour. Fictions de la vie sexuelle.* Paris: Albin.

Lacan, J. (1992 [1986]). *The seminar, book VII: the ethics of psychoanalysis, 1959–1960,* trans. D. Potter. New York, NY: Norton.

KEY WORDS Sexual love, ethics, jouissance, narcissism, neighbour.

NEO-SEXUALITY

LAURE BONNEFON-TORT

While it is well known to readers of Joyce McDougall, this strange term may seem hermetic to many others. If she introduced it in the context of her research into *sexualities,* it was because she was unsatisfied with the terms "perversion" or "deviation", which both have pejorative connotations. She wanted to be able to reflect and work on the different forms of sexuality which, while deviating from dominant norms, are practised between free and consenting adults, and thus sought to re-establish the possibility of neutral and benevolent listening by warning against the widespread tendency to take refuge in normative attitudes. She affirms, on the contrary, that clinically it is indispensable to preserve the patient from the possible value judgements of his analyst. On the theoretical level, this new expression also places emphasis on the creativity at work in the forms of sexualities. The term "neo-sexuality" is, as it were, for the analyst an invitation to engage in research, in other words to reconstruct with the patient the meaning of a sexual scenario rather than confining him from the outset to a pre-established category.

A young woman sought help in connection with difficulties in her love life linked to what she called a "disturbance of sexuality". Much sought after by men, she had a few adventures in order to put on a good show socially, but was, as it were, absent from herself. In these situations, she did not participate actively in the sexual relationship, but remained inert. Here sexuality was reduced in reality to solitary practices: images ran through her mind that she found unbearable, but which were the only vector that could bring her pleasure. It took her a long time to be able to speak about her favourite scenario, a sort of inversion of the biblical story of Susanna and the elders: she needed to be alone and to imagine that she was giving herself to very old, disgusting and dirty men. The more the scenario disgusted her, the more exciting it was.

Although this fantasy was totally opaque for her, she felt invaded by it and subjected to it as if it originated outside her and was imposed on her. She could no longer tolerate the indefinite repetition of this scenario that was a constraint and in which she humiliated herself. Confined within this autoerotic process, she feared that she would never be able to meet a man for real, as she wanted to do.

This patient's sexuality thus presented all the aspects of constraint and repetition that McDougall displaces from perversion to neo-sexuality. She had lost access to the meaning of this scenario which a part of her had nonetheless invented. One of the major difficulties for the analyst lay in the danger of letting herself be dragged down by the patient's words ("I don't understand anything about it"), and of abandoning her to the lack of meaning that would be the logical conclusion if the analyst saw the material as belonging to the category of perverse fantasies.

Following the perspective proposed by McDougall helped the analyst, on the contrary, to persevere in her quest for meaning, while keeping in mind the questions that McDougall asks: What does this scenario refer to? What gives it its erotic power?

The patient's associations gradually led to the reconstruction of the history of a little girl who had been humiliated by her father. He had neglected and ignored her, while at the same time explaining to her in crude terms how her mother remained his sole centre of interest because she was exciting. It was as if she did not exist other than as the witness of a primal scene that was constantly unfolding before her eyes.

Her scenario – of becoming in fantasy this young woman subjected to the assaults of lewd old men – had enabled this little girl to achieve a double victory over this narcissistic wound. On the one hand, she was able to identify herself with her mother by acquiring her charms; on the other, she humiliated her father, a powerful man, by picturing him in senile decline. However, when she reached adulthood, this construction outside time left her on the edge of the sexual scene: internally, she was still the little prepubertal girl doomed to experience the indifference of men. Although in reality she had become a beautiful woman, she could not allow herself to occupy this position and to enjoy the possibility of loving a man and of being loved by him.

She possessed the psychic resources necessary for analysing this scenario, for appropriating the meaning of it and thus for liberating herself from the constraint it exerted on her. This is not always the case and, in other situations, the neo-sexual solution remains the only recourse for a patient. Analysis can then help the patient to understand that he is not only the actor of these sexual scenes but also, and above all, the author, that they are his creations.

Further Reading

McDougall, J. (1980 [1978]). *Plea for a measure of abnormality*, New York, NY: International Universities Press.
McDougall, J. (1986 [1982]). *Theatres of the mind: Illusion and truth on the psychoanalytic stage.* London: Free Association Books.
Stoller, R. (1979). *Sexual excitement: dynamics of erotic life.* New York, NY: Pantheon Books.

KEY WORDS Fantasy, scenario, sexuality

THE MELANCHOLIC FEMININE

MICHEL VILLAND

She did not know why she had done it. Perhaps she had wanted to trouble her husband who was so sure of his ideas, so little inclined to doubt, thinking like his family, like his milieu of origin. Rather than letting himself be disturbed by the paradoxical thoughts of his wife, he always gave priority to this affiliation to his social class and his fidelity to tradition. For her part, she could see right through him as well as them, the members of his family, and her lucidity was unbearable for him. She could see just how much death was already present in their life. But it was not appropriate to think in ways that went beyond certain forms of propriety; one's thinking had to be "on the path", like chariot wheels following, without ever leaving them, the ruts left by their traces. The marriage had been consummated; she passed over on to the side of the "band" of those who knew the man. A life was awakening in her; she was not looked at for herself, but for what she represented: the continuation of the line. She wanted to die, and hoped that this life inside her would never awaken. When she gave birth, she did not take care of her daughter.

One day, out of fatigue, she failed to say anything when her husband made a mistake with his medication, taking twice the prescribed dose. He had fallen ill. Then, without knowing why, she gradually poisoned him. Perhaps it was so that he would be a little troubled, a little less sure of himself.

The reader will have recognised *Thérèse Desqueyroux*, the novel by François Mauriac published in 1927. Beyond the description of the Catholic bourgeoisie in Bordeaux, Mauriac depicts the female soul in which melancholia is allied with charm to exert their forces of attraction. Intelligence and lucidity are in the foreground, along with the weakness of narcissistic construction. Thérèse only thinks about herself; she cannot forget herself, even for the sake of taking care of her child. She is unable to explain it to her friend Anne: "She doesn't understand that I'm filled already with myself, that there's no room for anyone else. And Anne herself, she only wants to have children... But with me it's different, I always have to try to find myself again; I struggle to link up with myself" (Mauriac, 2005 [1927], p. 113).

Thérèse would like to leave, Thérèse would like to die. Which diabolical force is taking her so far away from her own source? To which destiny is she subjected? Mauriac notes a few possible paths: her maternal grandmother had disappeared, without explanation; her mother had died in childbirth; she was brought up by an old and deaf aunt who was completely devoted to her. Why did the personal alchemy of her development render her destiny tragic? We do not know.

Mauriac depicts the "melancholic feminine" by revealing a very subtle picture. He shows us that the murder of the other and of oneself is at the heart of melancholia (Chabert, 2003).

The deception felt by Thérèse following her marriage revived her oedipal disappointment. This marriage did not offer her the possibility of overcoming her original melancholia that made her so vulnerable to the excitation that the other provoked in her; the transformation imposed on her by the object was unbearable. Catherine Chabert has shown how melancholia impedes the flourishing of femininity, for the latter implies being able to be open to the other through constructive passivity. Melancholia, on the contrary, remains absolutely faithful to a past that does not pass and prevents openness and access to the novelty of the present.

The construction of the feminine welcoming the other is based on the construction of passivity of which the fantasy *A Child is Being Beaten* (Freud, 1919) is the paradigm: for Freud, this fantasy exemplifies the demand for love hidden behind the conviction that the one who is being beaten is oneself. It opens up the possibility of thinking about the excitation aroused by the other. Masochism becomes the guardian of life because it has the capacity to organise excitation and to promote construction. The capacity to welcome the other, which is essential in construction, implies the possibility of thinking about the excitation aroused by him, of tolerating constructive excitation and suffering, something Thérèse could not do.

Her father was her only hero; he condemned her no less than her in-laws and no less than herself. "She walked quickly, with the anxious heart of a wild animal," writes Mauriac (2005 [1927], p. 102).

Further reading

Chabert., C. (2003). *Féminin mélancholique.* Paris: Presses Universitaires de France (Series: Petite Bibliothèque de psychanalyse).

Freud, S. (1915). *Mourning and melancholia. S.E.* 14. London: Hogarth, pp. 237–258.

Freud, S. (1919). *A child is being beaten. S.E.* 19. London: Hogarth, pp. 179–204.

KEY WORDS Deception, melancholia, passivity.

11

NARCISSISM

THE SKIN-EGO

PATRICE BRUNAUD

"I'm going to read this book by Didier Anzieu, *The Skin-Ego"*, the patient said at the beginning of her session. She had had a dream that had interrupted her sleep and left her in a great state of anxiety: she was having her shower when, all of a sudden, her skin became detached from her body and covered the shower wall panels. At that time, she felt abandoned by everything: her husband was interested in another woman, her work colleagues wanted her to leave and she had had to undergo a biopsy for a dark spot on her skin that she feared might be a melanoma. All this made her feel depressed. The biopsy turned out to be negative, but there was a story connected with the dark skin. She was of mixed race, and her mother had found her too dark, darker than her brothers and sisters. When she was small, her mother had even advised her to drink a lot of milk to whiten her skin.

She was right to want to read Anzieu's (2016 [1985]) *The Skin-Ego.* Equally, her therapist was right not to count too much on this reading for reconciling her with her skin. If she had thought of a book to give meaning to her dream, it was perhaps because she did not feel well contained in her sessions. Was the "psychic skin" to which Anzieu refers lacking at this moment? In what respect could psychic treatment deprive her of her personal identity? Could the container, the shower closet, appropriate the content? She associated: "Did my mother want my hide? ("*Ma mere voulait-elle ma peau?*"). Psychic treatment recreates conditions that are favourable to such an experience of persecution through the great proximity that it affords, stimulating the "instinct for attachment", the baby's primitive instinct of attachment to its mother (John Bowlby, taken up by Didier Anzieu), but also the heart-wrenching feelings that can follow separations, if the attachment is formed in the pathological mode of "adhesive identification", according to Donald Meltzer. As the holidays were approaching, this patient said she felt "flayed alive", as a part of herself remained literally stuck to the treatment, to its setting, which deprived her of the capacity for taking advantage of her own existence, for "feeling well in herself" ("*être bien dans sa peau*"). Furthermore, when the treatment is limited to applying a dressing (Is it not often the case today that one has to treat quickly and superficially?), the "dressing sticks to the skin; the one who applies the treatment flays"; at least, if he is not attentive enough at the delicate moment of separation.

Thinking. As a young psychologist, Anzieu did a placement in a department of dermatology at the St-Louis hospital in Paris. Skin dressings were common practice there, and he was intrigued by what was expressed on the periphery of deep human suffering, but also of unrepresentable drives waiting to be put into words. At the same time, in the rue d'Ulm, at the *Ecole normale supérieure*, a thinker, Jacques Lacan, was fascinating the young member of his audience with his words, those of analysis and of Freud's texts. There was a link between the two of them, but they did not know it yet. An unconscious link? Anzieu's mother, who was insanely jealous, had tried to kill a famous actress. She was interned and treated by Jacques Lacan, who used the material for his inaugural "case of Aimée" in his medical thesis. From holes in skin to holes in words, there is much room for the unspoken: Anzieu, who had become a qualified philosophy teacher, underwent analysis with Lacan, and his mother was "placed" as a governess with Lacan's father! This eventuated in a rupture that was the outcome of violent conflicts, while at the same time the first split in the French psychoanalytic movement occurred.

Making links. Anzieu was now a teacher of psychology at the University of Nantes. His thesis, *Freud's Self-Analysis* (Anzieu, 1986) was published and enjoyed great success. He was also appreciated for his interest in transitional analysis, for the notions of gap and in-between, and their deployment in psychodrama and groups.

Albeit mindful of this dimension of groupality, of interpersonal and intrapsychic relations, he forgot nothing of his observations in the somatic, and more particularly, the dermatological domain. Drawing on Freud's work *The Ego and the Id* (1923), in association with post-Kleinian Anglo-Saxon studies (in particular, Wilfred Bion on the question of psychic containers), he put forward the hypothesis of a "skin-ego" with reference to four series of fundamental findings: ethological, group-related, projective and dermatological. This text, published in 1974 in the *Nouvelle Revue de psychanalyse* (Anzieu, 1974), appeared in its definitive form in 1985. Gradually, other publications completed this concept, described by the author himself as "a vast metaphor…capable of stimulating freedom of thought in psychoanalysts" (Anzieu, (2016 [1985]), p. 5). More recently, contributions by authors who were very close to Anzieu have been concerned with the question of limits (Chabert, Cupa, Kaës & Roussillon, 2007).

According to Anzieu's elaboration in 1974, the skin-ego has nine functions: (1) "maintenance" of the mind, with reference to D.W. Winnicott's concept of holding; (2) "containment", the skin-ego as a shell containing the drive nucleus; (3) the "stimulus barrier" as a protection against paranoid anxieties relating to psychic intrusion (these first three functions are indispensable for the rest); (4) "individuation" understood as, each person has his/her skin, with its major pathology, schizophrenia; (5) "intersensoriality", the lack of which is matched by fears of bodily fragmentation and, more precisely of dismantling (Meltzer, 1975); (6) "the support of sexual excitation", necessary for the localisation of the erogenous zones and for recognition of the difference between the sexes; (7) on the model of the sensory-motor tonus of the skin, the "libidinal recharge" of psychic functioning, with its major vagary, fear of the explosion of the psychic apparatus; and (8), this function is particularly worth our attention because it links up words with the skin. It is that of the "inscription" of sensory-tactile traces. "The skin-ego," writes Anzieu, "is the original parchment which preserves, like a palimpsest, the erased, scratched-out, written-over first outlines of an 'original' preverbal primal writing made up of traces upon the skin" (Anzieu, 1985, p. 105). Skin relates forgotten, poorly erased histories.

The double taboo on touching is the "condition for overcoming the skin-ego", as is shown in Chapter Ten of Anzieu's *The Skin-Ego*. Otherwise, there may be an evolution towards the ninth function of the skin-ego, "an anti-function, as it were, in the service of Thanatos, aimed at the self-destruction of the skin and of the ego". "I am struck, "he says "by the analogy between this auto-immune response and the negative therapeutic response of turning the drive against oneself, the negative therapeutic reaction, along with other attacks against linking in general and against psychic contents in particular... In the psychoses, especially schizophrenia, the paradox of allergic conditions reaches its peak... The imaginary skin that covers the Ego becomes a poisoned tunic, suffocating, burning and disintegrating. One may call this a *toxic* function of the skin-ego" (pp. 115–116).

This ninth function was modified subsequently by Anzieu. He replaced it with his studies on the void, inspired mainly by those that he called his three B's: Wilfred Bion, Samuel Beckett and Francis Bacon. Finally, it is Beckett that he evokes: "Speaking from one's heart gives one chunks of courage. Speaking from one's belly, from the inside of one's belly, or from this or that wounded or sick organ, from one's own flesh exposed beneath a torn skin, is what Beckett proposes and imposes as a necessity" (Anzieu, 1999, p. 127).

Further reading

Anzieu, D. (1994). *Le penser. Du Moi-peau au Moi-pensant.* Paris: Dunod.

Anzieu, D., et al., (2013). *Les enveloppes psychiques.* Paris: Dunod.

Chabert, C. (1997). *Didier Anzieu.* Paris: Presses Universitaires de France (Series: Psychanalystes d'aujourd'hui).

Chabert, C., Cupa, D., Kaës, R., and Roussillon, R. (2007). *Le Moi-Peau et la psychanalyse des limites.* Paris: Érès.

Kaës, R. (2011). *Penser l'inconscient. Développement de l'œuvre de Didier Anzieu.* Paris: Dunod.

KEY WORDS Attachment, Bacon, Beckett, Bion, containment, adhesive identification, inscription of traces, the unspoken, psychic skin.

THE PSYCHIC ENVELOPE

ÉVELYNE SECHAUD

This term constitutes an open model and covers various fields: sensorial envelopes (tactile, sonorous, olfactory, visual), memory envelope, dream envelope, envelope of excitation, envelope of suffering, envelopes of the psychoanalyst, etc.

The interest in psychic envelopes reveals a change of perspective: attention is turned away from psychic contents and focused on the containers. Incidentally, they are not passive receptacles but rather processual devices with a capacity for transforming what is received. We are indebted to Wilfred Bion for the first studies on the container/contained relationship and for the emphasis placed on the transformations that the maternal container (or analyst) can carry out on the child's projections (or the analysand's). The process is based on what he calls the capacity for reverie, which is an intuitive mode of thinking that makes it possible to transform unassimilable feelings (beta elements) into mentally assimilable elements (alpha elements).

Didier Anzieu developed the notion of psychic envelope into a real concept. Although the term appeared in 1976 in connection with the sound envelope of the ego, and the word "envelope" appears often in the first edition of *The Skin-Ego* in 1985, it was not until 1986 that the concept was fully developed.

Anzieu distinguishes essentially between two psychic envelopes, which differ in their structure and their form. The external layer, the stimulus barrier, which he considers as a membrane, is turned towards the outer world. The internal layer, considered as a sensitive pellicule, has a receptive interface function. It receives external and internal stimuli and brings them into relationship with each other by giving them a meaning; it is a surface of inscription.

The analytic frame presents in his view a homology with the structure of the psychical apparatus. The rule of abstinence corresponds to the stimulus barrier, and the rule of free association to the surface of inscription. For him the interlocking of the two instructions at the very heart of a fundamental rule reflects the original interlocking of the envelopes that are constitutive of the psyche. They make the latter an apparatus for thinking thoughts, for containing affects, and for transforming the instinctual drive economy.

The discourse of a patient on the couch had been iterative for several years: "I have nothing to say to you, any more than to the others… I have the feeling that it doesn't exist for me, and I don't want it to exist… I have no memory of my childhood; things don't register. Nothing gets to me; nothing affects me." This narcissistic shell hides and reveals her fragility. And then, one day she began to behave differently: she came to her sessions heavily perfumed; it was a strong, heady perfume whose excessive nature was overpowering. The persistence of the enveloping smell modified the analyst's listening: she ceased to listen to the content of her words and she had the growing conviction that with this patient she was experiencing a transference acting out without representation which aroused her interest and made her feelings of irritation disappear. The analyst finally said to her that, thanks to her perfume, they were now breathing and smelling the same air, and that that was no doubt the most important thing. She was taken aback. The analyst said to the patient that it was a way for her to communicate a sensation to the analyst that was perhaps also a form of emotion. A long silence followed which the patient finally broke by saying, "It's funny: you are talking about the air that we are breathing and smelling and now I've got a tune (*air*) running through my head. It's an old song, but I can't remember the words." The analyst asked her to hum the tune. She hesitated, said she felt ashamed, and then began to hum it. It was a song from her parents' generation in the 1930s. "Speak to me of love. Keep on telling me tender things. My heart will never tire of hearing your fine talk, provided you always repeat those wonderful words: I love you." It belonged to the common culture of the analyst and the analysand; it was a cultural envelope that respected and maintained the stimulus barrier and gave meaning to the olfactory and musical sensations. The words of the song, words from the parents' generation, words of love, made it possible to rediscover in the transference the affects and representations of the infantile relationship.

The analyst's words about the air that they were breathing sought to name the sharing of a sensation that was enveloping them and to lead to a representation and affect that hitherto were poorly differentiated. The sensation attested to a repression, but one it also maintained. It was the emerging trace of a buried relational mode of which only the body had retained a memory. The word "*air*" included in the interpretation was a verbal bridge that brought about an intrapsychic transition from one sensorial modality to another. Olfactory sensations as well as sounds participated in the fantasy of a common skin permitting the construction of a narcissistic envelope. In this sequence, the analytic work illustrates the path of intrapsychic and intersubjective transformation that is necessary for gaining access to meaningful speech. It leads here from the sensorial envelope to the content of unconscious representations.

Further reading

Anzieu, D. (2016 [1985]). *The skin-ego*, trans. N. Segal. London: Routledge.
Houzel, D. (2010). *Le Concept d'enveloppe psychique.* Paris: In Press.

KEY WORDS Setting, psychic envelope, skin-ego, sensorial.

THE PARTIAL OBJECT OR *OBJET (a)*

ISABELLE ALFANDARY

A young woman in analysis reported during a session a detail that had come to her attention in recent times: whenever she was reading a text in the context of her work or for pleasure, a syllable would stand out from time to time as she was reading. She noticed that she could not stop herself from paying attention to it, and that this experience, albeit fleeting, had affected and troubled her. She immediately associated this experience with the surname of her boyfriend from whom she had recently separated, which concerned the syllable in question. At the time of their relationship, she was vaguely aware of the attachment that she had to the name of this man, even if it was difficult for her to separate it from the feelings that she had for him. Since their separation, this name had continued to haunt her by reappearing in certain words of written language: she would see this syllable, a quite ordinary one in French, "flashing" in words she came across at random in her readings, and feel an emotion that she found difficult to explain other than by the fact that this combination of letters reminded her of the man she had loved.

During one session, she even wondered if this name had not contributed in part to the profound seductive effect that this man had had on her. In the course of the elaboration that followed, she recalled that this syllable, which can be found in many French words, was also present in her mother's maiden name. Another memory then came back to her concerning her mother's surname. When her mother had applied for naturalization, the surname had undergone a slight modification in its spelling at the precise position of this syllable. The civil status official, seeking to "give a French version" of the foreign name, had chosen to transcribe the surname in this way.

The syllable that kept cropping up in the name of the person she loved seemed to be indistinguishable from him, to get lost with him, but was also liable to turn up again in the world or in written language and exerted in a confused way seductive power over this subject, which is somewhat reminiscent of what Jacques Lacan called from 1960 onwards the *objet (a)*. What sometimes "flashes" while she is reading, as the analysand puts it very aptly, brings the subject back to her desire and seems obscurely to designate the object of desire, instead of representing it. Lacan designated by the term *"objet (a)"* what Elisabeth Roudinesco and Michel Plon (2006) define as "the object desired by the subject and which eludes him to the point of being unrepresentable or of becoming a non symbolisable remainder" (p. 739).

This object that Lacan calls partial and that only ever appears in a fragmented form, in this case practically detachable, is illustrated in the seminar on transference in the form of the *ágalma,* a Platonic notion developed in *The Banquet.* Lacan reported that it was in a verse from *Hecuba* by Euripides that this word had "struck" him. A statue of the gods, in Antiquity, the *ágalma* was a magic object of devotion or cult that made it possible to think about what he calls the "special power of the object", whose function as a fetish he notes, in this case a maternal fetish, but whose meaning he tries to understand beyond the function. The *ágalma* is linked to an idea of sparkle [*éclat*] which attracts irresistibly: "It is enough to indicate that *ágalma* has to do with the meanings *brillant* [sheen], and *gallant* [gallant], the latter coming from *gal*, meaning *éclat* in Old French. In a word, what is at stake here is the function we analysts have discovered that is designated by the term 'partial object'" (Lacan, 2005 [1991], p. 143). The *ágalma* to which the syllable bears witness points towards the *objet (a)*, as enigmatic as it is desirable, towards the lost object.

Further reading

Lacan, J. (2005 [1991]). *Transference. The seminar of Jacques Lacan: book VIII*, trans. B. Fink. Cambridge: Polity Press.

KEY WORDS *Ágalma,* fetish, object of desire, partial-object.

THE NARCISSISTIC CONTRACT

DOMINIQUE TABONE-WEIL

This is the name that Piera Aulagnier (2001 [1975]) gives to the "asymmetrical" contract linking the child and the parental couple from birth. The narcissistic foundations of the new subject result from this contract. It sets limits on the narcissistic cathexis that the parents bring to bear on a child whom they expect unconsciously to fulfil their unsatisfied desires and to embody their ideal. If its terms are respected, this contract enables the child to find his place in the continuity of generations, a place freed from the desire of objects and "independent of the parental verdict alone". For this to occur, the parental couple must be sufficiently engaged in the social field and respect its rules. Furthermore, society must be "sufficiently fair". For there is a breach of the narcissistic contract in the case of serious social failure on the part of the parents, but also in situations involving dictatorships, persecutions and totalitarian regimes. On the other hand, when its terms are recognised and it is applied, it underlines the adherence of each person to the human community and to respect for its imperatives that ensure protection and otherness (see Soulié 2002).

In the context of love, a similar contract is established. Each member of the couple must repair the narcissistic wounds of the other person. The contract is asymmetrical, but reciprocal. In bad cases, when all spirit of exchange has been lost and the contract deviates towards narcissistic perversion, one of the two members becomes for the other the target of a projective identification by means of which he gets rid of the parts of himself that he hates and strives to deny or split off.

The analyst often wondered when she was listening to N. whether there was not something of a narcissistic perversion in her husband. At other moments, it was in N. that she perceived a perverse mode of functioning, consisting of provocations, intrusions and manipulations with predominant projective defences. This amounts to saying that they were a fusional couple, as N. said herself, especially as they were unable to have children and each of them wanted in turn, or at the same time, to be the parent and the child of the other, which was not without its drawbacks. Their relationship took up a large part of the sessions. The central theme was one of betrayal. It came up again and again like a leitmotiv, with a few variations. N. and her husband met each other when they were adolescents, around the age of 17, when her parents were getting divorced. At the time, they seemed to play a role for each other that was assigned to each of them by the "narcissistic contract". Today, on the contrary, they saw everything in terms of betrayal.

The analyst was not deaf to the transference dimension of this singular experience. The question of knowing what she "did behind her back" during the sessions or with her other patients as soon as N. had her back turned could be heard, moreover, in the course of the patient's associations. In the transference, N. felt the analyst betrayed her like a weak and infantile oedipal father who was afraid of triggering the mother's anger if he showed his love for his children; or again when she became the mother who abandoned her in favour of a younger brother or, later on, the mother who took numerous lovers who occupied her much more than the difficulties or successes of her daughter.

It was precisely her husband's infidelity that made N. became obsessively jealous, to the point that she literally fell ill. Months went by and the wound did not heal. As soon as the situation between them calmed down a bit, it was as if she wanted to rekindle the tensions. "I will never be able to forgive him," she said. "He has broken something; it cannot be repaired. It's a breach of contract."

This was not the first time that this experience of a breach of contract had occupied the foreground, both at the professional level as well as on the level of relationships. The analyst wondered about its nature and what it was all about. Was she referring to the contract that had been established between herself and the analyst? Yes, in a certain way, because they had switched from a face-to-face therapy to a classical analysis, which she had experienced as a "betrayal" by the analyst as well as a "promotion", a mark of trust and consideration. It may also refer to all the contracts that had been broken in her life, notably by her parents: generous pseudo-gifts that she was asked to give back, serious social decline which shattered forever something in the child's self-image, cheating, lies, falsifications and, finally, her father's psychiatric collapse. He was both desocialised and delusional, and increasingly often hospitalised for psychiatric reasons, before he finally died of a neuroleptic malignant syndrome about 10 years before.

We are inevitably led to think about the young pre-adolescent and adolescent girl that she was, insecure and ill-at-ease, certain that she would never be able to "attract a boy", that she would never be chosen, to the point that even if a boy seemed interested in her, she saw it as a trap, a means of ridiculing her, and finally of rejecting her.

This was the case, anyway, until her future husband appeared on the scene. They chose each other, mutually, for better and for worse, as they say. She had no doubts this time and, with this encounter came the hope that everything would be repaired. More than hope, it was belief, finally, in the existence of a real "narcissistic contract". They would be the ideal couple and would found the ideal family. All the humiliations of puberty, her mother's rejections and the clear preference for her little brother, her father's collapse, the mockery of her girlfriends, the sense of exclusion, everything would be erased by this new relationship. This time she was the one who was preferred, chosen and loved. Her couple was poles apart from the picture that she had of the couple her parents had formed: they would be united, sharing everything, telling each other everything, without any possible obscurity or reserve. This requirement of idealness led her, moreover, to put up with many things on her husband's part, denying as far as she could his aggressive acts and various forms of misbehaviour, and to constantly see their common past as the unfolding of a fairy tale that had suddenly ended. (It is worth noting that this jealousy also seemed to have the function of concealing the first narcissistic trauma of the couple, the importance of which was denied, namely, the announcement of their sterility).

When the analyst interpreted the intensity of the pain felt by N. in connection with the breach of the narcissistic contract with her husband as an echo of the pain linked to earlier narcissistic wounds that had never really healed, it was an important moment for her, a source of *insight* and self-restoration. Her obsessive suffering abated, though it did not cease completely. The tonality of the sessions became richer and deeper. Real analytic work could now be done.

In this fragment of case history and analysis, the breach of the contract of which this patient speaks is clearly related to the breach of the narcissistic contract as defined by Aulagnier. Admittedly, it manifests itself within a loving relationship, but it also directly echoes the social failure of the parents, which was the mark of their deep psychic flaws and of their incapacity to establish their place fully in the social field. This was no doubt because for them society was a jungle in which, to survive, it was necessary to cheat, lie and be cleverer than others, and where the experience of belonging to the human community with the rights and duties that it implies was not accessible or barely accessible. The experience of betrayal that this patient manifested in her adult loving relationship was linked to the betrayal she had experienced in her relationship with her parents, but also to what they themselves had experienced and transmitted to her.

Further reading

Aulagnier, P. (2001 [1975]). *The violence of interpretation: From pictogram to statement*, trans. A. Sheridan. London: Routledge.

Kaës, R. (2009). *Les Alliances inconscientes.* Paris: Dunod.

Roussillon, R. (2013). Les niveaux de rupture du lien (paper read at the congress *Gypsy* in 2012). In: *Ruptures*, eds. Frydman, R. and Flis-Trèves, M. Paris: Presses Universitaires de France.

KEY WORDS Projective defences, denial, narcissistic flaw, reparation.

THE AMENTIAL UNCONSCIOUS

ISABELLE GERNET AND CHRISTOPHE DEJOURS

The investigation by psychoanalysis of the characteristic modalities of the psychic functioning of non-neurotic psychopathological organisations has contributed to the development of metapsychological propositions related to the topographical structuring of the psychical apparatus. The practical questions raised by patients presenting psychotic modes of functioning, narcissistic pathologies or somatic illnesses have led to the identification of heterogeneous sectors, enclaves or splits at the heart of the psychic topography. These conceptions, whose premises can be found in the last texts of Freud, *An Outline of Psychoanalysis* (1940a [1938]) and *Splitting of the Ego in the Process of Defence* (1940b [1938]), have made it possible to account for the coexistence of distinct modes of functioning within one and the same subject.

And yet, in these clinical configurations it appears that splitting cannot be reduced to a mechanism of defence aimed at protecting the ego; rather, it has a topographical dimension concerning the psychic topography as a whole. This bipartition of psychic life reveals in reality the coexistence of two distinct sectors of the unconscious: the repressed sexual dynamic unconscious and another sector designated as the "amential unconscious", which is formed not by repression but by the proscription of memory traces. (The term "amential" relates to Theodor Meynert's concept of *amentia*, with a view to insisting on the "thoughtless" mode of reaction of this unconscious, which takes the shape of the ego-disorganisation that is typical of mental confusion.)

In the context of analytic work, this other sector can make itself known through counter-transference manifestations that essentially take the form of what the analyst experiences as manoeuvres aimed at ensuring the immobility of the material and spatial frame of the session, but also through the patient's recourse to a concrete, logical, factual, "operational" form of thinking aimed at suffocating the associative thinking of the analysand and analyst alike. The domination and "mineralization" of the analyst reveal the constitution independent of any form of thought of the amential unconscious which, when it is activated, manifests itself in the violent mode of compulsion, taking the form of an acute somatic crisis, a delusion or an auto or hetero-aggressive *passage à l'acte.* Compulsive acting out may thus be seen as a form of reaction to the threat of "desubjectivation". Clinically, the existence of this sector constituted by elements resistant to any form of psychic metabolisation can be identified by the extinction of fantasy activity, in particular following interventions by the analyst that touch on these "silent" zones of the analysand's psychic life. What remains proscribed presents itself first in an affective form, in the body of the clinician, and implies a capacity to resist attempts at petrification before it can find possible forms of figuration.

A patient's invasive description of the bodily deficiencies of her body, which was a heavy burden for her, coexisted with the detailed presentation of the constraints of her time schedule and occupied for several months the space of the sessions. Her prepubertal physical appearance echoed the impasses of the adolescent process from which any form of conflictual expression was barred by the onset of an endocrinal pathology at the moment of puberty. While oedipal issues occasionally came to the surface thanks to relations marked by the stamp of the rivalry that she had with other students of her preparatory class for the *grandes écoles,* it was narcissistic issues related to her inability to go beyond a depreciated maternal figure that dominated the scene. Any aggressive manifestation towards her inaccessible mother who was essentially concerned with controlling the hygiene of her daughter's body, which sometimes involved being violent towards her, was regularly neutralised by the patient, who simply gave a continuous description of the factual content of her days. The unrepressed unconscious derivatives of adult violence manifested themselves at the clinical level by an extinction of fantasy activity and a reduction of associativity to silence, dominated by her impression of no longer "feeling anything", which also paralysed the analyst's associative capacity.

The appearance of a dysmorphophobic experience, following the evocation of a dream during which she failed the competitive entrance exam to her school would, however, reveal the feelings of hatred that her body, which she experienced as persecuting, aroused in her. She said she felt "distressed" by her imposing bust that she sought to cover up by various restrictive manoeuvres, before a new "defect" on her nose made her feel the need for corrective surgery.

The intensity of the alien character of the body that manifested itself in her may be analysed, classically, in terms of narcissistic disturbances linked with the impasses of the pubertal process. However, the dream also revealed the return, in a persecuting form, of the expressive and, in particular, aggressive functions of the body, proscribed by adult violence.

Further reading

Freud, S. (1940 [1938]). *An outline of psychoanalysis. S.E.* 23. London: Hogarth, pp. 139–207.

Freud, S. (1940 [1938]). *The splitting of the ego in the process of defence. S.E.* 23. London: Hogarth, pp. 271–278.

KEY WORDS Amentia, splitting, compulsion, violence.

IMPERFECT SEPARATIONS

CLAUDE ARLÈS

Not long after the birth of her first child, a woman began an analysis. This decision and her maternity resulted from the same wish to recover from the omnipresence of a dead father at the beginning of her adolescence. During her sessions, her constant mentions of her father remained consistently imbued with interminable criticisms that for a long time prevented any possibility of intervention. Through this suffering, which she clung to so strongly, she sought less to diminish her impulses than to maintain her attachment to the paternal imago without any possibility of accepting, for a while, the perspectives of change and separations envisaged in the analysis. She did not accept even the bare outlines of an interpretation, though one day the analyst managed to tell her that she seemed to be waiting for something from him, yet rejected obstinately everything that he was able to say to her. While they were both troubled by the suddenness and strangeness of these words uttered by the analyst, and by the term "mortified" assigned by her transference displacements and those of the analyst to this silent immobilism, she associated to the lively memory of her father and of her fantasy of never having found favour in his eyes in spite of all her efforts to satisfy him. This thought and her reference to the gaze of the other were striking. The analyst took the full measure at this moment of all the expectation and vitality that could sometimes be perceived in her eyes when she arrived for her session.

A few months later, this thought returned in a striking way. She had barely settled down on the couch when she once again asked the analyst if he could tell her the name of a reproduction in the waiting room. Faced with his silence and with the striking images that came to her mind, she said that she had been troubled for a long time by this abstract form that was evocative of her father's gaze. Suddenly, she seemed to be approaching what she was looking for in her analysis after having wanted for a while to bury it in the background of this painting or to taxidermise it in the complacent and silent immobilism of her analyst. It was no longer merely a painting that she was contemplating but, in a true reversal, her father who was looking at her. She recalled how, as a worried little girl, she had seen the anguished look of her father as he was dying and got a glimpse of her own gaze full of suffering because she had not been able, as was the case with the analyst up to the present moment, to tell him everything that she expected and hoped to obtain from him, and to hear what he had to say.

Michel Gribinski (2002),[1] a reader and translator of D.W. Winnicott, shared the same taste for simple words, those in which the poiesis of the *infans* remains apparent. The poetry of the expression "imperfect separations" attests to his exploration of this lapse of time, of this space between the image and the idea or between the word and the thing, a space that André Gide referred to as the habitat of poetic emotion. From different paths and angles, he envisages the innumerable separations in which human beings, the analyst and the analysand are confronted with their primal incestuous attachments and with the work disengagement or renunciation that is implied. In spite of the richness of his writing, he lays claim to a certain imperfection when the word, like that of the poet, gives a glimpse of the dazzling representative faculty which, like a squiggle game,[2] invites the interlocutor to participate in a creative game or an interpretative reverie. Recoiling from entering into explanations, his thought rarely allows itself to be reduced, except at the price of losing its substance and vitality. Like analytic work in sessions, only its movement, its force or its dazzling effects can be reported and above all transmitted.

By vocation, Gribinski reminds us, the transference repudiates separation. Like dreams, memories or symptoms, its aim is to maintain, in a disguised form and through a series of displacements, the presence of the object and the precious primal attachments that are linked to it. Transference and separation are consubstantial. The very essence of the analytic situation, moreover, is to favour its installation and the return of the object so as to take possession of it and, secondarily, to make separation from it possible. Beyond the working-through of the transference and a partial renunciation of the primal incestuous attachment, the separation is played out in several places and at different levels. In this respect, it can only be plural and imperfect. Just as internal as it is external, separation also affects the analyst when he tries to avoid or fill, somewhat hastily, the other gap between clinical work and theory. Sensitive to the work of the negative, Gribinski invites the analysand and analyst alike to let its imprint form itself in them. Beyond the wrenching emotional experience and transformation of the interpretative moment, he conceives the imperfection of separation, its awkwardness and its irreducibility, as the token of a living movement that continues in time, well beyond the session and the analysis. The analyst must also separate himself from his objects and give up his theoretical finery in order to be able to reweave a living theory out of rediscovered theoretical fragments, letting himself be touched by an inner voice, the signature of his transference onto the analytic situation. From its side, too, the transference becomes entangled, and separation, an opening onto the living, can only ever be incomplete, always a failure and fortunately imperfect.

Tolerating, and then recognising, the transference of representations onto the analyst or, more laterally, onto this painting bears witness to a shared psychic ordeal. For the analysand it is one of recognising herself in the pressing expectations of this little girl of her father and, in so doing, of accepting the outlines of a separation that she had hitherto refused. For the analyst it is one of extricating himself from the position of melancholic identification to which he has consented under the effect of the transference whose interpretation costs him by imposing a separation that an obscure part of himself always regards as incomplete, refuses to accept, and whose bite he experiences again in such moments. In this respect, as in every analysis, the analysis of this young woman bears witness to these "imperfect separations".

Notes

1 He was also the translator of *The Spontaneous Gesture: Selected Letters of D.W. Winnicott* (Winnicott, 1987).

2 A projective technique creating intimacy between the patient and his/her therapist, establishing an area of play between them.

Further reading

Gribinski, M. (2002). *Les Séparations imparfaites*. Paris: Gallimard. (Series: Connaissance de l'inconscient).

KEY WORDS Countertransference, imago, separation, transference.

LIVED EXPERIENCE

JEAN-YVES TAMET

The train was departing and the young girl, distraught at being taken away from her mother, looked at her standing on the station platform. Later, when she was also a mother, even though she herself had been neglected without understanding the reasons for it, she nonetheless let her mother take care of her own daughter. Why had people hit her and rejected her so often? Why had she been separated from this mother who was undoubtedly abusive, but whom she loved madly and found attractive? She was to ask herself this question for a long time. These distant events had taken place between women, in a world from which men were excluded and who did not seem concerned by what was going on under their noses. Here, life as a child was spent in childcare centres run by other women with daughters like her, who were isolated, often silent or suddenly violent. And then, one day, she was allowed to return home where the usual violence resumed, this time in her family. Soon, having grown older, she was the one who left; she was alone in another way, but at the time of her choosing. Until, that is, she returned home again as an adult, still alone, but with her own daughter. And there was the intolerable feeling, humiliating even, that repetition was at work, the repetition of a history that could only repeat itself.

A lot of time and sessions, but also long moments of troubled incomprehension, were necessary before this narrative could finally organise itself so simply and find the rhythm of its chronology by bringing together the fragmentary and painful traces. Words had to pass beyond blanks and tears, anguished silences and sudden rages against her mother who was a fighter, against him, her forgetful father, and against herself, the little girl who was too submissive, too submissive. The analysis helped her to give herself time and to make it her own time, where she could talk about herself and listen to herself, organising to some extent, with the support of words, the different images present in disorder in her head, where separations and wrenching experiences jostled. She had thus established her temporality, understood to some degree the weight of obscure forces, and finally she began to love herself better.

The analyst and his method were the guardians of this long process of giving shape to destructuring experiences: The slow work of putting things into words was facilitated step by step, word after word, during the sessions. When words were lacking or when they imposed the perception of the "muteness of language", the analyst drew on *la vivance,* a term often used by Edmundo Gómez Mango. It gave him the strength to continue listening without yielding to defeatism or to exhaustion. For their part, with courage and obstination, finding in analysis the strength to grapple with images that are present but terrifying, some patients construct the narrative of their broken journey and let "the mass of sensations without words of affective memory, the subterranean and simmering life of *Erlebnisse*, '*vivances*' or lived experiences" come to life (Gómez Mango, 2009, p. 195): they are often repeated in the transference with an obstinacy whose intensity is akin to the inaugural psychic drama.

Gómez Mango links the fragile words of the patient to the silent listening of analysis which thus establishes a situation in which the young child, an *infans* whose language is barely established, is confronted with the multitude of sensory and sensual traces far removed from any established process of thought. These experiences are constitutive of *vivances* which, sometimes as a violent and destabilising experience but also as a discovery of the world, constitute the foundations of the assumption of speech to come. By associating these experiences with the "muteness of language", hope opens up, according to Gómez Mango, and with it the hope that the captives can be liberated and the obstacles undone. For his part, he often draws on exile both as a personal experience and as an emblematic experience of what happens in the way of resistance in analysis. In effect, exile, especially if it is suffered more than chosen, echoes with this experience of transition between the world of childhood and that of adulthood, but also between the modalities of psychic functioning that Freud described in terms of primary or secondary processes. For, in analyses that are so often marked by the ordeal of desolation and the experience of sensory deprivation, the transference favours a new understanding of their psychic traces while making it possible to tolerate the primitive and wild character of the primary processes.

My initial remarks, a brief summary of a delicate clinical context, do not bear witness to the ordeals that this woman had to face so that, during this analysis, the different sequences of her memories scattered into many painful fragments could be established in the form of a narrative. Over the course of time, patients sought analysis who had gone through life experiences in which their capacity for living had been undermined and in which breakdowns had led them to rub shoulders with inhumanity. "This silent language" that the analyst and analysand discovered together as a specific feature of this analysis "is the metaphor for what language cannot reach but strives obstinately to express" (Gómez Mango, 2009, p. 195). This is one of the valuable lessons that can be drawn from this term *vivance,* which, thanks to the use of it suggested by Gómez Mango, wrenches words from formlessness. Resorting to what designates an existential experience makes it possible to bring into play numerous references to which it refers and to liberate in the analyst an area of creation.

Further reading

Apfelbaum, L. (2009). Histoire de cas. *Libres cahiers pour la psychanalyse,* 20: 7–17.

Gómez Mango, E. (2009). *Un muet dans la langue.* Paris: Gallimard (Series: Connaissance de l'inconscient).

Tamet, J.-Y. (1989). Il errait et il ne comprenait pas. *Nouvelle Revue de psychanalyse,* 40: 251–259.

KEY WORDS Construction, experience, narrative, silence.

12

OTHERNESS

THE RELATION TO THE UNKNOWN

PATRICK MEROT

A man who had been in analysis for a year had been talking in recent sessions about a painting he did a few years ago. One day, he arrived with a large painting with its front side facing his coat. The analyst said nothing and let him organise himself with it. After a moment of hesitation, he put the painting down at the end of the couch, leaning against the wall so that both he and the analyst could see it. It was a dark painting, glowing with light in places, showing two human forms whose faces were barely outlined other than as figures of death that were leaning in an oppressive way against a black mass in which everything was merged. Between this man and this woman – for one could clearly recognise a couple – a lighter mark of paint seemed to depict a child witnessing the scene.

He talked about the painting that was an attempt to evoke the memory he had of his grandparents killing an animal in a sort of unequal and confused fight. "I will have to do the painting again," he said, "so that the child can see better what's going on." That's how he saw himself – for the child half-hidden on the side of the scene was, of course, himself – fascinated by the dark area. Looking at this painting today, he was looking at it again, but from the other side of the mirror, at what he was still unable to see. Presenting all this in the session and in the particular setting that he had invented, he let himself be seen looking and looking at himself. In the plane of symmetry of this setting, between the background of the painting and the foreground of the spectators, in the undecipherable obscurity of the mass in the centre of the painting, was the terror of a hole, of flesh, of the sexual, and of death.

In this scene, different aspects constitutive of the relation to the unknown (*relation d'inconnu,* Rosolato, 1978a) are condensed: the enigma of death and sex depicted through an attempted sublimation which tries to give shape to the unrepresentable and, beyond the object, to circumscribe this unknown dimension of which the human world is constituted and towards which the subject unflaggingly turns his gaze.

The analysis of a female patient had for a long time presented an apparent oedipal configuration in which the mother's violence and the father's passivity had played a predominant role, particularly in adolescence, at a time when her awakening towards her father had been particularly intense. It subsequently emerged that this account which attributed great importance to her attachment to her father concealed a relationship with her mother that had been built in a context of the fear of abandonment. It turned out that this fear was still predominant in the present and that the patient had been trying to find a solution in a radical religious experience. It was not, however, until after several years of analysis that she was able to speak about her religious faith, because she considered that this domain was not the concern of analysis, that it was an unsharable matter of privacy, much more secret even than her sexual life. In periods of difficulty, what tormented her was the feeling that she was no longer loved by God. Her relationship with the other was only possible in the form of maximum idealisation: jouissance or prayer; she needed to find in this absolute other what the neurotic compromise did not permit. This concealment of her problems with her mother and of the religious question which amounted for her to an irresistible yearning for a superhuman beyond bore witness to the importance of the relation to the unknown. It was the consideration given to this dimension, marked here by a maximum idealisation of religious ideals, that permitted the analytic process to emerge from the impasse.

The relation to the unknown describes what may appear to be inaccessible, inexpressible, unimaginable, ungraspable, unreal and invisible. It stands in contrast with the object-relation, has its origin in the archaic relationship with the mother, and refers to an unchangeable relationship with the mother alone, a phallic, omnipotent and destructive mother.

The relation to the unknown is very present in ideals, whether religious, moral, philosophical, political or scientific, ideals whose realisation is supposed to bring the greatest jouissance, an echo of primordial times.

At the heart of myths – which deal explicitly with origins – it is present in religions through the maternal imprint that they conserve (including as a component of monotheistic religions) and is of decisive importance for mystics.

It participates in the course of desire, as being beyond the object-relation: "The relation to the unknown," writes Rosolato, "is the background, the hollow or the void against which the object-relation stands out" (1978a, p. 272). Elsewhere, he notes that if the drive implies an object, desire implies an unknown (Rosolato, 1996, p. 127).

The orientation of analytic treatment around the relation to the unknown leads to prioritising the dimension of the negative, where the focus is on the void, the hollow and loss (Rosolato, 1999, p. 215). We can also observe a tendency in analysis towards excluding any kind of approach to the unknown; this tendency is maximised in obsessional neurosis where the repetitive and factual way of speaking is aimed at never venturing into the unknown.

Further reading

Rosolato, G. (1977). Que contemplait Freud sur l'Acropole? *Nouvelle Revue de psychanalyse*, 15: 125–138.

Rosolato, G. (1978). La relation d'inconnu comme cheminement. In: *La Relation d'inconnu*. Paris: Gallimard (Series: Connaissance de l'inconscient), pp. 7–19.

Rosolato, G. (1978 [1968]). L'ombilic et la relation d'inconnu. In: *La Relation d'inconnu*. Paris: Gallimard (Series: Connaissance de l'inconscient), pp. 254–280.

Rosolato, G., et al., (2009). *L'Inconnu*. Paris: Presses Universitaires de France (Series: Petite Bibliothèque de psychanalyse).

KEY WORDS Desire, ideals, phallic mother, relation to the unknown, object-relation.

THE SITE OF THE STRANGER

OLIVIA TODISCO

Pierre Fédida (2009a) considers the psychoanalytic situation as a "site of the stranger", based on the foundational myth of the murder of the primal father. In Freud's work, the "event of the murder of the father" mainly concerns the origin of humanity and the constitution of a primitive ego, but Fédida, transposing it in an original way to analysis, sees it as both the point of origin and the horizon of every analysis. The patient's speech, depending on the phases and periods of the treatment, is addressed either to the primal father, whose murder (*meurtre*) is always "to come" – which he calls "*meurtralité*" – or to the father who is already dead, hence his theorisation of absence.

He thus puts "negative hallucination" at the centre of his theory of analysis: the analyst *is* the stranger and his presence is an "absent presence". That is why he does not answer the analysand in person and avoids any form of self-representation in the transference as father, mother, etc., leaving the place of the interlocutor empty. This conception of the psychoanalytic situation goes hand in hand with a preference for construction rather than interpretation. According to the author, construction is better suited to marking the separation between the scenes of the patient and the analyst. Fédida is thus opposed to a "communicational" and "interrelational" conception of analysis.

The site of the stranger is a place of passage, of transportation, that is marked not only by the strangeness of the analyst but also by other forms like that of the unconscious, that of language that welcomes it, a language worked on by transference regression, that of the fossil memory of the infantile, and, finally, that of the transference of which the dream is the paradigm, which can only be interpreted in a language where meaning and substance are one, that is, a language that restores through its enunciation the sensory imagination of words in attractive affinity with memory traces.

The following clinical fragment shows the necessity, for the analyst, of tolerating the transference of his patient, whatever it may be like, and of leaving empty the place of the interlocutor, whatever the cost may be.

For a long time, the analyst did not understand what had brought the patient to the analysis; she simply noted that he entered into the family of analysts in the same way as he had lived in his own, that is, with an occult science of affinities that had led him, as an adolescent, to his young homosexual cousin, and that had also led him today to her, a friend of an analyst who was close to his former editor. She was very quickly assailed by his transferences: depending on the day, she resembled the Jewish fiancée of Rembrandt or alternatively she possessed the pathetic innocence of Cécile de Volanges in *Dangerous Liaisons* (Choderlos de Laclos, 1782), the gentleness of the young psychologist who had helped his sister overcome her mutism, or the perversity of his editor – did she not have in her waiting room a book by Jean Genet? With time, it was this last transference that prevailed and, from being a woman "who liked homosexuals" she became homosexual, like his editor. She realised now that he had come I order to sort out a crisis that he had been going through for several years, ever since he had been ridiculed in public, following one of his lectures, by a friend of his editor. The latter had said – albeit speaking about another person – that he had "hidden sexual tendencies", but he *knew* that the friend was speaking about him. All this was in revenge for the fact that he had just been speaking to them about his father, a man who could not stand "queers with AIDS" and who had been delighted on hearing about the premature death of his cousin.

After recalling this "incident", while every other subject disappeared from his sessions, he finally committed an "unforgiveable" error by handing in an article on sociology from which it could be inferred that he was against the institution of marriage. Who would not see in it an allusion to "marriage for all"? Now, the whole of Paris and his editor "knew". Nothing could assuage his guilt, not even very considerable sums of money paid to Act Up from his father's legacy. His life then turned into a waking nightmare: "they" would massacre him; the whole world had it in for him; posters were being displayed in Paris for or against gay marriage; a man had approached him in the street; associations had sent him application forms to become a donor; a 4x4 had stopped alongside him when he was on his bike, a female friend had forgotten a book at his place, "guess by whom?" He begged the analyst to understand that it wasn't a fantasy, that he would soon be dead; he asked her to confirm that she was homosexual, that she would do everything she could to calm "them" down, that he was really the object of a conspiracy.

She said nothing.

Further reading

Fédida, P. (2009). L'interlocuteur. In: *Le site de l'étranger.* Paris: Presses Universitaires de France (Series: Quadrige Essais Débats), pp. 121–186.

Fédida, P. (2009). L'epos – le site. In: *Le site de l'étranger.* Paris: Presses Universitaires de France (Series: Quadrige Essais Débats), pp. 81–92.

Freud, S. (1913 [1912]). *Totem and taboo. S.E.* 13. London: Hogarth, pp. 1–161.

Freud, S. (1921). The group and the primal horde. In: *Group psychology and the analysis of the ego. S.E.* 18. London: Hogarth, pp. 122–128.

KEY WORDS Stranger, negative hallucination, murder, father.

THE MOTHER'S FATHER

JEAN-YVES TAMET

We are indebted to Little Hans for having erected the figure of his mother as the central character of the complex nature of the identifications between a child and his biological parents; but there is another specific bond, often passed over in silence, that also secretly organises a work of identification, namely, the mother's father and the configuration to which he is subjected once the woman has become a mother. As a central element with barely identifiable contours, this representation operates in silence.

A man called to speak about his grandson whom he liked a lot and about whom he was rather concerned; aged eight, the grandson had little interest in school, even though he had a sharp and curious mind. This caring man said, almost reluctantly, that this child reminded him of his daughter's difficulties: even though she was brilliant, she had had to make do with a job that, according to him, was well beneath her university qualifications. He felt she had failed to make the best of her capacities and then, sharing a second secret, he added, "As I did during my schooling." The analyst was all the more astonished in that neither he nor his daughter had a modest professional situation but it was undoubtedly a matter of the intimate perception that this man had of a trajectory that he felt was common to all three of them: he, his daughter and his grandson had all failed in the same domain of intellectual performance; there was something invisible uniting them. It was the case, moreover, that all three lived under the tutelary shadow of the grandson's somewhat overwhelming great-grandfather, a man who had been famous for playing a pioneering role in his discipline.

A little later, the analyst saw the child who presented a form of phobia of the written trace that stood in contrast with his bright and questioning mind, inventive even, as the analyst was gradually to discover. But, before this could happen, a specific phobia had to be overcome which prevented him from staying alone with the analyst. This obstacle was overcome by letting him decide how the meetings unfolded; then, the exchanges were organised around paper constructions made in front of the analyst; sometimes, as if by chance, the child asked what the spelling of certain words was that he wanted to write in order to be able to comment on his productions. At this stage, the idea of the registration or perpetuation of the trace seemed to be at the heart of the difficulties, even though he was not strictly speaking troubled by this! By way of following up on the initial telephone call, his grandfather often accompanied him and, each time, paid for the session with a cheque on which one could read the maiden name of his daughter, thus his own name attached to that of her husband.

Through this symptom, this child became part of a line of failures that had been experienced as such. Had not his grandfather himself practiced the same profession as his own father who had once been a famous, gifted and inventive pioneer, in short, a founder? Henri Normand (2007) has drawn attention to a singular clinical situation that could be useful for understanding this case. He points out that "the mother arrives in the world with a history and three loves, at least; she has been a daughter; she has had the love of another man, and finally she is the mother of a child" [in this case a son]... In addition, these three loves have grown through her love...for, and with, her mother" (p. 61). There is thus an intersection of the temporalities of the loves and of the disappointments concerning which the child becomes both the catalyser and the surface of registration. His psychic life is constituted and anchored to a meshwork that consists both of his mother's renunciation of her oedipal loves and of her adventure with the child's father. We cannot, however, overlook the fact that separation is also active on the side of the mother's father, who is faced with his daughter's moving away from him. These tensions are not exempt from pain, which creates the crucible of the identity of "this" child.

This little patient showed talent in creating three-dimensional objects in space: was he not trying to give concrete form to his perception of the delicate psychic proximities arising from the past loves of his mother: I thought that being inventive in front of me would help bring about in him a psychic liberation from the intellectual world of his mother who herself was very much behoven to her father's views. In effect, "a mother's loves are no jolly matter!", writes Normand (p. 62), because they expose the child at an early stage to tensions that he cannot decipher. In this case, they no doubt made intellectual work into a worthwhile task in which it would be good to be a devoted innovator like the ancestor had been. However, the mother's father saw himself as a castrated son in the intellectual domain and did not feel legitimate with regard to knowledge. The phantasmatic place of the mother is singular because it is often overlooked that, as a former daughter, she is the one who makes the psychic development of the son possible: it is the presence of incestuous projections that liberates the mother while playing a role in the sexualisation for the child. A situation had been established here whose outcome was unknown, but one on which the destiny of entry into the oedipal complex and, subsequently, its resolution, would depend. Normand thus situates renunciation along this trajectory that has its starting point in an archaic Oedipus. Could the male image that this woman presents to her son be an imago of her own father, with the conflicts of love that are associated with it?

It is interesting that none of the three spoke about the ancestor, but his name, borne by his son, immediately evoked in the analyst's mind the memory of his talent. If this case is concerned with a transmission between a mother and her son, it leaves open another destiny of transmission, namely, the impact that the mother's father has when the child is a girl.

Further reading

Normand, H. (2007). *Les Amours d'une mère.* Paris: L'Olivier (Series: Penser/Rêver).

KEY WORDS Love, identification, mother, representation.

THE ENIGMATIC MESSAGE

JEAN H. GUÉGAN

A young woman has been coming to talk for a few years. She often speaks about her intellectual and emotional journey with a constant air of astonishment at having succeeded so well. Each time she has success, she changes direction. For example, she completed her thesis but no sooner had she obtained it than she immediately turned her interests to quite another domain. When her analysis began, moreover, she was in the process of making a new conversion towards a plastic arts activity that interested her intensely. Remarkably, each of these changes constituted a definitive break, without further ado; the same was true in her emotional life which was marked by a succession of sudden and deliberate separations that even sometimes involved having an abortion. Each was followed by an immediate displacement towards other investments as if no working-through were possible, as if no experience could leave any traces. She then brought a dream: "The space of the session was transformed, the couch was in a different position and was stained with blood. The analyst then rushed towards the window, and opened it. The patient was afraid he might fall. In a further sequence, a surgeon explained that the act that he had just carried out could not be reimbursed by health insurance…as was the case here!" The patient associated quickly to a 2011 film by Pedro Almodóvar called *The Skin I Live In* (*La piel que habito*) in which, after multiple surgical interventions, a surgeon transforms a man into a woman with an ideal body. After a moment of silence, she added: "There is no treatment form here either, and I am becoming a woman; I come here to become a woman again." Becoming a woman again? The analyst took up this formulation whose impact made him listen more closely. Was he to see it as a new version of Freud's hypothesis according to which, on entering the phallic stage, "the little girl is a little man"? Or, alternatively, as a transference manifestation that had pushed the patient hitherto to think of herself as being loved as a boy by her male analyst, thereby repeating retroactively something of an unconscious message emanating from her parents? Gradually, the associations that unfolded reconfigured what she had said about her childhood, throwing light on the singularity of the "enigmatic message" of which she was the recipient. Indeed, when she was only five years old, her parents had separated "unexpectedly", suddenly, and with little explanation. She had then stayed alone with her father while her mother disappeared into a community with a very strong feminine (homosexual?) colouring, only forming a couple with a man again 10 years later. During all this time, the patient stayed with a "tender and attentive" father, but whose sexual choice was uncertain. The skin she lived in was affected by this. The disturbance manifested itself suddenly in the dream, as did the major sexual impact on her history of the enigmatic message delivered by her parents.

Before he can speak, the infant is from the outset thrown into a world governed by communication between him and another person whose active presence is made necessary by his disarray. A complex process then begins for, on the adult's side, cultural transmissions and bodily care are infiltrated by unconscious sexual phantasies. A dissymmetrical situation is thus created: the adult, who is the bearer of a sexual unconscious (which is an enigma for the recipient and for himself) transmits it to an *infans* who receives passively what he does not have the psychic capacity to integrate and translate because his topography is still only in a fledgling state. Such is the content of the enigmatic message, a term Jean Laplanche prefers to that of "signifier" to underline that prior to spoken language there is a heterogeneous communication to which the child is exposed as soon as he is born. In the parental messages, it maintains the tension of the non-organisation and enigma of infantile sexuality. Of course, in analysis the impact of these enigmatic messages on the infantile sexuality of a patient is only visible through the formations and deformations that organise themselves during the movements of the transference.

For the patient to whom I am referring here, the enigma of the sexual fantasies of the father and mother clearly plays a decisive role. It includes homosexual aspects which oblige her feminine position to find its place within the complex temporality of "becoming again" rather than of "becoming". This ambiguity of the parental message may in part have played an unconscious protective role, but it also constitutes a danger for her ego. Finally, it is also a source of ambivalence that can be seen in the mobility of her investments. In any case, the enigma of an enigmatic message can only be approached, at best. However, in each subject, it encourages greater complexity and diversification of the organisation of the original state of bisexuality.

Further reading

Beauvoir, S. de. (2009 [1949]). *The second sex*, trans. C. Borde and S. Malovany-Chevalier. London: Random House/Alfred A. Knopf.

Freud, S. (1933 [1932]). Femininity. In: *New introductory lectures on psychoanalysis. S.E.* 22. London: Hogarth, pp. 112–135.

Laplanche, J. (1989). *New foundations for psychoanalysis*, trans D. Macey. Oxford: Blackwell.

Laplanche, J. (2011). Gender, sex, the sexual. In: *Freud and the sexual.* New York, NY: International Psychoanalytic Books, pp. 159–202.

Laplanche, J. (2011). Starting from the fundamental anthropological situation. In: *Freud and the sexual.* New York, NY: International Psychoanalytic Books, pp. 99–114.

KEY WORDS Gender assignment, dream, infantile sexuality, transference.

THE DEAD MOTHER

LAURENT DANON-BOILEAU

A brilliant young academic had been in analysis for a long time. Recently, it seemed that the analysis was coming to an end: he was able to speak about the termination. And yet, on returning from the Christmas holidays, without any explicit reason, he came to his session feeling somewhat depressed. "It's strange," he said, "everything went very well, and I notice that I have discovered pleasure in living once again. What is happening is really quite pleasant. It was coming to see you that made me sad." Initially, he let himself associate freely, reviving various situations of separation and mourning that he had spoken about on many occasions, before concluding: "No, it's funny, what I feel this time is less heavy and at the same time deeper. It's as if you were staying by my side to help me cope with a sudden disappearance. You are both the one who disappears and the one to whom I would like to complain about it. Moreover, it's not really a disappearance. It's something else. When you opened the door, you seemed elsewhere. Maybe I don't interest you anymore. That would be normal, in fact, because I'm doing fine. After all, after eight years of analysis, it may be the right moment to stop. We should talk about it. Unless, that is, you have some personal worries."

The analyst waited a few moments, and then replied: "Being sad in order to have a good reason to continue the work with me and to distract me from my personal worries" After saying this, the analyst immediately felt that it was not right, *déjà vu, déja entendue.* The patient, moreover, did not fail to point this out: "Yes, I have thought about that. Moreover, we have often spoken about it, but this time, no, it's not that." Was it a denial on his part?

At the following session, he lay down on the couch and took up the thread of what he had been saying as if the session had not been interrupted since the last meeting: "There's something that I did not tell you last time. At one point, as I was speaking to you, there were two images of my mother in my mind. I didn't know what to do with them. The first was from a photo: I was three years old. We were on a beach, and I was playing with a shovel in the sand near the water. She seemed happy and was smiling at me. She was clearly having fun and so was I. I imagine the photo must've been taken by my father. And then this image faded away and another took its place. I don't think it was a photo; it was more a recollection. My mother was opposite me. Her hair was falling across her face. She was standing. I could not see her eyes. She was doing something, tidying up, as if she was folding clothes to put them in a cupboard. She said something to me that I didn't understand." This duality of his mother's face reappeared in his associations. Gradually, the patient evoked, more clearly than he had ever done before, a moment of his life as a child when he suddenly felt that something was changing. He never situated this moment precisely, but from that time on, it was if his mother had been elsewhere, absorbed by something that he could never name.

A short while later, on the occasion of a family gathering, he went by car to the country with his sister. She told him that she felt much the same way as he did; then she evoked a conversation with their mother in which the latter confessed that she had lost a child when she was two months pregnant. "I asked my sister if she remembered anything else, clothes, for example. But I was alone. She couldn't remember. Moreover, I don't even know if it's true." However, after these sessions, it became possible to link the sudden withdrawal of cathexis of which the patient felt he had been a victim due to his mother's mourning for her lost child to a nameable, historical event.

The work continued for a further year. The patient was able to see how much his mother's sudden disarray had laid the neurotic foundations of an impossible challenge in him: saving women from their depression. In his later life, he had often felt called upon to give back the taste for living to depressed women. But, as with his mother when he was a child, he never succeeded in providing them with solace. It was after having experienced this movement acutely in the transference (one day when the analyst had indeed been preoccupied) that something of this singular position of the dead mother and of the seduction that she exerts could be elaborated and then renounced.

In a paper given on 20th May 1980 at the Paris Psychoanalytical Society (subsequently taken up again in *Life Narcissism, Death Narcissism)*, André Green defines the complex of the dead mother as follows: "[a]n imago…has been constituted in the child's psyche, following maternal depression, brutally transforming the living object, a source of vitality for the child, into a distant, toneless and practically inanimate figure, deeply impregnating the cathexes of certain patients…and weighing on the destiny of their objected-related and narcissistic libidinal future" (2001 [1983] p. 170). A few lines further on, he adds: "the dead mother, contrary to what one might think, is thus a mother who remains alive but who is, so to speak, psychically dead in the eyes of the young child in her care" (p. 170). It is a matter of a sort of involuntary mistreatment by a mother who is suddenly overwhelmed and preoccupied by bereavement and the consequent process of mourning, whereas hitherto she had been "good enough" for the child. The suddenness of the withdrawal of cathexis, in addition to the material presence of the object, form an obstacle to the elaboration of a "depressive position" of quality. For the subject, this results in "psychic voids" both in the narcissistic and object-related register, even when these voids can be filled subsequently by secondary recathexes. It is in the transference, thus in the presence of the object, that the most specific characteristics of this configuration are deployed.

Further reading

Green, A. (2001 [1983]). *Life narcissism, death narcissism*, A. Weller. London: Free Association Books.

KEY WORDS Mourning, melancholia, dead mother, narcissism, separation.

THE FREUDIAN THING

ISABELLE ALFANDARY

A woman of foreign origins, who had been living in France for several years, reported during a session a conversation that she had had with one of her female friends on the subject of her expatriation dating back many years. The friend was astonished by the fact that, by leaving her country, she had left behind her loved ones, and also that she had voluntarily cut herself off from the culture, language and environment in which she had grown up and to which she remained deeply attached. Although this woman returned regularly to her country of origin, she recognised that she continued to wonder why she had made this change. This no doubt explains the fact that she had noted and heard in a very particular way a remark that was quite innocuous. In the course of the session, she said that she shared her friend's thoughts and acknowledged the "deep pleasure" that the familiarity of one's native country and the intimacy of one's mother language represent for each one of us. On several occasions during the session, she spoke of the "deep pleasure" linked to early childhood, to her experience more than her recollections of it, from which it is not easy to cut oneself off, and of which it was astonishing that one would want to deprive oneself. At the same time, it seemed to her that this "deep pleasure" was not exempt from feelings of anxiety that accompanied it in a way that was as manifest as it was inexplicable.

The reasons that can drive a subject to leave, to alienate himself, to avoid what he loves above all raise questions for psychoanalysis. In his seminar on the ethics of psychoanalysis, Jacques Lacan (1997 [1986]) takes up Freud's considerations on the prohibition against incest: "Freud designates the prohibition of incest as the underlying principle of the primordial law, the law of which all other cultural developments are no more than the consequences and the ramifications. And at the same time he identifies incest as the fundamental desire" (p. 67). Starting from Freud, Lacan endows the prohibition against, and the desire for, incest, with a philosophical name, the sovereign good, which he identifies with the mother who, for the child, is a possession subject to prohibition. This may explain the fact that a subject desires nothing so much as the proximity of which he deliberately deprives himself. The adjective "deep" (*profond*) chosen by the analysand to describe the said pleasure resides as much in the intensity as the archaism from which it proceeds. The pleasure principle is defined by Freud as one of the principles that governs the functioning of mental activity and aims to avoid the unpleasure that can result from excessive excitation.

Now Lacan argues that the object in relation to which primal experience is organised – the mother – is an object that, in certain cases, "literally gives too much pleasure" (p. 54). The deep pleasure of which the analysand speaks and which can also be understood as an alliance of words, which she associates with an infantile experience, points to excess, the too-much-pleasure that contact with the mother represents for the infant. The fact that a subject relates this "deep pleasure" to the question of his geographical displacement, to his voluntary exile, is elucidated by the relationship to the Thing (*das Ding*). Insofar as the subject structures himself and comes to himself in his relationship to the Thing, as Lacan calls it, he must protect himself against it all the more in that he feels deeply attracted by it. *Das Ding*, as Lacan conceives it, following Freud, has a function of structuring and psychic regulation that proves to be decisive: the subjective structures that we call neuroses can be deduced from the relationship of each subject to this Other described as "prehistoric, unforgettable" (p. 53).

Further reading

Lacan, J. (1997 [1986]). *Ethics of psychoanalysis, 1959–1960. The seminar of Jacques Lacan, book VII*, ed. J.-A. Miller, trans. D. Porter. New York: Norton.

KEY WORDS Anxiety, prehistoric other, prohibition against incest, mother.

INCESTUAL AND INCESTUALITY

JACQUES ANGELERGUES

We are indebted to Paul-Claude Racamier for these notions. Their success partly resides in their author's characteristic way with words, for what they designate seems immediately familiar and unusual. For Racamier, the terms incestual and incestuality can be employed when, in the subject's psychic history, something took place in the register of incest but "a genealogical distance was established in which the issues became confused" (Racamier, 1995, p. 98). For him, this situation is a source of destructiveness in a very particular mode. "Instead of a seism, it is a sort of fabric: instead of an aggressor and a victim, here it is two accomplices who meet up and gain satisfaction from their incestual relations" (p. 63). And he adds: "Above all, the incestual relationship is a narcissistic relationship. The incestual object is invested like an idol. But this investment is not at a loss: the idol necessarily has the function of illuminating the idolater in return" (p. 74).

It is no doubt in the register of transgenerational clinical work that the notion of incestuality is of most significant interest. Thus, in clinical work with infants, who immediately bring into play three generations, it helps to throw light on certain configurations of severe disorders in the early infant/mother relationship. Indeed, in the period of upheavals that accompanies the establishment of the relationship with their child, sometimes to keep an awakening of the incestual register at bay, and sometimes to reproduce it unconsciously, some mothers feel obliged to cathect their newborn baby immediately in a narcissistic mode without any restraint. It is often a defence in reaction to the revival of sufferings caused by certain "incestual" dimensions of their own history. No place is accorded to the real needs of their child; no place is given to the exigencies of its development. Massive disorders can result in the register of feeding, sleep, or at times of separation. In consultations, the mother is sometimes able to speak about early traumas that belong to the incestual register.

Take the example of an 11-month-old child suffering from primary anorexia. In the course of the consultations, the mother was able to speak about a particularly intrusive surgical operation that had awakened the profound alteration of her own relationship to her mother. Confined within the exigencies of maternal narcissism in an ideal dyad, but without space, her "marvellous" child's own needs were all denied. Reintroducing and recreating a place for the father of this child was a difficult, but salutary process.

Take the further example of a little insomniac girl, aged seven months, who was required by her parents to be an infant prodigy who knew how to walk and speak, even though her real needs were neither recognised nor supported. The small island of an ideal and fusional relationship that she had the task of forming with her mother soon proved to be hell. Thinking about the incestuality present in the family history of both parents helped, however, to give meaning to the defensive value of this movement of confinement. A difficult but progressive process began, allowing gradually for the recognition, through the careful interventions of the analyst concerning small events in the consultations, of the child's authentic needs. These interventions, in the form of words or gestures during play, were addressed to the little girl as a baby...but also to the parents.

Often, the idealisation of the relationship to the child serves defensively to "make up for internal presences that are lacking" (p. 75). The impact of the incestual register is found then in the quality of the narcissistic defences mobilised in those who are subjected to it and leads them to establish reciprocal relations of impingement with those who are close to them. For them, it is a fragile organisation of survival aimed at keeping at bay a trauma that is still active. This particularity makes the handling of representations a singularly delicate matter. The paths of symbolisation and sense-making must therefore be tackled very carefully. Through its empathic and metaphorising dimension, the therapeutic work between parents and their baby provides a possible way of overcoming the destructive tyranny that is sometimes imposed by the incestual register in the early stages of the relationship with the child.

Is it not also possible to speak of incestuality in connection with what opposed, in the analyst's office, a young provocative adolescent and his discouraged and aggressive mother? Major difficulties in the acquisition of basic skills, learning capacities, as well as his behavioural disorders, meant that he was on the verge of being excluded permanently from secondary school. When he was alone with the analyst, he was unusually provocative; when the mother and son were together, the analyst was the object of their convergent attacks on his powerlessness and uselessness, as soon as the mother stopped behaving aggressively towards her son in a way that was barely tolerable.

The analyst found a pretext for introducing the social worker into the exchanges: the latter would see the mother when he was alone with her son; and then, she would be present when he saw them together. This arrangement made possible new movements of identification: the mother could express her worries and disarray to this other woman who was a social worker. This colleague could intervene – in a slightly maternal way – in order to verbalise the mother's preoccupations for her son and the son's for his mother. The analyst kept quiet, while mother and son let her speak. An exchange was thus created in which they could express in front of each other what they were unable to say to each other or to say in the presence of the analyst alone. A slightly particular form of group functioning was established which calmed things down. The son's major difficulties at school led to pedagogical meetings at the school, which the analyst and social worker also attended.

Without going too much into the details of this situation, in the course of relatively peaceful consultations, the question of the father's place, or rather his absence, arose. The son's depression and resentment in connection with this absence could be expressed: usually he refused to do anything, but now he agreed to participate in a discussion group for adolescents. During a consultation between the mother, who had asked to see the analyst alone, and the analyst, she made the rather peculiar admission that she had invented a secret liaison with a man so that the boy "would not know that she did not have a man". The narcissistic dimension was in the foreground in this maternal fabulation and it attested to the incestual nature of the relationship. It is also fair to suppose that there was a transference of this incestual register in the confession that she made, thanks to the frame established with the presence of a third object: the "institutional" setting and its transference space made it possible to reintroduce a triangulation and a paternal superego presence for the son and mother alike, which probably changed the situation, transforming in passing the boy's school life.

The incestual has its roots in the narcissistic register: Racamier emphasises the caution that should guide our therapeutic undertakings: "Incest is all in the act, and the incestual is all in the relationship; I would say, then, that incestuality is all in the defence" (p. 99).

And he adds: "Is there not an incestual element hidden in very long analyses? Sometimes we think they are interminable… This cloak of silence is the work of the denials made by the mother" (pp. 222–223).

Further reading

Racamier, J.-C. (1995). *L'inceste et l'incestuel.* Paris: Editions du Collège.

KEY WORDS Destructiveness, incest, narcissistic relationship, transgenerational.

THE ALLERGIC OBJECT-RELATIONSHIP

MARIE SIRJACQ

A woman patient had been suffering from asthma since childhood, as her mother and grandmother had before her. On arriving for her sessions, she always asks how the analyst is ("Are you well?"). The analyst feels that the patient is scrutinizing every movement she makes and seems to be searching for her approbation and wanting to regulate her attitude in relation to that of her analyst. This dynamic of intense perceptual clinging makes evenly-suspended attention difficult.

In her daily life, she is unable to oppose anyone. She does not know how to say "no"; she invents exhausting stratagems to please everyone and hurt no one. Thus, she complains that she is unable to choose between two men. She lives with one of them without being able really to commit herself. He has a son from an earlier marriage and the relationship he has with his child is an insurmountable obstacle for her. She "cannot find her place there". "No place? or no place for you?", the analyst asked. Nor can she make up her mind to leave the man with whom she was living before. With regard to this man, she is in a situation of endless waiting: she would like him to be different, more attentive, more conciliatory, and capable of identifying with her needs. Everything, in other words, that her mother was not. Since her childhood, moreover, this patient has conformed scrupulously to her mother's wishes because she feared that, if she didn't, she would lose her love. We can see the manifestation of this in the transference when she adheres immediately to what the analyst suggests to her. It is a collage, a fascination, which evacuates any form of reflection and places her in a situation of absolute dependence.

One day, she had a dream: "I arrived at the time of my appointment, but it was another woman who opened the door and received me for the session. She was different from every point of view, but I did not pay attention to the difference, I acted as if it was you, I forgot that it wasn't you, except when I was leaving when I said to her that I didn't want to do that again, that she wasn't my therapist." In the dream, during the session, she said to herself "usually, she is not like that", but without considering that it might refer to her analyst who was neither exactly the same nor someone completely different.

Then she mentioned her mother again and her feelings about her, saying that she was either kind or nasty. There was no conceivable duality, it was either one or the other, it was impossible combine the two. As she was leaving on that day, the patient said: "Thank you for being what you are." To which the analyst replied: "And not someone else who you could oppose?"

The difficulties of this patient seem to result from an allergic relationship to the object as described by Pierre Marty (1958). It is a system of defence characterised by a subject who identifies closely with the object to the point of merging with it. The subject's behaviour is aimed at satisfying this object and excluding all conflict. In daily life, each real object that presents itself is cathected as a "*hôte*"[1] and can be decathected equally quickly. The object is immediately transformed into an idealised and all-powerful mother. Limits are erased, giving rise to a fusional relationship on the model of the mother/child dyad. Allergic subjects find it impossible to think for themselves or to make choices that would involve personal commitment and thus conflict, internal or external. Everything aims to avoid the representation of a united couple. In short, allergic subjects are allergic to the triangular relationship; they can only be in a relationship with one person at a time. Being faced with two equally cathected objects simultaneously can lead to a crisis: because the objects are distinct, they become incompatible.

Some children conduct themselves with great familiarity with the consultant who sees them for the first time. They are so at ease that they bring a smile to one's face. All those who meet them also find them likeable. In his ontogenetic reflections, René Spitz described the smile to all faces as the first organiser of the mind; the second being the reaction of anxiety provoked by the stranger's face. It seems that allergic patients act as if they only possessed the first organiser: they smile to everyone and are conflictual.

These patients do not make a differentiation between me (familiar) and not-me (strange) and so have no stranger anxiety. They have not made the transition from distress without an object to constituted object-anxiety (phobia of the stranger). The psychic mechanisms of repression (of the representation of the absent mother), of its displacement onto the face of the stranger, and then of anti-cathexis through fear, are not constituted. In clinical practice with allergic patients, this lack of stranger anxiety manifests itself in various ways: the search for complete confluence with the analyst, the inability to pass from one identification to another, an absence of ambivalence, or the impossibility of articulating maternal and paternal filiations in narrative form. In short, patients with allergic object relationships have a constant difficulty triangulating.

Note

1 Translator's note: a term used by Pierre Marty in his 1958 article "La relation objectale allergique"; the word *hôte* can refer either to a host or a guest in French; it is both the subject that inhabits the object and the subject inhabited by the object. It thus expresses an erasure of boundaries between subject and object.

Further reading

Le Guen, C. (1974). *L'Oedipe originaire.* Paris: Payot.
Marty, P. (1958). La relation d'objet allergique. *Revue française de psychanalyse,* 22(1): 5–35.
Spitz, R.A. (1965 [1958]). *The first year of life. A psychoanalytic study of normal and deviant development in object relations.* New York: International Universities Press.
Szwec, G. (1993). *La Psychosomatique de l'enfant asthmatique.* Paris: Presses Universitaires de France. (Series: Le Fil rouge).

KEY WORDS Absence of phobia of the stranger, difficulties of triangulation, me/not-me non-differentiation

13

DEFENCES

SELF-CALMING STRATEGIES

GÉRARD SZWEC

This patient is 14 years old, and suffers from migraines and abdominal pains. When he was three years old, he lost his sister, who was two years older than him, in a car accident. He is haunted by a repetitive image: the precise moment when he was thrown out of the car door during the crash. This scene had survived the period of latency without being subjected to sufficient repression. He spent his whole childhood playing indefinitely at provoking an accident between two small cars. This game did not become richer over the course of time and was more the expression of a traumatic neurosis than a real game. The exchanges at the beginning of the psychotherapy were extremely impoverished and trivial. The patient spoke only in response to questions. He had no perceivable affects or fantasies. There was no question of imagining anything. If the analyst tried to draw him away a bit from the factual and descriptive level, he replied: "The imaginary world is useless." He was stuck to reality, that's all.

The sessions were distressing. Finally, he livened up a little when speaking about a neighbour who played the drums. He said he listened to him playing for hours, without it being clear what sorts of thoughts went through his mind while he was doing this. In the end, he signed up for drum lessons. Practising playing the drums (in French this is called *répétition*) then took the place of the accidents he brought about with his little cars. He practised for hours and lived with constant noise. He played a sort of hard rock called The Dead. It is a violent, deafening, repetitive form in which the music is reduced to the minimum, in favour of speed. Pushed by this force, the death drive, he transformed his arms into a rhythmic, automated machine. By producing these sounds, he brought the accident back, as it were, while at the same time keeping it out of his mind.

This behavioural regression, which contrasts with a regression that gives rise to thinking, constitutes what we call a self-calming strategy. It involves mechanical or stereotyped repetitive behaviours that are motor or sensory discharges without representations. Self-calming strategies are precarious ego-defences that are employed when mental work (dreams, fantasies, elaboration, production of symptoms, etc.) cannot be deployed to relieve the psychic apparatus of excessive tensions due to excitation. It is a question of extinguishing the tension by more tension. And yet the calm brought about by the repetition of excitation only affords simple and brief relief, a very ephemeral return to a state of calm. That is why the strategy has to be indefinitely repeated, producing a process of mechanisation on both the physical and psychic levels.

Resorting to self-calming strategies confines the person to an untiring physical and psychic repetition that never brings satisfaction (in the sense of the satisfaction that a baby can feel after a feed). It may include an element of physical suffering and/or have the aim of seeking, through bodily exhaustion, the return to a state of calm. This mode of functioning can lead to a state comparable to that described by Gérard d'Aboville, who rowed across the Pacific in a boat: it is "always the same refrain, always the same metronome rhythm…the body works like a machine and the mind functions like a calculator" (Szwec, 2014, p. 19, drawn from an article in the newspaper *Libération* dated 22/11/92). It is a matter of repeating over and over again until one becomes a "voluntary galley slave". Those who use self-calming strategies seek, through their repetitive and quantitatively exaggerated practices, to "think about nothing", to "empty their heads" – expressions they often used to describe the experience. What they are seeking, in fact, and this is an essential point, is to do without the object, to abolish it, to be self-sufficient.

The quest for calm through the repetition of excitation is doomed to failure and there are sometimes misconceptions about this type of behaviour.

In the very young child, violent self-rocking at the moment of going to sleep, can, for example, be mistaken for autoerotic or hallucinatory activity, whereas the repetition has an automatic and untiring character that bears the mark of failure.

In children, a symbolic unconscious meaning is sometimes too easily attributed to fixed pseudo-games that are repeated almost automatically and are devoid of fantasy activity. The self-calming strategy is a sort of substitute for the wooden reel game, precisely because the fundamental process of this game (coming and going) could not be established and allow the preservation of the traces of the mother's presence. It constitutes an effort to maintain perception.

In adolescence, and in adulthood, the perpetual repetition of musical exercises or sports training exercises can be taken mistakenly for sublimation, an obsessional game or ritual. Yet it is the quantity that seems essential and not a symbolic meaning, which is lacking (no fantasies about object relations in which the adolescent or adult is loved, admired, or surpasses the oedipal rival).

Self-calming strategies must be distinguished from the motor activities discussed by Sándor Ferenczi, those acts of the psychopathology of everyday life that help to limit excessive excitation by means of muscular activity as a way of accompanying and promoting intellectual work, for example, pacing while thinking.

The muscular and perceptual sensations of self-calming strategies are different from those sought out by anorexic or bulimic patients or by drug addicts, but they have in common the function of replacing representations and affects.

When there are not good enough experiences of satisfaction of needs through contact with the object in early relationships, the infant is not able to hallucinate the satisfaction of his wishes by the object. This results in a failure to constitute an efficient stimulus barrier. The maternal object that has been internalised is not sufficiently reliable and helpful to permit the infant to psychically cope with the frustrating and traumatic experiences that he cannot elaborate. Because they are not registered psychically, these experiences are repeated through the self-calming strategy, while at the same time they represent an attempt to avoid the object by denying the need for help. Denying the lack of the object serves to prevent the arousal of destructive aggressiveness towards the object on contact with it.

Self-calming strategies are thus substituted for forms of autoerotism because they are delibidinalised and, rather than seeking continuity with the object, they seek avoidance of the object relationship. They aim to paralyse mental life in order to avoid the resurgence of a traumatic reality by maintaining the perception of the external object in place of its representation.

As pleasure is not their aim, self-calming techniques are not masochistic. On the contrary, they are substitutes for erotogenic masochism. They are neither forms of self-destruction nor forms of self-punishment inflicted by the superego. In these behaviour patterns, repetition is no longer in the service of symbolic binding as is the case, for example, in the repetition of the wooden reel game described by Freud. It undoes any attempts at binding and is more evocative of the repetition of the dream of the traumatic accident that gave rise to the neurosis. This is the model of a form of repetition "beyond the pleasure principle" that is traumatic and without symbolic meaning because it returns in the form of perceptions that are not linked to the representational network.

We find the two modes of fixation to trauma in self-calming strategies, repetition and flight described by Freud (1939) in *Moses and Monotheism*. We can recognise in them both the repetition-compulsion that drives the subject to repeat the initial trauma untiringly by making it part of perceptual reality, and a tendency to take flight from this trauma that leads to avoidance of its psychic inscription and representation. It should be noted that this avoidance differs from the reaction of psychic defence that can be found in inhibition and phobia and which becomes a modality of the object-relationship. This avoidance, which in my view is "pre-phobic", is both a form of motor behaviour, closer to the animal instinct of flight when faced with danger, and an avoidance of representation and thought, in particular thought about object relationships.

In the course of the psychotherapy conducted with this patient, a process of mentalisation was established. He began putting stickers and writing the names of musical groups on his workbook. The provocative nature of the names seemed to give him pleasure that he wanted to share by showing them. The drawings represented skeletons and skulls, decomposing corpses that seemed to come from hell.

He defined himself as a "hard guy"; he wore T-shirts and jackets with the names of hard-rock groups and sought the company of young people who liked the same music. Later, the analyst was able to show him the link between the accident and the representations of death in the phantasmagoria of hard rock. At this stage his interest in the most sadistic figures was a sign that the death instinct was entangled with the erotic drive. This opened the way to the expression of oedipal desires.

He talked about a horror film in which there was a car accident with a dead person who never died. By helping him to make a link with his own accident, this film enabled him to form a screen memory: his mother had been so worried about his sister and not at all about him.

Traumatic repetition gave way to a fascination for horror and terror, but with the pleasure of play (even if it was sadistic), and of "re-binding" fiction. His way of playing the drums was no longer underpinned by his traumatic vision, but was incorporated into a phantasmagoria that was compatible with the instrument. He began playing with others and in a more "nuanced" way. He also began to take real pleasure in the exchanges in the sessions, whereas before his discourse had been factual and devoid of affect.

Further reading

Szwec, G. (2014). *Les Galériens volontaires.* Paris: Presses Universitaires de France.

KEY WORDS Behaviour, excitation, mentalisation, motor functioning, perception, self-calming strategies, psychosomatics, repetition, trauma.

NEGATIVE HALLUCINATION

VINCENT PÉLISSIER

A patient who was in face-to-face therapy gave the analyst reasons to doubt for a long time, even though she herself had no doubts: she was enthusiastic, involved, persuaded as to the benefits of the work, whose effects she said she could distinctly measure and whose merits she bragged about to her friends and family. For her, it was "visible", undebatable. She was constantly looking to her analyst for approval, and he was an interlocutor implicitly taken as a witness. He struggled with this inwardly because the patient's detailed account of daily life and her discussions with those around her generally left very little room for fantasy, for unforeseen thoughts, or for the emergence of an elaborated preconscious. Her accounts were reduced to circumscribed recollections that were immediately "interpreted" and hence equally quickly classified. Things were clear for her, but obscure for the analyst.

It was only when something went wrong that the analyst's confidence returned. For instance, if she arrived late for a session or seemed embarrassed to speak, the analyst considered that maybe she should lie down so that she would be better able to play with associations, which one could now suppose were suppressed. She would no longer need to cling to the physical presence of the interlocutor to whom she clinged to validate her conclusive affirmations. During one of the rare moments when she talked about a difficulty in saying what came to her mind, the analyst decided to ask her if she had ever thought about using the couch. She responded very quickly: "It's really funny that you're mentioning that today because yesterday evening I said to my sister that since you changed your office at the beginning of the year *you no longer had a couch*. Previously, when I came into the room, it was obvious." It turned out later that she had noted, without paying attention, that a sofa had been replaced by an armchair in the waiting-room. An absence of perception was thus substituted with the perception of an absence. Very surprised, the analyst asked if this kind of "disappearance" had happened before. She paused for a moment and then recalled a somewhat sad evening at the home of a musician friend of hers: on leaving, she had been astonished by the absence in the living room of a harp that she had seen there for years, to the point that she even telephoned afterwards to make sure about it: no, the harp had not moved, something she was able to confirm for herself a few days later. As, exceptionally, during this session, she did not understand what was happening to her and was unable to rationalise this, the analyst ventured to point out that she had also deprived him of his instrument. She smiled, then, for the first time, and remained silent for the rest of the session.

Time was needed to bring this moment into perspective, to give it density. It was only much later, when she was using the couch that had returned, that she was able to link this episode to another denial of reality: during a first liaison she had had at the end of her adolescence, she had gotten pregnant and her family had encouraged her to have an abortion. "What's extraordinary," she remarked, "is that when my parents reproached me, I couldn't understand them; I was convinced we had simply been flirting, that I had remained a virgin. I had no recollection of penetration and even today, it's difficult for me to believe it." Listening to her, the analyst thought about a famous scene in a film: "*But, Madam, I swear to you that I have never slept with a boy!*" Like her parents' anger, his derision mirrored her incredulity. For both analyst and patient, each in their own way, the negative hallucination captivated, blinded and, above all, blocked out affect.

Months passed before what had disappeared could find its place, before she could feel the pain of the wound and mourning that had been neglected by the young girl who had secretly dreamed of being a mother. Christmas was approaching and though, ordinarily, the announcement of the analyst's holidays left her unmoved, she was worried out loud one day about an errand that she had to make after the session: the dry cleaner's… "I will not be returning to your area during the holidays and, in any case, they shut between Christmas and New Year, it's a pity." The analyst invited her to say more about this. Since the beginning of her analysis, she had been going to a dry cleaner that she had discovered nearby. She had left an item of child's clothing there the week before. "A white item of clothing – they're the only ones who can save it." Save her virginity? Whiten her fraudulent desires? Erase the pain? No doubt, but the denial of affect seemed to be the most important element at this moment and the analyst simply drew attention to the "closure of the shop" over Christmas and New Year. "Yes, but my children will not be there either; it doesn't matter, they are spending Christmas with their father this year." "No children for Christmas", the analyst noted. He then noticed that she was crying silently. It was only when we resumed in January that she told me that she had secretly given the child that she had once briefly carried the first name of one of her former dolls, a doll, moreover, that she had lost one day. "Perhaps during a move."

Negative hallucination, a phenomenon Freud observed early in his work, suffered for a long time from being a hybrid phenomenon, somewhere between a patent symptom and an unconscious process at the foundations of psychic life. If this is how it appears now most frequently, in the wake of the elaboration proposed by André Green, the phenomenon is also present in the shadows of many pathologies, from fetishism to drug addiction, from manic states to "operational" (*opératoire*) functioning.

Before Freud, a number of observers of hypnotic states or altered states of consciousness had noted the frequency of these moments in which a portion of external reality seems not so much repressed as not registered, not perceived. In his first metapsychological papers, Freud made a distinction between repression and a "gap" in the mind. He considered the latter as a more archaic defence against an unrepresentable traumatic reality, the consequence of an excess of massive excitation. The idea of a "non-cathexis" of the object of unpleasure was put forward in 1915.

There are two fundamental points to be emphasised here:

- For Freud, negative hallucination takes precedence over positive hallucination, the first having logical precedence, delimiting a "blank" space at the heart of which the second is an attempt to restore, admittedly in an altered state, a possible external reality that is compatible with the demands of the id and of the primary process.
- Negative hallucination may be likened to the processes of denial as a whole, but in a singular and radical form. Generally speaking, denial supposes the prior existence of a perception and a representation whose meaning, at the level of a split-off part of the ego, is subsequently withdrawn. Fetishism attests to this difference: if the subject faced with castration *cannot believe his eyes*, it is because he has really seen something. In this case, he is dealing with a perception of reality whose significant effects are the object of disavowal.

Negative hallucination, as a process, thus becomes the prerequisite for many noisy clinical conditions, such as delusion (we are reminded here of the famous Cotard's syndrome[1]). It is also the invisible platform of clinical organisations marked by an impoverishment of both affect and ideational content in patients whose negativism is, as it were, neutralised. This neutralisation is the result of an abrasion of inner perceptions of mood or an apparent lack of cathexis of relationships, of thought, of the frame, or of the object.

Negative hallucination may also appear in a sporadic, localised fashion. For example, it is not uncommon in an analysis for a word or an expression underlined by the analyst not to be heard initially – "What did you say? Could you repeat that please?" – and to leave the one who first uttered it in disarray: "Did I say that?"

It can thus be combined with repression or with denial when it is a matter of avoiding at all costs the conjunction between a perception and an unconscious representation.

Note

1 A syndrome described by Jules Cotard in the 1880s during which the patient in a delusional state may nourish ideas of immortality, damnation, negation of organs or even of the whole body. He may feel that his organs are putrefying and self-destructing; he may believe he is already dead. See, in particular, Cotard (1997 [1882]).

Further reading

Duparc, F. (1992). Nouveaux développements sur l'hallucination negative et la représentation. *Revue française de psychanalyse*, 56(1): 101–121.

Green, A. (1999 [1993]). *The work of the negative*, trans. A. Weller. London: Free Association Books.

KEY WORDS Splitting, negative hallucination, gap, non-cathexis.

CREATIVE HYPOCHONDRIA

JEAN-YVES TAMET

The medical approach to an intractable symptom often follows the following dual line of questioning: Is it of organic origin? Is it a psychic manifestation? This litigious duality underlies many endless debates on the question of the origin of symptoms and it is curious to note that a writer like Jean-Jacques Rousseau built part of his reflections around this line of reasoning to the point of sometimes getting lost in it and of not fearing the contradictions arising from this reasoning, even including the persistence of a procedural behaviour and a sensibility of someone who feels persecuted. In spite of that, as is often the case with him, he remains congenial for the reader because his painful questioning converges with our own when faced with physical ailments, great or small: hoping to find meaning in them is already part of the process of healing, often far removed from any scientific truth.

Rousseau's writing is haunted by evil and the quest for its origins, but it is also infiltrated by the account of physical pains and, ultimately, raises the question of salvation. His experience of these questions was intense and his thought was influenced by the dimension of persecution that marked his relationship to the world and, first and foremost, to the torments linked to the functioning of his body. Rousseau, somewhat complacently, often gives many details about his suffering or about his states of illness, but always with a certain reserve and a veil of mystery that maintains a distance between himself and what he is recounting: he is in search of a healer or an interlocutor in order to feel understood, but equally exhibits an attitude of proud refusal; he thus wavers between discretion and the exhibition of his states of suffering. "I came into the world almost dead;" he writes, "they had little hopes of preserving me." (Rousseau, 1790 [1783], p. 5).

This situation made it possible for him to meet a figure who is very present in the Western world, namely, a suffering healer whose gains and advances are only achieved at the price of painful and tragic experiences consisting of solitude and ordeals. Anyone who has gone through these ordeals is then listened to with respect. A man of sorrows, Rousseau was such a case and, lastingly, for the enigma of his illness caused a lot of ink to be spilt both in his lifetime and after his death. Commentaries on his work emphasise, moreover, the view taken by critics of the close relations between the work and the man: is it really necessary to know the state of an author's health to appreciate what he has created? Curiosity looks for something obscene, indecent, and, once the issue has been uncovered, judgement concerning it becomes reductive and it becomes highly tempting to link the whole of his creation to symptomatology: if it sufficed to be ill to have talent, this would have been known long ago. Rousseau gave rise to such a following that one current of thought, considering him as degenerate, tried to discredit the whole of his work by highlighting the persecuted and ill person, the hypochondriac suffering from necropathy, to the detriment of the visionary, the reformer or the pedagogue. Rousseau played on this in his own way by calling, for example, for his own autopsy. The emerging psychology, from Pierre Janet to René Laforge, had a field day with his exuberant personality, and doctors, from René Leriche to Emmanuel Régis, explored with steadfastness all available paths in an attempt to identify his urinary disorder. To no avail, for it continues to remain an enigma, including with regard to its consequences on the possibilities of his achieving paternity. Was Rousseau the biological father of his numerous children?

There was a time when literary criticism turned to medicine, psychology, and then psychoanalysis, in an attempt to understand the origins of the singular genius of the creator. In Rousseau's case, it was a matter of understanding how he coped with his state of illness alongside his project of sincerity, since *The Confessions* claimed to say everything, including the darkest, most revolting aspects of the self. In so doing, he opened the doors to calumny and suspicion and encouraged the search for other much less flattering confessions: in short, his enemies called into doubt this possibility of "saying everything". In this regard, Rousseau wanted to remain an exception and this was how he presented himself: physical illness was a central element of his personal theatre thrown to the mercy of the public, and sometimes exhibited, which made him extraordinary in his own eyes.

The body as an irrefutable argument, anatomy as evidence, and physiology as experience, are the scenes that were frequented by Rousseau's genius. Even today, they still play a role in stirring appreciation for his work: no, clearly we can neither escape the idea of the trial with Jean-Jacques nor the nagging question of origins!

The term of somatisation elicited by hypochondriacal disorders is one of the consequences of the interest analysts have shown in the relations uniting the life of the mind and bodily functioning: following earlier traces with the study of hysterical conversion, they turned the debate towards internal illnesses with so-called somatoform disorders (Rousset, 2013). It should be pointed out that a solution is possible by placing the disorders at the heart of an artistic creation.

We are indebted to the genius of Jean Starobinski, armed with medical, psychiatric and literary training, as well as his broad erudition which brought him into contact with psychoanalysis, for having established that Rousseau's illness was something constitutive of his being and that it had its place at the heart of his personality. What other destiny can there be for the hypochondriac than to be able to think about his suffering in itself rather than projecting it wastefully into an external space that would paradoxically distance him from himself? Rousseau, like many hypochondriacs, claimed to be exceptional, and his illness belonged to his project of constructing such an original destiny. In this sense, Jean Starobinski's essay helps us to understand this pathology, a frontier between melancholia and paranoiac attacks: the discourse on the body occupies the writer's mind in the same way as a loving relationship, even if tragic, takes hold of the mind.

Further reading

Apfelbaum, L. (2006). L'alliance de la littérature et de la psychanalyse. *Les Cahiers pour la psychanalyse*, 13: 127–135.

Rousseau, J.J. (1790 [1783]). *The confessions of J.J. Rousseau, book I.* London: J. Bew.

Rousset, H. (2013). La tentation hypochondriaque. *Les Cahiers pour la psychanalyse*, 28: 111–118.

Starobinski, J. (1987). La maladie de Rousseau. In: *Jean-Jacques Rousseau: la transparence et l'obstacle.* Paris: Gallimard.

KEY WORDS Literature, paranoia, Rousseau, somatisation.

FUNCTIONAL SPLITTING

GÉRARD BAYLE

Functional splitting is a temporary and very widespread emergency defensive process. It contributes to the self-withdrawal that the subject must initiate when the order of psychic and event-based realities disturbs the equilibrium of his ego and overwhelms his protective capacities. Unable to cope with the trauma, the ego divides itself into two parts: one part continues to carry out the usual functions of this agency, while the other is isolated from it. The latter contains the affective impacts of the trauma and keeps them at a distance, thereby creating efficient conditions for warding off immediate exigencies.

So it was for this patient. She had many faithful friends, but could not engage in a satisfying love life. Broken relationships were frequent. She was even astonished that she was only attracted by "good for nothings".

From the very beginning of the consultation, the analyst found her very likeable. Then he forgot about her totally until the second interview.

When the analyst was led to tell her that what she was saying concealed deeper thoughts, her face decomposed under the pressure of mounting pain. She shut herself away in silence, a response the analyst respected. Then she tried to talk, but couldn't. The analyst suggested that she waited, that she should only say what she felt was tolerable for her and for him. Several sessions passed in silence interspersed with confused evocations referring to an old and deep wound that she had never spoken about, except to her parents, who had not known what to say to her. Gradually, bit by bit, she revealed that when she was 10 years old, she had been raped by a stranger who had threatened to kill her. Her parents took her to see a doctor, but left it at that. She did not dare speak about what had happened. In order to avoid a destructuring traumatic experience leading to moments of depersonalisation, derealisation and desymbolisation, the patient and her parents organised a common disavowal (Freud, 1927) around what had happened. They decathected the affects linked to the trauma and the trauma itself. They kept silent out of an unformulated concern to mutually protect themselves. Due to the denial, the episode faded into the background.

However, this defence turned out to be costly. The unconscious mistrust infiltrated by her hatred for the aggressor made way for bad choices in love.

This patient's psychic organisation was organised around a second decisive element that reinforced the splitting and the denial of the trauma: this was a reaction formation which led her to engage with courage and energy in brilliant studies, and then in a demanding profession in the service of an international humanitarian cause. She became fanatical about friendships, outings and dangerous excursions. Her spontaneous impulses of hatred for the aggressor, and also for her parents, were repressed by this reaction formation arising from a double "reversal", the first, a "turning-round into its opposite" (idealisation of the love of human beings), and the second, a "turning-round upon the subject's own self" (she is a good, friendly, and likeable friend, which reinforces earlier pleasant personal dispositions). In view of the brilliance of the reaction formation, the trauma faded even more deeply into the background. Although it was never forgotten, equally it was never felt.

The challenge of this face-to-face therapy was to enable the subject to experience this trauma without being radically overwhelmed by it. This patient's successes were not only for her own benefit, but also for the benefit of her parents, her friends and her analyst. The organisation of functional splitting consumed psychic energy and a constant and considerable amount of narcissistic libido. In the transference, the analyst was supposed to benefit from this, like the parents and friends. There came a moment, then, when he questioned her position as a potential abuser, revealing to her thereby the obligation she felt to satisfy all those around her, despoiling her legitimate narcissistic gains in a form of "diversion" neurosis (*névrose d'intendance*). This process resembles that of a neurosis; it has the taste of it, but rather than hiding a guilty wish, it is a matter of maintaining a split within a common disavowal that includes the analyst.

During the sessions, the patient's narrative took on a certain associative consistency. She calmed down and had a dream. She was in a room whose walls were covered with mosaics. One of them was in a different colour from the others. She felt disturbed: this mosaic had been before her eyes during the rape, when she cut herself off from her sensations. The refuge she had taken in a certain degree of negative hallucination had ultimately made way for a perceptual clinging to a colour.

Her disturbance worried the analyst because it suggested the porosity of splitting. The danger of a sudden breakdown of this splitting could not be excluded. The risk of a spillage of the split-off material would be like the rupture of a dam. However, the context of a dream reassured him because the narcissistic restoration that makes it possible to face up to the consequences of the trauma is often marked by a dream, a sign that elaboration is possible. From that moment, the splitting gradually diminished. The therapeutic work continued with caution and determination.

After two years of weekly sessions, she was able to see the damage caused by the shared disavowal and to take part with her parents in family therapy. Later on, she did a classical analysis. The news that the analyst received from her subsequently showed that the fanatical idealisation had given way to original personal values and that the denial had diminished sufficiently for her to be able to enjoy a romantic life of quality.

For 20 years, she had maintained a functional split that was indispensable in the situation of emergency felt during and after the rape, but it had persisted in a way that was burdensome for her because of her illusory hope that she would be able to forget about it and obtain broader family protection.

In the talking cure and thanks to the basic transference made possible by the availability of the patient and analyst, the process of putting things into words lifted the anti-cathexes of affects, allowing for their controlled return, that is, in a variable and temporally staggered way over the course of the sessions. In this way the retroactive reliving of savagery was avoided as well as the falseness of a potentially watered-down fictional account that would have turned the patient into a victim, without restoring to her responsibility for her defences and for their cost.

Further reading

Bayle, G. (1988). Traumatismes et clivages fonctionnels. *Revue française de psychanalyse*, 52(6): 157–174.

KEY WORDS Functional splitting, denial, idealisation, management neurosis.

DIVERSION NEUROSIS

GÉRARD BAYLE

The "diversion" neurosis (*névrose d'intendance*) consists in diverting the libidinal trend of a neurosis (conversion hysteria, anxiety hysteria, obsessional neurosis) in favour of a struggle against narcissistic wounds. Its symptomatology is based on that of neurosis exploited for narcissistic ends that are identifiable by the psychic pain and fatigue stemming from the wound itself. It is no longer only a matter of the neurotic expression of an oedipal conflict, but of an economic struggle for psychic and somatic integrity.

In the classical neuroses, the oedipal conflict exposes the ego to contradictory demands. The returns of the repressed, veiled resurgences of incestuous and murderous wishes, result from libidinal pressure with a constant flux of charge, characteristic of a repetition-compulsion. Thanks to this energy, the neuroses nourish actualisations of hate and love with objects of substitution specific to each one of them. The struggle, both exciting and co-exciting, for the conquest of the object, which often has to be repeated over and over again, is played out in the ego that is subject to the demands of reality, to the inextinguishable wishes of the id, and to the dangers of the superego. In spite of the repetitive aspect of the vicissitudes of this secondary defensive struggle linked to the oedipal conflict, the substitutive and temporary satisfactions contribute largely to the fluctuations in self-esteem, that is, to the subject's secondary narcissism. A portion of the libidinal energy engaged in these conflicts can, however, be desexualised thanks to a few more or less stable renunciations. The desexualised narcissistic libido has a fundamental aim: binding. The more narcissistic libido one has, the more it is possible to create links, both for coping better with the hazards of everyday life and for sublimatory aims.

In the case of a significant trauma, the signs of which are psychic or physical pain and a loss of self-confidence, narcissistic libido is immediately mobilised to contain and patch up, as far as possible, the psychic breach. If the force of the trauma is too significant or if the narcissistic libido that is mobilisable in an emergency is lacking, the wounded ego has to react by means of a new defensive strategy: splitting. On one side there is the narcissistic wound; on the other, what remains of the ego. Through a denial of the existence of what is affecting it, it withdraws, abandons the territory of the wound and isolates it by means of a set of interconnected defences.

These auxiliary defences of denial, motor discharge, negative hallucination and projective identification are costly in terms of narcissistic libido and may even result in attacks on linking between thoughts, and between thoughts and their accompanying affects. The struggle against the truth of the traumatic experiences is not only carried out as a matter of emergency but also over the long term. Fatigue is always present. The struggle to create a split in the ego and to maintain it can be exhausting.

The lack of narcissistic libido can be compensated for by resources in sexual libido. The uncensored returns of the repressed allow large quantities of sexual libido to enter the ego. Clinically, this is translated by new neurotic disorders or by an accentuation of those already present, but we must not delude ourselves; this new energy is put in the service of the economy of splitting and its annex defences. Furthermore, this failure of repression deprives the id of new ideational contents and thus favours the fixedness of defences and regression of a libidinal colouring. It is thus a diversion neurosis, because the thwarted desire is not for an object other than oneself, but rather for the deficient object of narcissism.

Faced with such a situation, it is important to contribute to the reinforcement of narcissism through access to a basic transference, without however committing the error of interpreting the transference on to the analyst as a neurotic transference, without confusing a narcissistic need and a neurotic wish. Here is an example.

This patient was doing research. He sought help a year ago on account of anxieties about a variety of illnesses. The classical picture of a phobic neurosis is based on traces of an infantile neurosis. His demand was moving because his anxieties tired him out so much. However, his physical fatigue, a certain degree of shame and very swift improvement during the preliminary interviews made it possible to accord importance to a process of mourning that had not taken place for two years. It concerned a colleague who was a little older than him, who had always supported and encouraged him in their research work; in short, a friendly and demanding mentor.

The analysis showed how much the patient tended to place the analyst in equally benevolent dispositions towards him. A denial of the importance of the death of his mentor showed that he had isolated his grief and that he had not engaged in the work of mourning.

At the same time as he regained a sense of well-being, he threw himself with zest into successful professional and amorous ventures. The analyst noted that this "analytic honeymoon" lasted for an abnormally long period, but the energy emerging from the positive transference that could serve to interpret movements of negative transference was extensively used in his new activities. At the same time, his phobia of mice had returned, a disorder that was not very troubling for someone living in comfortable circumstances in which animals were absent. Here is a neurosis that brings him more benefits than costs, and which is evocative of a diversion neurosis, the analyst said to himself. In spite of the multiple indications, the analysis of condensations and displacements suggesting such a phobia, the analyst abstained from venturing an interpretation of any kind. He noted that the patient had a split that was tenacious. It was necessary to wait until the patient could take the risk of beginning a work of mourning.

A year and a half went by like this. One day, he arrived at his session feeling very moved; he had dreamed about his colleague and began to speak about him. An entire year that was calmer, albeit sadder at times, showed that the work of mourning was underway. Gradually, elements of negative transference onto the analyst showed the very great ambivalence that governed his feelings towards this colleague. This negative transference was gradually interpreted, which helped to enrich the work of mourning; at the same time, the patient's infantile neurosis was reactivated in the form of a real transference neurosis, thereby leading towards the end of the analysis.

Further reading

Bayle, G. (2012). *Clivages, moi et défenses*. Paris: Presses Universitaires de France.

KEY WORDS Splitting, motor discharge, denial, negative hallucination, projective identification, idealisation, neurosis, diversion neurosis, projection, repression of affects.

MASOCHISM AS THE GUARDIAN OF LIFE

EVELYNE CHAUVET

We owe this concept to Benno Rosenberg (1991), who clearly highlighted masochism's function as a guardian of life. Starting from erotogenic masochism and from its primordial form, *primary erotogenic masochism* – the source of all the others – Rosenberg made it the specific expression of the process of drive fusion with which it is indistinguishable and of which it is the result. Its presence at the heart of every psychic phenomenon was evidence for him of the "masochistic dimension of existence" for, owing to its effect of binding the drives, masochism is in the service of the life drive.

This conceptualisation is an extension of Freud's (1924) discovery in "The economic problem of masochism", where he recognised the "scandal" that pain, considered as an object of satisfaction in itself, represented for rationalised thought and morality. Freud was then obliged to modify his first drive theory in which the discharge of the tension of excitation was considered as a source of pleasure: he replaced this short path centred on the quantitative factor with along path of psychic elaboration involving masochism and the capacity that it implies to endure the tension of unpleasure. This was the famous "turning-point of 1920", paving the way for the second drive theory in which a nuanced principle of pleasure reigns, placed under the aegis of a *qualitative* factor that is articulated with the reality principle by integrating temporality, waiting and endurance, in which masochism plays a present and vital role. But, before a new metapsychological ensemble could be organised, Freud had to be bold enough to advance the hypothesis of a death drive operating against the interests of the ego, and which was therefore the antagonist of the life drives. The vital necessity of taming these drives of destruction would be the task of Eros, tasked with a work of *binding* or fusion through masochism, a work of vital *alloying* that would ensure the necessary "eroticization" of destructiveness by mixing a portion of pleasure with unpleasure.

Primary erotogenic masochism is constituted at the heart of primary narcissism with the help of the object whose quality of presence promotes the development of a capacity to tolerate excitation. It is a founding element of psychic life, of fantasy life, via a hallucinatory satisfaction which, secondarily, paves the way for thought.

But this autoerotic narcissistic base implies its opposite, active self-destructiveness when Eros is no longer able to carry out its work of binding and leaves the field free for the death drive. The deadly masochistic process arising from drive unbinding then leads to a decathexis of the object, endangering not only psychic life but the preservation of the subject. The clinical and therapeutic implications of the presence and functionality of this primary masochistic nucleus are thus fundamental.

When masochism "succeeds too well" (Rosenberg's expression), deadly masochism prevails. This is the case in severe mental anorexia, where the tension of excitation is maintained and sought after to the point of sacrificing all satisfaction, in a state of omnipotence and denial of need as well as of the object that can even result in death.

At the other extreme, if it has not been possible for primary erotogenic masochism to organise itself for lack of a reliable internal object, an addictive pathology may materialise. In such cases, dependence on real objects is intolerable because it is seen as a narcissistic slight. So it is replaced by a self-controlled dependence on "available" substitutes that can give *satisfaction without delay*. Waiting and the capacity to tolerate deferring satisfaction is impossible because the masochism that is necessary for tolerating frustration has not been constituted. A female patient, whose eagerness for relationships and intolerance of emotions and the object's absence led her to engage in dangerous addictive behaviours, said after a long separation during the holiday period: "I have gorged myself with all the forms of mother that I could find. When they are not there all the time, they become bad, and I go downhill."

Another configuration shows that self-destructiveness can remain controllable thanks to the presence of an internal eroticised and eroticisable object that maintains the efficacy of "masochism as a guardian of life". I am thinking of depressive and post-traumatic states in which the spectre of melancholia and suicidal outcomes is looming. The eroticisation of destructiveness through masochism protects against the risk of drive unbinding and its consequences.

This was the case of a patient who sought help because she feared she could no longer control invasive ideas of death in spite of her will and powers of endurance. The sessions were for a long time taken up with unhappy accounts of her childhood, of the privations and humiliations she had tolerated without complaining, as well as of her impoverished and hardly satisfying world. In the course of the sessions, she exhibited, not without perceived and recognised excitement, her guilt and her "mediocrity". One day, finding everything that she was "inflicting" on her analyst intolerable, she confessed that she had planned to commit suicide, but that feelings of shame had prevented her from carrying out her plan. Her complaints and this admission called for interpretations of her sadistic aggressive feelings towards the analyst and of her self-destructive masochistic impulses. Privileging the narcissistic axis during this early stage of the treatment, the analyst said to her: "You are telling me all that in order to tell me who you are and how you developed yourself *with* and *around* this suffering; it's like an identity for you."

For this patient, masochism really served as the guardian of her psychic life by permitting the restoration of a narcissistic autoerotic position in order to maintain an internal continuity over and beyond the traumatic cracks.

Every analytic situation can always be turned around in favour of the accomplishment of masochistic fantasy. Its resolution requires the elaboration of its defensive and narcissistically protective aspect just as much as its links with the object and with infantile sexuality. For as long as these are maintained, which implies maintaining an internal link with the object and thus a continuity of object-cathexis, we are still on the terrain of psychoanalysis and its purposes. On the other hand, if these links with the sexual and with the object are loosened, decathexis will dominate and masochism will lose its function as the guardian of life, and instead become deadly.

Further reading

Freud, S. (1924). *The economic problem of masochism. S.E.* 19. London: Hogarth, pp. 155–170.

Green, A. (2001 [1983]). *Life narcissism, death narcissism.* trans. A. Weller. London: Free Association Books.

Pontalis, J.-B. (1977). *Entre le rêve et la douleur.* Paris: Gallimard. (Reprinted in the series Tel, 1983).

Rosenberg, B. (1991). *Masochisme mortifère et masochism gardien de vie. Monographies de la Revue française de psychanalyse.* Paris: Presses Universitaires de France.

Rousillon, R. (1999). *Agonie, clivage et symbolisation.* Paris: Presses Universitaires de France.

KEY WORDS Binding of the drives, erotogenic masochism, death drive, temporality.

PRE-PSYCHOSIS

MARIE-LAURE LÉANDRI

This concept advanced by René Diatkine expresses the perplexity of the clinician when faced with a child for whom the threat of psychosis in adolescence or in adulthood cannot be excluded entirely. It does not indicate therefore a more or less vague resemblance with the register of psychosis, but rather a prognostic concern. It relates to questions about the evolution of the processes of the child's psychic equilibrium during his development and the way in which he will be able to deal on a lasting basis with the excitation by which he is besieged.

A young girl was in psychotherapy on a twice a week basis. Her massive inhibition in learning to read and a certain excitability were a source of concern for her parents. She presented herself as a little woman, a miniature woman, the miniature of her mother. What was suggestive of pre-psychosis was the constant excitation of her thought and the fact that her recourse to play and narrative gave her little relief.

She explained: "At school I sometimes feel I have all the dead animals in my feet. Once, I was going down the stairs, and it bothered me; I was afraid that they would make me fall because they were in my feet, I could feel them. In class too, I could feel them in my back, in the back of my chair, and I asked a friend if she could see them. It stops me from working to feel them like that." While she was talking, she took a piece of pink modelling clay and rolled it. The phallic vermicelli, grew longer between her fingers, almost mechanically, then she took it in both hands and reduced it, then thickened it, shortened it, placed it vertically on the table, and crushed the base of it; the vermicelli had changed in appearance. Finally, she lifted it up with its base, turned it round and said: "It's a mushroom!" This manipulation made the analyst feel ill-at-ease. The pink vermicelli was not playing its usual role. In spite of its name "mushroom", there had been no displacement. It was almost a penis that she was caressing. Independently of this word "mushroom", she seemed caught in the symbolic equation described by Hanna Segal, when the sign becomes for the subject who is manipulating it the fantasized thing that it should only represent. In this child, sexual excitation was not only manifested in this way. Sometimes, it emerged in speech. Thus, a little later on in the same session, she opened the folder of her old drawings, looked attentively at one of them and said: "In that one, I kept the males a long way away." Finally, when she evoked the moment of going to bed in the evening, excitation took hold of her again: "When I go to bed, my little sister cries, Daddy makes a lot of noise, he hoovers between the floorboards, that makes a lot of noise." Behind these noises one can sense once again an exciting evocation of the primal scene.

What is striking is the economic force of the primary processes and the disorganisation that they engender. According to René Diatkine (1969), "no one is safe, in particular circumstances, from a disorganisation of the neurotic defences, suddenly failing, resulting in a sudden activation of primary processes" (p. 423). It may be that this was the case for this young patient during the session reported here. What makes one think of the concept of pre-psychosis is the volatile character of the thought processes: the invasion by the almost delusional conviction of dead animals, the manipulation of the phallic vermicelli (in spite of its relative cancellation by the use of the word "mushroom", and the evocation of invasive noises assailing her at bedtime). The sole recourse to the primary process obliged her to effect constant reversals, but the excitation could not find relief through fantasy activity. The equilibrium between primary processes and secondary processes is not sufficiently stable to enable her to deploy associativity, representations and appropriate games.

For René Diatkine, this dominance of the primary processes often leads to "a particular alteration of the narcissistic cathexis", a sort of discontinuity of the cathexis of oneself. The clinical picture that results from this is particularly contrasted. While in certain children, in spite of a relatively discrete symptomatology, a clearly psychotic turn is observable, in others, on the contrary, it is too much conformity in a "false self" mode that masks a certain denial of the place of internal objects and a "disconcerting absence of curiosity concerning what their parents are hiding" (p. 427).

Further reading

Angelergues, R (1978). Continuité/discontinuité: psychose de l'enfant – psychose de l'adulte. Réflexions après-coup consecutives à la journée d'étude sur le devenir des psychoses de l'enfant et à quelques autres discussions avec des psychiatres d'enfants. In: *Le Devenir de la psychose de l'enfant*. Paris: Presses Universitaires de France, pp. 269–280.

Diatkine, R. (1969). L'enfant prépsychotique. *La Psychiatrie de l'enfant*, 12(2): 413–446.

Diatkine, R., Kestemberg, E., and Lebovici, S. (1958). Bilan de dix ans de pratique psychodramatique chez l'enfant et l'adolescent. *La Psychiatrie de l'enfant*, 1(1): 63–180.

Diatkine, R., and Simon, J. (1972). *La psychanalyse précoce.* Paris: Presses Universitaires de France.

Lebovici, S. (1985). La solution délirante chez l'enfant. *Les Cahiers du Centre de psychanalyse et de psychothérapie*, 15: 45–64.

KEY WORDS Neurosis, primary process, secondary process, psychosis.

14

PROCESS

THE CENTRAL PHOBIC POSITION

DANIEL IRAGO

The central phobic position as conceived by André Green (2000) corresponds to a mode of psychic functioning marked by the negativisation of thought processes that occurs at the heart of analytic communication. It is a thought phobia that affects borderline patients for whom associative thinking as such represents a danger; a phobia that does not reveal mechanisms of symbolisation or displacement that would make it possible to circumscribe anxiety within a neurotic symptom.

The patient seeks to avoid the intersection of different associative lines of thought, because when they are brought into relationship with each other, it amplifies the traumatic charge. It is the resonance between the different themes that represents a danger. It is a matter, then, of preventing their revival and deployment in consciousness, for bringing them explicitly into relationship with each other represents a danger for the ego's integrity. Non-meaning then becomes the only defence.

This has the effect of short-circuiting the production of meaning and of blurring the analyst's understanding. It is as if the patient, anticipating forthcoming meanings, virtually present in the associations that he has already formulated, carried out an abortion of what has been fertilized in the very context of the analysing situation. This associative braking is accompanied by a discursive vagueness that often neutralises the analyst's listening and the elucidation of the transference issues.

And yet this anti-processual disposition cannot be dissociated from the dynamics of the transference. The central phobic position corresponds, in effect, to a situation in which it is the analytic situation itself that is attacked by the negativising processes operative in the patient. In this respect, it constitutes a transferential phobic position. When he is confronted with it, the analyst feels obliged, in the countertransference, to think about these mechanisms of the destruction and erasure of meaning. The difficulty for the analyst is then one of "thinking about the thought disorder" of his patient.

Starting from the session understood as a basic cell for studying the analytic process, the author proposes a model of free association integrating the findings of clinical experience of borderline states. Green argues that the associative network is deeply affected by effects of irradiation coming from the unconscious that shatter the linearity of the discourse. The associative network is thus worked on permanently by effects of retroactive reverberation: when one element is evoked, it echoes various earlier contents. At other times, certain themes acquire an anticipatory value in relation to contents to come (effects of anticipatory enunciation). It is thus a model that integrates both the functioning and dysfunctioning of the associative process.

A man aged about 30 sought analysis as a result of overwhelming anxiety attacks and a sense of malaise going back far into childhood. His emotional life was frozen and professionally he was struggling to survive as a self-employed worker. He described a childhood marked by the depression of his father and the intrusions of his mother. The indication of analysis was made after his last anxiety attack, which had occurred on the same date as the tragic death of a cousin a few years earlier, had been put into a context of meaning.

In the initial period of the analysis, the deployment of very rich associative material nourished the analytic process. Each session led to a sort of acceleration of meaning that gave great intensity to the analysis. This stage enabled the patient to elaborate a very ambivalent relationship with his mother. Now, it was when this relationship with his mother appeared to serve as a shield against a much more difficult and complex relationship with his father that the analysis was infiltrated by negativity and by the least neurotic aspects of the patient.

A period of difficult work then began because he did not come to his sessions when his associations led him to advance too quickly in gaining understanding of his paternal transference. Discontinuity was indispensable for him in order to be able to tolerate the transference relationship with the analyst and to inhibit awareness of new contents.

The analytic situation clearly became a menace from the moment he no longer had recourse to the incestuous relationship with his mother as a protection against the homosexuality linked to the paternal complex and reactualised in the relationship with the analyst. At the centre of his thought avoidances, which were at the origin of his excesses in the form of acting out, there was this unthinkable relationship with his father in both its erotic and aggressive aspects.

The analysis underwent an evolution that is reminiscent of the central phobic position. For the analyst, it was a matter of preserving the frame, of following the meanderings of a transference that had, at times, become negative, and above all of maintaining a reflexive position in relation to an atmosphere marked by acting out and an opposition to a work of thinking.

Further reading

Bournova (K.) et Suarez-Labat (H.) eds. Psychophobies. *Revue française de psychanalyse*, 78, 2014/3.

Green, A. (2002). *Key ideas for a contemporary psychoanalysis. Misrecognition and recognition of the unconscious*, trans. A. Weller. London: Routledge, 2005.

Green, A. (2005 [2000]). The central phobic position. A new formulation of the free association method. *International Journal of Psychoanalysis*, 81: 429–452; also in: *Psychoanalysis: A Paradigm for Clinical Thinking*, trans. A. Weller. London: Free associations Books, pp. 133–167.

KEY WORDS Free association, borderline states, negative, thought phobia.

PSYCHIC GENERA

VIRGINIA PICCHI

Where do those intuitive moments of inspiration and creativity in which ideas seem to fall from heaven come from? Why do some patients manage to overcome the effects of trauma and repetition and succeed in building a rich and evolving psychic life? Christopher Bollas (1992) offers an answer to these questions by proposing the existence of a receptive capacity at the heart of the unconscious from which what he calls "psychic genera" emerge. Psychic genera are unconscious, dynamic and evolving productions arising from the encounter between unconscious ideas and real experiences. Including both processes and contents, the term *genera* refers to the capacity for engendering psychic movement and new internal and external experiences making it possible to extend the subject's associative network. Psychic genera are formed in moments of resonance between the unconscious and the external world, moments when intuition is predominant. Fruitful meanings then well up that become attached to other groups of already existent unconscious ideas – which Bollas calls psychic "matrixes" – and acquire a new form. Unlike traumatic representations that generate deadly repetition and inhibition, this receptive dynamic of the unconscious facilitates the process of giving living meaning to the internal movements of the subject. This does not mean that psychic genera are devoid of negative dimensions. What characterises them is not the positive or negative quality of the contents that they bring into play, but their capacity to promote new links and a broader spectrum of meaning. Bollas places this concept of psychic genera in the tradition of Wilfred Bion's K function and of Freud's life drive.

A patient who had been in treatment for three years reported that the evening before he had watched a very interesting documentary on the British Crown Jewels. He thought that it was a fascinating way of looking at the history of the monarchy. As a result, he had spent the whole night researching into the jewels and their history. However, his account of this interest remained relatively succinct: he had spent quite a lot of time which had distracted him from more important things that he ought to have done, and furthermore he did not even know why he was speaking about that. The theme of the crown jewels seemed to fleetingly run through the session like a simple event of daily life, without being the subject of associations or any elaboration. It seemed to be just a fact, nothing more.

At the time, the patient was going through an important period of professional and financial change. Although he was determined and usually succeeded brilliantly, now he felt invaded by an unbearable sense of passivity: "I don't even want to get up. I am unable to get out of this state."

"Crown jewels, family jewels…", thought the analyst without saying anything, while following two associative threads. First, the question of money: the patient's father had squandered the family heritage, and currently the patient's salary was supporting everyone; second, the question of object-choice: the patient remained hesitant in his sexual orientation.

A few weeks after this episode, this patient spoke about his father who, as usual, had called him to ask him for some money. He talked about the burden of feeling financially responsible for everyone. He had a grudge against his father for expecting him to support him. Moreover, when his father called, he didn't return the call. He didn't feel able to cope with his requests for help. He didn't want to do anything: neither to work nor to return his father's call. He wanted to change profession, start over afresh. He should've been an artisan, he said. If he was doing what he was doing, it was only because he had to earn money for everyone. The analyst then said to him that he perhaps dreamed of having nothing so that he didn't have to give anything to anyone anymore. He stayed silent a moment, then replied: "I had a strange dream, last night. I dreamt about the Queen of England. She was wearing all her jewels, her family jewels."

The theme of the crown jewels and family jewels, which had first appeared to be anecdotic, without any link to the manifest content of the sessions, was gradually enriched by various signifiers whose polysemy made it possible to work on the patient's central conflicts at this moment in the analysis. It was possible to begin to elaborate the passive resistance that was playing such an important role in his life. It also enabled the link to be made between his passive response to his current relatively precarious situation (castration anxiety) and the loss of the virile paternal object.

From Bollas' perspective, we could say that the creation of psychic genera around representations of family jewels/crown jewels gave new impetus to the analytic process.

Further reading

Bion, W.R. (1962). *Learning from experience.* London: Heinemann.
Bion, W.R. (1963). *Elements of psychoanalysis.* London: Heinemann.
Bollas, C. (1992). *Being a character.* New York: Harper Collins.
Bollas, C. (2008). *The evocative object world.* London: Routledge.
Freud, S. (1920). *Beyond the pleasure principle. S.E.* 18. London: Hogarth, pp. 1–64.

KEY WORDS Genera, matrix, unconscious ideation, trauma.

OEDIPUS AS AN ATTRACTOR

MICHEL ODY

This metaphor is at the crossroads of two orders of reflections. First of all, there is a question about what can become of the Oedipus today, at a time when appeal is so easily made to early traces and fixations in the mind to approach the pathology of patients. Then there is the dialogue with chaos theories that allow us to consider that a portion of determinism remains compatible with a certain appearance of chaos, a determinism underlying this appearance, and is represented by the notion of attractor.

Oedipus as an attractor includes four constantly interacting tendencies. Two of them are inherent to the subject ("inside"): that of basic triangulation – here, the concepts of the "other of the object" (Green, 2011), or of the "non-mother" (Le Guen, 2007), must be linked up with the notions of the depressive position (Klein, 1935), of sixth or eighth-month-anxiety (Spitz, 1965 [1958]), etc., – and that of the Oedipus complex, with its own four tendencies, which are themselves reactualised and reorganised during the second phase corresponding to puberty and adolescence. Two other tendencies are inherent to the environment ("the outside"): that of the psychic functioning of each of the parents or of their substitutes – whatever form it takes this functioning has in any case itself been permeated by the Oedipus; it is here that we can identify what is generally called the "transgenerational"– and that of collective functioning in general, which is what Freud's group psychology refers to. This tendency concerns the space in which the symbolic order has been established throughout human history, an order that towers above the individual and the collective order of the moment; it is situated at a distance as well as being an object of reference, including at the unconscious level.

In each individual, these different dimensions organise a unique, specific and singular hypercomplex ensemble. And, of course, it fluctuates and is modified in the course of the subject's evolution. The expression of Oedipus as an attractor connotes a hypercomplexity and marks the fact that consideration of the Oedipus cannot be reduced to its complex alone. It is part of a larger ensemble that nonetheless remains qualifiable by the nominalization itself of Oedipus.

In the session, preserving the hypercomplexity of the Oedipus, particularly in moments when the transference/countertransference situation encourages simplification, is an essential technical requirement.

To illustrate what this means, I will borrow from Fatima Cabral the example that she gave during a workshop of the 2012 Congress for French-Speaking Psychoanalysts (CPLF) in Bilbao. The theme was precisely that of Oedipus as an attractor.

At this point in the analysis, the patient had begun to feel able to fantasise in the analyst's presence. One day, after an initial silence, he said he felt embarrassed by what had come to his mind. Then he brought associations to repeated childhood nightmares in which he would see abstract forms moving away from him before they returned violently. When his analyst evoked them during the workshop, I understood them for my part as a sort of abstract transformation of unrepresentable primary "figures", comparable to those that we sometimes see in children's drawings which constituted "primary scars" that they can only mentalise very summarily.

The patient continued. He realised that he had told the analyst this dream in connection with something that had just escaped him. His analyst, from his position of Oedipus as an attractor, had an overview of the two phases of this process (the first in which he felt embarrassment and the second in which he narrated his dream). She then reminded her patient that before speaking about his nightmares, he had first evoked a sense of embarrassment. She suggested to him that this embarrassment might be linked to the fact that he felt her to be "either very far away or very close". At this moment, with great emotion and some difficulty, the patient managed to take up again the evocation of the "images" that had come to his mind.

Their description opened out on to striking signifiers, in the maternal register, which also brought into play various symbols. In the course of his associations these symbols took on a sexualised connotation, to the point of bringing infantile sexuality into play. As the analysis progressed, drawing on this type of movement of primary triangulation established in the transference, various representations of paternal figures gradually manifested themselves.

Further reading

Ody, M. (1990). Oedipe comme attracteur. In: *Revue française de Psychanalyse (Monograph: La psychanalyse Questions pour demain)*. Paris: Presses Universitaires de France, pp. 211–219.

Ody, M. (2015). Oedipe attracteur, une étape à Bilbao. *Revue française de Psychanalyse*, 5: 1587–1593.
Pragier, G. & Faure-Pragier, S. (2007). *Repenser la psychanalyse avec les sciences*. Paris: Presses Universitaires de France.
Stewart, I. (1992). *Dieu joue-t-il aux dés?* Paris: Flammarion.

KEY WORDS Thirdness, triangulation.

NORMOPATHY

DOMINIQUE TABONE-WEIL

The notion of normopathy was introduced by Joyce McDougall in an article of 1972, taken up again in the last chapter (bearing the same title) of her book, *Plea for a Measure of Abnormality* (McDougall, 1992 [1978]), originally published at a time when questions of madness, mental illness and norms were boiling joyfully in the cauldron of thought, whether analytic or not. Our conception of normality has since changed, so that this text probably seems more subversive today than it did at the time.

The question of whether one is normal or not nonetheless lingers in many people's minds, even in our era when what once seemed transgressive now appears quite ordinary. Joyce McDougall traces this question back to castration anxiety which persists, even if it manifests itself differently depending on the state of mores. "It has simply found new disguises," she says (1992 [1978], p. 478).

Of normality erected as an ideal, she says that it is a symptom, a defensive character formation against the fear of existing and of having to confront reality. In other words, asking oneself whether one is normal or not, trying to be normal at any price, irrespective of the norms, avoids having to ask oneself questions about one's own desires and fantasies, having to recognise "all that is most painful and scandalous in the depths of our being – not only the forbidden erotic desires but also our infantile avidity for what we do not possess, unsuspected selfishness, our childlike narcissism, and our murderous aggression" (p. 480). An analysis confronts us precisely with what is most alien and most intimate in ourselves. And, she adds, not only does analysis lead us to discover not only that "I is another" (*Je est un autre*) … "but worse, that the I may dissolve, making way for nameless anxiety. Why should anyone seek to possess this knowledge? Who wants to question all that he knows, all that he is?" she continues (p. 480).

We might be led to think here about Eichmann, whom Hannah Arendt described, at the time of his trial, as an "incredibly mediocre and insignificant", "terrifyingly normal" little man confined within a glass booth, twitching and quibbling over anecdotic details (hours, dates), while he was accused of having taken part in one of the greatest crimes committed against humanity. In her article "Thinking and moral considerations" (Arendt, 1971) she writes: "Clichés, stock phrases, adherence to conventional and standardised codes of expression and conduct have the socially recognized function of protecting us against reality, that is, the claim on our thinking attention that all facts and events make by virtue of their existence. If we were to respond to the claim that we should think when we speak all the time, we would soon be exhausted; the difference in Eichmann was only that he clearly knew of no such claim at all" (p. 161), echoing McDougall.

In the same book she also says that the "banality of evil" "could not be traced to any particularity of wickedness, pathology or ideological conviction in the doer, whose only personal distinction was perhaps an *extraordinary shallowness*" (p. 159, author's emphasis). Absence of pathology or normopathy? In her report *Eichmann in Jerusalem: A Report on the Banality of Evil* (Arendt, 1963) she describes him as a "failure in the eyes of his social class, of his family and hence in his own eyes as well" (p. 32), a man whose life was full of frustrations, who was rejected, excluded, sent away from everywhere and for whom his "engagement" in the Nazi Party and the SS was an opportunity to belong to something. He himself, explaining during his trial what he had felt on 8th May 1945 said: "I sensed I would have to live a leaderless and difficult individual life, I would receive no directives from anybody, no orders or commands would any longer be issued to me, no pertinent ordinances would be there to consult, in brief, a life never known before lay before me" (p. 32).

For McDougall, "the so-called normal individual does in fact "create a protective shield we call normality. Such a person respects the ideals that have been handed down to him, as he respects the rules of society" (1992 [1978], p. 480). For her part, Arendt explains: "Non-thinking…teaches people to hold fast to whatever the prescribed rules of conduct may be at a given time in a given society. What people then get used to is less the content of the rules, a close examination of which would always lead them into perplexity but rather the possession of rules under which to subsume particulars. If somebody appears who, for whatever purposes, wishes to abolish the old 'values' or virtues, he will find that easy enough, provided he offers a new code. He will need relatively little force and no persuasion – i.e. proof that the new values are better than the old – to impose it" (1978, p. 177).

Thinking, she writes, is an activity that is an endless process that produces no settled results, a quest for meaning that accompanies life, and, like "Penelope's web, it undoes every morning what it has finished the night before" (p. 88), a definition that could equally well apply to analysis.

Eichmann could be seen as a clinical case of normopathy in a society where the norm is inverted and where the commandments say "Thou shalt kill", "Thou shalt steal", "Thou shalt not feel any compassion" and, finally, "Thou shalt not think"; he could be seen as embodying the experience of being subjected to the terror of being rejected into outer darkness and of being excluded from the "group". This banal figure can also help us, following McDougall, to see how ignorance of one's own unconscious can lead one to project its contents on to others whom, ultimately, one then follows blindly (the Führer embodying the ideal ego, the superego and the ego ideal all at once) or exterminates (the Jews embodying evil, denied in oneself). Psychoanalysis, which in principle encourages listening to one's own unconscious, could thus help to find paths of elaboration and resolution for conflicts other than the negation of oneself and otherness.

All this invites us to reflect further on the abysses to which blind submission to the idea of a norm or an authority, whatever it may be, can lead, especially when one is a psychoanalyst, that is, necessarily belonging to a group, to a "society", and when one is often required to decide what is normal and what is not.

Further reading

Arendt, H. (1963). *Eichmann in Jerusalem: A report on the Banality of evil.* London: Penguin.

Arendt, H. (1971). Thinking and moral considerations. *Social Research,* 38(3): 419–446.

Arendt, H. (1978). *The life of the mind.* London: Secker & Warburg.

McDougall, J. (1992 [1978]). *Plea for a measure of abnormality.* New York: Brunner/Mazel.

Von Trotta, M. (Director & Writer). (2012). *Hannah Arendt* [Motion picture]. Germany/Luxembourg/France: Heimatfilm.

KEY WORDS Banality of evil, ignorance of oneself, pathology of character, submission to authority.

THE ANTI-ANALYSAND

DOMINIQUE TABONE-WEIL

The concept of anti-analysand was suggested by Joyce McDougall in 1972. She describes patients who seem to accept and respect scrupulously the formal aspects of analysis, but with whom the analytic process does not get underway. The anti-analysand is punctual and assiduous; he never misses a session, but remains at the level of factual narrative. Gradually, a hatred for thinking and an indifference to the internal world and to psychic life is revealed, accompanied by a denial of affects which seem frozen, except for constant mute feelings of anger towards his entourage, which is held responsible for everything that is wrong. Anti-analysands reject links, associations, and the transference relationship. In this picture we can recognise certain characteristics of narcissistic problems in which unconscious rage and destructiveness predominate. They have extracted the tangible, living nucleus of their conflict with the other; all that remains is the outer surface which is impenetrable to pain. This mode of functioning is thus akin to the "operational" mode of thinking (*pensée opératoire*) described by Pierre Marty and Michel de M'Uzan in psychosomatic patients. Like the patient, the analyst ends up withdrawing too, losing curiosity, no longer investing in the analysis.

Is such a patient really an anti-analysand? The analyst always has the tendency to ask himself when feeling boredom or the desire to withdraw if it is not he who is at certain moments, and/or with certain patients, an anti-analyst? Perhaps this is how one recognises in the countertransference the anti-analysands that McDougall speaks about.

Be that as it may, the patient I am referring to here respected scrupulously the analytic protocol: he was assiduous, punctual, regular, etc. He never missed a session. The detailed factual narrative was not disagreeable to listen to because he put all his talent for narrating into it in order to keep the auditor spellbound, but he was often conventional and cold in an improbable style between a horror film and a new novel, perhaps. His courtesy bordered on obsequiousness, the sign of tangible hatred that was especially great in that he clung to his sessions like to the apple of his eye. His rage no doubt stemmed from the sense of dependence he felt towards the object that the analyst represented (reminiscent of the destructive envy of the infant for the breast, according to D.W. Winnicott, welling up at the very moment when the milk spurts and satisfies the need). He did not deny the importance of his analysis, and even had the feeling that it was of vital importance, but if the analyst ventured a transference interpretation, he would reject it immediately: "Ah that? You want to speak about those things, the transference and all that, in which I supposedly take you for my mother? No, I don't believe in all that. In any case, it doesn't mean anything to me at all." Listening to him, one might almost feel embarrassed to admit that, yes, one "stills believes in all that nonsense". The same was true for free association, the pertinence of which he constantly rejected, preparing no doubt a long time in advance what one might call his "session discourse".

What the analyst understood was that he could not allow himself to feel negative affects directly towards her, because they were much too violent and destructive. These affects manifested themselves through his attacks on the foundations of the analysis, even if he did not see them as such. They also found expression in the account he gave of violent, sadistic fantasies and forms of behaviour that he had difficulty controlling and which he recounted in detail and with suspense to boot, often making the analyst shudder (which was no doubt the effect he wanted to create). He was inevitably addicted to pornography as well to excesses of all kinds (cigarettes, cannabis, speed, alcohol, including before driving his motorbike). His self-destructiveness in the form of these addictive behaviours, which put his own life in danger, was a source of concern. During the analysis, he developed an autoimmune disease that was uncurable but treatable, with which he "played" a great deal, always teetering on the edge of decompensation.

It was a little child with severe deficiencies that the analyst had on her couch, who was struggling not to fall into psychosis, to survive psychically, and not to destroy his objects. He had a vital and frantic need to find and create through his analysis an acceptable primary environment, a containing mother, neither too exciting nor rejecting, who would allow him to exist while denying the affective dimension of this relationship – and also to meet a father who was neither indifferent nor full of hatred, who would set some limits and "safeguards". The hatred and rage that were expressed abundantly during the sessions could not be recognised as affects towards the analyst, because he could not take the risk of attacking the benevolent object that he needed to see in her and the "haven of peace" that the session was for him, a place where he was reconstructing his life by giving an account of it, however factual it was. Not for the time being, at least. Likewise, he was unable to recognise the scale of the relational catastrophe with his parents in early childhood, even though is effects and signs were clearly visible in his current relationship with them.

The transference love could not be recognised as such either. The analyst was there to help him understand and restore something, but in an intellectual way, he thought. At best, the analyst was a sort of technician of the soul, a repairer of history, a mender of the past, and at worst a services provider towards whom he consciously had no passionate or burning feelings.

Contrary to the canonical description by McDougall, this patient was not psychically dead; but he had not extracted the tangible nucleus of his conflict with the other. For this he paid a very high psychic price and the analyst was there to help him keep this central nucleus alive in a bearable way.

It cannot really be said that an analytic process was underway, but nor was it simply a matter of providing support, even if the analyst's interventions amounted to little more than psychotherapy. Were the changes that occurred in his life in the register of *acting* or did they bear witness to an evolution in his internal world *via* the evolution of the transference relationship? We may wonder. In any case, the analyst felt discouraged and had major doubts. She even often felt afraid: the catastrophe had perhaps already taken place in the past, but that did not mean that another one was not possible at any moment. Sometimes, however, he was ready to recognise what was happening within him, to accept this violence, this hatred, this rage as being his own, as symptoms of his madness, of his suffering, directed against an object of the past rather than "provoked" by the other in the present who was allegedly the cause of it and for whom the analyst sometimes trembled.

However that may be and whatever the reasons for it were, the idea, as McDougall puts it, that he "cared about his analytic adventure", even if he also insisted on denying its specificity, on attacking its foundations, gradually prevailed over the analyst's sense of discouragement. As André Green said, and like the captain in Joseph Conrad's *Typhoon,* the essential thing for the analyst is sometimes to stand firm or, in Winnicott's terms, to remain a living object.

Further reading

Conrad, J. (1902). *Typhoon*. New York: Putnam.
Freud, S. (1920). *Beyond the pleasure principle. S.E.* 18. London: Hogarth, pp. 1–66.
Green, A. (1986). *On private madness*. London: Hogarth.
McDougall, J. (1992 [1972]). The anti-analysand in analysis. In: *Plea for a measure of abnormality*. New York: Brunner/Mazel, pp. 219–247.
McDougall, J. (1992 [1978]). *Plea for a measure of abnormality*. New York: Brunner/Mazel.
Winnicott, D.W. (1971). *Playing and reality*. London: Tavistock.

KEY WORDS Attack, denial of the transference, narcissistic rage, risk of decathexis.

THE NEGATIVE THERAPEUTIC REACTION

DOMINIQUE TABONE-WEIL

In *Analysis Terminable and Interminable,* Freud (1937) speaks of the negative therapeutic reaction, linking it to the effects of the death drive, after having linked it in his earlier writings (*The Ego and the Id,* 1923) to unconscious guilt, masochism, the need for punishment and the resistances of the superego.

Anyway, it is defined as a paradoxical aggravation during the course of a treatment, occurring after an improvement and particularly, says Freud, when one has drawn the patient's attention to this improvement. It is considered as a particularly tough resistance, which, like a quicksand in which the analyst is caught, sucks and traps him all the more as he increases his efforts (interpretations) to escape from it.

Nevertheless, it is not the equivalent of a failure of the analysis, although it can be a cause, due to a rupture or to getting bogged down in an interminable treatment. It bears witness to a specific psychic organisation of narcissistic problems of identity, with a relationship to the primary object that is marked by pain, frustration and failure to adjust to the patient's needs (including the failure to recognise the child as a distinct individual). It is the transference reactivation of this unbearable pain which raises a radical opposition to the transformative potential of the analysis. The patient clings hatefully and desperately to the analyst, who is experienced as a reincarnation of this passionately cathected primary object whom there can be no question of losing, but to whom there can equally be no question of "yielding". The patient "reacts" to the analyst by opposing every "action" on the latter's part, because to change, to be transformed, would feel like submission to the object and a defeat of identity. "Change!" the patient hears the analyst saying. "Renounce your suffering!" "I would rather die!" replies the patient. "Rather die than be healed, give in to you, give you pleasure, lose you."

"To get better" would be to lose the object: not only the internal object to whom complaints reproaches, resentment and hopelessness are addressed tirelessly (sometimes through a desire for vengeance, but also in the hope of obtaining at long last recognition and love or at least compensation for harm suffered), but also the object's transferential incarnation, which the patient would no longer meet in reality as a result of the end of his treatment.

A patient I had been seeing for about a year had been in therapy with a colleague for severe melancholic episodes. When he first came to see me, he had been on antidepressants for several months and said of his previous treatment that his therapist and he had decided by common consent to stop, because "they were going round in circles" which "no longer served any purpose".

The disaster of his existence was impressive: an unhappy marriage in which he was inextricably entangled, two adolescent boys who were doing badly, a job, certain aspects of which he liked more or less secretly, in which he was performing very well, but for which he did not feel recognised. He was clearly experiencing mental pain which gradually diminished as the months went by, without it being clear whether it was the effect of his current medical treatment or of his sessions following on from his previous therapy.

There was a heavy atmosphere of immobility and massive refusal. The analyst felt that the patient was making her pay for what he considered as the failure of his previous therapy and a rejection by his therapist. He also rejected many interventions, seeming to say that his case was desperate and that the analyst could do nothing for him. Every sign of improvement was dismissed as insignificant or announcing the worst. He fiercely defended everything that caused his woes about which he complained vociferously. "Stay out of it!" he seemed to say. "I am the only person who has the right to look at my woes, for which I am not responsible and in which I will always be stuck". In short, he presented himself as one of those patients of whom one says, "They cling to their symptoms" and seem determined not to get better, even if it means engaging in a merciless battle with their analyst to prove their incurability.

The analyst was sometimes tempted to withdraw narcissistically in *reaction* to the repeated rebuffals (if he set so much store on his misfortune, then, after all, let him keep it or if the analyst was not good enough for him, then let him go and see someone else) but she did not have too much difficulty in avoiding this temptation. At the same time, she was careful not to "take up the challenge" that he was secretly issuing. She made sure that she preserved a flexible inner attitude, talking to him freely, formulating some of her questionings out loud, without playing the one who "knows it all" – that is to say, without pretending to be the omniscient and omnipotent object who *ipso facto* would provoke negative reactions. After all, she said to herself, are we not all to some extent hung up on our symptoms, on our secret illness, on the secret object of our desire? As the sessions progressed, the sense of boredom and heaviness faded away. It cannot be said that they were overflowing with life, but something was moving and an authentic contact had been made between analyst and patient.

During one session, he was talking, as he often did, about his work. He wanted to change his job, he was looking for something else and someone had offered him a very interesting post which, however, he had more or less decided to refuse because the salary on offer was the same as that of the position he currently had. He does not want to be "taken for a ride". He did not want to "prove them right", to "give them that pleasure". "They" were his current bosses, who did not recognise his real value, and he wanted to make them pay for this henceforth by doing the bare minimum. "They" were also his possible future bosses who thought they could "have" him without paying him properly.

The analyst pointed out to him that, in doing this, it was above all he himself that he was depriving and punishing. Especially as in his current job, he was beginning to be caught up in negative interactions that were likely to get worse, as well as his bitterness and resentment that were poisoning him more than his managers.

At the same time, she wondered what he was saying to her about *their* work. By his "current work", was he referring to his previous therapy, during which he was told that he was "going round in circles"? Or did he mean *their* work together, which he seemed to value whilst subtly denigrating it. Was the analyst charging enough compared to her colleague whose fees were higher? In the transference, was she the maternal object to whom he turned for comfort after being subjected to his father's anger? An object at once idealized and devalued, because what counted, what he would have liked to have obtained, was the love and recognition of his terrible father, who was omnipotent, violent and rejecting and who preferred his younger brother, just as bosses today prefer "young" people.

While remaining on the manifest level of his discourse, the analyst also pointed out to him that he had wanted a change for some time, and that the pleasure he would take in a new job, in new exchanges, in a new mode of functioning and relationships that would not be spoiled by old resentments, could perhaps counterbalance the absence of a salary increase.

At the same time, it was clear that he was afraid to leave his boss, "that asshole" by whom he was "getting screwed", he said, his homosexual sadomasochistic relationship with him, and a familiar way of relating that caused him suffering, for sure, but which he endured as a necessity.

The point of view that the analyst put forward did, however, make him think. "Perhaps you are right" he finally said. "Perhaps it would be better." Knowing him, she told herself that he was only giving in order to do better next time, and that perhaps she would have done better to keep quiet. She continued to wonder about the meaning of these possible or impossible changes, and what they really meant for him.

Anyway, it was the end of the session and the analyst was still left with her questions.

> "Good", he said, "OK, I'm ready to try and change."

A silence followed.

> "But then," he added, looking at the analyst with great attention, "if I change, I will not be able to come to see you anymore. Because if I have a new job, I will not be able to leave two hours early in the evening. We will have to stop!"

The analyst was quite stunned by this outcome that she might have anticipated and through which he exposed his dilemma in a remarkably concise and clear way. It is not suffering, writes J.-B. Pontalis, that the "negatives" do not want to give up. What they do not want is to *lose*, in both senses of the word: not losing the object and not being the loser.

Further reading

Pontalis, J.-B. (1983). *Perdre de vue*. Paris: Gallimard. (Series: Connaissance de l'inconscient).

KEY WORDS Unconscious guilt, to lose, refusal to change, narcissistic identity disorder.

THE DYNAMIC APRÈS-COUP

ROSINE JOZEF PERELBERG

One could distinguish between the descriptive idea of après-coup and the concept of a dynamic après-coup. The first is widely present in French psychoanalysis and simply means "after". The concept of a dynamic après-coup implies different temporalities such as the notions of fixation, regression, compulsion to repeat, and the return of the repressed. These different temporal notions refer to the heterochrony in psychoanalysis, developed in particular by André Green. In addition, the concept of dynamic après-coup is part of a network constituted by other concepts, such as trauma, castration, passivation and infantile sexuality, which gives it its metapsychological and "third" dimension.

The operation of après-coup is a dynamic movement that brings the temporalities of the subject into play in a constant to-and-fro. In what way does this point of view illuminate clinical practice and make it possible to establish new links between different types of material? In the following example, a link is established between a painting, a dream, the here-and-now of the transference, and a childhood memory. They are gradually organised into a chain that makes sense in the situation of the transference and enriches the echoes of the actuality of the session.

A woman, a renowned sculptor in her fifties, petite and brunette, came to do an analysis. She walked lightly, as if suspended, with a rare elegance. She wanted, she said, to do an analysis because she was afraid of losing her memory and at times felt unable to think. She had undergone many medical examinations to see if her concerns had any basis, but nothing organic had been found. She had already done an analysis and felt that it had helped her. She was married and had two daughters.

During the last few sessions, she had had dreams in which the presence of celebrities indicated her tendency to idealise the analyst and her narcissistic identification with her. She had read a chapter of a book the analyst had recently written and found that the style was clear, that she could understand it. She added that she had the same impression in the sessions. She felt that the analyst spoke in an "embodied" way, and that it was no doubt her way of being, unlike her previous analyst whom she felt was too "cerebral".

During the session in question, the patient first spoke of her admiration for the analyst, but also of the terror she inspired in her because she knew so well how to write and teach. She also talked about meetings at work with other colleagues she admired enormously. She suffered in front of them when she felt stupid and had nothing to offer. She went on to mention a weekend in Salzburg, where she had seen statues of Mozart. In this city, there are no end of statues to his glory, he is an absolute idol. The analyst then pointed out that her way of putting her colleagues and herself on a pedestal left her empty, without anything. This was followed by a period of silence. Then the patient talked about a painting she had seen that morning in an exhibition, depicting a woman and an eight-year-old girl. It was revolting eroticism. The woman was standing over the little girl and kissing her on the lips. The girl, head back, was in a position of total abandonment. Yet she was also being singularly active in this kiss. The girl had red lips and eyelashes thick with black mascara, as if this make-up was the signature of the kiss that this woman had laid on her mouth. "And it was also as if the girl had suddenly become an adult woman", the patient finally exclaimed. "A totally erotic painting". A vibratory silence settled in the space of the session.

After a moment, the patient said that all this made her think of her relationship with her mother. She had never previously thought about it like this. She could recall her passionate feelings towards her. During an argument, as a teenager, she had even told her one day: "You will end up kissing me to death". This, then, was the movement in the session: first, the idealisation of the analyst which left the patient emptied, then a second defeat, erotic this time, and the repetition of the sensation of being kissed to death, abandoned to the kiss that depicts in her fantasy the exchange between analyst and patient during the session.

The analyst then said to her: "When you abandon yourself to me during the session, you do not simply feel empty, but that you are being kissed to death."

Even though she had thought about what she was going to say, she felt surprised when she said it. They both stayed silent for a while. There followed what certainly seemed to be a dynamic après-coup. During the session, there were indeed echoes of very different temporalities, and it was in this respect that there was a dynamic après-coup: starting from the actuality of the session, the movement then focused on the evocation of the painting, then on the patient's memory of her experience of her relationship as a little girl to her mother (the kiss), then on the dispute in adolescence, throwing new light retrospectively on the experience of this little girl. All these moments constituted a source of light and new perspectives for deploying the analytical experience of the here-and-now of this session.

In short, it is the establishment of the link between the actuality of the transference experienced in the session and the affective experience of the past elucidated by a memory of adolescence, then the return in a loop to what is being played out in the present session, that constitutes the essential movement of the dynamic après-coup. Four dimensions of time are gathered here: the abandonment/defeat in front of the analyst in the actuality of the session, the erotic image of the painting of the woman and the little girl, the memory of the passion of the patient as a child for her mother, that of the adolescent's quarrel with the latter and her statement: "You will end up kissing me to death". In the here-and-now, both the present and the past may be experienced and understood as an après-coup in the experience of "fragmented time" (*le temps éclaté*).

Further reading

Althusser, L., et al. (1970 [1968]). *Reading capital*, trans. B. Brewster. London: New Left Books.

Chervet, B. (2009). L'après-coup. La tentative d'inscrire ce qui tend à disparaitre. *Revue française de psychoanalyse*, 78: 1361–1442.

Chervet, B. (2009). L'après-coup. *Prolégomènes. Revue française de psychoanalyse*, 70: 671–700.

Donnet, J.-L. (1995). *Le Divan bien tempéré*. Paris: Presses Universitaires de France.

Donnet, J.-L. (2006). L'après-coup au carré. *Revue française de psychoanalyse*, 70(3): 715–725.

Green, A. (1982). Après-coup, l'archaique. *Nouvelle Revue de Psychoanalyse*, 26: 195–216 ("L'archaique").

Green, A. (2002). *Time in psychoanalysis: Some contradictory aspects*, trans. A. Weller. London: Free Association Books.

Perelberg, R.J. (2006). Les controverses et l'après-coup. *Revue française de psychanalyse*, 70(3): 647–670.

Perelberg, R.J. (2009). Après-coup dynamique: implications pour une théorie de la clinique. *Revue française de psychoanalyse*, 73(5): 1583–1589.

KEY WORDS Descriptive après-coup, dynamic après-coup, castration, heterochrony, infantile sexuality, trauma.

RECOVERY

LUCETTE NOBS

The "fitness effect": this is how a patient ironically described the immediate experience of effort and pleasure in the session. It is a defensive formula, obviously excluding presence, the relationship with the other and the analyst, unless the latter is confined to a "mirror effect" whose purpose is to bring the narcissistic claim to its term; and unless time, space and the object of the transference are incarnated in everything, the space of the session, the fixed framework and the rhythm, and that the purpose is to induce the subject to engage in associativity, providing him with a field of tonic wandering between the inside and the outside, an autonomous and autoerotic field almost without danger. Can lightness and movement be considered as acceptable gains of analysis? Would recognition of well-being then only be possible by running the risk of denying the most fundamental gain of analysis? For if analysis permits the patient to a better conscious sense of well-being, can it change the patient's relationship to his feminine attachment figures, incarnated by the object of the transference? Does this flaunted sense of well-being not signify that the subject refuses to play an honest game, to rely on the other and to resist him, to desire to be loved and to fight against the abandonment that this desire implies? In order to be effective, does the method not require the acceptance of a certain state of dependence of the ego with regard to the drive impulse aimed at the object-analyst? It is certainly necessary for a sufficiently libidinalised and tolerable cathexis of the shared work to develop, but can this be expressed in terms of well-being? Are we not in a logic of avoidance?

The question is no less pertinent when the atmosphere of the session and the flow of words follow the opposite course, when associativity is irregular, constrained and anguished. The liberating effectiveness of the work and its healing power are no longer assured. Thus, to provide an image of his life and to probe what we could share, another patient referred to literary texts. By evoking them, he found an ephemeral way to give shape to the pain and the shame of his own story. The fictional narrative provided him with a more dignified access to the understanding of the disaster of his life, and to the play of forces that fate had violently confronted him with.

Yet he was suffering from this recourse to the images and words of another in order to construct a "view" of his own story. He felt dispossessed. Moreover, to organise his suffering in narrative form was also to risk giving meaning to the complaint he was addressing to his analyst and a way of overcoming the confusion of the spaces between himself and the other. The image of the wandering rat in the labyrinth under the indifferent gaze of the observer was often reflected in his remarks. It said much about the anguished picture he had of an inhuman therapeutic relationship and his catastrophic experience of dissymmetry.

Two logics of resistance oppose recovery: the compelling need for "something to happen" and, conversely, the terror that it will not happen. In all cases, we could say with Jean-Luc Donnet that the patient "clashes" with the method and that it is on the possibility of overcoming this clash that acceptance of the idea of recovery and the psychic change that it implies depend.

For Nathalie Zaltzman (1998), psychoanalytic recovery inevitably raises the question of the difficulty for man to live at the level of what determines him, namely, his relationship to the other, his libidinal structure, and his condition of being cultural. She boldly points out that in the psychoanalytic sense of the term "recovery" (*la guérison*) can be nothing but a strictly personal matter, if only due to the unavoidable and immortal instinctual drive determinations of the patient and to his affiliation to a human reality shared by all subjects. Moreover, if illness is indeed, as she asserts, the final narcissistic bulwark against the risks of the sexual dimension, then it has to be accepted that recovery implies the recognition of the movements of this sexual dimension within the therapeutic relationship. "Analysis does not set out to make pathological reactions impossible but to give the patient's ego *freedom* to decide one way or the other" Freud wrote in *The Ego and the Id* (1923, p. 50, note 1). This freedom of choice is assured all the better in that it enables the subject to initiate a movement that permits him to transform his subjective experience into common knowledge capable of constituting a capital of sharable reason.

Further reading

Freud, S. (1923). *The ego and the id. S.E.* 19. London: Hogarth, pp. 13–66.

Zaltzman, N. (1998). *De la guérison psychanalytique.* Paris: Presses Universitaires de France. (Series: Épîtres).

(1978). *Nouvelle Revue de Psychanalyse,* 17 ("L'idée de guérison"). Paris: Gallimard.

(2002). *Monographies de psychoanalyse,* ("Quelle guérison, quelle normalité"). *Revue française de psychanalyse.* Paris: Presses Universitaires de France.

KEY WORDS Recovery, infantile, object, resistance.

15

CREATION OF THE THIRD

THE ANALYTIC THIRD

VIRGINIA PICCHI

We are indebted to Thomas Ogden for the concept of the analytic third. It refers to the intermediary, intersubjective analytic space that emerges between an analyst and a patient through a process of unconscious exchange during a session. The analytic third is a space where thoughts, fantasies and affects that may have otherwise remained silent are mobilised and manifested. Although it emerges from a process of co-creation, the form and content of this "third" element are primarily determined by the patient's internal object world, his unconscious fantasies and defence system. This notion is reminiscent of the concepts of potential space of D.W. Winnicott (1960) and the analytic object of Andre Green (1975).

In order to access this co-creation, the analyst must be able to draw on his most banal reveries. For this, he must be able to tolerate his own uncomfortable sensations and feelings: feeling lost, frustrated, angry or confused, for instance. The analytic third can only really be constituted and thought about retrospectively, often long after being experienced in the session. It is not an event experienced identically by both participants, but an unconscious and asymmetrical co-creation that gives structure to the analytic relationship.

A patient usually came to her sessions having prepared herself in advance; she would begin with an exhaustive list of what she had done, thought about and felt since the last session. She expressed all this without the slightest affect, in an almost sterile manner, as if she were establishing an autopsy report on her psychic life, taking care to enumerate each element without providing the slightest elaboration. This approach to sessions sometimes left the analyst feeling trapped and helpless, as if the patients factual, pragmatic narrative accounts prevented the analyst from thinking, associating or being receptive to her own reveries or those of the patient.

The patient described her parents as absent. Her father was never home, her mother who neglected her for her father. Her parents would go out night after night, leaving her alone in bed. She would stay awake, waiting for their return and fearing in advance the violent scenes between her parents in the early morning.

One day, the patient started the session with her usual list of what had happened that week. The analyst felt bored and withdrew internally, checking the clock to watch the passing time. And all of a sudden, she had a memory of a night she had spent in a mountain hut: a long row of tightly aligned beds in a huge dormitory with only two small windows. A feeling of oppression and claustrophobia overcame her: those small beds, the narrow windows, the feeling of being locked up with no escape.

At that moment, the patient spoke of her need to feel the physical presence of her companion to be able to fall asleep. That was why, she said, with the analyst she did not want to lie on the couch. She needed visual contact to be able to see what the analyst might be thinking and feeling, and to be able to orient herself in the space of the session.

The analyst then said to herself: "I am stuck here like a pinned butterfly." Then she associated inwardly with her cousin who collected butterflies. When they were children, she was jealous of him. He was so precise and careful! She admired his way of classifying and organising everything. And yet, thinking today of the way in which this cousin had sunk into alcoholism, she could not refrain from feeling a certain sense of triumph.

The patient continued by describing how she scrutinised the slightest gestures of her companion. "And if you were to let go of him a little bit?" thought the analyst, annoyed. The day before, they had quarrelled. He never did things as she would like them to be done! "Sometimes I do not exist for him," she said, "and it makes me want to leave at once." The analyst, responding to the transference allusion to an insatiable demand for attention, intervened: "It's as if his inattentive presence just left you stuck there like some kind of decoration, trapped, pinned down, and the only thing you can think of is running away, getting out of there."

At that moment in the session, the analyst's reverie linked up with the content of the patient's associations. This led to a memory on the part of the patient: she was in bed, stuck in her blankets, trapped and panicked. Her father came into the room to comfort and reassure her. He adjusted the covers and calmed her down. This is the first time in the course of the treatment that her father has appeared as an empathic paternal presence.

In this session, a situation was created between the patient and the analyst which cast the pervasive feeling of affectless immobility in a new light and led to a verbal elaboration of new material. In retrospect, the analyst understood her reveries during the session—the images (the dormitory, the butterflies, the word "anarchic') and the various uncomfortable feelings they evoked in her (claustrophobia, repulsion, confusion, aggression)—as ideational and sensorial elaborations occurring in articulation with the archaic unconscious feelings of nocturnal terror, abandonment and non-differentiation of the patient. The gradual unfolding of this intersubjective experience led to the emergence, in the transferential context, of the representation of a differentiated, benevolent paternal object.

Further reading

Green, A. (1975). The analyst, symbolisation, and absence in the analytic setting (On changes in analytic practice and analytic experience). *Memory of D.W. Winnicott, International Journal of Psychoanalysis*, 56: 1–22.

Ogden, T. (1994). The analytic third: Working with intersubjective clinical facts. *International Journal of Psychoanalysis*, 75(1): 3–19.

Ogden, T. (1996). Reconsidering three aspects of psychoanalytical technique. *International Journal of Psychoanalysis*, 77: 883–899.

Ogden, T. (2005). Le tiers analytique: les implications pour la théorie et la technique psychoanalytique. *Revue francaise de psychoanalyse*, 69: 751–774.

Winnicott, D.W. (1960). The theory of the parent/infant relationship. *International Journal of Psychoanalysis*, 41: 585–595.

KEY WORDS Intersubjective and interpersonal fields, unconscious co-creation.

CENSORSHIP OF THE WOMAN-AS-LOVER

ANNE MAUPAS AND
ALETH PRUDENT-BAYLE

Michel Fain (1971) elaborated this concept in his article "Prelude to fantasy life". It was developed and deepened with Denise Braunschweig throughout their joint work.

"The censorship of the woman-as-lover is the censorship introduced by the mother of the child when part of her erotic libido refuses to be a mother" (Fain, 1971, p. 292). This censorship is exercised when the mother suspends her role as a mother to resume her role as a woman. At this point, she decathects her child in favour of a third who can be the object of her fantasy. The mother's capacity to share herself between her baby and her other cathexes creates the necessary conditions for the child's symbolic capacity and serves as the basis of oedipal organisation.

The analyst heard a knock at the door, and opened it. There was nobody there! It was systematic. This patient, hidden in the hallway, always appeared with a slight delay. This ritual seemed more like a game of "Hello, it's me!" than the expression of a neurotic discomfort related to the oedipal fantasy of the primal scene with the intention of disturbing it. What did she fear? "I'm so boring," she said, "that I'm always surprised you're there".

She had come for a consultation in connection with somatic symptoms: asthma and eczema. She was the daughter of parents who had separated very early on and, for her, the couple did not exist. She was desperately and hatefully attached to a mother described as distant, always ready to abandon her. "She preferred working," she said, "to caring for her daughter." Now that she was a mother herself, how could she escape the fate of this identification that would turn her, too, into a 'bad mother'?" To prevent this misfortune, she established a fusional relationship with her baby. This was the only means she had of maintaining a "good maternal image" of herself. She could not leave her daughter day or night, keeping an eye on her as she slept. The baby's insomnia worried her, but reassured her at the same time because "a sleeping child may not wake up". These paradoxical thoughts were constant and disturbing; she suffered from being stuck to her child and constantly failed to give herself any credit. The analyst offered this thought: "Whether a mother is good enough or unsatisfactory, it only concerns the mother. A woman who has a baby is simply a mother who has ousted the woman and the lover. And, by the way, where did your baby come from?"

Not being able to think of herself as different from the "abandoning" maternal imago, this patient felt obliged to constantly cathect her child's ego. However, the decathexis of the child's ego by the mother is the condition for "the child's escape" (the state of hallucination and reverie) which leads to hallucinatory wish-fulfilment, the discovery of autoerotisms, and the representation of the absent object. These representations resonate with primal fantasies and thus constitute the nucleus of the unconscious. However, by sticking to her daughter, she does not transmit to her, at the moment of falling asleep, the double message that every mother transmits to her child: one charged with the life drive, which encourages self-preservation ("It's important that you sleep in order to be healthy") and the other with the death drive ("I want you to sleep so that I can be rid of you"). The quality of this essential time in the relationship depends on the pulsional weaving *(intrication pulsionelle)* of the two sides of the message.

Michel Fain differentiates between an adequate mother and a "calming" mother: the adequate mother can keep displeasure and the associated disagreeable representations at bay when soothing the child, while the "calming mother" *("mere operatoire")* soothes the child with continuous and mechanic rocking which is, in fact, overstimulating.

After the holidays, the patient once again told the analyst that she should really throw her out because she, the patient, "was going to bore her" and would no longer be able to "satisfy" her. The analyst said: "If I am absent, you prefer to think you are unsatisfactory rather than to imagine me wanting to be with a satisfying companion who would distance us from each other for good! It may be such thoughts that you dread attributing to your baby when you are in your bedroom with your husband."

During the course of the treatment, the patient initially managed to step back from the invasive maternal imago and was gradually able to free herself from the fusional relationship with her baby. The patient recognised that her own mother could be invested, at the same time, in her life as a mother, as a lover, as a friend and as a professional. She was then able to accept that she herself could have other interests outside of the realm motherhood. She became more attractive and more seductive. She was newly invested in her love life. In her professional activities, she could rely on a paternal imago independent of her mother. Finally, she was able to renounce the idea of being all things to her baby, the messages transmitted to the baby became less discordant and she ceased her night-time visits. The baby began to sleep through the night. The maternal function was conflictualised, a third object was introduced, and the process of symbolization, in the mother and the child, was revived.

In a later development of this theory, Braunschweig and Fain (1975, *La Nuit, Le Jour)* suggested that the censorship of the woman-as-lover helps the child develop a double identification. In contact with its mother who once again becomes a woman, the child will develop an identification both with the penis desired by the mother (penis of an absent third party, distinct from the baby/penis), and with the mother herself desiring this penis. This is how the psychic bisexuality that characterises hysterical identification is constituted. For Fain, this is the neurotico-normal functioning mode of reference when the child cathects, without realising it, the mother's sexual partner.

Further reading

Braunschweig, D., and Fain, M. (1975). *La Nuit, Le Jour.* Paris: Presses Universitaires de France. (Series: Le Fil Rouge).

Braunschweig, D., and Fain, M. (2013). *Eros et Antéros.* Paris: In Press.

Fain, M. (1971). Prelude to fantasy life. *Interpretation*, 5(2–3): 22–104.

KEY WORDS Censorship, hallucinatory function, calming mother, adequate mother, third.

THE DOUBLE TABOO ON TOUCHING

FRANÇOISE LAURENT

A patient suffering from an obsessional neurosis had often evoked the memory of an everlasting nightmare going back to his infancy in which a black cat looked at him with terrifying luminous eyes. A detail, emerging late in the treatment, had helped him understand this better. As a young child, he had always wanted to touch his mother, especially her hair. Nobody could stop him. The doctor consulted had recommended that they buy a cat. And this trick had succeeded! He had thenceforth ceased to annoy his mother, accepting the cat as a substitute.

However, after telling this story in the session, he was overcome by a rush of rage: his quest for meaning and his analysis were not leading to anything concrete, leaving him just as miserable as ever. Fascinated by mythology, he then compared the permanence of his suffering to the punishment of Ixion, who was condemned to turn for eternity, chained to a wheel of fire, for having betrayed his benefactor Zeus by wanting to kiss his wife Hera. The punishment was all the more cruel and humiliating because the cunning Zeus, having guessed his intention, had created a lure, a cloudy form in the shape of Hera, so that Ixion had embraced only a cloudy form.

"Embracing a cloudy form" described both the impossibility of satisfying his oedipal desire for his mother and the frustration inherent in the transference love, both united by the theme of unconscious guilt. The myth of Ixion even illuminated his complaint about analysis, which he described as "a bed of embers". The patient had found in this myth of sexual desire and its frustration a means of bringing thoughts hitherto forbidden to associativity into contact. Interpretation, wherever it comes from, makes this contact real, this touching of words and being touched by words. The patient understood this well, because he had wanted, in a previous session, to hand the analyst a collection of poems written during his analysis. The latter's refusal to accept them had surprised him, and even hurt him, but it had given rise to the emergence of the memory. Experiencing this new associativity, he had realised at the same time that in order or this to be possible he had had to accept and submit to the need to use language, and this had caused the return of his infantile rage against the prohibited.

Deploying the skin-ego metaphor in all possible directions, Didier Anzieu (2016 [1985]) showed the fecundity of the taboo on touching and its fundamental value in psychic life as well as in the intervention of psychoanalysis. The discovery of the Oedipus complex and the introduction by Freud of the analytic situation were indeed concomitant to his renunciation of touching patients. When, in *Inhibitions, symptoms and anxiety,* Freud (1926 [1925]) was considering one of the oldest injunctions of obsessional neurosis, the "taboo against touching", he realised that it had two aspects: it applied as much to aggressive impulses as to libidinal impulses. Their goal is always to touch the object physically. He linked the "taboo against touching" with the mechanism of isolation, so that now it operated on the psychic level to avoid the return of a repressed impulse in consciousness; isolation is opposed to associative contact, to the "touching of thoughts" between themselves.

From the psychogenic and metapsychological perspective of Anzieu, the taboo on touching makes it possible to go beyond the skin-ego, derived from the illusion of a common skin with the mother, in favour of a psychic ego founded on the activity of thought. It takes place when excitation, which is unable to find a path of discharge through "skin-to-skin" contact, must find outlets through language. This is a "double" taboo in several respects and in several registers; primarily, it is a taboo on pressing against the mother's body, while, secondarily, it limits manual touching, and leads to the oedipal prohibitions of incest and parricide. Concerning in a combined manner father and mother, as well as libidinal and destructive impulses, the taboo against touching introduces a new duality into the Oedipus complex (immediately pointed out by Freud). Finally, it applies as much to the object (mother, father, adult, analyst) as to the subject. Thus, by filtering and channelling the stimuli coming from outside as well as from within, it establishes separation between the ego and the object, and establishes the intrapsychic topographical differentiation between the ego, the id and the superego.

Further reading

Anzieu, D. (1975). Le transfert paradoxal. De la communication paradoxale à la réaction thérapeutique négative. *Nouvelle revue de psychanalyse*, 12: 49–72.

Anzieu, D. (2013). Les signifiants formels et le Moi-peau. In: *Les enveloppes psychiques*, eds. Anzieu, D. et al. Paris: Dunod.

Chabert, C. (1996). *Didier Anzieu*. Paris: Presses Universitaires de France. (Series: Psychoanalystes d'aujourd'hui).
Freud, S. (1909). *Notes upon a case of obsessional neurosis. S.E.*, 10. London: Hogarth, pp. 151–249.

KEY WORDS Interpretation, isolation, skin-ego, obsessional neurosis, taboo against touching.

REFUSAL

CLAUDE ARLÈS

For a long time the patient refrained from opening himself up to someone else about the pain lodged in his soul. Yet everything seemed to be going well for him: he had achieved brilliant studies, enjoyed rude health, and acquired material comfort acquired early on in his life, and above all he had a loving companion with whom a good future seemed to be taking shape, albeit darkened by this painful breach. When, finally, he had made a decision to do so, after a few sessions he accepted without frowning the framework and the method: free association and the payment of all sessions. A window onto his internal world, this silent presence that the analyst faced him with and imposed on himself, exposed the patient to his perplexity when faced with the expectations of the other: the other in himself, but also its echo or its extensions in the analyst. In the course of the sessions, he talked about his phobia of marriage and even more his phobia of becoming a father. With the same restraint, he evoked the tensions and dissensions between him and his colleagues, his friends, his parents or his companion, with whom he was now reluctant to speak, as he no longer accepted her way of revealing allusively his sadness and his depression. Quite clearly, this complaint was addressed to the analyst and was the hallmark of his transference neurosis. And yet the analyst refused to respond to this illusory demand: it would be premature to want to name or silence the tormenting pain that he was complaining about.

After a few months, somewhat embarrassed, the patient handed the analyst a letter from his father. Although he had often mentioned his admiration for his parents, their qualities, their vital force, and how they had overcome during his adolescence the death of a younger sister, the analyst now discovered that the father was a medical professional. At the next session, the analyst learnt that he had kept this letter for several weeks in his back pocket, unable to decide whether to hand it over. In so doing, the patient had also made it his own and showed that he intended to ensure that his sessions were refunded by social security; but above all, on the stage of the transference, this letter testified to the emergence of a conflict of ambivalence that was always held back with the aim of sparing his bereaved parents.

The patient was torn apart by this conflict of fidelity, but also derived pleasure from seeing how the analyst would oppose his father; he arrived half an hour late for the following session and warned the analyst with a completely new sense of assurance that if he agreed to pay him, it would certainly be the last time. Although he was sensitive to his "professionalism" and the efficiency of a method that was nonetheless so enigmatic, the patient considered his therapist as a man who was too self-serving, stubborn, and even narrow-minded. Troubled as much by what the patient had said as he was after reading his letter, the analyst refrained from responding, letting his annoyance unfurl deep down inside him. He then heard the echo of the words often used by the patient to describe his father: "obstinate" and "diligent". Their ambivalence and the resonance of this analogy pushed him to say to the patient, "Slam the door today just as you might have done in the past in your parents' home?" After a brief silence, tears and words, so long held back, welled up from this painful breach on mentioning the boarding school to which he had been sent after the death of his sister, but especially when he recalled the ambivalent and terribly painful feeling that was aroused in him as much by the fact of wanting to flee the family home as by that of being turned out or rejected.

By establishing free association, the fundamental rule also requires certain "refusals" *(refusements)*: for example, that of using the couch, ensuring the analysand does not see the analyst, or that of suppressing acting in favour of speech. It also implies that the analyst imposes certain refusals on himself: that of leaving in suspense his own feelings or emotions in order to examine them and put them into words in his inner discourse, but also that of not answering questions, requests for advice, expectations or impulses of the analysand, except with a certain neutrality. This neutrality, described as "benevolent", seeks to welcome the unconscious manifestations of the analysand by refusing to give priority to one representation over another. Ideally one would listen to the patient in each session as if it were the first. The generally accepted translation of *Versagung* by "frustration" was crtiticised by Jacques Lacan as early as 1956, and then by Jean Laplanche and J.-B. Pontalis. Instead, the word *refusement* was resurrected from old French by Laplanche and the translators of the *Oeuvres complètes* in 1989. Closer in its different meanings to Freud's thought, this translation extends for both protagonists the idea that the analytic situation is based on the fact that there is a movement of confrontation with the enigma that the analyst represents as a result of the framework he establishes and the refusals that he maintains.

Although the importance and the theoretical-clinical consequences of such refusals are fairly obvious and unanimously accepted for classical analysis, they have long fuelled a controversy between the various analytic societies around training and the so-called question of didactic analysis. For example, at the end of a long period of reflection arising in 1963 from questioning and theorisation concerning the training of analysts, crystallized by the controversy and the split with Lacan, Laplanche and Pontalis proposed in 1970 that the French Psychoanalytical Association (APF) should renounce didactic analysis. Concerning the central idea of a real *refusal* this choice was accepted on the grounds of the extraterritoriality of analysis, that is to say to avoid the recruitment of analysts trained according to a particular institutional ideal. In so doing, the institution refused to entertain any point of view on the validity of a request for analysis, which, by moving from the outset to a request to become an analyst, would deprive the analysand of part of his/her analysis as a consequence of this inaugural "advice" and of immediate or deferred participation in training (seminars, etc.). It is a matter of extraterritoriality once again, in that the institution refuses, at any level, to intervene in the analysis itself. At the level of its theorization and the framework of its training, the institution does not seek to meet the future analyst in training before his/her analysis has started or even to require that it be done with an analyst of a particular tradition.

Further reading

Laplanche, J. (1987). *New foundations for psychoanalysis*, trans. D. Macey. City/Publisher, pp. 156–157.

Laplanche, J. (1987). *Problematiques V, Le Baquet. Transcendance du transfert.* Paris: Presses Universitaires de France, pp. 288–292.

Laplanche, J. (1989). "Refusement", terminologie raisonnée. In: *Traduire Freud*, eds. Bourgignon, A., Cotet, P., Laplanche, J., and Robert, F. Paris: Presses Universitaires de France, pp. 133–135.

KEY WORDS Extraterritoriality, frustration, silence.

ETHICAL SUFFERING

CHRISTOPHE DEMAEGDT AND CHRISTOPHE DEJOURS

In *Civilization and its Discontents*, Freud (1930) admits that "it is not possible, within the limits of a short survey, to discuss adequately the significance of work for the economics of the libido" (p. 80, note 1). Classically, and in the absence of the question of what work is from a metapsychological point of view (Lantos, 1952), ordinary working conditions are considered pathogenic only because of the fragility of the psychic apparatus, whilst the organisation of work is perceived as a stage on which pre-existing conflicts emerging from the history of childhood are revealed.

Today, the pertinence of this question is based on the discussion initiated by the clinical analysis of work, in particular the dimension of ethical suffering (Dejours, 1998). The latter occurs when the subject carries out orders of which he/she nevertheless disapproves. For some, engaging in work they disapprove of, participating in "dirty work", can produce various moral feelings such as shame, unworthiness, or guilt. On the other hand, other subjects are exempt from it and display an apparent normality and/or somatic disorders. Thus, in contrast to the repression of sexual desire, which characterises "civilized sexual morality", it is the thorny problem of the psychopathological impact of repression of the moral sense in the workplace that is raised here.

During his first interviews, a man complained mainly about diffuse musculoarticular pains, accompanied by fatigue that was resistant to rest and psychotropic substances. He wanted to get rid of the vertigo and bouts of distress that hampered his family life and "weakened" him from a professional point of view. As a manager in the retail distribution field, he had climbed the ladder step by step before being demoted without any reason. He insisted on his loyalty and cryptically evoked a robbery, but also a hoped-for promotion accompanied by increasing investment, embezzlement, dismissals, and so on. His story became animated and the chronological sequence was difficult to follow.

He vehemently denounced "inhumane" practices and those friends who had turned their backs on him and now wanted his skin. Various defensive solutions governed by splitting allowed him to prevent himself from thinking about this too much, in a more or less temporary or transitory way, by separating sectors of life or thought in order to save the anguish. Some elements remained juxtaposed, conflictual, until certain things he had hitherto taken for granted were suddenly called into question: "What I committed to in passionately yesterday is destroying me today." He was destabilized, embarrassed. The tension of contradictory ideas initiated a process of clarification, which was accompanied by a progressive sedation of his multiple disorders. It was not only the fact of having participated in certain management practices that proved to be problematic for him, but the gradual elaboration of a link between the treatment he once inflicted on his colleagues or his customers and from which he was suffering today.

Taking into consideration the ambiguity of his commitment no longer allowed him to pose as a passive victim of a harmful system or a malicious manager, since it forced him to get a glimpse of the combination of shame and enjoyment that coloured his arbitrations in the face of the contradictions of work. The erotisation of suffering at work, one's own or that of others, frequently allows one to bear the constraints, and even to find satisfaction or derive enjoyment from them by binding the excitement that resists sublimation. Of this, the patient, just like others, could only speak with difficulty. To do this, listening attentively to the material obstacles of his work was necessary. What cannot be talked about and which, moreover, is also obscured by the intervention of the defences, can be found behind the denunciatory projections, the contempt of the other, or various forms of otherness, namely hatred of oneself.

From this perspective, self-hatred is not to be considered as the strict residue of a superego-related or archaic guilt. It is the theoretical link that makes it possible to go back to the roots of ethical suffering. Manifestations of unconscious guilt, at the forefront of which is the need for self-punishment, derive from the patient's treatment of conflicts that pertain in the first place to activity and are related to working conditions.

The evolution of clinical practice imposes technical adjustments on the psychoanalyst. The acquisition of knowledge about the psychic issues at stake in work and its collective determinations informs the listening process with a view to understanding in what ways the patient may be actively involved in the extremely powerful and unprecedented forms of domination that lie behind the discontents in contemporary culture.

Further reading

Dejours, C. (1998). *Souffrance en France. La banalisation de l'injustice sociale.* Paris: Seuil.

Freud, S. (1930). *Civilisation and its discontents. S.E.*, 21. London: Hogarth, pp. 59–145.

Lantos, B. (1952). Metapsychological considerations on the concept of work. *International Journal of Psychoanalysis*, 33(4): 439–443.

KEY WORDS Self-hatred, jouissance, moral sense, work.

CULTURAL REFERENCE AND ANTHROPOLOGICAL MEDIATION

GILBERT DIATKINE

Cultural reference plays an important role in every analysis, but more often than not it remains silent. It is because the analyst and the patient both speak almost the same language that a discreet anomaly in the patient's discourse lifts in the analyst a preconscious repression of previous episodes in the analysis, which can lead him to offer an interpretation; and it is because they share many of the same customs and live in the same city that the analyst may become aware that an apparently factual account of the events of the previous day is at the same time referring to him/her. Without this common cultural reference, analytic work would be impossible.

When the worlds of the patient and the analyst are extremely different, the use of cultural mediation, that is to say anthropology, can greatly facilitate the work of the psychoanalyst.

The patient that Georges Devereux (1951) named Jimmy Picard was a veteran of the Second World War, during which he had suffered a cranio-cerebral trauma. His symptoms and behaviour were so strange that the psychiatrist at the Topeka Clinic in Kansas wondered if he was not psychotic. However, as Jimmy was a Plains Indian, the psychiatrist asked Georges Devereux, who had been attached to the clinic as an anthropologist a short time earlier, if his quirks of personality and behaviour were not explicable by a culture gap? Devereux quickly realised that Jimmy's peculiarities were not symptoms of schizophrenia, but that they had a meaning deeply related to Plains Indian culture. He then took Jimmy into face-to-face psychotherapy on the basis of one session per day.

At the end of the first week of the treatment, Jimmy said he had dreamed he was going hunting with Devereux. The latter was not armed, but had advised the patient to use only one bullet at a time. He failed to shoot a bear, but killed a fox, which turned into a baby. He pointed out that Devereux was with him in the dream.

To interpret the role that Jimmy attributed to him in the dream, Devereux was led to use a cultural reference. He said: "In this dream, I am exactly like the protective animals of the warriors of old and whose protection gave them courage".

The protective animal embodied "the guardian spirit", a supernatural being with whom the Indians come into contact at the end of the initiation ritual of puberty. During this initiation, the young man would withdraw to an isolated place, submit to a "genuine debauchery of exhibitionist torture" and ask the supernatural beings to take pity on him. He then usually had a vision in which a supernatural being adopted him and gave him a "talisman", that is to say, a bag of disparate symbolic objects, which gave him magical power.

Georges Devereux used a cultural element to interpret the double reference. This interpretation was followed by an opening up of Jimmy's associative network. He mentioned the fox which he had successfully shot in his dream. Several of his associations led to the idea that the fox represented the sexual organs of a woman. Devereux asked him if, in old Indian language, "*shooting*" had the same sexual sense as in English ("shooting off"). Jimmy responded with a typical denial – "I don't think so"[1] – and then came back to the rest of the dream in which he "let the baby down" after shooting a fox. Devereux asked him what this "let down" meant – "letting down a friend"? Jimmy then went on to speak of a major trauma during his adolescence. He reproached himself for letting down the girl he loved, who was pregnant by him, and never caring for the child (1951, pp. 139–140).

Mediation through culture created a space in which the transference became interpretable and where word-presentations began to associate with each other. The work on word-presentations (first, "shooting", then, "let down") allowed for an early elaboration of unconscious thing-presentations related to the traumas that Jimmy had suffered not only in the war but in his teens and his childhood.

Note

1 Translator's note: In the original text there is a note here saying "when speaking English the Cheyenne refer to ejaculation as 'the gun going off'."

Further reading

Devereux, G. (1951). *Reality and dream. Psychotherapy of a Plains Indian.* International Universities Press.

Green, A. (1984 [1983]). Le langage dans la psychoanalyse. In: *Langages, Deuxièmes Rencontres psychoanalytiques d'Aix-en-Provence*. Paris: Les Belles Lettres.

Moro, M.-R. (2007). *Aimer ses enfants ici et ailleurs: Histoires transculturelles*, Paris: Odile Jacob.

KEY WORDS Cultural countertransference, double reference, language, representation.

CULTURAL REFERENCE AND SEDUCTION

GILBERT DIATKINE

In an ideal analysis, the patient and the analyst, protected by the frame, would be totally cut off from the influences of the outside world. The analyst would listen only to the free associations of the patient, his/her attention would be aroused only by the interruptions in the patient's discourse, the changes of direction towards lateral paths and repetitions. This ideal model would be realised if they could use something other than language to communicate. Unfortunately, every utterance is linked to the whole system of the language and opens the door wide to cultural differences. A shared cultural reference can be at the source of a connivance that is both decisive and dangerous.

In a megapolis of India, a lawyer entered analysis with the psychiatrist who had been treating her in psychotherapy since her hospitalisation for a depression when she was an adolescent. She was a young woman from a traditional Indian background who had become a senior executive in a large multinational company. Her analyst came from a background very similar to hers. He had attended the same sort of university as her, knew the particularities of her hometown, the problems of religion, caste and emancipation of women that arose there, and which were different from those of the megapolis where the analysis was taking place. Naturally, the analysis took place in English, which the analyst and patient spoke perfectly. But they had another language in common: Hindi, the language of their early childhood and their material life. The interpretations often focused on cultural references of a sociological nature, for example on the patient's efforts to make a guru out of her analyst. They also used the double meaning of words in English, for example that of the word *hot*, when she found that the ventilation was not cooling her analyst's office sufficiently, while at the same time the transference was getting a little too "heated". The patient overcame her depression and her inhibitions, her interests in the real world multiplied, she made a partly conventional and partly "modern" marriage, and was now pregnant.

For one session, she arrived 10 minutes late. Her sister had just arrived from her hometown and she had to be there to welcome her. Her mother had sent her some homemade food. Her vomiting had diminished since she had started taking medicine twice a day and she had even been able to find the time to play Xbox in her company relaxation room. It did her good. Her midwife told her that the medication she was taking was acting on the "oesophageal sphincter". She added, "You should grow a tree in your courtyard, like that, you would have car park in the shade! The mangos of this city are not as sweet as those from my hometown."

ANALYST: "This city is not so sweet?
THE PATIENT: "At least its mangoes."
ANALYST: "It reminds me of that old song by S. D. Burman (famous Indian musician and director): "My universe is in the folds of your mother's sari. [...] The shaded car park is the mother."

The patient laughed and nodded. The session continued around the conflict between her desire to "stay in the car park" and to have a more independent existence that would also allow her to go out and enjoy herself with other people.

The double sense of cold and warmth, which described both the transference and the ambient temperature, was easily expressed in English. But the abrupt transition to Hindi, the reference to the song by S.D. Burman and the interpretation given in Hindi of the maternal transference, had a much more open associative potential than if the analyst had flatly said in English that the shaded parking area imagined by the patient made him a welcoming mother. The word-presentations associated with the folds of the mother's sari and the mangos of her hometown were brought into relationship with the unconscious thing-presentations related to her inability to separate from her mother at the time of her adolescence, and from the crisis that took her to the psychiatric hospital.

The use of cultural mediation is sometimes essential to create a space of play between the patient and the analyst. Like play with a child, it has a dimension of seduction that it is not always possible to anticipate. It is listening to the patient's associations that shows how he reacts to what is always a countertransferential *Agieren* of his analyst. In this case, the analyst was constantly confronted with the need to be aware of his positive countertransference towards his patient when he switched from English to Hindi.

Further reading

Green, A. (1984 [1983]). Le langage dans la psychoanalyse. In: *Langages, Deuxièmes Rencontres psychoanalytiques d'Aix-en-Provence*. Paris: Les Belles Lettres.

Sparer, E. (2013). L'inconscient du moi. *Revue française de psychanalyse*, 1: 194–209.

KEY WORDS Cultural countertransference, representation, seduction.

THE WORK OF CULTURE

BRIGITTE DOLLÉ-MONGLOND

A patient returned to see her analyst after several years of analysis simply to reflect on what she was living through: she had a cancer recurrence. She trivialised her illness, but was very angry; she felt lonely even though she had a companion and her daughter, who was still young. She spoke mainly about this family environment, but also about her parents who did not understand her, the reactions of relatives, clumsy caregivers, her noisy and gnawing feelings of bitterness, and her resentment. Through the evocation of her daily life, burdened by illness, one could hear her extreme difficulty in taking stock of what might well be the end of her life. This approaching end of her life was as denied as it was omnipresent in her decision to return see the analyst, as were her painful moments of wavering that she could barely perceive. "A place to think about my life", she would say, over the course of several sessions.

How can she continue to inhabit her life, the analyst asked herself as she was accompanying her, as an articulation between culture and death. Whether it was a case of her anger, her despondency, or her multiple emotions and life reviews that were not named as such, all these thought processes between the analyst and the patient constantly navigated between the exploration of her own internal mysteries and the vestiges in her of her relations to the other. In this process the key moments of her own life that were also bound up with a collective memory emerged. Within the emotion of these sessions the following trend of thought was present in a veiled form: there is something of me in the other and something of the other in me; but there is also this need to "prepare yourself for death" – to use Montaigne's words. All this concerned the two protagonists involved and confronted them with the same term, provided that the analyst did not resist, even deeply within herself, this approach of the depths in each of them.

If culture, with respect to civilization, is difficult to define in its individual and collective sense, the work of culture, of which Freud posited certain premises, refers to a polysemic concept, interpreted differently by certain authors from their reading of Freudian contributions on this topic. We may recall in particular the famous Freudian assertion referring to the notion of *Kulturarbeit*: "Where id was, there ego shall be. It is a work of culture – not unlike the draining of the Zuider Zee" (Freud, 1933, p. 80). Freud thus placed the therapeutic efforts of psychoanalysis at the forefront by describing a transformative process that works through the psychic in the individual and interferes by its very essence with the collective scene. Beyond the classical individual/collective opposition, the two terms belong to a continuum despite the epistemological difficulties that this entails; light is thrown on this dimension of psychoanalysis involving a subject whose psychic reality is at once singular and common, who is referred back to these phylogenetic traces, and who, through his unconscious contents, drive and identificatory cathexes, is a member of humanity as a whole.

For Nathalie Zaltzman, this notion becomes a guiding thread, inherent in the very work of analysis. It stimulates reflection on how the analyst conceives his practice starting from a certain vision of the subject: the subject cannot be apprehended in isolation, without reference to other human beings, as though outside the world. This change *a minima* brought about by the work of culture is based on an enrichment of the awareness that man acquires concerning what is beyond him; and these microscopic movements are necessarily linked to the macroscopic evolution of the human species, since all general changes have no other path of transformation than that of the individual psyche. This potentiality gives the analytic discipline a particular cachet, distinguishing it from other therapeutic approaches, namely, a mission of humanization which will thus contribute to the objectives of civilization.

Thus she emphasises the irreversible significance of the Freudian contribution in its interpretation of both individual destiny and the human species, the inextricable knotting between ontogenesis and phylogenesis owing to the preservation in oneself of the memory traces of an archaic collective inheritance, and the dialogue between our discipline and the works of culture. She nevertheless questions some forms of inheritance inherent in *Civilization and its Discontents*. Where Freud (1930) poses an antagonism between the interests of the individual and the interests of the species, Zaltzman discerns a single path, questioning the "absence of a common derivation" between the two levels postulated by Freud, choosing instead to illuminate the similarities of the individual process and the cultural process of humanity to the point of identifying them with each other regarding the work of culture. She thus designates an agency of psychic lucidity where it is a matter of arousing and accompanying an evolution in the life of the mind, a capacity for discernment enabling one to think about one's life but also about the surrounding world. What is implemented in an analytic process is thus like learning a new mode of attention, of presence to oneself, to the other, and to the world, where it is a question of making intelligible to oneself what is presented in repetition, opacity, and "without meaning". Analysis sets in motion the exploration in oneself of foreign lands, of one's own depths of baseness and barbarism, familiarization with these dark forces of bad thoughts, the acceptance of the psychic reality in its worse aspects, and these internal emergences have a value of culturation, beyond the mere aim of instinctual drive renunciation that Freud himself renounced. In the same tone, she highlights some insidious slippages within analytic practice: how were psychoanalysts able to move away from this conception of the intrapsychic that was always marked by the work of the collective, and to give ground, in part at least, concerning the therapeutic effects of the treatment?

She was thus to reconcile two paths, the work of culture and recovery, in a singular axiomatic centred on the death drive, in order to grasp what the work of analysis can be, bearing witness at the same time to a difference of nature when compared with other therapeutic approaches. "Not only individual history is changed through each analytic process, but the history of the ascendants and descendants of this life" (Zaltzman, 1998, p. 44). In other words, every step accomplished in an analytic treatment creates a spiral of effects in those around and in relations to the other, filters and transforms what has been inherited and will necessarily be a legacy in turn.

In connection with clinical practice, this notion has a heuristic tone in that all analytical work must deal with the "bedrock of human reality", not just the subject as a person in his psycho-pathological dimension, but as a subject of the human condition. For the analyst, it can become a central paradigm that directs his/her listening and influences his/her interpretive mode, an inclination that allows him/her to re-examine the singularity of his/her action and responsibility. "The way we conduct an analysis is not the same depending on whether we associate or, on the contrary, dissociate individual psychic interests and collective psychic interests" writes Nathalie Zaltzman (1998, p. 50).[1]

It seems to me that the clinical tone of this concept should be emphasised on the analyst's side, as an internal disposition, as a backdrop that determines, to a large extent, the direction he/she gives to his/her practice. My own clinical associations testify to this intertwining of the individual and the collective. Thinking about this "bedrock", I recalled in particular this singular clinical work which took place in a face-to-face analytical situation, where the impact of my personal conviction was reinforced by the reading of Zaltzman.

Note

1 On these questions, the reader may also like to refer to Dollé-Monglond (2011).

Further reading

Dollé-Mongland, B. (2011). Prendre la mesure de sa condition d'humain. In: *L'Esprit d'insoumission*, ed. G. Lévy. Paris: Campagne Première.

Freud, S. (1930). *Civilization and its discontents. S.E.* 21. London: Hogarth, pp. 64–145.

Lévy, G. (Ed.). (2011). *L'Esprit d'insoumission* (Part 1: "Le travail de culture, entre individuel et transindividuel"). Paris: Compagne Première.

KEY WORDS *Kulturarbeit,* progress of the mind, bedrock of human reality, phylogenetic traces.

Appendix

PRESENTATION OF THE AUTHORS

Isabelle Alfandary is a psychoanalyst, a member of the Société de Psychanalyse Freudienne (SPF) and a university professor of Foreign Literature at the New Sorbonne University

Jacques Angelergues is a psychoanalyst and child psychiatrist in charge of parent/baby consultations at the Alfred Binet Centre in Paris. He is a member of the Paris Psychoanalytical Society (SPP).

Claude Arlès is a psychoanalyst in Lyon. He has recently published "Un amour lointain", *Le moi et l'objet, Libres cahiers pour la psychanalyse*, 29, Spring 2014, Paris: In Press.

Jean-Louis Baldacci is a psychiatrist, psychoanalyst and full training member of the Paris Psychoanalytical Society (SPP); he is also the head doctor of the Jean-Favreau Centre for Psychoanalytic Consultations and Treatments. He has recently published "Sublimation et processus de pensée" *in* Emmanuelli, M. and Nayrou, F. (Eds.) *La Pensée*, Paris, Presses Universitaires de France (Series: Monographies et débats de psychanalyse), 2015.

Alice Bauer is a psychoanalyst and member of the Paris Psychoanalytical Society (SPP). She practices at the Centre Claude Bernard. She is also a translator (English to French) and works as a secretary of edition for the European Federation of Psychoanalysis.

Gérard Bayle is a psychoanalyst in Paris and a full training member of the Paris Psychoanalytical Society (SPP). He has a training role in the Étude et traitement analytique par le psychodrama (ETAP)

within the Société parisienne d'aide à la santé mentale (SPASM). He has recently published "La haine faute de mieux" *in* Cohen de Lara, A. and Danon-Boileau, L. (Eds.) *La Destructivité chez l'enfant,* Paris, Presses Universitaires de France (Series: Monographies et débats de psychanalyse), 2014.

Thierry Bokanowski is a psychiatrist and psychoanalyst in Paris, and a full training member of the Paris Psychoanalytical Society (SPP). Recent publications: *The Analytic Process: Journeys and Pathways,* London, Karnac, 2017.

Laure Bonnefon-Tort is a psychoanalyst in Paris and a member of the Paris Psychoanalytical Society (SPP). Recent publications: "Obituary Joyce McDougall (1920–2011)" *The International Journal of Psychoanalysis*, December, 2012, 93: 1533–1540.

Patrice Brunaud is a psychiatrist and psychoanalyst in Lyon.

Evelyne Chauvet is a psychiatrist and psychoanalyst in Paris, and a full training member of the Paris Psychoanalytical Society (SPP). Recent publications include: "Penser pour ne pas penser", *Revue française de psychanalyse,* Les psychophobies, 2014/3: 643–657; "L'ombre de la bonne parole" *Revue française de psychanalyse,* Consolation, 2015/2: 445–457.

Brigitte Chervoillot-Courtillon is a psychoanalyst in Paris.

Nicolas de Coulon is a psychiatrist and psychoanalyst in Lausanne and a training member of the Swiss Psychoanalytical Society. Recent publications: "La psychanalyse à Lausanne, entre crise de filiation et construction groupale", with Lucette Nobbs, *Le Coq-Héron,* 218, 2014; "Le chemin des souvenirs perdus" *in* Manzano, J. and Abella, A. (Eds.) *La Construction en psychanalyse. Récupérer le passé ou le réinventer?* Paris, Presses Universitaires de France (Series: Le fil rouge), 2011.

Laurent Danon-Boileau is a psychoanalyst and member of the Paris Psychoanalytical Society (SPP). He is also a Professor Emeritus in linguistics at the Paris-Descartes University and a writer. Recent publications: "La force du langage", *Revue française de psychanalyse,* 2007/71: 1341–1409; *Voir l'autisme autrement,* Paris, Odile Jacob, 201, *Le Non-Moi*, Paris, Gallimard, 2017.

Christophe Dejours is a psychiatrist and psychoanalyst, a teacher at the *Conservatoire national des arts et des métiers* in Paris, and a member of the French Psychoanalytical Association (APF). Recent publications include: *Le Corps d'abord. Corps biologique, corps érotique et sens moral,* Paris, Payot, 2001; *Les dissidences du corps,* Paris, Payot, 2009.

Christophe Demaegdt is a clinical psychologist, with a doctorate in psychology, practising in Charleroi and in Brussels. He is an associate member of the Laboratory of Clinical Psychology, Psychopathology and Psychoanalysis at the University of Paris-Descartes. Recent publications: L'embarras du travail dans l'étiologie psychanalytique des névroses de guerre, *L'Information psychiatrique,* 89, 2013/8: 651–659.

Gilbert Diatkine is a psychoanalyst in Paris and full training member of the Paris Psychoanalytical Society (SPP). He is also associate director of training at the Han-Groen-Prakken Institute of Psychoanalysis of Eastern Europe.

Brigitte Dollé-Monglond is a psychoanalyst and president of the Fourth Group (Quatrième Groupe) in Paris. She has a doctorate in Letters and is a clinical psychologist by training. Recent publications include: "Une écoute de la vie amoureuse", *Actes,* 4, 2015, Paris, In Press; "Le Dialogue intérieur avec *Les Yeux de l'âme* de Jean-Claude Rolland", *le Coq-Héron,* 213, 2013.

Jean-Luc Donnet is a psychiatrist and psychoanalyst in Paris, and a full training member of the Paris Psychoanalytical Society (SPP). English publications: *The Analysing Situation,* trans. A. Weller, London: Karnac, 2009.

Jean-Philippe Dubois is a psychoanalyst in Bordeaux and a full training member of the French Psychoanalytical Association (APF). Recent publications: "Complaisance de la langue", *Libres cahiers pour la psychanalyse, En deçà des mots,* 27, 2013, Paris: In Press.

Haydée Faimberg is medically trained psychoanalyst in Paris and a full training member of the Paris Psychoanalytical Society (SPP). Recent publications: "The as yet situation in Winnicott's *Fragment of an Analysis* (1955): 'Your father did not make you the honour of… *yet*'", *The Psychoanalytic Quarterly, 82,* 2013/4, pp. 849–875; "The paternal function in Winnicott. The psychoanalytic frame", *The International Journal of Psychoanalysis, 95,* 2014, pp. 629–640; "'Well, you better ask them': the countertransference position at the crossroads", Chapter Three in R. Oelsner (Ed.) *Transference and Countertransference Today*, London: New York, Routledge, 2013.

Bernadette Ferrero-Madignier is a psychoanalyst in the Lyon region at Dardilly, and a member of the French Psychoanalytical Association (APF). She has recently published: "L'amour non médecin", *Transferts d'amours, Libres cahiers pour la psychanalyse,* 2011/23: 45–61, Paris, In Press.

Mireille Fognini is a psychoanalyst, clinical psychologist, and participant in the Fourth Group, (OPLF: *Organisation psychanalytique de langue française*) in Paris. She is also a researcher attached to the UTRPP (Paris University 13–Sorbonne-Cité) and a member of the editorial committee of the journal *Le Coq-Héron.* Recent publications include: "Identité et plagiat" *in* J.F. Chiantaretto (Ed.) *Écriture de soi. Écriture des limites,* Paris, Hermann, 2014; editor of the volume *Wilfred Bion. La psychanalyse en devenir, Le Coq-Héron,* 216, 2014; "De l'acte d'écrire et de sa public-action", *Ce que la littérature fait des psychanalystes, Les Lettres de la SPF*, 27, 2012, Paris, Compagne première.

Isabelle Gernet is a clinical psychologist in Paris and lecturer at the University Paris–Descartes. Recent publications: "Théorie de la seduction généralisée et topique du corps", *Psicologia Em Estudo,* 17, 2012/3, pp. 383–391.

Jean H. Guégan is a psychoanalyst in Nantes and member of the French Psychoanalytical Association (APF).

Jean-Michel Hirt is a psychoanalyst in Paris, a full member of the French Psychoanalytical Association (APF) and a university lecturer in psychopathology and clinical psychology. Recent publications include: *Paul, l'apôtre qui 'respirait le crime'",* Arles, Actes Sud, 2014; *La Dignité humaine, sous le regard d'Etty Hillesum et Sigmund Freud,* Paris, Desclée de Brouwer, 2012; *L'Insolence de l'amour,* Paris, Albin Michel, 2007.

Daniel Irago is a psychoanalyst in Paris and a member of the Paris Psychoanalytical Society (SPP).

Claude Janin is a clinical psychologist in Lyon and training member of the Paris Psychoanalytical Society (SPP).

René Kaës is a psychoanalyst and group analyst in Aix-en-Provence, and Professor Emeritus of psychology and clinical psychopathology at the University Lumière–Lyon 2. Recent publications: *L'Extension de la psychanalyse*, Paris, Dunod, 2015; *Le Malêtre*, Paris, Dunod, 2012.

Laurence Kahn worked as an anthropologist of Ancient Greece before becoming a psychoanalyst and training analyst at the French Psychoanalytical Association (APF). She was co-editor of the *Nouvelle Revue de Psychanalyse* and of the *Fait de l'analyse,* and president of the APF from 2008 to 2010. Recent publications: *Le psychanalyse apathique et le patient postmoderne,* Paris, L'Olivier (Series: Penser/Rëver), 2014.

Réal Laperrière is a clinical psychologist and psychoanalyst in Montreal, and a member of the Montreal Psychoanalytical Society (Canadian Psychoanalytical Society). Recent publications: "Le témoin", *Filigrane,* 19, 2010/2, pp. 75–80.

Françoise Laurent is a psychiatrist and psychoanalyst in Lyon, and a member of the French Psychoanalytical Association (APF). Recent publications: "*En courant*", *Psychanalyse, les traverses,* APF Annual, 2013, Paris, Presses Universitaires de France.

Marie-Françoise Laval-Hygonenq is a psychoanalyst in Paris and full member of the Paris Psychoanalytical Society (SPP). Recent publications include: "Nouveaux développements en psychanalyse. Autour de la pensée de Michel de M'Uzan", *Revue française de psychanalyse*, 78, 2014/4, pp. 1181-1190; "Le travail de trauma. Son actualisation dans la cure", *Revue française de psychanalyse,* 78, 2014/5, pp. 1678–1683.

Marie-Laure Léandri is a psychologist and psychoanalyst at the Alfred-Binet Centre and the Evelyne and Jean Kestemberg Centre in Paris.

Anne Maupas is a psychoanalyst and member of the Paris Psychoanalytical Society (SPP); she is also a psychosomatician and member of the IPSO-Pierre Marty Association. She practices at the Alfred-Binet Centre and at IPSO in Paris.

Patrick Merot is a psychoanalyst in Nogent-sur-Marne and full member of the French Psychoanalytical Association (APF). He has recently published *Dieu la mère. Trace du maternel dans le religieux,* Paris, Presses Universitaires de France (Series: Le Fil rouge), 2014.

Nicole Minazio is a psychoanalyst in Brussels and a training member of the Belgian Psychoanalytical Society. Recent publications: "Après-coup, le traumatique", *Revue de la Société belge de psychanalyse,* summer 2014.

Lucette Nobs is a psychoanalyst in Lausanne and a psychologist by training. She is a member of the Swiss Psychoanalytical Society and of the Editorial Committee of the journal *Tribune psychanalytique.* Recent publications: "L'Amour limite", *Tribune psychanalytique,* 11, 2013.

Michel Ody is a psychoanalyst in Paris, honorary training member of the Paris Psychoanalytical Society (SPP), and honorary teacher at the Association of Mental health in the 13th district of Paris (ASM13). Recent publications: *The Psychoanalyst and the Child,* London: Routledge, 2018.

Nicole Oury is a psychoanalyst in Lyon and full member of the French Psychoanalytical Association (APF). Recent publications: *Inquiétude des amours enfantines* in collaboration with Jean-Yves Tamet and Michel Villand, Paris, Presses Universitaires de France (Series: Le Fil rouge), 2012.

Michael Parsons is a training analyst at the British Psychoanalytical Society and a member of the French Psychoanalytical Association (APF). Recent publications include: *The Dove that Returns, the Dove that Vanishes: Paradox and Creativity in Psychoanalysis,* London, Routledge, 2000*; Living Psychoanalysis. From theory to Experience,* London, Routledge, 2014.

Vincent Pélissier is a psychoanalyst in Paris and member of the Paris Psychoanalytical Society (SPP).

Rosine Jozef Perelberg is a full member and training analyst at the British Psychoanalytical Society, and a guest lecturer at University College. She is the present president of the British Psychoanalytical Society.She was voted one of the 10 women of the year in 2006 by the Brazilian National Council for Women. She practices in London. Recent publications: *Violence et Suicide,* Paris, Presses Universitaires de France, 2004.

Virginia Picchi is a psychoanalyst with a doctorate in clinical psychology, a member of the Paris Psychoanalytical Society (SPP), and director of Psychological Services (INSEAD).

Jacques Press is a psychoanalyst and psychosomatician, training analyst at the Swiss Psychoanalytical Society and president of the Geneva Association for Psychosomatics (AGEPSO). Recent publications: *La Construction de sens*, Paris, Presses Universitaires de France (Series: Le Fil rouge), 2010; main author of the collective volume of AGEPSO, *Corps culturel, corps malade,* Geneva, Georg (Series: Perspectives psychosomatiques), 2014; "Il transfert del negative, storio di una possession Bianca", *Psiche*, 2, 2014 (subsequently published in 2015 in the *Revue française de psychanalyse,* 79(4): 1123–1135, under the title, "Le transfert du négatif. Histoire d'une possession blanche"); "Metapsychological and clinical issues in psychosomatics research", *International Journal of Psychoanalysis,* 97(1):89–113, 2016; "Lire Winnicott", *Revue française de psychosomatique,* 45:67–78, 2015.

Aleth Prudent-Bayle is a psychoanalyst in Paris, member of the Paris Psychoanalytical Society (SPP), training analyst in psychoanalytic psychodrama for ETAP (Étude et traitement analytique par le psychodrama) at the Société parisienne d'aide à la santé mentale (SPASM) and member of the IPSO-Pierre Marty Association.

Rachel Rosenblum is a psychiatrist and psychoanalyst in Paris and member of the Paris Psychoanalytical Society (SPP). Recent publications: "Peut-on mourir de dire? Sarah Kofman, Primo Lévi", *Revue française de psychanalyse,* 2000, 64(1): 113–137; "Cure ou repetition du trauma, 2006, 28: 69–90; Commentary on "Presenting the past: psychoanalysis and the sociology of misremembering", *Revue française de psychanalyse,* 2004, 2: 691–698; "Un destin-écran, ou l'homme qui avait deux destins", *Revue française de psychanalyse,* 2001, 65(3): 845–860; "Carrère et les retours", *Esquisses,* 2008; "Postponing trauma. The dangers of telling", *International Journal of Psychoanalysis,* 2009, 90(6): 1319–1340; "The Shoah and psychoanalysis", *Psychanalyse internationale,* 18, 2010.

Évelyne Sechaud is a psychoanalyst in Paris, former president of the French Psychoanalytical Association (APF) and of the European Federation of Psychoanalysis (EPF). Recent publications: "Le féminin du site", APF Annual, *Psychanalyse. Les Traversées,* Paris, Presses Universitaires de France, 2013.

Marie Sirjacq is a psychoanalyst in Paris and member of the Paris Psychoanalytical Society (SPP). She is also a psychosomatician and member of the IPSO-Pierre Marty Association. Recent publications: "Le caractère, pour quoi faire", *Revue française de psychanalyse,* 2014, 78(4): 1010–1022.

Gérard Szwec is a psychiatrist and psychoanalyst in Paris, and a full training member of the Paris Psychoanalytical Society (SPP). He is the former medical director of the Léon Kreisler Centre for child psychosomatics (Institute of Psychosomatics) and former director of the *Revue française de psychosomatique.*

Diana Tabacof is a clinical psychologist and psychoanalyst in Paris. She is an adhering member of the Paris Psychoanalytical Society (SPP) as well as a psychosomatician and member of the IPSO-Pierre Marty Association.

Dominique Tabone-Weil is a psychiatrist and psychoanalyst in Paris, and member of the Paris Psychoanalytical Society (SPP).

Jean-Yves Tamet is a psychoanalyst in Lyon and full member of the French Psychoanalytic Association (APF). Recent publications: *Inquiétudes des amours enfantines,* in collaboration with Nicole Oury and Michel Villand, Paris, Presses Universitaires de France (Series: Le Fil rouge), 2012; "Différenciation sexuelle et identités", *Clinique, art, et littérature,* Paris, In Press, 2012.

Olivia Todisco is a psychoanalyst in Paris and member of the French Psychoanalytic Association (APF). Recent publications: "Le visage dans la littérature érotique" *in Le Visage et la Voix,* Paris, In Press, 2004.

Joseph Torrente is a psychiatrist and psychoanalyst in Paris, a full member of the Paris Psychoanalytical Society (SPP), and head of the ESAT Bastille (SPASM). Recent publications: *Le Psychiatre et le Travailleur. Cheminement de la psychopathologie du travail d'hier à demain.* Paris, Doin (Series: Thématiques en santé mentale, 2004.

Claire Tremoulet is a psychiatrist and psychoanalyst in Paris. Recent publications: "Notes de lecture de 'La conviction'", APF Annual, *Le carnet psy,* Boulogne-Billancourt, Cazaubon, 2015.

Michel Villand is a psychiatrist and head doctor of child psychiatry in Lyon. Recent publications: *Inquiétudes des amours enfantines,* in collaboration with Nicole Oury and Jean-Yves Tamet, Paris, Presses Universitaires de France (Series: Le Fil rouge), 2012.

Felipe Votadoro is a psychoanalyst in Paris and full member of the French Psychoanalytic Association (APF).

References

Anzieu, D. (1974). "Le Moi-Peau". *Nouvelle Revue de psychanalyse*, 9: 195–203.

Anzieu, D. (1986). Freud's self-analysis, trans. P. Graham, *International Psychoanalytic Library*, 118. London: Hogarth, pp. 1–596.

Anzieu, D. (1987). Les signifiants formels et le moi peau. In: *Les enveloppes psychiques*. Paris: Dunod, pp. 19–41.

Anzieu, D. (1999). *Beckett*. Paris: Gallimard. (Series: Folio Essais).

Anzieu, D. (2016 [1985]). *The skin-ego*, trans. N. Segal. London: Routledge.

Arasse, D. (1992). *Le Détail. Pour une histoire rapprochée de la peinture*. Paris: Flammarion.

Arasse, D. (2006a). Heurs et malheurs de l'anachronisme. In: *Histoires de peintures*. Paris: Gallimard pp. 145-152.

Arasse, D. (2006b). Secrets de peintres. In: *Histoires de peintures*. Paris: Gallimard, pp. 111–124.

Arendt, H. (1963). *Eichmann in Jerusalem: A report on the banality of evil*. London: Penguin.

Arendt, H. (1971). Thinking and moral considerations. *Social Research*, 38(3): 419–446.

Arendt, H. (1978). *The life of the mind*. London: Secker & Warburg.

Aulagnier, P. (2001 [1975]). *The violence of interpretation: From pictogram to statement*, trans. A. Sheridan. London: Routledge.

Aulagnier, P. (1979). *Les Destins du plaisir*. Paris: Presses Universitaires de France.

Aulagnier, P. (1984). *L'Apprenti-historien et le maître sorcier: du discourse identifiant au discourse délirant*. Paris: Presses Universitaires de France.

Aulagnier, P. (1986). *Un interprète en quete de sens*. Paris: Presses Universitaires de France.

Balint, M. (1968). *The basic fault: Therapeutic aspects of regression*. London: Tavistock.

Benjamin, W. (1934). Excavation and memory, trans. R. Livingstone. In: *Selected writings*, eds. Jennings, M. Eiland, H, and Smith, G., vol. 2, Pt 2, 1931–1934. Cambridge, MA: Harvard University Press.

Beradt, C. (2002). *Rêver sous le IIIe Reich*. Paris: Payot.

Bion, W.R. (1962). *Learning from experience*. London: Heinemann.

Bion, W. (1970). *Attention and interpretation*. London: Tavistock.

Bollas, C. (1992). *Being a character*. New York: Harper Collins.

Botella, C. (2001). Figurabilité et regrédience. *Revue française de psychanalyse*, 65(4): 1149–1239.

Bouvet, M. (1959). *Le Transfert. Œuvres psychanalytiques*, vol. 2. Paris: Payot.

Braunschweig, D., and Fain, M. (1975). *La Nuit, Le Jour*. Paris: Presses Universitaires de France. (Series: Le Fil Rouge).

Chabert., C. (2003). *Féminin mélancholique*. Paris: Presses Universitaires de France. (Series: Petite Bibliothèque de psychanalyse).

Chabert, C., Cupa, D., Kaës, R., and Roussillon, R. (2007). *Le Moi-Peau et la psychanalyse des limites*. Paris: Érès.

Choderlos de Laclos, P. (2007 [1782]). *Dangerous liaisons*. London: Penguin Classics.

Cotard, J. (1997 [1882]). *Du délire des negations aux idées d'énormité*. Paris: L'Harmattan.

Denis, P. (1997). *Emprise et satisfaction. Les deux formants de la pulsion*. Paris: Presses Universitaires de France (Series: Le Fil rouge).

Denis, P. (2012). *Le Narcissisme*. Paris: Presses Universitaires de France.

Dejours, C. (1998). *Souffrance en France. La banalisation de l'injustice sociale*. Paris: Seuil.

Devereux, G. (1951). *Reality and dream. Psychotherapy of a Plains Indian*. New York: International Universities Press.

Diatkine, R. (1969). L'enfant prépsychotique. *La Psychiatrie de l'enfant*, 12(2): 413–446.

Donnet, J.-L. (1995). *Le divan bien tempéré*. Paris: Presses Universitaires de France (Series: Le Fil Rouge).

Duras, M. (1980 [1958]). *Moderato cantabile*. Paris: Minuit.

Fain, M. (1971). Prélude à la vie fantasmatique. *Revue française de psychanalyse*, 35(2–3): 291–364.

Fédida, P. (2009a). *Le site de l'étranger*. Paris: Presses Universitaires de France.

Fédida, P. (2009b). Le soufflé indistinct de l'image. In: *Le Site de l'étranger*. Paris: Presses Universitaires de France, pp. 187–220.

Fédida, P. (2009c). La régression. In: *Le site de l'étranger.* Paris: Presses Universitaires de France, pp. 221–244.

Fédida, P. (2009d). Restes diurnes. In: *Restes de vie. Crise et contre-transfert.* Paris: Presses Universitaires de France, pp. 45–66.

Ferenczi, S. (1955 [1928]). The problem of the termination of the analysis. In: *Final contributions to the problems and methods of psychoanalysis.* London: Hogarth, pp. 77–86.

Ferenczi, S. (1955 [1933]). Confusion of tongues between adults and the child. The language of tenderness and passion. In: *Final contributions to the problems and methods of psychoanalysis.* London: Hogarth, pp. 155–167.

Fognini, M. (2008). Exploration de l'autre en soi dans le récit mythique de Gilgamesh. *Le Coq-Héron*, 1: 48–56. Paris: Érès.

Freud, S. (1900). *The interpretation of dreams. S.E.* 4-5. London: Hogarth.

Freud, S. (1905). *Three essays on the theory of sexuality. S.E.* 7. London Hogarth, pp. 135–244.

Freud, S. (1907). *Delusions and dreams in Jensen's 'Gradiva'. S.E.* 9. London: Hogarth, pp. 1–95.

Freud, S. (1911). *Formulations on the two principles of mental functioning. S.E.* 12. London: Hogarth, pp. 218–226.

Freud, S. (1912). *The dynamics of transference. S.E.* 12. London: Hogarth, pp. 99–108.

Freud, S. (1913). *Totem and taboo. S.E.* 13. London: Hogarth, pp. 1–161.

Freud, S. (1914a). *Remembering, repeating and working-through. S.E.* 12. London: Hogarth, pp. 145–156.

Freud, S. (1914b). *On narcissism: An introduction. S.E.* 14. London: Hogarth, pp. 67–102.

Freud, S. (1915). *Observations on transference love. S.E.* 12. London: Hogarth, pp. 159–171.

Freud, S. (1917). *A metapsychological supplement to the theory of dreams. S.E.* 14. London: Hogarth, pp. 217–222.

Freud, S. (1918 [1914]). *From the history of an infantile neurosis. S.E.* 17. London: Hogarth, pp. 1–122.

Freud, S. (1919). *A child is being beaten. S.E.* 19. London: Hogarth, pp. 179–204.

Freud, S. (1920). *Beyond the pleasure principle. S.E.* 20. London: Hogarth, pp. 1–66.

Freud, S. (1922). *Some neurotic mechanisms in jealousy, paranoia and homosexuality. S.E.* 18. London: Hogarth, pp. 223–232.

Freud, S. (1923a). *The ego and the id. S.E.* 19. London: Hogarth, pp. 13–66.

Freud, S. (1923b [1922]). *Remarks on the theory and practice of dream-interpretation. S.E.* 19. London: Hogarth, pp. 109–121.

Freud, S. (1924). *The economic problem of masochism. S.E.* 19. London: Hogarth, pp. 155–170.

Freud, S. (1925). *Negation. S.E.* 19. London: Hogarth, pp. 235–239.

Freud, S. (1926 [1925]). *Inhibitions, symptoms and anxiety. S.E.* 20. pp. 75–174.

Freud, S. (1927). *Fetishism. S.E.* 21. London: Hogarth, pp. 147–158.

Freud, S. (1930). *Civilisation and its discontents. S.E.* 21. London: Hogarth, pp. 59–145.

Freud, S. (1933). *New introductory lectures on psychoanalysis. S.E.* 22. London: Hogarth.

Freud, S. (1937). *Analysis terminable and interminable. S.E* 23. London: Hogarth, pp. 216–231.

Freud, S. (1939). *Moses and monotheism. S.E.* 23. London: Hogarth, pp. 1–137.

Freud, S. (1940a [1938]). *An outline of psychoanalysis, S.E.* 23. London: Hogarth, pp. 139–207.

Freud, S. (1940b [1938]). *The splitting of the ego in the process of defence. S.E.* 23. Hogarth, pp. 271–278.

Freud, S. (1992 [1905]). *Le Mot d'esprit et sa relation à l'inconscient*, trans. D. Messier, preface by Jean-Claude Lavie. Paris: Gallimard.

Gómez Mango, E. (2009). *Un muet dans la langue*. Paris: Gallimard. (Series: Connaissance de l'inconscient).

Gómez Mango, E., and Pontalis, J.-B. (2012). *Freud avec les écrivains*. Paris: Gallimard. (Series Connaissance de l'inconscient).

Granoff, W. (1975). *Filiations: L'avenir du complexe d'Œdipe*. Paris: Minuit.

Granoff, W. (1978). *La pensée et la féminin*. Paris: Minuit.

Green, A. (1975). The analyst, symbolisation, and absence in the analytic setting (on changes in analytic practice and analytic experience). In *Memory of D.W. Winnicott, International Journal of Psychoanalysis*, 56: 1–22.

Green, A. (1980). Intervention. *Revue française de psychanalyse*, 5–6: 1092–1093.

Green, A. (2001 [1983]). *Life narcissism, death narcissism*, trans. A. Weller. London: Free Association Books.

Green, A. (2005 [2000]). The central phobic position. A new formulation of the free association method. *International Journal of Psychoanaysis*, 81: 429–452; also in: *Psychoanalysis: A paradigm for clinical thinking*, trans. A. Weller. London: Free Associations Books, pp. 133–167.

Green, A. (2011). *Du signe au discours*. Paris: Ithaques.

Gribinski, M. (2002). *Les Séparations imparfaite*. Paris: Gallimard (Series: Connaissance de l'inconscient).

Jacob, M. (1921). *Le Laboratoire central*. Paris: Au Sens Pareil.

Kaës, R. (2001). L'analogie du groupe et du rêve: implications et développements. *Psychologie clinique et projective*, 7(1): 3–16.

Kaës, R. (2002). *La Polyphonie du rêve. L'expérience onirique commune et partagée*. Paris: Dunod.

Klein, M. (1932). *The psychoanalysis of children*. London: Hogarth.

Klein, M. (1935). A contribution to the psycho-genesis of manic depressive states. *International Journal of Psychoanalysis*, 16: 145–174.

Klein, M. (1946). Notes on some schizoid mechanisms. In: *Envy and gratitude and other papers, 1921-45. The writings of Melanie Klein*, vol. III. London: Hogarth Press, pp. 1–24.

Kohut, H. (1971). *The analysis of the self*. New York, NY: International Universities Press.

Lacan, J. (1997 [1986]). *Ethics of psychoanalysis, 1959–1960. The seminar of Jacques Lacan, book VII*. ed. J.-A. Miller, trans. D. Porter. New York: Norton.

Lacan, J. (2015 [1991]). *Transference. The seminar of Jacques Lacan: book VIII*, trans. B. Fink. Cambridge: Polity Press.

Lantos, B. (1952). Metapsychological considerations on the concept of work. *International Journal of Psychoanalysis*, 33(4): 439–443.

Laplanche, J. (2013). Le genre, le sexe et le sexual. In: *Sur la théorie de la séduction, Libres cahiers pour la psychanalyse, Etudes*. Paris: In Press, pp. 69–103.

Lavie, J.-C. (2002). *L'amour est un crime parfait*. Paris: Gallimard.

Le Guen, C. (2007). Comment ça naît, un moi? *Revue française de psychanalyse*, 71(1): 11–26.

Lebovici, S. (1994). Empathie et 'enactment' dans le travail de contre-transfert. *Revue française de psychanalyse*, 58(5): 1551–1561.

Lewis, R. (1993). *Evolution man: Or: How I ate my father*. London: Pantheon Books.

Marty, P. (1958). La relation d'objet allergique. *Revue française de psychanalyse*, 22(1): 5–35.

Marty, P. (1985). *L'ordre psychosomatique: Les mouvements individuels de vie et de mort*, vol 2. Paris: Presses Universitaires de France.

Marty, P. (1990). *La psychosomatique de l'adulte*. Paris: Presses Universitaires de France.

Marty, P., de M'Uzan, M., and David, C. (2010 [1963]). *L'Investigation psychosomatique*. Paris: Presses Universitaires de France. (Series: Quadrige).

Mauriac, F. (1968 [1964]). *The inner presence: Recollection of my spiritual life*, trans. H. Briffault. Indianapolis: Bobbs Merrill Co.

Mauriac, F. (2005 [1927]). *Thérèse Desqueroux*, trans. R. McKenzie. New York, NY: Rowman & Littlefield Publishers Inc.

McDougall, J. (1992 [1972]). The anti-analysand in analysis. In: *Plea for a measure of abnormality*. New York: Brunner/Mazel, pp. 219–247.

McDougall, J. (1992 [1978]). *Plea for a measure of abnormality*. London: Routledge.

Meltzer, D. (1975). *Explorations in autism*. London: Karnac.

Milner, M (1955). The role ofillusion in symbol formation. In: *Psychoanalysis and art. Kleinian perspectives*, ed. Gosso, S. London: Karnac, pp. 85–109.

Milner, M. (1979). Le rôle de l'illusion dans la formation du symbole. *Revue française de psychanalyse*, 43(5–6): 841–874.

Molière (real name Jean Poquelin). (2014 [1660]). *Le Bourgeois gentilhomme*. Paris: Flammarion.

M'Uzan, M. de. (2003). La séance analytique, une zone érogène. *Revue française de psychanalyse*, 67(2): 431–439.

M'Uzan, M. de. (2013 [1976]). Countertransference and paradoxical system. In: *Death and identity: Being and the psycho-sexual drama*, trans. A. Weller. London: Karnac, pp. 17–32.

Neyraut, M. (2004 [1974]). *Le Transfert*. Paris: Presses Universitaires de France.

Normand, H. (2007). *Les amours d'une mere*. Paris: L'Olivier. (Series: Penser/Rêver).

Oury, N. (2013). Sonner à plain souffle du cor! Paper read at a meeting of analysts of the l'Association Psychanalytique de France (APF) in Lyon, 16 March 2013 on the theme "L'appel du vivant".

Parat, C. (1976). A propos du contretransfert. *Revue française de psychanalyse*, 40(3): 545–560.

Pommier, G. (2002). La fin relative de l'analyse. *Figures de la psychanalyse*, 6(1): 123–143.

Pontalis, J.-B. (1983). *Perdre de vue*, Paris, Gallimard (Series: Connaissance de l'inconscient).

Pontalis, J.-B. (1986). *L'amour des commencements*. Paris: Gallimard.

Pontalis, J.-B. (1990). *La force d'attraction*. Paris: Hachette.

Pontalis, J.-B. (1997). *Ce temps qui ne passe pas*. Paris: Gallimard.

Pontalis, J.-B.. (2001). Le laboratoire central. *Revue française de psychanalyse* (Special edition, pp. 311–317).

Pontalis, J.-B. (2012). *Le Laboratoire central*. Paris: L'Olivier. (Series: Penser/ Rêver).

Proust, M. (2015). In the shadow of young girls in flower. In: *In search of lost time*, vol. 2, trans. C.K. Scott Montkrieff. Yale University Press: New Haven.

Racamier, J.-C. (1995). *L'inceste et l'incestuel.* Paris: Editions du Collège.

Reid, W. (2008). Un nouveau regard sur la pulsion, le trauma et la méthode analytique. Première partie: une théorie de la psyche. *Filigrane*, 17(1), pp. 68–94.

Rey, A. (2005). *Dictionnaire culturel en langue française.* Paris: Le Robert.

Rimbaud, A. (2009 [1972]). *Correspondances, Œuvres complètes.* Paris: Gallimard. (Bibliothèque de la Pléiade).

Rolland, J.-C. (1998). *Avant d'être celui qui parle.* Paris: Gallimard.

Rolland, J.-C. (2002). Sur le discours intérieur. In: *Penser les limites. Écrits en l'honneur d'André Green.* Paris: Delachaux et Niéstle.

Rosenberg, B. (1991). Masochisme mortifère et masochism gardien de vie. *Monographies de la Revue française de psychanalyse.* Paris: Presses Universitaires de France.

Rosenfeld, H. (1987). *Impasse and interpretation: therapeutic and anti-therapeutic factors in the psychoanalytic treatment of psychotic, borderline, and neurotic patients.* New York, NY: Tavistock/Routledge.

Rosolato, G. (1967). Étude des perversions sexuelles à partir du fétishisme. In: *Le Desir et la Perversion.* Paris: Seuil, pp. 9–40.

Rosolato, G. (1969a [1965]). Difficultés à surmonter pour une esthétique psychanalytique. In: *Essais sur la symbolique.* Paris: Gallimard., coll. Connaissance de l'inconscient, pp. 121–128.

Rosolato, G. (1969b). *Essais sur la symbolique.* Paris: Gallimard., coll. Connaissance de l'inconscient, 1969 (reprinted coll. Tel, 1979).

Rosolato, G. (1969c [1963]). Les arts plastiques dans un système des beaux-arts. In: *Essais sur la symbolique.* Paris: Gallimard., coll. Connaissance de l'inconscient, pp. 129–138.

Rosolato, G. (1969d [1960]). Technique d'analyse picturale. In: *Essais sur la symbolique.* Paris: Gallimard., coll. Connaissance de l'inconscient, pp. 139–157.

Rosolato, G. (1978a). *La Relation d'inconnu.* Paris: Gallimard. (Series: Connaissance de l'inconscient).

Rosolato, G. (1978b [1968]). L'ombilic et la relation d'inconnu. *La relation d'inconnu.* Paris: Gallimard.

Rosolato, G. (1985). *Élements de l'interprétation.* Paris: Gallimard.

Rosolato, G. (1992). Comment s'isolent les signifiants de démarcation. *Topique*, 49: 65–79.

Rosolato, G. (1993 [1985]). John Cowper Powys: l'extase préméditée. In: *Pour une psychanalyse exploratrice dans la culture*. Paris: Presses Universitaires de France, pp. 113–122.

Rosolato, G. (1996). *La Portée du désir ou la psychanalyse même*. Paris: Paris: Presses Universitaires de France.

Rosolato, G. (1999). *Les Cinq axes de la psychanalyse*. Paris: Paris: Presses Universitaires de France.

Roudinesco, E., and Plon, M. (2006). *Dictionnaire de la psychanalyse*. Paris: Fayard.

Rousseau, J.J. (1790 [1783]). *The Confessions of J.J. Rousseau, book I*. London: J. Bew.

Rousset, H. (2013). La tentation hypochondriaque. *Les Cahiers pour la psychanalyse*, 28: 111–118.

Roussillon, R. (1991). *Paradoxes et situations limites de la psychanalyse*. Paris: Presses Universitaires de France.

Roussillon, R. (1999). *Agonie, clivage, symbolisation*. Paris: Presses Universitaires de France.

Soulié, M. (2002). *Dialogues*. Paris: Érès.

Spitz, R. (1965 [1958]). *The first year of life: A psychoanalytic study of normal and deviant development in object relations*. New York: International Universities Press.

Stewart, S. (2009 [2002]). *Mémoire de l'humain: du trauma à la créativité*. Paris: Campagne Première.

Stoller, R. (1968). *Sex and gender. The development of masculinity and femininity*. London: Karnac.

Surget, A. (2001). *La rivière aux castors*. Paris: Calligram.

Szwec, G. (2014). *Les Galériens volontaires*. Paris: Presses Universitaires de France.

Tamet, J.-Y., Oury, N., and Villand, M. (2012). *Inquiétudes des amours enfantines*. Paris: Presses Universitaires de France.

Widlöcher, D. (1998). De l'empathie à la co-pensée. *Revue de psychothérapie psychanalytique de groupe*, 30: 9–15.

Widlöcher, D. (2003). La personne du psychanalyste et les processus d'empathie et de co-pensées. *Bulletin de la FEP*, 57: 89–96.

Widlöcher, D., and Delattre, N. (2003). *La psychanalyse en dialogue*. Paris: Odile Jacob.

Winnicott, D.W. (1958 [1948]). Reparation in respect of mother's organized defence against depression. *Through paediatrics to psychoanalysis: Collected papers*, London: Tavistock, pp. 91–96.

Winnicott, D.W. (1960). The theory of the parent/infant relationship. *International Journal of Psychoanalysis*, 41: 585–595.

Winnicott, D.W. (1971). Creativity and its origins ("The split-off male and female elements to be found in men and women"). In: *Playing and reality*. London: Tavistock, pp. 72–79.

Winnicott, D.W. (1974). Fear of breakdown. *International Review of Psychoanalysis*, 1: 103–107.

Winnicott, D.W. (1987). *The spontaneous gesture: Selected letters of D.W. Winnicott*. Harvard: Harvard University Press.

Wu, D. (2005). *Romanticism: An anthology*. Oxford: Blackwell.

Zaltzman, N. (1979). La pulsion anarchiste. *Topique*, 24: 25–64.

Zaltzman, N. (1998). *De la guérison psychanalytique*. Paris: Presses Universitaires de France. (Series: Épîtres).

Index